I0884985

Utilizing Blockchain Technologies in Manufacturing and Logistics Management

S. B. Goyal
City University, Malaysia

Nijalingappa Pradeep
Bapuji Institute of Engineering and Technology, India

Piyush Kumar Shukla
University Institute of Technology RGPV, India

Mangesh M. Ghonge
Sandip Institute of Technology and Research Centre, India

Renjith V. Ravi
MEA Engineering College, India

A volume in the Advances in Business Information Systems and Analytics (ABISA) Book Series

IGI Global
PUBLISHER of TIMELY KNOWLEDGE

Published in the United States of America by
IGI Global
Business Science Reference (an imprint of IGI Global)
701 E. Chocolate Avenue
Hershey PA, USA 17033
Tel: 717-533-8845
Fax: 717-533-8661
E-mail: cust@igi-global.com
Web site: http://www.igi-global.com

Copyright © 2022 by IGI Global. All rights reserved. No part of this publication may be reproduced, stored or distributed in any form or by any means, electronic or mechanical, including photocopying, without written permission from the publisher. Product or company names used in this set are for identification purposes only. Inclusion of the names of the products or companies does not indicate a claim of ownership by IGI Global of the trademark or registered trademark.

Library of Congress Cataloging-in-Publication Data

Names: Goyal, S. B., 1978- editor. | Pradeep, Nijalingappa, 1977- editor. | Shukla, Piyush Kumar, 1976- editor.
Title: Utilizing blockchain technologies in manufacturing and logistics management / S. B. Goyal, Nijalingappa Pradeep, Piyush Kumar Shukla, Mangesh Manikrao Ghonge, and Renjith V. Ravi, editors.
Description: Hershey, PA : Business Science Reference, [2022] | Includes bibliographical references and index. | Summary: "The key objectives of the book are to explore the strengths of blockchain adaptation in manufacturing industries and logistics management, presenting different use cases of and future research trends"-- Provided by publisher.
Identifiers: LCCN 2021040467 (print) | LCCN 2021040468 (ebook) | ISBN 9781799886976 (hardcover) | ISBN 9781799886983 (paperback) | ISBN 9781799886990 (ebook)
Subjects: LCSH: Manufacturing industries--Technological innovations. | Industrial management--Technological innovations. | Blockchains (Databases)
Classification: LCC HD9720.5 .U85 2022 (print) | LCC HD9720.5 (ebook) | DDC 658.5--dc23/eng/20211007
LC record available at https://lccn.loc.gov/2021040467
LC ebook record available at https://lccn.loc.gov/2021040468

This book is published in the IGI Global book series Advances in Business Information Systems and Analytics (ABISA) (ISSN: 2327-3275; eISSN: 2327-3283)

British Cataloguing in Publication Data
A Cataloguing in Publication record for this book is available from the British Library.

All work contributed to this book is new, previously-unpublished material. The views expressed in this book are those of the authors, but not necessarily of the publisher.

For electronic access to this publication, please contact: eresources@igi-global.com.

Advances in Business Information Systems and Analytics (ABISA) Book Series

Madjid Tavana
La Salle University, USA

ISSN:2327-3275
EISSN:2327-3283

Mission

The successful development and management of information systems and business analytics is crucial to the success of an organization. New technological developments and methods for data analysis have allowed organizations to not only improve their processes and allow for greater productivity, but have also provided businesses with a venue through which to cut costs, plan for the future, and maintain competitive advantage in the information age.

The **Advances in Business Information Systems and Analytics (ABISA) Book Series** aims to present diverse and timely research in the development, deployment, and management of business information systems and business analytics for continued organizational development and improved business value.

Coverage

- Algorithms
- Strategic Information Systems
- Information Logistics
- Data Strategy
- Business Information Security
- Business Decision Making
- Performance Metrics
- Business Process Management
- Business Systems Engineering
- Forecasting

IGI Global is currently accepting manuscripts for publication within this series. To submit a proposal for a volume in this series, please contact our Acquisition Editors at Acquisitions@igi-global.com or visit: http://www.igi-global.com/publish/.

The Advances in Business Information Systems and Analytics (ABISA) Book Series (ISSN 2327-3275) is published by IGI Global, 701 E. Chocolate Avenue, Hershey, PA 17033-1240, USA, www.igi-global.com. This series is composed of titles available for purchase individually; each title is edited to be contextually exclusive from any other title within the series. For pricing and ordering information please visit http://www.igi-global.com/book-series/advances-business-information-systems-analytics/37155. Postmaster: Send all address changes to above address. Copyright © 2022 IGI Global. All rights, including translation in other languages reserved by the publisher. No part of this series may be reproduced or used in any form or by any means – graphics, electronic, or mechanical, including photocopying, recording, taping, or information and retrieval systems – without written permission from the publisher, except for non commercial, educational use, including classroom teaching purposes. The views expressed in this series are those of the authors, but not necessarily of IGI Global.

Titles in this Series

For a list of additional titles in this series, please visit: www.igi-global.com/book-series

Business Applications in Social Media Analytics
Himani Bansal (Jaypee University, Solan, India) and Gulshan Shrivastava (National Institute of Technology, Patna, ndia)
Business Science Reference • © 2022 • 330pp • H/C (ISBN: 9781799850465) • US $195.00

Achieving Organizational Agility, Intelligence, and Resilience Through Information Systems
Hakikur Rahman (Ansted University Sustainability Research Institute, Malysia)
Business Science Reference • © 2022 • 350pp • H/C (ISBN: 9781799847991) • US $195.00

Handbook of Research on Applied Data Science and Artificial Intelligence in Business and Industry
Valentina Chkoniya (University of Aveiro, Portugal)
Engineering Science Reference • © 2021 • 653pp • H/C (ISBN: 9781799869856) • US $425.00

Using Strategy Analytics to Measure Corporate Performance and Business Value Creation
Sandeep Kautish (Lord Buddha Education Foundation, Nepal)
Business Science Reference • © 2021 • 287pp • H/C (ISBN: 9781799877165) • US $225.00

Adapting and Mitigating Environmental, Social, and Governance Risk in Business
Magdalena Ziolo (University of Szczecin, Poland)
Business Science Reference • © 2021 • 313pp • H/C (ISBN: 9781799867883) • US $195.00

Innovative and Agile Contracting for Digital Transformation and Industry 4.0
Mohammad Ali Shalan (Aqarat Real Estate Development Company, Saudi Arabia) and Mohammed Ayedh Algarni (Information and Documents Center, Institute of Public Administration, Saudi Arabia)
Business Science Reference • © 2021 • 415pp • H/C (ISBN: 9781799845010) • US $225.00

Opportunities and Strategic Use of Agribusiness Information Systems
Ferdinand Ndifor Che (W3-Research, USA & APPC Research, Australia) Kenneth David Strang (W3-Research, USA & APPC Research, Australia) and Narasimha Rao Vajjhala (University of New York Tirana, Albania)
Business Science Reference • © 2021 • 333pp • H/C (ISBN: 9781799848493) • US $195.00

Integration Challenges for Analytics, Business Intelligence, and Data Mining
Ana Azevedo (CEOS.PP, ISCAP, Polytechnic of Porto, Portugal) and Manuel Filipe Santos (Algoritmi Centre, University of Minho, Guimarães, Portugal)
Engineering Science Reference • © 2021 • 250pp • H/C (ISBN: 9781799857815) • US $225.00

IGI Global
PUBLISHER of TIMELY KNOWLEDGE

701 East Chocolate Avenue, Hershey, PA 17033, USA
Tel: 717-533-8845 x100 • Fax: 717-533-8661
E-Mail: cust@igi-global.com • www.igi-global.com

Table of Contents

Detailed Table of Contents

Renjith V. Ravi, MEA Engineering College, India
Mangesh M. Ghonge, Sandip Institute of Technology and Research, India
P. Febina Beevi, MEA Engineering College, India
Rafael Kunst, University of Vale do Rio dos Sinos, Brazil

Blockchain technologies have lately risen to the top of the academic and industry agendas, owing to their potential advantages across a wide range of sectors. This is due to their practical skills in resolving many problems that are presently impeding progress in different industrial sectors. These problems include securely capturing and exchanging transactional data, creating automated and efficient supply chain procedures, and improving transparency throughout the whole value chain. Blockchain provides an effective method to address these problems using distributed, shared, secure, and permission transactional ledgers. The uses of blockchain technology in the manufacturing and logistics sectors have been examined in this chapter. The study shows many possibilities for using blockchain in different industrial sectors; nevertheless, certain obstacles must be solved before this technology can be fully used. This chapter also covers case studies and difficulties encountered in the industrial and logistics sectors while using blockchain.

Manimaran A., Madanapalle Institute of Technology and Science, India
Chandramohan Dhasarathan, Thapar Institute of Engineering and Technology, India
Arulkumar N., CHRIST University (Deemed), India
Naveen Kumar N., Madanapalle Institute of Technology and Science, India

The internet of things (IoT) represents rapid development in research and industry that enables both virtual and physical objects to be linked and transfers information in order to produce various services that enhance our excellence of life. Traditional security and privacy methods are not applicable for IoT, mostly due to their topological constraints and versatility of IoT devices. Blockchain technology has started to fascinate younger generations because it works especially well in the digital world. Blockchain is suitable for internet of things applications. Advancements in IoT have propelled distributed systems. The blockchain concept demands a method for exchanging and storing data that is managed by a decentralized network. The rise of IoT applications is hindered by these obstacles. One option to fix these problems is to use a distributed ledger technology using blockchain technology. This chapter gives a comprehensive overview of blockchain's strengths and weaknesses with its applications.

The chapter's fundamental goal is to discover and feature the job of blockchain technology in inventory networks including its benefits and impediments. The idea of the examination depends on auxiliary information and data. The necessary information and data have been gathered from different sites, magazines, and media reports. Supply affixes the need to confront difficulties as far as quality, cost, and speed. These boundaries can be accomplished effectively with blockchain in the inventory network of the executives.

This chapter studies blockchain technology logistics and supply chain adoption in four manufacturing firms. Semi-structured interviews are conducted, and the results are analyzed using case study methods. Four manufacturing firms are selected for the study. First firms deal with consumer electronics manufacturing, second firms deal with auto components manufacturing, third firms deal with paint manufacturing, and fourth firms deal with consumer electronics, manufacturing, wearables manufacturing. The case study is analysed using cross-case analysis and withing case analysis.

The main purpose of this chapter is to present the need to use the mutual recognition mechanism (MRM) of electronic signatures based on the DVCS oracle in the blockchain platform for the global supply chain. The authors begin their research by comparing a single-domain traditional supply chain with a multi-domain global supply chain. In the second case, the necessity of using an MRM electronic signature based on the DVCS oracle is justified. Various options for constructing MRM are discussed. The chapter provides a comparative assessment of the electronic signature validation protocols and the rationale for using the DVCS protocol to implement the blockchain oracle. As a result, the authors propose to use a well-tested software and hardware complex of the Litoria DVCS as a DVCS oracle and illustrate its use with practical examples.

Supply chain management (SCM) is a system to manage the flow of goods and services, and from transforming the raw into finished products, it has challenges that are needed to be achieved like good quality services to the consumer, reducing labor cost, etc. Industries need to digitize real assets and make distributed, immutable transactions possible to trace assets from manufacture to supply. To overcome the lack of transparency and traceability of the products in the enterprise resource planning system in supply chain (SC) and logistics issues, there is a solid need to employ a method that can efficiently track assets from production to supply decentralized, immutable records of all transactions. A blockchain (BC) is a decentralized software network that follows a digital ledger to exchange entities digitally and a way through which it makes secure transactions. Thus, this chapter proposes integrating BC in logistics and SC monitoring by giving a template on how Python and Flask can be used for BC with the SCM system to improve traceability without involving any intermediary.

As logistics companies continue to expand due to the revolution of Logistics 4.0, the complexity of the multiple connected organizations makes it impossible for a clear view of logistics operation. Since customer information is shared between companies, unauthorized access to personal information is inevitable, and it poses several threats to customers. To address this challenge, blockchain with some fascinating properties like enhanced security and transparency will be deployed. Blockchain is a technology that can be used to improve efficiency, visibility, and security in logistics management. This chapter will explore the current applications of blockchain in logistics management based on an analysis of the findings of several scholars. The change from traditional logistics to digital logistics, digital logistics issues, as well as blockchain principles, this study also provides useful insights into how blockchain can disrupt conventional operations in logistics management. It also lays the groundwork for future study into blockchain's applicability in digital fleet management.

As supply chains become more dynamic, incorporate a scope of partners, and intensely depend on an assortment of outside counterparties, blockchain has arisen as a feasible possibility to de-tangle all information, archives, correspondence exchanges that exist inside the production network organization. Each production network will have enormous measure of information being traded between different stages in a supply chain network. To deal with colossal of measure of information and guarantee its security, supply chain can consolidate IoT and blockchain. This will help in further developing security, usefulness, proficiency, and benefit of the production network. This chapter examines the foundation of blockchain, IoT, and a portion of the issues confronting present day supply chain. The significant advantages for supply chains utilizing IoT and blockchain are analyzed, and future examination heading for Integration of IoT and blockchain for supply chain management are discussed.

Ankur Agrawal, Sharda University, India
Swati Bansal, Sharda University, India
Monica Agarwal, Sharda University, India
Reema Agarwal, Lloyd Institute of Management and Technology, India
Mohammad Rumzi Tausif, Prince Sattam Bin Abdulaziz University, Saudi Arabia

The concept of blockchain is prevalent globally in today's times. It has shown remarkable growth and has shown a lot of achievement by executing systems of peer-to-peer cryptocurrency. The cryptocurrency was introduced in 2009 but created hype about digital currency around the world in 2017. Blockchain works on the concept of a "distributed ledger/database." The transactions are recorded and replicated to all the participating parties chronologically. Blockchain has verified to be immutable and provides accountability, integrity, and quite a lot of confidentiality through a pair of private and public keys. Various sectors have started using blockchain due to its salient features. Asset management is also one of the areas where blockchain can reduce transaction costs, approval waiting time, and increase transparency. The complicated processes of asset management can be automated by unifying permissioned and permissionless blockchain. This chapter discusses how asset management firms can use blockchain opportunities to harness its benefits.

Poshan Yu, Soochow University, China & Krirk University, Thailand
Zhiruo Liu, Independent Researcher, China
Emanuela Hanes, Independent Researcher, Austria
Jabir Mumtaz, Capital University of Science and Technology, Pakistan

This chapter will focus on the combination of supply chain management and digital technology. Starting from the popular digital terms in the current market, the authors examine the current environment of the development, including Chinese government policies and the industry situation, and then compare the different characteristics of Industry 4.0 before and after digitization by combining the two digital technologies (i.e., blockchain and internet of things [IoT]). Moreover, the advantages of the integration of internet of things and blockchain in supply chain management will be highlighted. At the same time, according to the changes brought by digitization, the added value of IoT and blockchain integration will be analyzed from the perspective of different stakeholders. In addition, some Chinese case studies will be introduced to show the innovative performance of and benefits for enterprises, to provide references for enterprises, and to implement IoT for smart economic growth.

The author considers the main purpose of this chapter to be the presentation of a modern approach to the digital transformation of traditional business processes in the gas industry. Using the example of a pilot project successfully implemented in the gas industry, the author shows the process of synthesizing a high-tech supply chain infrastructure based on blockchain. The presentation begins with a description of the main business processes of the supply chain. The functions for all participants of the system are described and visualized in detail. The main components of the system are considered: digital dispatcher, supply monitor, interaction interfaces, and production environment. A comparative analysis of the security of modern blockchain platforms is provided. The author carefully analyzes the technologies for creating and ensuring the security of smart contracts and offers a step-by-step method for implementing secure smart contracts. At the end of the chapter, the results of choosing the most secure blockchain platforms are presented.

The purpose of this chapter is to broaden the discussion about the various logistics solutions used by industrial firms to improve customer satisfaction and to assess their effect. This study seeks to discover and suggest new connections between logistics management solution theory and customer satisfaction using semi-structured interviews. Twelve small and mid-sized Algerian industrial firms from various industries participated in the semi-structured interviews. Their 22 top supply chain and logistics managers were questioned to determine their perceptions of what is essential to their suppliers and how logistics management is crucial for them to be happy customers. In today's highly competitive global economy, businesses are under increasing pressure to discover innovative methods to generate value and deliver it to their consumers.

Preface

Blockchain technology is a digitalized public ledger, which was initially used only for cryptocurrency transactions. Blockchain is one of the cutting-edge technologies that have the potential to utterly transform the manufacturing industry. Blockchain technologies have the potential to radically change manufacturing supply chains and irradicate the middleman, streamline processes, and improve security on the whole—as well as simplify data management.

Manufacturers across the globe are facing challenges with forecasting demand, controlling inventory, managing manufacturing plant capacity, ensuring Return-On-Investment, and accelerating digital transformation to cater the challenges of changing market dynamics and evolving customer expectations. Also, the limited operational visibility due to complex and expansive supply chains spread across geographies – which make it difficult to track and trace the movement of raw material, finished products and spare parts, as they make their way through production facilities, warehouses, distributors and sales outlets. Blockchain is the one way secured and traceable solution to pertinent challenges being faced by the manufacturing industries.

Now a days, manufacturers are developing blockchain implementations that have the potential to cater them in streamline operations, gain greater visibility into supply chains and track assets with unprecedented precision. Blockchain has potential to revolutionize how manufacturers design, engineer, make and scale their products. Blockchain is gradually proving to be an effective "middleware" solution for enabling seamless interoperability within complex supply chains. Due to its technological nature, blockchain enables secure, transparent and fast data exchanges as well as allowing for the creation of immutable records databases

The main advantage of Blockchain in Manufacturing Industries is product traceability, supply chain transparency, compliance monitoring, and auditability. Moreover, leveraging blockchain technology into a manufacturing enterprise can enhance its security and reduce the rates of systematic failures. So, blockchain is now used in various sectors of the manufacturing industry, such as automotive, aerospace, defense, pharmaceutical, consumer electronics, textile, food and beverages, etc. Hence, Blockchain should be seen as an investment in future-readiness and customer-centricity, not as an experimental technology – because the evidence is overwhelming.

This book serves as an instant ready reference to researchers and professionals working in the area of blockchain technology especially in Supply Chain Management and Logistics Management.

ORGANIZATION OF THE BOOK

The book is organized into 12 chapters. A brief description of each of the chapters follows:

Chapter 1

Blockchain technologies have lately risen to the top of the academic and industry agendas, owing to their potential advantages across a wide range of sectors. This is due to their practical skills in resolving many problems that are presently impeding progress in different industrial sectors. These problems include securely capturing and exchanging transactional data, creating automated and efficient supply chain procedures, and improving transparency throughout the whole value chain. Blockchain provides an effective method to address these problems using distributed, shared, secure, and permission transactional ledgers. The uses of blockchain technology in the manufacturing and logistics sectors have been examined in this chapter. The study shows many possibilities for using blockchain in different industrial sectors; nevertheless, certain obstacles must be solved before this technology can be fully used. This chapter also covers case studies and difficulties encountered in the industrial and logistics sectors while using blockchain.

Chapter 2

The Internet of Things (IoT) represents rapid development in research and industry that enables both virtual and physical objects to be linked and, transferred information's with each other in order to produce various services that enhance our excellence of life. Traditional security and privacy methods not applicable for IoT, mostly due to its topological constraints and versatility of IoT devices. Blockchain technology has started to fascinate younger generation because it works especially well in the digital world. Blockchain is suitable for Internet of Things applications. Advancements in IoT have propelled distributed systems. Blockchain concept demands a method for exchanging and storing data that is managed by decentralized network. The rise of IoT applications is hindered by these obstacles. One option to fix these problems is to use a distributed ledger technology using Blockchain technology. This article gives a comprehensive overview of blockchain's strengths and weaknesses with its applications.

Chapter 3

Blockchain can possibly develop to be the bedrock of the overall record-keeping frameworks yet was dispatched only ten years prior, it was made by the obscure people behind the online money cash Bitcoin, under the pen name 'Satoshi Nakamoto' Blockchain can be the foundation of the digitized inventory network. It really helps the clients and organizations track their item from the hour of pickup to the time it arrives at the end customer. The chapter's fundamental goal is to discover and feature the job of Blockchain Technology in inventory network the board and its benefits and impediments. The idea of the examination is engaging, which depends on auxiliary information and data. The necessary information and data have been gathered from different sites, magazines, and media reports. Supply affixes need to confront difficulties as far as quality, cost, and speed. These boundaries can be accomplished effectively with blockchain in the inventory network of the executives.

Chapter 4

This research paper studies blockchain technology logistics and supply chain adoption in four manufacturing firms. Semi-structured interviews are conducted, and the results are analyzed using case study methods. Four manufacturing firms are selected for the study. First firms deal with consumer electronics manufacturing, second firms deal with auto components manufacturing, third firms deal with paint manufacturing, and fourth firms deal with consumer electronics, manufacturing, wearables manufacturing. The case study is analysed using cross-case analysis and withing case analysis.

Chapter 5

The main purpose of this chapter is to present the need to use the Mutual Recognition Mechanism (MRM) of electronic signatures based on the DVCS oracle in the blockchain platform for the global supply chain. The authors begin their research by comparing a single-domain traditional supply chain with a multi-domain global supply chain. In the second case, the necessity of using an MRM electronic signature based on the DVCS oracle is justified. Various options for constructing MRM are discussed. The chapter provides a comparative assessment of the electronic signature validation protocols and the rationale for using the DVCS protocol to implement the blockchain oracle. As a result, the authors propose to use a well-tested software and hardware complex of the Litoria DVCS as a DVCS oracle and illustrate its use with practical examples.

Chapter 6

Supply Chain Management (SCM) is a system to manage the flow of goods and services, and from transforming the raw into finished products but it has challenges that are needed to be achieved like good quality services to the consumer, reducing labor cost, etc. Industries need to digitize real assets and make distributed, immutable transactions, possible to trace assets from manufacture to supply. To overcome the lack of transparency and traceability of the products in the Enterprise Resource Planning system in Supply Chain (SC) and logistics issues, there is a solid need to employ a method that can efficiently track assets from production to supply decentralized, immutable records of all transactions. A blockchain (BC) is a decentralized software network that follows a digital ledger to exchange entities digitally and a way through which it makes secure transactions. Thus, this chapter proposes integrating BC in Logistics and SC Monitoring by giving a template on how Python and Flask can be used for BC with the SCM system to improve traceability without involving any intermediary.

Chapter 7

As logistics companies continue to expand due to the revolution of logistics 4.0, the complexity of the multiple connected organizations makes it impossible for a clear view of logistics operation. Since customers' information is shared between companies, unauthorized access to personal information is inevitable and it poses several threats to customers. To address this challenge, Blockchain with some fascinating properties like enhanced security and transparency will be deployed. Blockchain is a technology that can be used to improve efficiency, visibility, and security in logistics management. This paper will explore the current applications of Blockchain in logistics management, based on an analysis of the findings of several scholars. The change from traditional logistics to digital logistics, digital logistics issues, as well as Blockchain principles, this study also provides useful insights into how Blockchain can disrupt conventional operations in logistics management. It also lays the groundwork for future study into Blockchain's applicability in digital fleet management.

Chapter 8

As supply chains become more dynamic, incorporate a scope of partners, and intensely depend on an assortment of outside counterparties, blockchain has arisen as a feasible possibility to de-tangle all information, archives, correspondence exchanges that exist inside the production network organization. Each production network will have enormous measure of information being traded between different stages in a supply chain network. To deal with colossal of measure of information and guarantee its security, supply chain can consolidate IoT and blockchain. This will help in further developing security, usefulness, proficiency, and benefit of the production network. This chapter examines the foundation of blockchain, IoT and a portion of the issues confronting present day supply chain. The significant advantages for supply chains utilizing IoT and blockchain would be analyzed and future examination heading for Integration of IoT and blockchain for supply chain management would be discussed.

Chapter 9

The concept of blockchain is prevalent globally in today's times. It has shown remarkable growth and has shown a lot of achievement by executing systems of peer to peer cryptocurrency. The cryptocurrency was introduced in 2009 but created hype about digital currency around the world in 2017. Blockchain works on the concept of a "distributed ledger /database". The transactions that are recorded and replicated to all the participating parties chronologically. Blockchain has verified to be immutable and provides accountability, integrity, and quite a lot of confidentiality through a pair of private and public keys. Various sectors have started using blockchain due to its salient features. Asset Management is also one of the areas where blockchain can reduce transaction costs, approval waiting time and increase transparency. The complicated processes of asset management can be automated by unifying permissioned and permissionless blockchain. This chapter discusses how asset management firms can use blockchain opportunities to harness its benefits.

Chapter 10

This chapter will focus on the combination of supply chain management and digital technology. Starting from the popular digital terms in the current market, we will examine the current environment of the development, including Chinese government policies and the industry situation and then compare the different characteristics of Industry 4.0 before and after digitization by combining the two digital technologies i.e., Blockchain and Internet of Things (IoT). Moreover, the advantages of the integration of Internet of things and blockchain in supply chain management will be highlighted. At the same time, according to the changes brought by digitization, the added value of IoT and blockchain integration will be analyzed from the perspective of different stakeholders. In addition, some Chinese case studies will be introduced to show the innovative performance of and benefits for enterprises, to provide references for enterprises considering to implement IoT for smart economic growth.

Chapter 11

The author considers the main purpose of this chapter to be the presentation of a modern approach to the digital transformation of traditional business processes in the gas industry. Using the example of a pilot project successfully implemented in the gas industry, the author shows the process of synthesizing a high-tech supply chain infrastructure based on blockchain. The presentation begins with a description of the main business processes of the supply chain. The functions for all participants of the system are described and visualized in detail. The main components of the system are considered: digital dispatcher, supply monitor, interaction interfaces and production environment. A comparative analysis of the security of modern blockchain platforms is provided. The author carefully analyzes the technologies for creating and ensuring the security of smart contracts and offers a step-by-step method for implementing secure smart contracts. At the end of the chapter, the results of choosing the most secure blockchain platforms are presented.

Chapter 12

The purpose of this article is to broaden the discussion about the various logistics solutions used by industrial firms to improve customer satisfaction and to assess their effect. This study seeks to discover and suggest new connections between logistics management solution theory and customer satisfaction using semi-structured interviews. Twelve small and mid-sized Algerian industrial firms from various industries participated in the semi-structured interviews. Their 22 top supply chain and logistics managers were questioned to determine their perceptions of what is essential to their suppliers and how logistics management is crucial for them to be happy customers. In today's highly competitive global economy, businesses are under increasing pressure to discover innovative methods to generate value and deliver it to their consumers.

Acknowledgement

We wish to acknowledge the help of all the people involved in completing the book and, more specifically, the authors (contributors) and reviewers who contributed active role in the contributing chapter and in review process respectively. Without their support, this book would not have become a reality. We thank God for the opportunity to pursue this highly relevant subject at this time, and each of the authors for their collective contributions. My sincere gratitude goes to all the chapter authors who contributed their time and expertise to this book. We wish to acknowledge the valuable contributions of all the peer reviewers regarding their suggestions for improvement of quality, coherence, and content for chapters. Some authors served as referees; we highly appreciate their time and commitment. A successful book publication is the integrated result of more people than those persons granted credit as editor and author.

S. B. Goyal
City University, Malaysia

Nijalingappa Pradeep
Bapuji Institute of Engineering and Technology, India

Piyush Kumar Shukla
University Institute of Technology RGPV, India

Mangesh M. Ghonge
Sandip Institute of Technology and Research Centre, India

Renjith V. Ravi
MEA Engineering College, India

Chapter 1
Need, Role, and Impact of Blockchain in the Manufacturing and Logistics Industries

Renjith V. Ravi
https://orcid.org/0000-0001-9047-3220
MEA Engineering College, India

Mangesh M. Ghonge
https://orcid.org/0000-0003-0140-4827
Sandip Institute of Technology and Research, India

P. Febina Beevi
MEA Engineering College, India

Rafael Kunst
University of Vale do Rio dos Sinos, Brazil

ABSTRACT

Blockchain technologies have lately risen to the top of the academic and industry agendas, owing to their potential advantages across a wide range of sectors. This is due to their practical skills in resolving many problems that are presently impeding progress in different industrial sectors. These problems include securely capturing and exchanging transactional data, creating automated and efficient supply chain procedures, and improving transparency throughout the whole value chain. Blockchain provides an effective method to address these problems using distributed, shared, secure, and permission transactional ledgers. The uses of blockchain technology in the manufacturing and logistics sectors have been examined in this chapter. The study shows many possibilities for using blockchain in different industrial sectors; nevertheless, certain obstacles must be solved before this technology can be fully used. This chapter also covers case studies and difficulties encountered in the industrial and logistics sectors while using blockchain.

DOI: 10.4018/978-1-7998-8697-6.ch001

Copyright © 2022, IGI Global. Copying or distributing in print or electronic forms without written permission of IGI Global is prohibited.

INTRODUCTION

Blockchain introduces new, complex functionality to the business and industrial sectors. Many existing commercial and industrial processes can benefit from these features, which can help them improve, optimize, secure and simplify their operations. They also enable the development of new business models that were difficult to achieve just a few years ago. These new business models impact numerous industries, including banking, medical care, manufacturing and logistics. While the Internet has helped create many of today's business and service models, safe registration and ensuring commercial transactions between different parties always have problems. Companies and people may now record and preserve their contracts signed by the blockchain advent.

Blockchain uses a variety of methods to maintain a distributed ledger among users (organizations, businesses, individuals, software agents, etc.). Its content is agreed upon by all parties concerned. All transactions are safe and can't be changed once they've been added. It also enables comprehensive transaction monitoring, measuring, and tracing. Without a governing authority, Blockchain allows a group of companies to agree on a specific transaction and record that agreement. Blockchain can be used to record, secure and communicate their agreed actions. A cash transaction from one member to another, a purchase, a voting engagement, or a patient's medical lab test entry are examples of agreed upon activities. Multiple parties collaborating on a particular job, contract agreements, and supply chain logistics are just a few examples of such operations.

Blockchain technology combines the features and benefits of peer-to-peer networks with cryptographic techniques to ensure that completed agreements are legitimate. No approved or registered activity may be altered without the participation of the other participating organizations. This functionality is ideal for facilitating other commercial agreements amongst a group of organizations from various locations. In addition to preserving the sequence of events, blockchain can guarantee the accuracy of recorded transactions over time. It is virtually difficult to falsify records or reject an agreement since no one can independently change any recorded transactions. Consequently, numerous sectors and companies are contemplating adopting blockchain, and more research is being conducted to use blockchain in these areas successfully.

For the commercial and industrial world, blockchain introduces additional advanced functionalities (Nakamoto, 2008). Many existing commercial and industrial processes can benefit from these features by improving, optimizing, securing and simplifying them. They also enable the development of new business models that were previously difficult to develop. These innovative business models impact areas such as finance, healthcare, manufacturing, and logistics. While the internet has contributed to the development of many of today's business and service models, concerns remain about how to securely register and guarantee agreements between the numerous parties involved in commercial transactions. With the advent of blockchain technology, businesses and individuals can now record and preserve their transacted agreements with each other. The typical applications of blockchain technology are shown in Figure 1.

Blockchain technology, which heralds the start of a new age in decentralized information technology, is a life-changing invention. Its usefulness extends well beyond digital currencies and financial assets, as it was created as part of Bitcoin's fundamental design in 2008 (Nakamoto, 2008) . The technology is still in its infancy and has yet to be adopted by the general public or businesses. There have been numerous improvements, new use cases, and applications as the technology have risen in recent years (Bogart & Rice, 2015). The possibilities for Blockchain applications are endless, ranging from digital money to

Blockchain-enabled legal contracts (Buterin & others, 2014), with the most promising applications still being researched.

Figure 1. Typical Applications of Blockchain Technolgy (Casino, Dasaklis, & Patsakis, 2019)

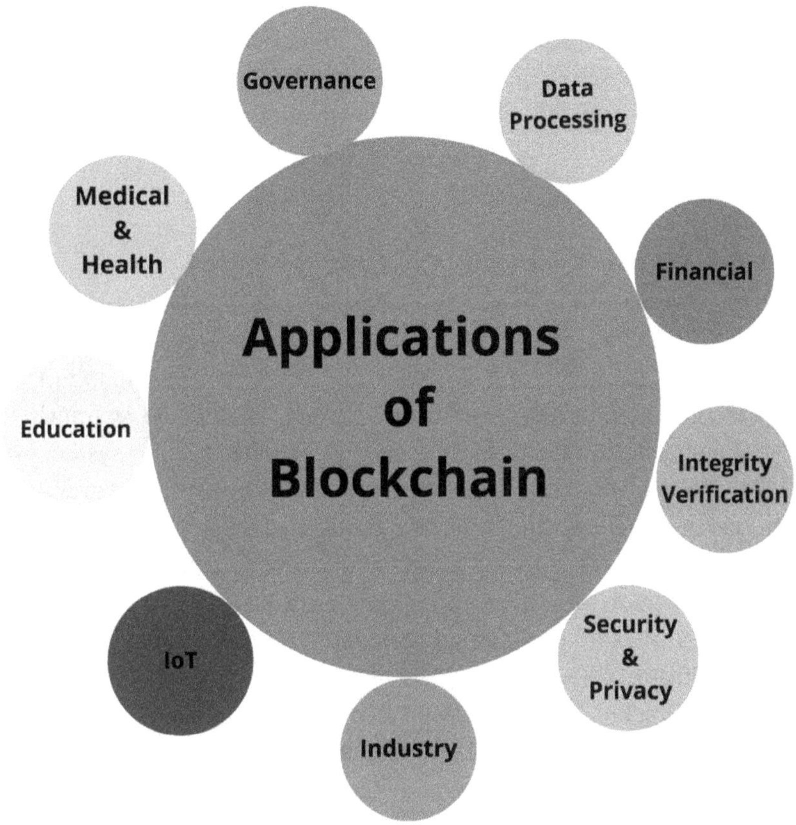

A blockchain uses a variety of techniques to establish a shared ledger between the users such as organizations, businesses, individuals, software agents, etc. Its content has been agreed upon by all parties involved. All transactions are secure and cannot be changed once they are entered. It also allows for accurate transaction tracking, measurement, and tracing. Blockchain allows parties to agree on a specific activity and record that agreement in the absence of a governing body. Blockchain technology has the potential to be used to record, secure, and transmit agreed-upon actions. A cash transaction from one member to another, a purchase activity, a vote activity, or a medical lab test entry for a patient are all examples of agreed-upon activities. Collaboration on multi-party projects, contract negotiations, and supply chain logistics are some of the other activities. To guarantee the validity of completed agreements, blockchain technology benefits peer-to-peer networks with cryptographic techniques. Without the involvement of the other participating entities, none of the authorized and registered actions may be altered. This functionality is ideal for facilitating other commercial agreements amongst a group of companies from various locations. Furthermore, in addition to preserving the order of events, blockchain can verify the accuracy of documented transactions over time. Therefore, it is almost hard to falsify records or reject an agreement since no one can independently modify any recorded transactions. As a result, numerous sectors and organizations are contemplating adopting blockchain, and more research is being conducted to use blockchain in these fields successfully.

The use of blockchain in many sectors is investigated in this study. This contains a review of blockchain's industrial uses, as well as its pros and drawbacks. Financial, healthcare, logistics, manufacturing, energy, agriculture and food, robotics, entertainment, and other industrial sectors are among the applications addressed. The article also discusses the essential criteria for using blockchain in industrial applications and some unresolved challenges.

HISTORY OF BLOCKCHAIN

Blockchain technology must be one of the greatest innovations of the twenty-first century, given its effect on a wide range of industries, from banking to manufacturing and education (Iredale, 2020). Many people are unaware that Blockchain dates back to the early 1990s.

Stuart Haber and W. Scott Stornetta came up with the idea for the blockchain in 1991. Their original goal was to establish a cryptographically secure chain of blocks that would guarantee that no one could tamper with the timestamps on documents. Merkle trees were added to their system in 1992, increasing efficiency and allowing them to store more documents on a single block. However, due to the efforts of one individual or group known as Satoshi Nakamoto, Blockchain History begins to acquire significance in 2008. Blockchain technology is attributed to Satoshi Nakamoto as the brains behind it. Individuals think Nakamoto may be a person or a group of people that worked on Bitcoin, the first use of digital ledger technology, but very little is known about him (Rathee, 2020). The Figure 2 depicts the history of blockchain technology from 1990s to 2018.

Nakamoto invented the first blockchain in 2008, after which the technology has developed and found applications outside of cryptocurrencies. In 2009, Satoshi Nakamoto published the first whitepaper on the technology (Iredale, 2020). In the whitepaper, he explained how the technology was particularly well suited to bolstering digital trust because of the decentralisation component, which meant that no one could ever control anything. The digital ledger technology has evolved since Satoshi Nakamoto left the scene and turned over Bitcoin development to other core developers, resulting in additional applications that make up the blockchain History.

BLOCKCHAIN TECHNOLGY AN OVERVIEW

A blockchain is a growing collection of linked documents, referred to as blocks, linked and protected using encryption techniques (Bogart & Rice, 2015). The connections established from one block to the next are the key to the efficacy of this list, making it impossible to alter any block once it has been put to the list. As a result, the term "blockchain" comes from the fact that it is essentially a chain of data blocks. This list is a password-protected online register for recording agreed-upon and completed transactions between various companies or organizations. Financial, commercial, industrial, and system operations are all examples of activities that produce recorded transactions. The transaction blocks are typically timestamped, encrypted, and duplicated across many locations, and they cannot be changed.

Figure 2. History of blockchain (Atlam & Wills, 2019)

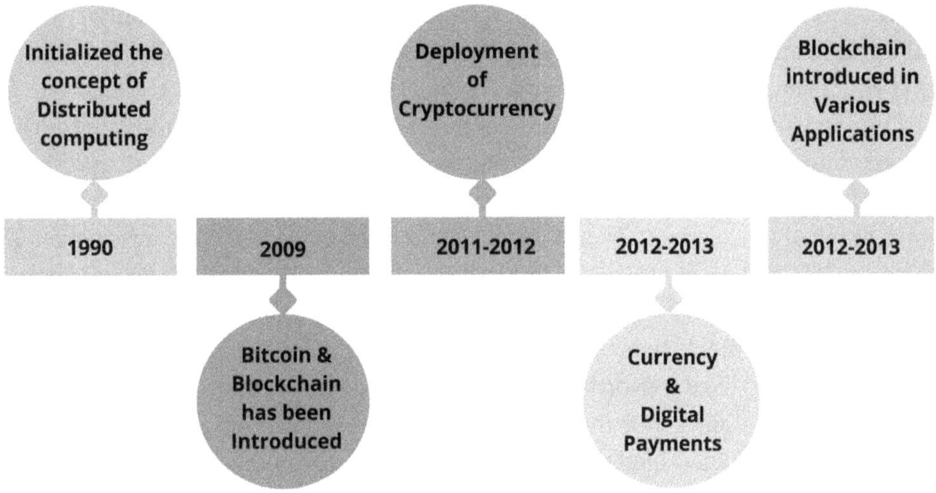

Blockchain can record certain transactions by connecting individuals or companies through a network (activities). Members of the group can typically view previously recorded transactions, but no one can edit or delete them. As a result, Blockchain keeps an immutable record of the group's actions. This history is shared with all or part of the group. All recorded transactions have a high degree of traceability and transparency, and anyone involved can view them. However, it is ensured that these records (or blocks) cannot be changed by anyone in the group that created them, nor by anyone else. The group agrees on the logical relationships between transactions, but changing them is difficult because they are irreversible.

One of the most significant aspects of blockchain technology is that it permits two or more organisations to securely record an agreement for specified acts over a public network like the Internet without the participation of a third party like a licenced firm or government agency. The parties may or may not be acquainted, and they most certainly do not trust one another. They can still agree, document the transaction, and have it added to the chain. As a result, when the agreement is attached to the chain, none of the parties involved may change, cancel, or deny the agreement's record. The authenticity and integrity of the executed agreements added to the chain is ensured through a process known as mining. This crucial function was not accessible before the blockchain's introduction. As a result, blockchain is the most important facilitator of the Internet of Transactions (Abeyratne & Monfared, 2016), (Mainelli & Milne, 2016) and is required to support a wide range of industrial applications.

Blockchain is a developing technology that was first used in the Bitcoin space (Chuen, 2015), but it has a wide range of industrial uses, some of which we will examine and explore in this article. IBM is a firm believer in blockchain's potential in the broader business and industrial sector, investing significantly in the field and developing various improvements and applications (Abeyratne & Monfared, 2016). Before we get into the specifics of these applications, we'll go through the essential characteristics and functions of blockchain, which are the primary facilitators of the studied industrial applications.

In recent years, DLT (Distributed Ledger Technology) has attracted much attention. DLT is a decentralized, secure, and transparent data storage and transmission system that does not rely on a centrally trusted third party. A distributed ledger is a decentralized database that is maintained by a peer-to-peer network of numerous nodes. Each node verifies and replicates the ledger. One kind of DLT is blockchain.

On the blockchain, data is split into blocks and connected by an append-only structure. The most common DLT data structure is the chain-based block structure, although it is far from the only one. DLT may be implemented using other data structures, such as Directed Acyclic Graph (DAG).

BlockDAG and Transaction DAG are the two types of DAG-based DLT (TDAG). The BlockDAG structure is a DAG in which each block may refer to many preceding blocks. Inclusive Two examples of blockDAG systems are BlockDAG (Lewenberg, Sompolinsky, & Zohar, 2015) and Spectre (Sompolinsky, Lewenberg, & & Zohar, 2016). Transactions are immediately added to a graph in the TDAG-based DLT, creating a graph of transactions. Therefore, each transaction refers to many prior ones. Two typical TDAG systems are IOTA (Xie, et al., 2019) and Byteball (Xie, et al., 2019). Because blockchain is the most commonly used distributed ledger system, we will concentrate on it in this article.

There are three types of blockchain systems: private blockchain, public blockchain and consortium blockchain (Cui, et al., 2017). The consortium and private blockchains are both permissioned, whereas the public blockchain is permissionless. On the public blockchain, anybody may join the network, participate in the consensus process, read and send transactions, and keep track of the shared ledger. Permissionless blockchain systems are used by the majority of cryptocurrencies and open-source blockchain platforms. Bitcoin (Li, et al., 2010) and Ethereum (Steiner, Baker, Wood, & Meiklejohn, 2015) are two of the most well-known public blockchain platforms. Satoshi Nakamoto, the creator of Bitcoin, the most well-known cryptocurrency, developed it in 2008. Another well-known public blockchain example is Ethereum that uses Turing-complete smart contract programming languages to allow large decentralized applications.

Architecture of Blockchain

Like a traditional public ledger (Chuen, 2015), blockchain (Zheng Z., Xie, Dai, Chen, & Wang, 2018) (Zheng Z., Xie, Dai, Chen, & Wang, 2017)is a series of blocks that contain a complete transaction record list. A blockchain is shown in Figure 1 as an example. A block has just one parent block if the block header contains a last block hash. Uncle blocks' hashes (children of the block's predecessors) would likewise be recorded on the Ethereum blockchain. The genesis block is the initial block in a blockchain that has no parent block. This architecture is shown in Figure 3.

Figure 3. A blockchain example consists of a continuous block series. (Zheng Z., Xie, Dai, Chen, & Wang, 2018), (Zheng Z., Xie, Dai, Chen, & Wang, 2017)

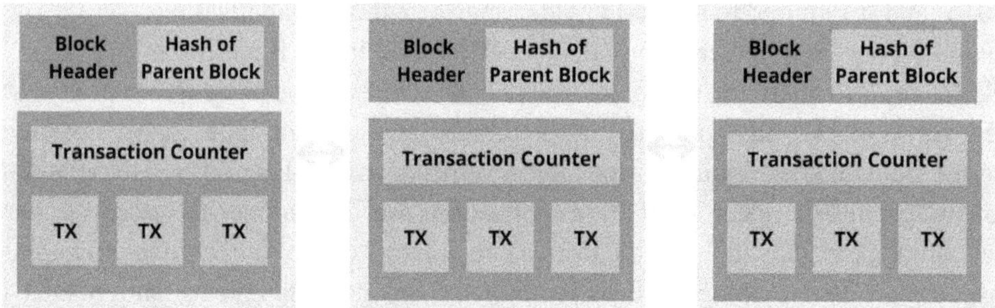

Block

As illustrated in Figure 4, a block comprises of a block header and a block body. The block header, in particular, contains the following information:

Figure 4. Block structure (Zheng Z., Xie, Dai, Chen, & Wang, 2018) (Zheng Z., Xie, Dai, Chen, & Wang, 2017)

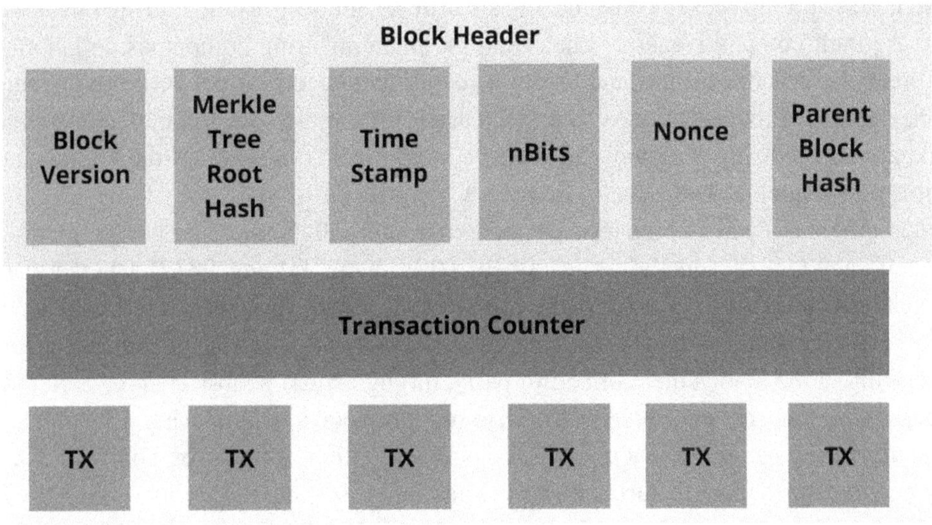

Block version: The block version specifies which set of block validation criteria should be used.
Merkle tree root hash: the sum of all transactions in the block's hash value.
Timestamp: Since January 1, 1970, the current time is expressed in seconds in universal time.
nBits: A valid block hash goal threshold.
Nonce: a 4-byte field, typically beginning with 0 and increasing in every hash computation (will be explained in detail in Section III).
Parent block hash: a 256-bit hash value that points to the previous block.

The block body consists of a counter and transactions for transactions. The maximum number of transactions that may be included in a block depends on the size and size of the block. To authenticate transactions, blockchain employs an asymmetric cryptography mechanism. In an unreliable context, asymmetric cryptography is used to create a digital signature.

BLOCKCHAIN IN THE MANUFACTURING INDUSTRY

The manufacturing industry is making significant progress toward smart manufacturing and automated/automized processes, and blockchain may help in various ways. For example, logistics management, which we covered previously, is an essential topic. Logistics management is critical for every company to guarantee fair pricing and timely delivery of raw material and supplies for its operations. It also aids in the effective and timely distribution of their goods to meet their consumers' requirements. Using blockchain for industrial logistics management may decrease time delays, management expenses, and human mistakes, just like any other logistics management program (Buterin & others, 2014). As a result, businesses may lower their production costs while also becoming nimbler and more competitive.

In addition, blockchain may be utilized to facilitate the efficient, equitable, and secure sharing and use of its social production resources by manufacturing companies' social networks (SMNs). Social manufacturing is a fast-evolving production process and commercial activity aiming to deliver more personalized goods and services to consumers. Using this technique, manufacturing businesses may be able to increase their competitiveness. When multiple manufacturing companies collaborate to share their social manufacturing resources and create a social manufacturing network for the benefit of all members, the success of this technique can be increased. With more social manufacturing resources in this network, a manufacturing company can produce more precise and professional items that meet the unique desires of consumers (Ding, Jiang, Leng, & Cao, 2016).

Nonetheless, there is always a high level of concern in this collaborative network regarding security, fairness, and efficacy. One such method is described in (Liu, Jiang, & Leng, 2017), where Liu et al. developed a blockchain-based Product Credit Mechanism (PCM) to safely, equitably, and effectively manage cross-enterprise partnerships in their social manufacturing network. This Management is accomplished peer-to-peer, without the involvement of a third party, through smart contracts and a credit system.

Blockchain technology has enormous potential to support cloud manufacturing. Cloud manufacturing is a new manufacturing paradigm that combines cloud computing, Internet of Things (IoT), SOA, and virtualization to transform manufacturing resources and processes into a network of digitally linked and managed manufacturing services (Li, et al., 2010). In this regard, blockchain technology should enable the development of a secure decentralized cloud manufacturing architecture (Barenji, Li, & Wang, 2018) and the secure exchange of information for manufacturing design, such as the creation and redesign of injection moulding (Li, Liu, Barenji, & Wang, 2018).

Another use of blockchain is to improve copyright and anti-counterfeiting procedures in additive manufacturing. For example, Kennedy et al. (Kennedy, et al., 2017) devised a physical counterfeit detection method that may be used to validate the validity and quality of 3D-printed components. In this approach, nanomaterial chemical signatures are applied to these components, and their provenance is verified using blockchain based on their many nanomaterials chemical signatures.

Some of the primary benefits of utilizing blockchain to verify the authenticity of components in production are that it allows for healthier manufacturing supply chains and reduces the dangers of employing counterfeit parts (Holland, Nigischer, & Stjepandić, 2017). In addition, before being utilized to construct additional goods, each part may be authenticated through an automated procedure.

The Genesis of Things is working on a platform that combines 3D printing, blockchain and the Internet of Things to create more advanced manufacturing processes. This enables more efficient customization by decreasing bespoke items generated by 3D printing and automating various manufacturing and associated operations. Another advantage is the ability to communicate and share manufacturing data across cooperating firms securely. Data must be protected and tracked and regulated in these cases to guarantee adequate access and prevent unauthorized modifications or tampering.

The Impact of Blockchain Technology on Manufacturing

Blockchain may be used to improve other emerging technologies but also to change fundamental business operations which, as we know, will develop the manufacturing industry (Xcube, 2020). For example, blockchain's intrinsic openness creates confidence amongst stakeholders at every production process, from raw material purchasing through floor operations to distributing final products to clients. As a result, you can enhance procedures such as:

- Contract drafting and implementation
- Monitoring of the supply chain
- Detection of falsification
- Management of intellectual property
- Tracking and monitoring of assets
- Management of stock
- Quality control
- Compliance with regulations

Blockchain technology can speed up a company's time to market by streamlining a variety of business processes. Supplier order accuracy, product quality, and delivery rates all improve due to blockchain applications, leading to greater customer satisfaction and income.

Figure 5. Elimination of a Manufacturing Firm's Verification Costs when using blockchain (Ko, Lee, & Ryu, 2018)

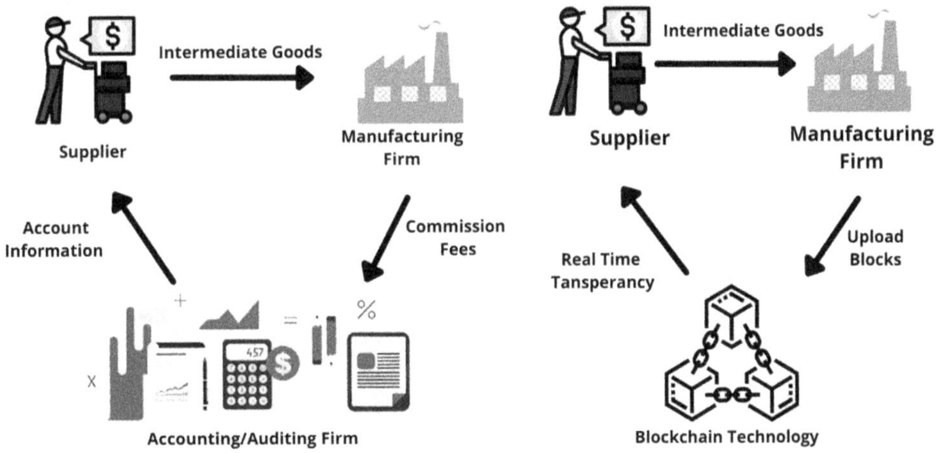

The Advantages of Using Blockchain in Manufacturing

Although blockchain was created to enable bitcoin transactions, the underlying technology is adaptable. Here are a few examples of how blockchain technology may assist the manufacturing industry:

Reduced Administrative Expenses and Entry Barriers

Blockchain can drastically decrease the overhead expenses involved with running a manufacturing business, lowering entry barriers. Machines as a Service (MaaaS) is a business concept based upon blockchain, allowing manufacturers to pay for the output of the equipment used instead of the machine itself, thereby lowering expenses. By using this business model, new manufacturers and designers will sell their goods without substantial start-up costs (Xcube, 2020). Smart contracts automate different business processes, from procurement to payment, which usually require time and effort from team members that may be utilized better elsewhere. A model which shows the elimination of verification costs in manufacturing industry is depicted in Figure 5.

Stability and Resilience

Because of COVID-19, manufacturers have been focusing on business continuity and resilience for the last year. While there is no one "cure" for a worldwide epidemic, blockchain is a fantastic way to assist a manufacturing company to develop resilience.

The decentralization of blockchain is crucial since it includes a distributed ledger visible to all network participants. This implies that even if one of the nodes fails or one of the parties quits the network, the blockchain will continue to function normally (Xcube, 2020). Thus, manufacturing firms striving toward a robust business model will benefit from the stability provided by blockchain technology.

Improved Transparency and Trust

A blockchain is an excellent tool for businesses that establish trust amongst many stakeholders. The distributed directory includes a single, unchangeable version of information, which is always available to all network participants (Xcube, 2020). In addition, the network must verify each transaction or modification to enhance its credibility.

Improved Safety

The sophisticated encryption code needed to consolidate the system's safety is part of what makes blockchain special. The transparency of blockchain must be tempered with cryptographic signature requirements for each transaction that improve tamper prevention (Xcube, 2020). The storage of the network is decentralised too, thereby reducing cybersecurity risks and the data it holds.

Blockchain Applications in the Manufacturing Sector

Blockchain is a versatile technology used in a variety of operations across a wide range of industries. Here are a few examples of how it is utilized in manufacturing.

Management of Supply Chain

Supply chain management is one of the most important jobs faced by businesses, and blockchain technology is being used to help with it. Blockchain increases the tracking function of many firms to identify the whereabouts of materials, components and products utilized in everyday operations in previous and present situations (Xcube, 2020). The capacity of blockchain to offer a clear end-to-end route for components and products increases trackability and ensures correctness and reduces production process mistakes.

Smart Contracts

Smart contracts enabled by blockchain technology are proving to be a game-changer in the manufacturing sector. Instead of paper contracts or unstable digital copies of paper contracts, smart contracts live as a computer program on a blockchain. The smart contract encapsulates all of the benefits of blockchain technology: it is immutable and accessible to all stakeholders at all times.

Smart contracts' capacity to automate otherwise complicated commercial processes is a benefit to their security (Xcube, 2020). The data in the terms and conditions stored on the blockchain may be used to manage inventories, monitor the supply chain, schedule and execute payments, and more.

Automating procedures that were previously done manually saves time, effort, and money. Employees' skills can better serve the company's objectives using smart contracts.

Shop-Floor Operations

The shop floor is probably the most important part of any manufacturing operation, as well as one of the most difficult to optimize. The blockchain is being used to improve shop-floor operations. For example, blockchain apps are being used to monitor and report the health of particular equipment, providing operators with data that may help them plan maintenance rather than depend on costly emergency repairs (Xcube, 2020). With a technique known as machine-controlled maintenance, blockchain may potentially be used to automate servicing to equipment. A manufacturer collaborates with a third-party servicer to install shared software, including a blockchain system, that monitors equipment via a digital duplicate of the machine. Without requiring any human intervention, blockchain monitoring may identify when planned maintenance is required, generate a service request, purchase any components required for the equipment, and process payment after the order is completed.

Quality Control and Regulation Compliance

The inherent security of blockchain technology and its capacity to monitor a single version of a piece of data make it ideal for quality control and regulatory compliance in the manufacturing industry. The quality control process is streamlined by machine-level monitoring and accurate track-and-tracing of materials and components, reducing mistakes (Xcube, 2020). As a result, there are fewer recalled goods, less waste, and total income.

In addition, the blockchain ledger creates an immutable record of data regarding equipment, processes, materials, and other things. Internal auditors may utilize these records to verify that the premises are safe and that rules are followed. The logs may also be used as proof of compliance in the event of an external inspection.

Blockchain's Potential in the Manufacturing Industry

Many innovation-driven firms in the sector perceive the considerable potential for improvement in many processes via blockchain development (Xcube, 2020). 49% think that blockchain can improve compliance with current and future regulations, 31% say that blockchain can improve product sales in new areas, and 28% think that blockchain can decrease product reminder risk.

Whether it's suppliers, procurement, procurement, store and production, blockchain provides a new business method and is a perturbing solution for different industrial activities. As manufacturing blockchain is becoming more and more widely accepted, specialists estimate that usage of blockchain is likely to record an AGRC of around 78% in production.

Use Cases of Blockchain in Manufacturing

The manufacturing sector, which accounts for 17% of global GDP, has long struggled with quality control, inefficiencies, and other issues. By providing insight across all aspects of production, blockchain can completely revolutionize it (Xcube, 2020). Here are some examples of how blockchain technology might be used in manufacturing:

Tracking and Traceability Improved

An IoT-powered system can monitor the provenance of a manufactured component from the point of manufacture to retail destinations, improving transparency and traceability for all parties involved in the value chain. IoT-sensor data may be put into the blockchain so that there is a common perspective and no gaps in handling products while moving through the supply chain (Xcube, 2020). The Blockchain implementation may considerably enhance the many procedures involved, such as documentations, certification acquisitions, timestamps and quality checks.

Efficient Procurement of Products

Inefficient product procurement has been one of the leading reasons of financial loss for firms. Organizations are often exposed to risks and unwelcome costs as a result of their complicated supply chain (Xcube, 2020). Companies may use Blockchain technologies to simplify and automate their supply chain and speed up the procurement process, including ordering products and the payment process.

Better Payment Process

Manufacturers often experience delayed payments and a lack of transparency in the payment process since many parties are engaged in confirming and issuing payments (Xcube, 2020). Payments get blocked at different points throughout the supply chain. Blockchain's smart contract feature automates the payment process and guarantees faster and more reliable payment to suppliers.

Efficient Inventory Management

Everyone in the network may view the data since blockchain allows you to connect with every participant in the supply chain-supplies, distributors, and even retailers (Xcube, 2020). This implies that everyone has a copy of the information, reducing the amount of misunderstanding in the supply chain. This makes inventory planning and Management easier.

Increased Consumer Involvement

Blockchain datasets may be examined and utilized to make forecasts and predictions, reduce supply chain delays, and improve customer experience by guaranteeing product origin and manufacturing process transparency. Grocery shops, for example, may make specific information available to consumers, such as the source of supplies that proves the food was produced organically (Xcube, 2020). Sharing this information fosters transparency, which leads to consumer loyalty and long-term relationships.

Better Data Security

Using conventional methods to communicate information such as invoices and contract data in any supply chain may be extremely hazardous. This is where blockchain comes in to assist protect the data using the most advanced cryptographic methods (Xcube, 2020). The risks of being hacked are removed since information blocks are nothing more than chronologically stored copies of documents connected to the preceding block.

Payments to Suppliers are Made Automatically

The transfer of money directly between the payer and payee in any part of the globe, swiftly and securely, is made possible by blockchain. Even an hour of waiting time is no longer necessary- it's that simple (Xcube, 2020). Smart contracts start the payment process as soon as the digitally secure transaction data is included in blockchain agreements and your network agrees to the terms and conditions.

Supply Chain Dependability

Manufacturers place a high value on the quality of the supplies they buy. Reputable providers are increasingly seeking to get their brands documented and recognized. This requirement is addressed with the assistance of blockchain technology, which allows manufacturers to get information on suppliers to ensure that they receive exactly what they bought and that the goods are in excellent condition and free of faults (Xcube, 2020). Smart contract implementation also ensures standards, protects intellectual property, and allows for safe payments.

Manufacturing Plants and Blockchain

For planned maintenance, several industrial facilities have already used IoT and machine learning. When combined with blockchain technology, data on machine component lifespans may be collected and kept in a blockchain network, and replacement parts can be purchased and paid regularly by smart machines.

When equipment fails and parts must be purchased manually, this minimizes downtime, making predictive maintenance more effective (Xcube, 2020). Manufacturers may utilize the blockchain network to store their data and connect their ERP systems to their suppliers' systems.

Management of Warranties

False claims, fraudulent goods, misunderstandings regarding coverages, and other issues plague businesses regarding warranty management (Xcube, 2020). Manufacturers must take steps to avoid fraud, save expenses, and provide a better consumer experience.

By bridging the information gap between manufacturers, warranty providers, and other supply chain players and protecting the chain of custody, blockchain can help expedite the warranty lifecycle, guaranteeing no counterfeits enter the supply chain and no fraudulent claims are submitted.

How Companies are Using Blockchain in Manufacturing?

Some businesses have already begun to investigate the possible use cases of blockchain to address the many problems encountered by manufacturers worldwide (Xcube, 2020).

- Samsung Electronics developed a distributed ledger system to monitor overseas shipments and save 20% on transportation expenses. According to a Bloomberg article, the blockchain-based system will enable the company to save costs like shipping paperwork and react more rapidly to market changes.
- The IBM Blockchain project encourages supply chain openness and accountability. Shipping and logistics stakeholders may utilize a shared ledger to automatically update a process as it happens, increasing confidence throughout the supply chain network and establishing a reliable platform for cooperation.
- To improve security in additive manufacturing, the US Air Force partnered with SIMBA Chain, a blockchain as a service business. The United States Navy Department utilized blockchain to manage its 3D printers.
- The world's biggest container shipping company, MAERSK, using blockchain technology to share event data and manage document processes throughout industrial supply chains.
- The **Bank of America Corp. and Mastercard, Inc.** are using blockchain technology and have more than 48 patents and applications connected with blockchain.

LOGISTICS INDUSTRY

Software solutions that assist coordinate raw materials, goods, and services between producers/sellers and consumer destinations are known as logistics management applications. These may all be part of the same organization or spread among various organizations and entities. These apps may benefit from blockchain's strong support. The participation of numerous businesses in the operations is one of the difficulties in logistics management. Many coordinated sub-activities conducted by various businesses, such as manufacturers, storage companies, shipping companies, and regularity agencies, may also be included. Any logistics management program must have a set of features for planning, scheduling, coordinating, monitoring, and validating completed tasks. Blockchain can effectively and securely support such tasks (Al-Jaroodi & Mohamed, 2019). Time delays, administrative expenses, and human mistakes may be reduced by using blockchain's shared distributed ledgers to verify, record, and audit logistics transactions.

Furthermore, using smart contracts would make it easier for businesses to reach agreements and establish binding contracts quicker and cheaper. Blockchain is expected to significantly affect the logistics sector due to these advantages (Hackius & Petersen, 2017). Many startups are offering blockchain-based logistics management systems and apps in this space. Provenance (Steiner, Baker, Wood, & Meiklejohn, 2015), for example, is a traceability system that connects customers and suppliers for various logistical operations. Hijro is another example, which provides an application platform for worldwide supply chain management.

The Logistics Industry Benefits from Blockchain

One of the most important aspects of modern business is logistics. It guarantees that goods get to their destination in the shortest amount of time, for the lowest cost, and with the least amount of damage. In a nutshell, it is concerned with the planning and execution of complicated procedures for moving products from one location to another (generally from the point of origin to consumption). The roles of blockchain in supply chain in shown in Figure 6.

Figure 6. Supply chain roles (actors) interacting with blockchain distributed ledger technology (Litke, Anagnostopoulos, & Varvarigou, 2019)

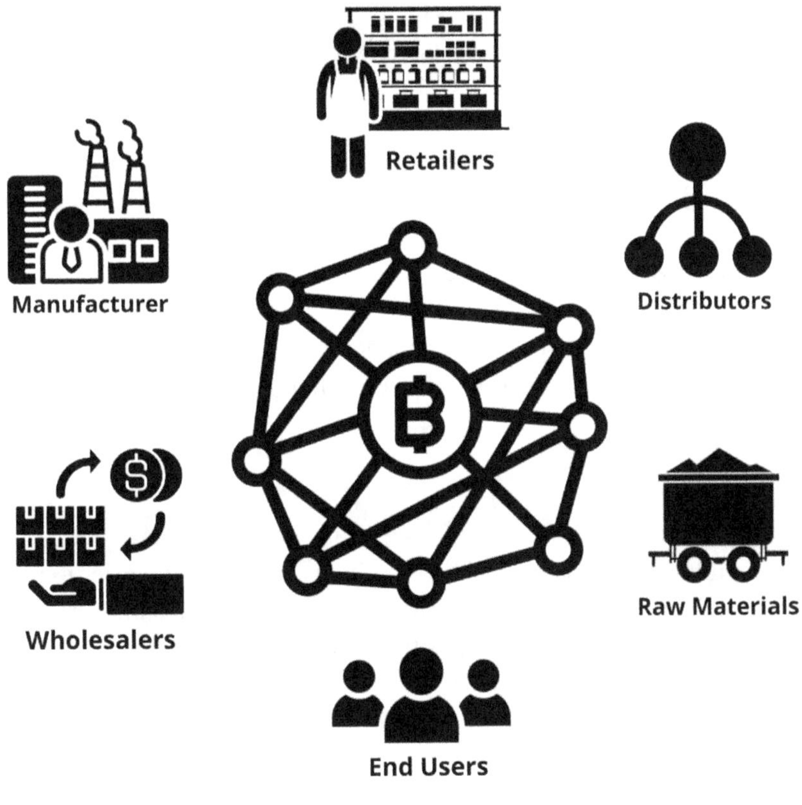

The logistics business is massive right now! In the year 2020, the United States alone generated \$791.7 billion in income. In terms of statistics, it's staggering, and that makes the logistics sector one of the most complicated in the world (Blockchains, 2020).

Blockchain technology creates a decentralized network in which peers may connect and transact without relying on a central authority. Immutability, transparency, and security are just a few of the advantages of its decentralized nature. Furthermore, it is well-suited to the logistics sector.

Because the transaction data on the blocks cannot be changed or falsified, the transaction data is highly reliable. You may also substantially increase work speed by using smart contracts that can automate transactions under specific circumstances. Blockchain technology is being used to innovate in the logistics industry, where activities need a lot of paperwork.

MAERSK Line, a Danish shipping company, conducted a blockchain proof of concept in 2016, estimating a 20% decrease in transportation costs if the blockchain is used to carry products from East Africa to Europe. Blockchain isn't simply another new technology; it's anticipated to play a significant role in helping logistics companies maintain stable growth. As a result, there must be a debate regarding the role of blockchain technology in the logistics industry (Thistlethwaite, 2018).

Several stakeholders are engaged in logistics when it comes to delivering raw materials or finished goods to consumers. To guarantee the transaction's credibility, all logistical transactions are conducted using numerous papers. Work is done in global commerce using conventional trade papers, while in face-to-face exchanges, there are generally no trust problems since the buyer pays after seeing the goods.

Because worldwide commerce transactions rely entirely on records, the risk is frequently significant because you never know whether the other party will deliver you the goods or if the importer will pay you. Furthermore, when quality assurance papers are needed in the event of global commerce, these documents may be changed or falsified (Thistlethwaite, 2018). Unless you phone or send an email, there is no way to know what tasks or procedures the other person is working on in real-time. However, blockchain technology ensures that transaction data on blocks is resistant to fraud or alteration, resulting in a trustworthy ecosystem.

Blockchain is anticipated to cause a paradigm change in logistics in the future. It will speed up the transaction verification process and aid in the supply of goods and services by fostering mutual confidence among participants. It may take many years for this procedure to be fully implemented in logistics.

Use Cases of Blockchain in Logistics

Many applications of blockchain logistics are available. Let's look at five blockchain logistical uses to gain a better idea. It will also assist you in comprehending the logistical advantages of blockchain technology (Blockchains, 2020).

Better Freight Tracking

The use of blockchain in logistics systems and supply chains may make it easier to track down freight. Same-day and on-demand delivery are on the rise at the moment (Blockchains, 2020). Since a result, it may rapidly become a strain for logistics firms, as they cannot fulfil these burgeoning demands.

Many trucking firms are attempting to invest in superior tracking technology; however, the security of these systems is under doubt.

Furthermore, these systems lack a safe authentication procedure. As a result, hackers or bad actors take use of the network's data at all times (Blockchains, 2020). The blockchain has the potential to alter the situation. No one can tamper with the data since blockchain provides a suitable authentication route with verification. Also, since you can keep track of all your deliveries and monitor them in real time, it may help the logistics sector better customer experience.

Increased Efficiency in the Shipping Process

The first area where blockchain will enhance logistics is shipping and freight. In a nutshell, it may be utilized to enhance both international and local delivery processes (Blockchains, 2020). It will also encourage them to increase their products volume and process efficacy.

Maersk recognizes the value of blockchain and has already used it into its procedures and operations. They are one of the biggest container transport companies in the world (Blockchains, 2020). The ultimate aim is to monitor the cargo as closely as possible by collaborating with other agencies. IBM and Maersk are also collaborating to enhance global commerce infrastructure.

Security for IoT Devices to Boost Efficiency

Many companies are now using Internet of Things sensors to track inventory and guarantee constant quality. However, these IoT gadgets are susceptible to assaults since they rely on cloud servers to interact (Blockchains, 2020). Consequently, blockchain in logistics and supply chain can secure these IoT devices while simultaneously monitoring all of the data they produce. It may also aid in the analysis and categorization of all data from these devices in order to make business strategy changes.

Better Transparency

Transparency is one of the most important characteristics of blockchain. When properly deployed, blockchain for supply chain provides more openness, which impacts logistics transparency (Blockchains, 2020). It allows businesses to have greater faith in one another. Better openness, less worker exploitation, and lower auditing expenses will result in fewer billing disputes.

In addition to the consumer, owing to its increased trust and integrity, the B2B industry is imploding. Because of the trust, auditing expenses, invoice disputes, and other forms of conflict will be significantly minimized, if not eliminated entirely.

Companies are already investing in improving transparency (Blockchains, 2020). One such firm is Provenance, which has performed a case study to examine how blockchain, including the supply chain, might enhance logistical elements.

Inventory Tracking

Inventory management is a difficult task. Companies invest a significant amount of money to make it flawless and efficient (Blockchains, 2020). Even then, it presents a slew of issues. As a result, inventory monitoring is one of the sectors' primary concerns. Companies pay millions of dollars to handle it. Blockchain technology may help address the issue by allowing businesses to control their goods at the macro level and at the micro level. Companies, for example, may maintain a close eye on logistics by monitoring it closely. IBM's blockchain-based technology is one such example. It allows businesses to monitor and report on food products throughout the transaction process (Blockchains, 2020). Large corporations such as Nestle, Walmart, Unilever, and others have already joined the initiative and are assisting in achieving the best possible outcome. The end-users will benefit the most since they will always get fresh, ready-to-eat food. This is one of the best example of corporate blockchain use cases in this industry.

Settling Disputes

Another use of blockchain in logistics is the resolution of freight transportation disputes. Cargo transportation is prone to disagreements (Blockchains, 2020). This may occur if the items are lost or arrive late. Disputes are difficult to settle and may take weeks to resolve. All of this requires the business to spend additional resources.

With the assistance of immutable data and real-time cargo information, blockchain can help settle conflicts more quickly (Blockchains, 2020). Many conflicts may be resolved in minutes thanks to automation and reliable data. It also aids businesses in resolving consumer complaints.

Invoicing and Payments

Finally, via an effective and protected system, blockchain may assist enhance invoicing and payments. When done on a big scale, invoicing may be a significant problem (Blockchains, 2020). As a result, you'll come across invoicing and payment methods that are efficient.

Smart contracts may be used by businesses to automate the complete process and make it error-free and crystal clear. Invoicing and payments will be much more efficient as a result of this.

Blockchain in Logistics: Implementation Challenges

Companies must overcome many obstacles to adopt blockchain. The following are some of the difficulties. The following are some of the difficulties (Blockchains, 2020).

- **Various applications of data storage model:** To cooperate on the blockchain, not all businesses or systems use the same data model.
- **Embedding blockchain technology within the current IT environment** Integration of blockchain into the current IT environment will always be difficult.
- **Evolving blockchain technology:** Working with blockchain is the last obstacle. Blockchain is a relatively young technology that is rapidly developing. Implementing blockchain today will result in future implementation difficulties.
- **The flow of Information:** Another significant issue in logistics is controlling the flow of information between the various organizations. When a transaction is multinational, the procedure gets more complicated since additional entities are involved.

Ways Blockchain Can Improve Logistics

Efficiency

Blockchain technology has the ability to transform the way transportation and freight are handled. Blockchain has the potential to enhance the delivery process and boost the efficiency of logistics businesses by efficiently monitoring goods. To create an efficient logistics system, it is essential to collaborate internationally and openly in order to guarantee and optimize product delivery amongst partners while also protecting information and financial activities (Scand, 2020). Logistics has poor transparency and a fragmented structure due to the industry's competitive character, unstandardized procedures, data silos, and different degrees of technology advancement.

Blockchain has the potential to enhance global trade efficiency by removing complexity from administrative procedures. Multiple parties and a massive quantity of paperwork may be eliminated with an automated procedure that provides a systematic approach to monitoring the product lifecycle from its origin to the shop shelf while also enabling all ownership transfers between producers, retailers, and purchasers.

Security

Because current systems are centralized, a malevolent attacker may gain complete control over them once they get access. Any data saved inside the system may be altered or erased by such an invader.

There is no central authority over the whole system in blockchain networks (Scand, 2020). However, unlike other competing solutions, blockchain provides a higher level of security since no third party may alter the data recorded in the chain. Furthermore, blockchain networks may use cryptographic security methods to make hacking the data chain extremely difficult.

Transparency

Blockchain improves security and transparency. It allows companies to monitor and document all changes, including what was changed, why, who made the changes, and when (Scand, 2020). Furthermore, since every entity on the chain uses the same ledger version, there is no misunderstanding regarding chain transactions, and the transaction process becomes more efficient.

The data will be logged on the public ledger after the products have been delivered and digital smart contracts have been signed. The data is saved with information about who created it and when it is impossible to change. Businesses can keep track of products and identify who owns them at any given moment thanks to access to this ledger (Scand, 2020). The data will be recorded on the public ledger once the items have been delivered and digital smart contracts have been executed. The information regarding who made it and when it was made is preserved, making it very impossible to alter. Companies with access to this ledger can keep track of the goods and see who owns them.

Real-Time Asset Tracking and Inventory Management

Blockchain technology may be coupled with IoT and mobile-based technologies to build real-time delivery monitoring systems. Tracking does not have to be done manually anymore; instead, electronic sensors can monitor goods from beginning to end of the supply chain. Logistics firms may use blockchain and IoT to decrease delivery times, improve transparency in the logistics sector, and keep a closer watch on the goods they carry (Scand, 2020). Furthermore, small sensors attached to goods or objects may assist organizations in maintaining accurate and up-to-date inventory. Such "smart" inventories may provide a wealth of information about the items, such as their previous locations, the length of time they've been stored at the facility, and more. Detailed inventory auditing may be simplified using IoT sensors, lowering the risk of missing goods, incorrect storage, and other issues that impact total profitability.

Smart Contracts

Every day, $140 billion is locked up in transportation payment issues. It takes an average of 42 days to settle an invoice in full, which is a waste of time and money. A smart contract is a blockchain-based technology that enables supply chain legal binding agreements to be automated. Smart contracts allow businesses to track the stages in a logistical process and enforce adherence to the transaction's pre-determined standards, lowering the chance of the other party failing to fulfill an agreement (Scand, 2020). This is especially useful for enabling smaller and less known businesses, such as start-ups, to enter the supply chain industry without a prior reputation or references. Smart contracts, by ensuring transparency, may help to mitigate this problem.

Performance History Monitoring

The carrier's and suppliers' performance histories may be tracked using blockchain. Additionally, companies may analyse the performance of individual vehicles in the fleet and past carrier performance, such as on-time pickups and deliveries, among other things (Scand, 2020). This information enables better decision-making and, as a result, supply chain improvement. Businesses may create faster routes and eliminate needless stages in the shipping process using important data.

CONCLUSION

We covered just a few blockchain use scenarios in the manufacturing industry. The technology is still far from being extensively adopted, and there are numerous obstacles such as industry-wide standards and more. However, one thing is that blockchain may change how manufacturers are doing business. The slow-moving, unsecured, manual system is being revolutionized into a digital, safe, quick, and automated network run on a single platform. In terms of process change, money transfers, supply chain monitoring, guarantee management and more, we may anticipate more blockchain until we ultimately see an entire, decentralized manufacturing system. Although we see a blockchain revolution occurring mainly now in white papers and papers, but as more and more companies are piloting their cases of use to disrupt the manufacturing industry, we can be sure that most companies will soon embrace it to try to survive when the fourth industrial revolution comes into being. Logistics is one of the major problems in today's company development. But the entire ball game is different if you are a member of a logistics business. Important players include manufacturers, suppliers, 3PLs, long-haul carriers, short-haul carriers, warehouses, and consignors. The use of various data storage strategies, integration with the present ecosystem, the development of blockchain technology, and information flow are the primary difficulties facing the logistics business right now. Inventory tracking, increased transparency, dispute resolution, and invoicing and payments are some of the logistics use cases for blockchain. Nonetheless, even in these cases, blockchain offers many success factors in logistics.

REFERENCES

Abeyratne, S. A., & Monfared, R. P. (2016). Blockchain ready manufacturing supply chain using distributed ledger. *International Journal of Research in Engineering and Technology*, *5*(09), 1–10. doi:10.15623/ijret.2016.0509001

Al-Jaroodi, J., & Mohamed, N. (2019). Blockchain in Industries: A Survey. *IEEE Access: Practical Innovations, Open Solutions*, *7*, 36500–36515. doi:10.1109/ACCESS.2019.2903554

Atlam, H. F., & Wills, G. B. (2019). Chapter One - Technical aspects of blockchain and IoT. In S. Kim, G. C. Deka, & P. Zhang (Eds.), *Role of Blockchain Technology in IoT Applications* (Vol. 115, pp. 1–39). Elsevier. doi:10.1016/bs.adcom.2018.10.006

Barenji, A. V., Li, Z., & Wang, W. M. (2018). Blockchain cloud manufacturing: Shop floor and machine level. *Smart SysTech 2018: European Conference on Smart Objects, Systems and Technologies*, (pp. 1–6). Academic Press.

Blockchains. (2020, February). Benefits of Blockchain In Logistics Industry. *Benefits of Blockchain In Logistics Industry*. Retrieved July 17, 2021, from https://101blockchains.com/blockchain-in-logistics/

Bogart, S., & Rice, K. (2015). The blockchain report: Welcome to the internet of value. *Needham Insights*, *5*, 1–10.

Buterin, V., & Associates. (2014). A next-generation smart contract and decentralized application platform. *White Paper, 3*.

Casino, F., Dasaklis, T. K., & Patsakis, C. (2019). A systematic literature review of blockchain-based applications: Current status, classification and open issues. *Telematics and Informatics*, *36*, 55–81. doi:10.1016/j.tele.2018.11.006

Chuen, D. L. (2015). *Handbook of Digital Currency*. Bitcoin.

Churyumov, A. (2016). *Byteball: A decentralized system for storage and transfer of value*. https://byteball. org/Byteball. pdf

Connor, T. (2001). *Still waiting for Nike to do it*. Global Exchange.

Cui, G., Shi, K., Qin, Y., Liu, L., Qi, B., & Li, B. (2017). Application of block chain in multi-level demand response reliable mechanism. *2017 3rd International Conference on Information Management (ICIM)*, 337–341.

Ding, K., Jiang, P., Leng, J., & Cao, W. (2016). Modeling and analyzing of an enterprise relationship network in the context of social manufacturing. *Proceedings of the Institution of Mechanical Engineers. Part B, Journal of Engineering Manufacture*, *230*(4), 752–769. doi:10.1177/0954405414558730

Elder, S. D., Zerriffi, H., & Le Billon, P. (2013). Is Fairtrade certification greening agricultural practices? An analysis of Fairtrade environmental standards in Rwanda. *Journal of Rural Studies*, *32*, 264–274. doi:10.1016/j.jrurstud.2013.07.009

Frentrup, M., & Theuvsen, L. (2006). *Transparency in supply chains: Is trust a limiting factor?* Tech. rep.

Hackius, N., & Petersen, M. (2017). Blockchain in logistics and supply chain: trick or treat? *Digitalization in Supply Chain Management and Logistics: Smart and Digital Solutions for an Industry 4.0 Environment. Proceedings of the Hamburg International Conference of Logistics (HICL)*, 23, 3–18.

Holland, M., Nigischer, C., & Stjepandić, J. (2017). Copyright protection in additive manufacturing with blockchain approach. In *Transdisciplinary Engineering: A Paradigm Shift* (pp. 914–921). IOS Press.

Iredale, G. (2020, November). History of Blockchain Technology: A Detailed Guide. *History of Blockchain Technology: A Detailed Guide*. Retrieved July 17, 2021, from https://101blockchains.com/history-of-blockchain-timeline/

Kennedy, Z. C., Stephenson, D. E., Christ, J. F., Pope, T. R., Arey, B. W., Barrett, C. A., & Warner, M. G. (2017). Enhanced anti-counterfeiting measures for additive manufacturing: Coupling lanthanide nanomaterial chemical signatures with blockchain technology. *Journal of Materials Chemistry. C, Materials for Optical and Electronic Devices*, *5*(37), 9570–9578. doi:10.1039/C7TC03348F

Ko, T., Lee, J., & Ryu, D. (2018). Blockchain Technology and Manufacturing Industry: Real-Time Transparency and Cost Savings. *Sustainability*, *10*(11), 4274. doi:10.3390u10114274

Lewenberg, Y., Sompolinsky, Y., & Zohar, A. (2015). Inclusive block chain protocols. *International Conference on Financial Cryptography and Data Security*, 528–547. 10.1007/978-3-662-47854-7_33

Li, B.-H., Zhang, L., Wang, S.-L., Tao, F., Cao, J. W., Jiang, X. D., ... Chai, X. D. (2010). Cloud manufacturing: A new service-oriented networked manufacturing model. *Jisuanji Jicheng Zhizao Xitong*, *16*, 1–7.

Li, Z., Liu, L., Barenji, A. V., & Wang, W. (2018). Cloud-based manufacturing blockchain: Secure knowledge sharing for injection mould redesign. *Procedia CIRP*, *72*, 961–966. doi:10.1016/j.procir.2018.03.004

Litke, A., Anagnostopoulos, D., & Varvarigou, T. (2019). Blockchains for supply chain management: Architectural elements and challenges towards a global scale deployment. *Logistics*, *3*(1), 5. doi:10.3390/logistics3010005

Liu, J., Jiang, P., & Leng, J. (2017). A framework of credit assurance mechanism for manufacturing services under social manufacturing context. *2017 13th IEEE Conference on Automation Science and Engineering (CASE)*, 36–40.

Mainelli, M., & Milne, A. (2016). *The impact and potential of blockchain on the securities transaction lifecycle*. Academic Press.

Moore, M. (2012). 'Mass suicide' protest at Apple manufacturer Foxconn factory. *The Telegraph, 11*.

Nakamoto, S. (2008). *Bitcoin: A peer-to-peer electronic cash system*. Decentralized Business Review.

Punter, A. D. (2013). *Supply chain failures. A study of the nature, causes and complexity of supply chain*. Academic Press.

Rathee, P. (2020). Introduction to blockchain and IoT. In *Advanced Applications of Blockchain Technology* (pp. 1–14). Springer. doi:10.1007/978-981-13-8775-3_1

Scand. (2020, September). *6 Ways Blockchain Can Improve Logistics*. Retrieved July 17, 2021, from https://scand.com/company/blog/blockchain-for-logistics/

Sompolinsky, Y., Lewenberg, Y., & & Zohar, A. (2016). SPECTRE: a fast and scalable cryptocurrency protocol. *IACR Cryptol. ePrint Arch.*

Steiner, J., Baker, J., Wood, G., & Meiklejohn, S. (2015). *Blockchain: the solution for transparency in product supply chains*. Available at: provenance. org/whitepaper.

Taylor, E., & Cremer, A. (2016). *Volkswagen takes 18 billion hit over emissions scandal*. Tech. rep., Reuters.

Thistlethwaite, G. (2018, July). *How blockchain is changing the logistics industry*. Retrieved July 17, 2021, from https://www.gbnews.ch/blockchain-logistics-industry/

Tschorsch, F., & Scheuermann, B. (2016). Bitcoin and beyond: A technical survey on decentralized digital currencies. *IEEE Communications Surveys and Tutorials*, *18*(3), 2084–2123. doi:10.1109/COMST.2016.2535718

Xcube, L. A. (2020, April). *How Companies Worldwide are Using Blockchain Technology in Their Manufacturing Processes*. Retrieved July 17, 2021, from https://www.xcubelabs.com/blog/how-companies-worldwide-are-using-blockchain-technology-in-their-manufacturing-processes/

Xie, J., Tang, H., Huang, T., Yu, F. R., Xie, R., Liu, J., & Liu, Y. (2019). A Survey of Blockchain Technology Applied to Smart Cities: Research Issues and Challenges. *IEEE Communications Surveys and Tutorials*, *21*(3), 2794–2830. doi:10.1109/COMST.2019.2899617

Xu, R., Zhang, L., Zhao, H., & Peng, Y. (2017). Design of network media's digital rights management scheme based on blockchain technology. *2017 IEEE 13th international symposium on autonomous decentralized system (ISADS)*, 128–133.

Xu, Z., Liu, Y., Zhang, J., Song, Z., Li, J., & Zhou, J. (2019). Manufacturing Industry Supply Chain Management Based on the Ethereum Blockchain. *2019 IEEE International Conferences on Ubiquitous Computing Communications (IUCC) and Data Science and Computational Intelligence (DSCI) and Smart Computing, Networking and Services (SmartCNS)*, 592-596. 10.1109/IUCC/DSCI/SmartCNS.2019.00124

Yu, F. R., & He, Y. (2019). A service-oriented blockchain system with virtualization. *Trans. Blockchain Technol. Appl.*, *1*, 1–10.

Yu, F. R., Liu, J., He, Y., Si, P., & Zhang, Y. (2018). Virtualization for distributed ledger technology (vDLT). *IEEE Access: Practical Innovations, Open Solutions*, *6*, 25019–25028. doi:10.1109/ACCESS.2018.2829141

Yuan, Y., & Wang, F.-Y. (2016). Towards blockchain-based intelligent transportation systems. *2016 IEEE 19th international conference on intelligent transportation systems (ITSC)*, 2663–2668.

Zheng, Z., Xie, S., Dai, H., Chen, X., & Wang, H. (2017). An overview of blockchain technology: Architecture, consensus, and future trends. 2017 IEEE international congress on big data (BigData congress), 557–564.

Zheng, Z., Xie, S., Dai, H.-N., Chen, X., & Wang, H. (2018). Blockchain challenges and opportunities: A survey. *International Journal of Web and Grid Services*, *14*(4), 352–375. doi:10.1504/IJWGS.2018.095647

Chapter 2
A Comprehensive Review on Blockchain-Based Internet of Things (BIoT):
Security Threats, Challenges, and Applications

Manimaran A.
Madanapalle Institute of Technology and Science, India

Chandramohan Dhasarathan
https://orcid.org/0000-0002-5279-950X
Thapar Institute of Engineering and Technology, India

Arulkumar N.
https://orcid.org/0000-0002-9728-477X
CHRIST University (Deemed), India

Naveen Kumar N.
Madanapalle Institute of Technology and Science, India

ABSTRACT

The internet of things (IoT) represents rapid development in research and industry that enables both virtual and physical objects to be linked and transfers information in order to produce various services that enhance our excellence of life. Traditional security and privacy methods are not applicable for IoT, mostly due to their topological constraints and versatility of IoT devices. Blockchain technology has started to fascinate younger generations because it works especially well in the digital world. Blockchain is suitable for internet of things applications. Advancements in IoT have propelled distributed systems. The blockchain concept demands a method for exchanging and storing data that is managed by a decentralized network. The rise of IoT applications is hindered by these obstacles. One option to fix these problems is to use a distributed ledger technology using blockchain technology. This chapter gives a comprehensive overview of blockchain's strengths and weaknesses with its applications.

DOI: 10.4018/978-1-7998-8697-6.ch002

Copyright © 2022, IGI Global. Copying or distributing in print or electronic forms without written permission of IGI Global is prohibited.

INTRODUCTION

The market has seen an exponential increase in IoT devices over the last decade. The number of IoT devices on the market is reaching 25 billion and is anticipated to reach 50 billion by the end of 2025. These devices feature sensors to connect to the network and provide data to a reserved node. Many devices in our daily lives are becoming wirelessly compatible with low-power wireless devices. A wide range of objects (or physical equipment) may be easily interacted via the IoT, including monitoring sensors, household appliances, security cameras and automobiles (Khan et al., 2018). These applications leverage massive amounts of data created by objects to assist individuals, governments, and businesses.

One of the most emerging technologies of this century, the Internet of Things (IoT) is a hyper-connected IoT is basically anything connected to the Internet. IoT devices are characterized by low power, limited storage, and low computing capacity. IoT devices are connected to the internet via "gateways" that allow the devices to "talk" to each other. IoT improves the global connectivity of people and their surroundings by bringing intelligence and greater efficiency to everything in the globe. Many "things" are being connected, thereby increasing the amount of data generated. These additional data help to further connect people and the environment, therefore enabling us to increase the intelligence of our surroundings. For instance, data may be gathered to support tailored services for customers. The popular IoT is now seeing fast expansion in both industry and research. A large number of well-known companies, like Amazon and Google, have invested billions of dollars to construct IoT platforms, like the Amazon AWS IoT and Google Cloud IoT (Agrawal et al., 2018).

Blockchain, a digital ledger technology that has lately captured the attention of the world and it is a database which records transactions. With respect to blockchain identification and accessibility, there are three broad categories: public, private, and consortium. Blockchain transactions, which are blocks of information, are used to securely store information. This aspect of blockchain is completely different from anything else. Decentralized consensus is very resilient because to its ability to stay consistent, continue operating, and automatically resolve any faults.

The new Blockchain technology may be used in a broad range of industries. Blockchain may be used in the IoT sector to share and exchange network data, validation, and security service between devices. Blockchain technology faces a few important problems that are being studied with an emphasis on security of cyber-physical systems in the IoT sector. A lot of legitimate companies are doing their best to guarantee there is appropriate connectivity, privacy, and security in the IoT network. Blockchain and cloud computing have been used to empower many entities. The technology improves the IoT information system by making it more transparent, reliable, and well-governed (Kumar et al., 2018).

Governments are using Blockchain in IoT applications to revolutionize data modelling. Because it is good at separating, safeguarding, and transferring IoT data and services, it is the best option for these kinds of programs. Many IoT technologies utilize blockchain nowadays. IoT services often experience risks and complications. Blockchain is a solution to many IoT cyber-physical system challenges. Management in smart communities and all of the associated elements must be described according to individual benefits (Da Xu et al., 2021).

Security is a key problem as we progress towards decentralization, persistence, anonymity, and auditability. This article gives an overview of blockchain characteristics and cyber-physical system security threats. It also discusses existing solutions and blockchain applications for various issues that may arise. Blockchain technology's decentralization, durability, anonymity, and auditing features have captivated industry and academia. This survey examines the use of blockchain technology in various applications and discusses the problems involved.

BACKGROUND

Drastic increase in attacks have been announced due to mixture of physical world and the growth of internet which are leading to difficult security inference. This section deals with potential benefits of integrating blockchain with IoT architectures. IoT has vast number of nodes at the network edge and they are more vulnerable to enormous range of attacks. IoT offers centralized configurations for its service availability and which is highly impactful threat. Authorization and confidentiality services are also bigger threat because of central failure point architecture which may leads to misuse of user's data.

Security aspect is of utmost dominant factor for IoT smart devices. At Present, third party based security solutions are provided and are centralized. We can achieve better security solutions without utilizing third party support by integrating block chain technology. Block chain provides auditability, fault-tolerant design and decentralized public key infrastructure for fighting with vast variety of attacks, in addition to that it can deliver security to transactive networks such as Bitcoin. Blockchain protocols are well capable of preventing unauthorized users from DoS attacks because transaction amount is necessary to pay each time while making empty transactions. Hence, Blockchain has more powerful techniques to provide improved security to the IoT stack. Fig. 1 depicts the Blockchain based IoT Security services.

The Blockchain is a decentralized transaction and data management technology designed for Bitcoin that lets consumers and businesses to store and exchange value without financial intermediaries. Transparency, efficiency, and security are key features of this new technology. Blockchain technology uses a globally distributed ledger to verify and approve transactions. The distributed ledger contains immutable, chronologically ordered transaction records that are accessible to all network participants. Because blockchain is globally distributed, the historical documents cannot be changed without network consensus. Immutable distribution promotes network trust.

Access Control

Several academics have published ideas for incorporating blockchain into access control systems without a third party, for IoT devices. The researchers, (Hashemi et al., 2016), advocate a multi-layered blockchain architecture, which enables data storage and has inbuilt data access and permission mechanisms. There are three separate parts to the Blockchain decentralized data storage facility, a control mechanism for accessing user data, and a negotiation function to allow the two parties to access each other's information. The data that is kept in the Blockchain is encrypted, and it is only accessible to privileged users who have authorization to decode it.

(Zhang et al., 2017), developed a token-based technique to assigning various access responsibilities to different individuals as well as individual access rights. The authors, according to (Shafagh et al., 2017), concentrate on off-chain decentralized hash tables for data storage with access rights to different users and nodes to facilitate the hash table for access control.

Figure 1. Blockchain based IoT security services

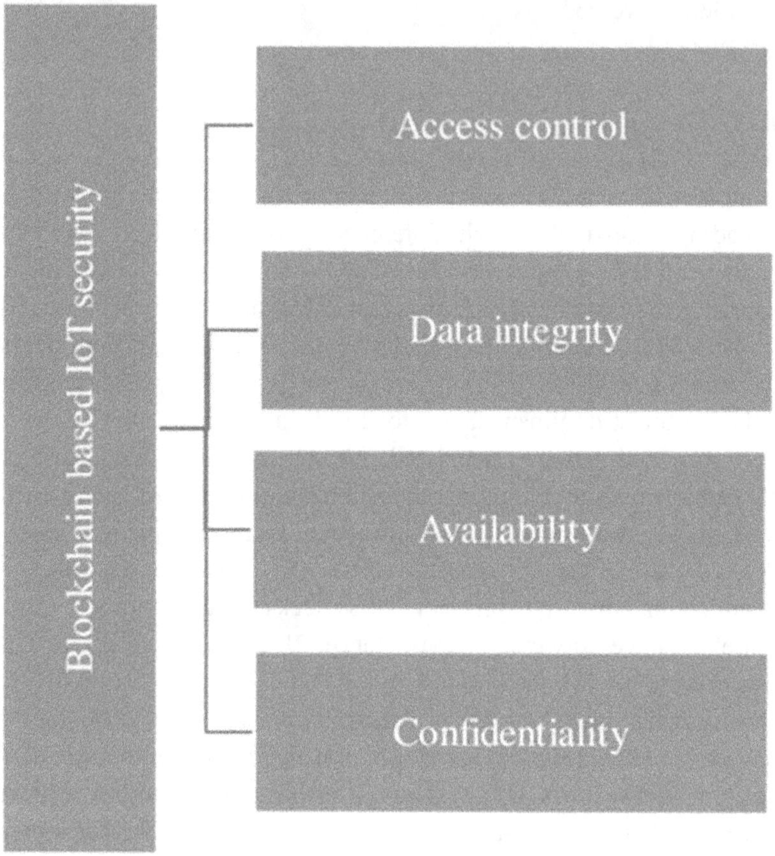

Data Integrity

Blockchain may be able to help with data integrity problems. It protects the database's file integrity. It also offers transaction auditing, security, and authentication features. Blockchains were designed to be resistant to changes in data. Since blockchain ledgers are uneditable, they're the ideal choice for handling everything that needs to be trusted. This includes recording important information (e.g., medical records), providing trustless online identities, and confirming the validity of important documents.

In a Blockchain-powered IoT system, a malicious actor has tried to inject fabricated blocks. In contrast, when using traditional shared ledger, blockchains aren't able to leverage real-time data due to the complexities involved. (Shafagh et al., 2017), described a decentralized hash table technique that uses persistent blockchain records as a data storage model. Blockchain keeps data safe from tampering and provides access to many kinds of data with proper control over who can access the data. (Liu et al., 2018), suggested a blockchain data integrity protocol that handles query-based integrity checks, without requiring any third-party involvement. In order to identify loss of information, the blockchain uses record verification.

Availability

Blockchain provides in-built higher data availability due to its decentralized data storage in order to protect data from vulnerable points. In addition to that, off-chain storage mechanism is also implemented to provide improved data availability. (Chakraborty et al., 2018), proposed multi-layered blockchain solutions to handle resource constrained issues of IoT devices. Higher data storage and higher computational tasks are taken care of higher level nodes and resource controlled nodes situated at the lower layers, Higher layer nodes enables the data communications with lower level resource constrained nodes. (Bahga et al., 2016), introduced blockchain oriented manufacturing system which provides flexibility for delivering straight manufacturing commands during transactions. This type of approach gives more advantage for numerous applications like, supply chain tracking, machine fault identification and on-demand manufacturing. Distributed nature of nodes arrangement assures the network availability and keep them as live node forever.

Confidentiality

Confidentiality feature in blockchain is enabled by its strong usage of issuers private key for each and every transaction. (Axon et al., 2017), suggested blockchain based Public Key Infrastructure(PKI) to commendably manage the IoT devices. Proposed approach used to issue orders like recording energy usage information and altering working policies in a secured way by implementing smart contracts.

(Aitzhan et al., 2016), proposed energy transacting smart grid based security schemes to implement confidentiality. This proposed approach enables the confidentiality by hiding the energy producer's identity along with their data communication. (Cha et al., 2018), worked on signature based blockchain which gains access of Ethereum blockchain to maintain confidentiality among IoT gateways and wearable devices.

BLOCKCHAIN ATTACKS

A variety of threats evolved with blockchain technology progresses. These assaults or hazards may be coming from inside the organisation or outside its boundaries. Data storage and transmission protection has emerged as an increasing concern due to the rising number of blockchain-powered applications. Double spending attacks, network attacks, mining pool issues, and security concerns in wallets are the primary challenges in blockchain security today.

Double Spending Attacks

If a person is performing several transactions with one cryptocurrency, they're more vulnerable to this assault. Below, we describe the many methods double spending assaults may be launched (Begum et al., 2020).

Race Attack

When an attacker sends two or more confusing transactions at once, this counterattack is deployed. PoW-based blockchains may be attacked using this simple method. Opponents make an instant payment to the seller, who ships the goods before receiving a confirmation. While this is happening, the bad actor submits another transaction that the bitcoin nodes receive openly and deems the coins that the merchant receives as having no value. The double spending attack is launched rapidly because the adversary utilises the time that is required to complete two transactions.

Suggested solutions: Upon seeing a new transaction, peers inspect the blockchain's memory pool to see if the currencies used in the transaction have been used before. The coins are first sent to peers, who add them to their memory pool before forwarding them to the network. If they have been sent to other parties before, they are only passed on if it is discovered in the previous transaction. The double-spending detection strategy is mostly on finding the double-spend assault rather than stopping it.

51% Attack

51% attack is an attack in which a group of miners have 51% of the mining hash rate or processing power. In the event of an attack, the perpetrator may block further transactions from being verified, thereby hindering payments to users. It may even reverse transactions, spending bitcoin twice. For bitcoin transactions to be settled, nodes or computers are required to first examine newly generated blocks. This may follow with a block addition (Sayeed et al., 2019). A public ledger of all transactions may be found on the blockchain. Decentralization is when no one person or organisation has control, thus that is the case with this system. A wider hash rate is obtained because nodes and computers operate in parallel to mine.

Suggested solution: The inability to approach 50% of the entire hash rate means that miners cannot monopolise the system's overall computational power and perform this attack.

Finney Attack

The Finney attack is an example of double-spending. The attacker inserts a transaction in the block that transfers part of his money back to himself without disclosing it. If he discovers a pre-mined block, he transfers the same coins again. Other miners will reject the second transaction, but this will take time. To avoid this attack, the vendor should hold the items for six blocks.

Vector76 Attack

The Vector76 attack combines the Race and Finney attacks, allowing even one confirmation transactions to be reversed. It involves a miner creating two nodes, one linked to the exchange node and another to well-connected peers in the blockchain network. As a result, the miner generates two transactions. The attacker then pre-mines a high-value transaction. On block announcement, he transmits the pre-mined block to the exchange. The attacker submits a low-value transaction to the blockchain network, which rejects the high-value transaction. As a consequence, the compromised attacker's account receives the high-value transaction. Incoming connections may be disabled and only well-connected nodes can be joined.

Network-Based Blockchain Attacks

In order to utilise the blockchain, nodes must comply with the network protocols. There are two kinds of nodes on the bitcoin network: users and miners. One node type produces blocks and accepts incoming TCP connections while the other makes transactions and sends them to the bitcoin network. The subdivisions below describe several kinds of network challenges (Bose et al., 2019).

Distributed Denial of Service Attack

DDoS attack on a blockchain server aim to use the server's processing power to generate excessive requests. To dismantle the crypto economy, hackers target blockchain technology pools, wallet platforms, and exchange houses. A DDoS attack at the application layer may also be used to hack a blockchain.

Timejacking

Timejacking is a kind of cybercrime that takes use of a potential weakness in Bitcoin's timestamp processing. Timejacking is a kind of attack in which a hacker changes the network time counter of a node, forcing the node to accept an other blockchain. An attacker may do this by adding numerous bogus peers to the network with erroneous timestamps, which are then removed. A timejacking attack, on the other hand, may be avoided by limiting the acceptable time ranges or by utilising the system time of the node.

Transaction Malleability Attack

The Bitcoin protocol's vulnerability lies in its origins. When a victim falls for the transaction malleability attack, their belief that a certain transaction has failed results in that transaction being replayed on the bitcoin network with a new transaction hash ID. In a situation when the adversary is not the one initiating the transaction, an attack of this kind is known as an alternate double spending attack.

Routing Attack

A routing attack may have a negative effect on both individual nodes and the whole network. The goal of this attack is to tamper with transactions before they are sent to peers for approval (Sengupta et al., 2020). Because the hacker splits the network into divisions that are unable to interact with one another, it is virtually difficult for other nodes to notice the tampering. Rather than being one attack, routing attacks are really two distinct attacks:

A partition attack is one in which the network nodes are divided into different groups.

A delay attack, which interferes with the propagation of messages and transmits them to the network.

Sybil Attack

This attack has one goal: to destroy the trust network by using false names to get into a Peer to peer network. Anonymous identities are used to gain influence and disrupt the authentication scheme by building large amounts of influence in a network. Due to the reason that even PoW struggles to prevent sybil attacks, which are possible in almost all scenarios excluding impractical and unrealistic scenarios where the entities have extreme resources, PoW cannot combat these attacks.

A preventative measure put forward, which, amongst other things, overcomes timing-based inference attacks, denial-of-service attacks, and the sybil attack through a two-party decentralised mixing protocol.

Mining Pool Attack

Individual miners are unable to benefit from Bitcoin, therefore they form mining pools, groups that use their pooled computer capacity to solve Bitcoin's algorithms (Chen et al., 2020). They mine more blocks and, as a result, everyone receives a piece of the prize. Bitcoin's top three mining pools, as of now, are BTC.com, AntPool, and ViaBTC.

Selfish Mining Attack

A selfish miner is someone who uses his hash power to block or censor a block, allowing the selfish miner to "steal" other people's blocks. Some methods to help avoid these attacks include the use of random mining assignments, preference of blocks with a more recent timestamp, and limiting the allowed duration to generate a block (Chicarino et al., 2020). Block withholding is another name for this kind of attack.

Suggested solution: The Freshness Preferred (FP) method to thwart selfish mining attacks utilises block headers to detect recently mined blocks and ensure their freshness. Because previously mined blocks are competing against the unmined blocks, the selfish mining incentive is diminished. Because of this, honest miners will consider the authenticity of private blockchains reported by dishonest miners with the time it was hashed and published to the network.

Block Stretching Attack

In a mining pool attack that discards blocks, dishonest miners are prevented from publishing mined blocks for their own gain, preventing them from undermining pool income. Miners (who do the work) and pool administrators (who organise the mining process) are generally the kinds of users found in a mining pool.

The role of the pool manager is to transfer unfinished assignments to miners who will produce PoW and submit that work to the pool manager. The pool management then uses this fresh block as an opportunity to advertise to the whole network. In this type of attack, the pool management would employ some of its miners to disguise itself as a normal miner of the target pool by using the mining software. When intruding miners transmit PoW to a victim pool, the attacker discards the PoW and doesn't contribute to victim income. In this situation, the attacker's mining strength is lowered, but he enjoys more income because of his other pool infiltrations.

BLOCKCHAIN BASED IOT APPLICATIONS

Blockchain technology has the power to involve in many application areas. The growth of blockchain started with Version 1.0 of Blockchain (Bitcoin), then progressed towards the Version 2.0 (Smart contracts) and later on moved to Version 3.0 (Efficiency applications). Blockchain can be used in IoT applications such as sensor devices, cyber security, crowd sensing, wearable devices, timestamping services, identity management, intelligent transportation system, healthcare field, and smart home (Lockl et al., 2020). Fig. 2 represents various applications of BIoT.

Figure 2. Blockchain based IoT (BIoT) applications

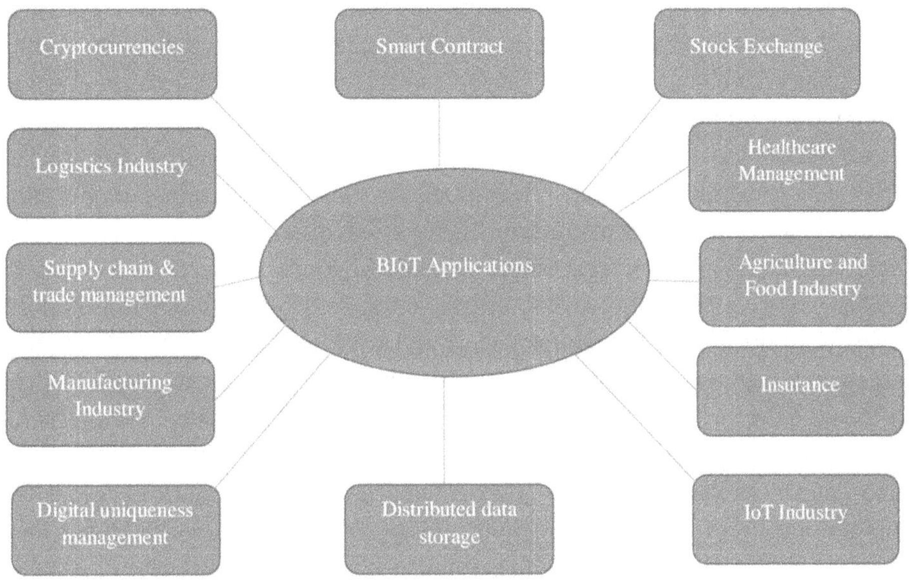

Logistics Industry

Logistics management applications help control the flow of goods and services between producers/sellers and consumers. These can be part of a single organization or spread over several. Multi-company engagement is one of the logistical challenges. This may comprise synchronized sub-activities by factories, storage businesses, shipping companies, and regularity regulators. Any logistics management application must have functions to plan, schedule, coordinate, monitor, and validate activities. Blockchain may effectively and safely support such functions. Using blockchain to verify, store, and audit logistics transactions reduces delays, costs, and human errors. Using smart contracts can also help companies reach agreements faster and more affordably. With these advantages, blockchain is expected to have a big effect on logistics (Jain et al., 2020). Many startups in this field are developing blockchain-based logistics management systems and applications. Provenance offers a traceability system that connects customers and suppliers for various logistical operations.

New business models emerged from automation and the shared economy. Online and automated networks are replacing human-facilitated physical systems. The sharing economy has established a platform ecosystem that has increased efficiencies and offered new opportunities. These trends are fueled by existing and emerging technologies. These technologies are SMAC (Social, Mobile, Analytics, and Cloud), AI, Internet - of - things, Autonomous Vehicles, Drones, Robotics, VR, AR, and 3D Printing. Numerous operations are automated to make them more economical as businesses like retail and finance digitise. The future competitive edge will go to those who hold this valuable data and use it to produce a better consumer experience.

Manufacturing Industry

Manufacturing is moving towards smart manufacturing and automated/autonomous processes, which may benefit from blockchain in many ways. As previously said, logistics management is an essential topic. In order to guarantee fair pricing and timely delivery of raw materials, logistics management is critical. It also ensures effective and timely delivery of goods to meet consumer requirements. Using blockchain for industrial logistics management may decrease time delays, costs, and human mistakes (Tian et al., 2021). This allows producers to be more flexible and competitive. Also, blockchain can help manufacturing companies share and utilise their social manufacturing resources efficiently, equitably, and securely. With social manufacturing, businesses may create more customised goods and services for consumers. Using this strategy, industrial firms may improve their competitiveness. In order to maximise the effectiveness of this strategy, several manufacturing companies should work together to share resources and create a social manufacturing network. A manufacturing company with more access to social manufacturing resources may create more accurate and professional goods targeted to particular customer needs. This collaborative network is constantly a source of security, fairness, and efficacy issues.

In addition to using blockchain to manage the manufacturing cloud, it may assist cloud manufacturing operations. This new paradigm, called cloud manufacturing, is defined as the collection of manufacturing services that will use computer and networking resources to be intelligently integrated and controlled. Using blockchain, cloud manufacturing architecture may be more secure, and knowledge exchange for injection moulding production design can be enhanced. For example, additive manufacturing may be enhanced with blockchain technology to fight counterfeiting and piracy.

Blockchain's ability to authenticate the authenticity of components in production improves supply chains and lowers the threats of utilising imitation parts. Parts may be authenticated by an automated procedure and then reused to create new products. An revolutionary platform from a new firm, Genesis of Things, seeks to blend 3D printing, blockchain, and IoT to create advanced manufacturing processes. Lowering the cost of 3D printed customized goods and automating the manufacture and other functions lead to better customised products (Tian et al., 2021).

Cryptocurrencies

Cryptocurrency is the first application of Blockchain technology. It has vast variety of dimensions such as Bitcoin-cash, Litecoin, Dash, Ripple, Monero, Zcash and many others. Cryptocurrencies are acceptable by many companies like Microsoft, Expedia, Wikipedia, Burger King, KFC, Subway, Norwegian Air, Home Depot, Shopify, Newegg, Starbucks, Apple, and more. According to HSB's survey, one third of small businesses accepts cryptocurrency and they are supporting digital currencies. ATMs for exchanging Cryptocurrencies into cash are widely available across 63 countries globally (Wang et al., 2020). Several countries are working towards owning their own central bank digital currencies for making transactions on intra-bank and government purpose.

Smart Contract

A smart contract is governed and enforced by a computer programme rather than a third party such as a lawyer (Szabo et al., 1997). It automatically executes contracts when the program's criteria are fulfilled. Blockchain support makes smart contracts safe and easy. In addition to financial and smart contracts on the blockchain may provide additional services like as voting, library, and notary services (Bartoletti et al., 2017). Smart contracts are novel blockchain transactions. Currently, Ethereum has approximately 14 million smart contracts (Pinna et al., 2019). A transaction may fund a smart contract or call its functionalities. To execute transactions, smart contracts may communicate with one other. Solidity is a programming language used in Ethereum to create smart contracts.

Stock Exchange

Blockchain is used to make investments. Tokens that represent real-world stocks can be traded across a peer-to-peer network, making them easier to buy and sell. Digital stocks, like digital cash, have a real-time value. The stock market is struggling with a number of challenges today, including high frequency trading and short sales. Many of these problems could be resolved with just an exchange where trading was totally done through peer-to-peer (Bhandarkar et al., 2019). When purchasing and selling assets and stocks, the traditional method involves plenty of additional fees, risk, and several intermediaries. In the face of these challenges, blockchain could offer a solution. Blockchain technology will completely reshape stock exchange marketing, according to Microsoft. Although banks don't actually sell shares, blockchain enables secondary marketplaces to trade shares.

Healthcare Management

Data inconsistency, duplicate records, and the inability for patients to manage their own records are just a few of the numerous concerns present in the current healthcare administration system. Blockchain has the potential to overcome these healthcare problems. For healthcare management, Blockchain is currently employed to share and protect data. Files are uploaded to the blockchain for increased data access, confidentiality, Different medical organisations could more effectively interoperate and exchange information with no difficulties caused by dissimilar databases or controlling parties. Estonia has pioneered in the field of healthcare by putting all of its medical records on the blockchain. Some major healthcare corporations like Gem and HealthBank are using blockchain to offer services like record sharing and preventing counterfeits. Healthcare applications using blockchain were found to be categorised into four classes, including: keeping medical records, dealing with medical insurance, clinical and biomedical research, and blockchain projects which help to connect healthcare providers (Abou-Nassar et al., 2020).

Insurance

More insurance businesses are using blockchain technology. Putting insurance data on blockchain avoids fraud and lets insurers share data and operate on a centralized database. Using the same insurance policy from multiple firms protects customers from double-dipping. A startup named Everledger uses blockchain to provide diamond certification histories. An example of blockchain in insurance is Etherisc, Insurwave, and MedRec (Xiao et al., 2020).

IoT Industry

Blockchain solutions establish a decentralised network of Internet of Things devices, preventing the requirement for a single site to manage device communication. Blockchain technology is an attractive alternative for IoT security, as it provides robust protection against data manipulation and unauthorised access to IoT devices. Blockchain has gained interest for application in IoT devices because IoT devices require human participation. A good number of practical applications using the blockchain have evolved for IoT, including IBM's ADEPT, Filaments, GSF, and Share&Charge. With ADEPT, IoT devices may do repair, upgrades, and updates on their own, which can help solve issues faster (Mazzei et al., 2020).

Distributed Data Storage

There is an inherent risk connected with data security and centralization when using cloud storage services from sources like Google and Dropbox. Security and privacy breaches occur often since these previous versions of monolithic systems were all centralized. Decentralizing personal data storage via blockchain technology allows owners to take ownership of their data. Blockchain storage has many benefits: it's fast, protected, flexible, and affordable. Storj is a distributed, blockchain-based cloud storage network that can be accessed easily, keeps data private, and is very safe. So now is another blockchain storage solution out there called Gaia that has similarities to Blockstack (Abou-Nassar et al., 2020).Other blockchain-based storage networks include Swarm, Sia, IPFS, and SAFA.

Digital Uniqueness Management

Governments and organisations are looking at new ways to utilise blockchain's identity management. In the past, authorities like the government issue identification documents such as passports, IDs, and certificates to help people prove who they are. Identity management in the earlier was weak since it was easy to loose money, theft, and fraud. Now identities are safer, because they're better controlled through blockchain, which means they are independent and don't need a central authority.

Zero-knowledge proof and blockchain are helpful in making identity information on the blockchain private while maintaining accuracy and traceability. The e-Identity of Estonia is a commonly known application case for blockchain-based identity. Other nations have undertaken blockchain experiments for identity management, including the USA, Japan, Switzerland, India, and Finland. The platform Tykn employs blockchain technology to assist with identity management and other services. Microsoft and Accenture developed a model of the United Nation's global refugee identity system, which is based on blockchain technology and was presented at the United Nation's ID2020 Summit in New York (Mazzei et al., 2020).

Supply Chain and Trade Management

Blockchain, which improves upon standard information sharing, offers customers increased trust, quicker transactions, and lower costs. People might record trades and information about the deliveries of items in a blockchain in order to keep better track of things and be able to easily verify them. All relevant parties are aware of the location of their items and of recent trades. Without relying on central authority, data is collected considerably faster. This can happen because central authorities can be potentially harmful. Items and documents could be preserved via blockchain technology. There are around 20 different blockchain-based supply chain networks in development, and one of the most significant ones, TradeLens, was developed by Maersk and has received over 70% of the worldwide shipping firms as partners.

Governance

Blockchain-enabled applications may disintermediate transactions and record keeping, changing local or state government operations. The transparency, automation, and security that blockchain provides for public documents could help fight corruption and improve government services. Blockchain could be used to securely connect physical, social, and business infrastructures in a smart city environment. Blockchain governance aspires to provide the same services as the state and its public authorities. Registration, legal documents, attestation, identification, marriage contracts, taxation, and voting are examples. World Citizen is an example of a decentralized passport service to identify global citizens. Also, public services like marriage registration, patent administration, and taxation can leverage blockchains. Other efforts focus on delegated democracy, where delegates vote instead of parliamentarians.

Agriculture and Food Industry

Generally, Information and Communication Technology (ICT) plays a key role in increasing agriculture and food sector activities. ICT helps e-agriculture, which allows farmers to increase their profit margins by reducing risks and increasing their food security. E-agriculture focuses on aiding farms in becoming more productive, safe, and preventing possible hazards through promoting information exchange about farming. Blockchain is capable of making this information exchange more effective. In the context of agriculture, using blockchain technology makes it possible to increase participants' confidence in each other, which in turn benefits participants' agricultural operations by using supplied e-agriculture servers. The new services are going to increase the cost-effectiveness of food service, increase food safety, and decrease uncertainty and risk.

Blockchain may be used in the food sector to increase the safety of food. It may be combined with RFID to provide a system for traceability in the agri-food supply chain. Food safety in every production, manufacturing, and sales phase may be guaranteed with the help of an information system that securely collects and communicates data throughout the agri-food supply chain. Blockchain is used with many IoT technologies and other established ideas like Hazard Analysis and Critical Control Points to make sure food is safe from the source all the way to the plate.

Every country's economy depends on agriculture, and all food products are made from agricultural raw materials. However, the agriculture sector has been encountering challenges with weather, traceability, finances, and resource updates. Using the blockchain in agriculture can help alleviate this issue. The blockchain connects all agriculture-related sectors in a decentralized network. No field officer is required to go to the field to check whether the farmer is submitting accurate information, for example. If field inspectors and farmers are on the same network, both parties can operate rapidly. Because each event is available in a distributed network, everyone in the system can easily track its progress. If the weather department links in agriculture, the weather authority can warn the farmer. Blockchain can connect regional and national agriculture departments, allowing it to solve problems across regions and nations.

In China, Walmart has partnered with IBM and the Tsinghua University to use blockchain to build a supply chain application focused on the pork market. They said they got a great benefit by shortening the amount of time it takes to trace food from days to minutes. A better way to ensure food safety has better consumer approval since customers feel safer with it (Lin et al., 2020). Blockchain helps with food-related endeavours including boosting transparency, creating better flows, eliminating waste, preventing fraud, and ensuring that consumers can trust the food whatever they eat.

Table 1 summarizes the different types of blockchain systems, language support, data model and its related application areas.

Table 1. Comparisons of various blockchain systems

Blockchains	Language of Smart contract	Data Model	Applications
Litecoin	• C++, Golang	• Transaction-based	• Crypto-currency
Ethereum	• Serpent, Solidity	• Account-based	• General applications
Monax	• Solidity	• Account-based	• General applications
Quorum	• Golang	• Account-based	• General applications
Dfinity	• Serpent, Solidity	• Account-based	• General applications
Corda	• Kotlin, Java	• Transaction-based	• Digital assets
Multichain	• C++	• Transaction-based	• Digital assets
BigchainDB	• Python	• Transaction-based	• Digital assets
Tezos	• Serpent, Solidity	• Transaction-based	• Smart Contracts
Stellar	• C++	• Transaction-based	• Crypto-currency

CHALLENGES

These challenges are more obvious and raise further considerations for important mission applications. Blockchain integration leads to further technical and operational constraints due to the complexity of the BIoT applications (Zachariadis et al., 2019). The key factors affecting the development of the BIoT application are detailed in subsequent paragraphs.

Energy Efficiency

The most critical thing is permitting long-term deployment, since end nodes are resource-constrained. This necessitates giving a priority to energy efficiency. But this Peer to peer(P2P) connection and mining is costly and consumes a lot of energy. Because of its consensus method, bitcoin uses a lot of electricity throughout the mining process. P2P connections could end up leading to wasteful energy use due to continuously-powered devices.

Privacy

No one can be sure they are anonymous when using blockchain as all users are known by their hash or public key, and their transactions are shared with others so third parties can guess and find out their real identities. When considering IoT, privacy is more complicated due to private user data possibly being exposed by IoT devices. A challenge with IoT applications is to provide identity certification. In their work, (Kravitz et al., 2017), has suggested using permissioned blockchains to manage and secure IoT nodes by enabling them to serve as an identity management solution that features an asymmetric key rotation system which can help them to avoid attacks. Private blockchains assume the neutrality of their access controllers and eliminate risk. Furthermore, it presents additional communication complications. Zero knowledge proof is a system that gives a degree of identification without disclosing the user's name during a transaction.

Another privacy preserving technique was introduced by (Hayouni et al., 2016), who suggested using homomorphic encryption. Using a secure communications protocol, the data doesn't have to be exposed to third-party IoT services as the transaction can be performed by them. However, IoT devices have a limited resource capacity, therefore this limits the practical use of these strategies.

Security

Confidentiality, integrity, and availability are three fundamental aspects of ensuring secure systems. One benefit of using traditional Iot devices is that their validity is kept, as long as system robustness against leaks and attacks and centralised infrastructure managers is preserved. While a blockchain-based system is decentralised and hence doesn't fall apart if some nodes are hacked, an application in the old centralised model fails if some nodes are compromised.

The usage of certificates for public key infrastructure protects third party trust. Authorities in general do an adequate job of protecting everyone, but they have a critical flaw in some conditions. The last necessary part of an IoT application is ensuring data integrity. (Liu et al., 2017), suggested a blockchain-based framework for cloud-based IoT applications that replaces reliance on a third party. It seems there are major attack surfaces in IoT systems, but these systems are also extremely vulnerable to an array of security problems. The most dangerous exploit for an IoT system is a 51 percent attack, when one entity has control over the majority of IoT devices. A single miner can get control of the entire blockchain and process transactions as they like in an attack such as this.

Lack of Adoption

Blockchains are ecosystems that require widespread adoption. For supply chain tracking, a firm would need to establish a blockchain network, as would its suppliers. APQC revealed that only 29% of organisations are experimenting or completely deploying blockchain. Blockchains' efficacy and scalability will be restricted without wide adoption.

But there are reasons to be positive about blockchain adoption. Companies are increasingly building blockchain working groups to address common issues and develop solutions that benefit all without compromising sensitive information (Liu et al., 2017).

Before the COVID-19 epidemic, several prominent pharmaceutical companies formed the Blockchain for Clinical Supply Chain Industry Working Group with Consultants. The organisation created KitChain along with blockchain developer LedgerDomain. The tool allows organisations to track bundled drug deliveries, which helps safeguard the supply chain, reduces dependency on paper records, and secures medical trial data.

Blockchain Interoperability

As more businesses use blockchain, many will design their own systems with unique features (governance rules, blockchain technology versions, consensus models, etc.). These various blockchains don't communicate, and there is no single standard for interoperability. Interoperability is sharing, seeing, and accessing data across blockchain networks without an intermediary or central authority. Interoperability issues can make mass adoption challenging.

With post-pandemic business collaboration across functions, suppliers, and customers necessary, blockchain interoperability is critical. It is the only approach to boost the impact of blockchain assets. The scary part is that interoperability projects have increased in number during the last year. Many of them attempt to join internal network or global blockchains. Less reliant on blockchain networks and cryptocurrency-related tools, these platforms will eventually be more beneficial to company executives. Other difficulties with blockchain technology include interoperability, privacy, energy usage, selfish mining, security, and regulatory policy. The challenge of interoperability emerges as a result of the absence of a standardized framework for implementing and integrating blockchain-based solutions across businesses. Additionally, privacy leakage may occur within the blockchain, despite the fact that the system purports to be extremely secure due to the fact that users only conduct transactions using digital signatures that include public-private key encryption. (Liu et al., 2017).

Blockchain has an Identity Problem

Many people associate blockchain with cryptocurrencies. Especially crypto has a bad reputation due to scammers and hackers that abuse the technology. This bad reputation reflects on the blockchain technology system as a whole, making people hesitate to use it. Before widespread acceptance, the public must comprehend bitcoins, other crypto-currencies, and blockchain. Cryptocurrencies are one of several uses of blockchain technology. This will remove certain negative consequences and may enhance desire to use technology. Meanwhile, a rising number of blockchain-based collaboration efforts across industries are bringing about change. This interdependence may be the key to progress.

Some organisations dislike the disruptive nature of blockchain. Some fear losing market share or perhaps becoming obsolete. Blockchain is 80% business process change and 20% technology. It is a radical departure from the norm. This includes industries that already have undergone major digital revolution (Dorri et al., 2016).

Scarcity in Blockchain Developers

The problem is that there aren't enough skilled personnel to manage the complexities of blockchain networks. Blockchain technology also requires more technical expertise and training. Blockchain technology is still in its childhood and is in the process of growing and expanding. Introducing blockchain to developers and academic institutions will take time, as both groups have to start incorporating technology into their lives. The improvements are likely to benefit the public, but it will take time before the advantages can be recognized since the students must complete their studies before anything significant happens (Dorri et al., 2016).

CONCLUSION

IoT has improved people's lives in many ways, including as exchanging data and helping to make significant decisions. On the other hand, it causes security and privacy problems at the same time. The possibilities that blockchain could use to handle these security and privacy challenges in IoT. Blockchain can connect companies, governments, and even nations. The decentralized and peer-to-peer nature of blockchain technology is generally recognized and valued. The review paper's key lesson is that the authors thoroughly investigated many blockchain threats and security vulnerabilities. We examine IoT's well-known security and privacy vulnerabilities in this research article. Then, the use of blockchains is recommended to help resolving those problems. This paper also explored many security difficulties, obstacles, weaknesses, and threats that restrict the expanding usage of blockchain technology. We also summarized various blockchain applications and benefits, as well as commercial potential. Finally, we discussed existing security solutions and research issues.

REFERENCES

Abou-Nassar, E. M., Iliyasu, A. M., El-Kafrawy, P. M., Song, O. Y., Bashir, A. K., & Abd El-Latif, A. A. (2020). DITrust chain: Towards blockchain-based trust models for sustainable healthcare IoT systems. *IEEE Access: Practical Innovations, Open Solutions*, *8*, 111223–111238. doi:10.1109/ACCESS.2020.2999468

Agrawal, R., Verma, P., Sonanis, R., Goel, U., De, A., Kondaveeti, S. A., & Shekhar, S. (2018, April). Continuous security in IoT using blockchain. In *2018 IEEE International Conference on Acoustics, Speech and Signal Processing (ICASSP)* (pp. 6423-6427). IEEE. 10.1109/ICASSP.2018.8462513

Aitzhan, N. Z., & Svetinovic, D. (2016). Security and privacy in decentralized energy trading through multi-signatures, blockchain and anonymous messaging streams. *IEEE Transactions on Dependable and Secure Computing*, *15*(5), 840–852. doi:10.1109/TDSC.2016.2616861

Axon, L., & Goldsmith, M. (2017, July). PB-PKI: A Privacy-aware Blockchain-based PKI. In SECRYPT (pp. 311-318). doi:10.5220/0006419203110318

Bahga, A., & Madisetti, V. K. (2016). Blockchain platform for industrial internet of things. *Journal of Software Engineering and Applications*, *9*(10), 533–546. doi:10.4236/jsea.2016.910036

Bartoletti, M., & Pompianu, L. (2017, April). An empirical analysis of smart contracts: platforms, applications, and design patterns. In *International conference on financial cryptography and data security* (pp. 494-509). Springer. 10.1007/978-3-319-70278-0_31

Begum, A., Tareq, A. H., Sultana, M., Sohel, M. K., Rahman, T., & Sarwar, A. H. (2020). Blockchain attacks analysis and a model to solve double spending attack. *International Journal of Machine Learning and Computing*, *10*(2), 352–357.

Bhandarkar, V. V., Bhandarkar, A. A., & Shiva, A. (2019). Digital stocks using blockchain technology the possible future of stocks? *International Journal of Management*, *10*(3). Advance online publication. doi:10.34218/IJM.10.3.2019/005

Bose, A., Aujla, G. S., Singh, M., Kumar, N., & Cao, H. (2019, August). Blockchain as a service for software defined networks: A denial of service attack perspective. In 2019 IEEE Intl Conf on Dependable, Autonomic and Secure Computing, Intl Conf on Pervasive Intelligence and Computing, Intl Conf on Cloud and Big Data Computing, Intl Conf on Cyber Science and Technology Congress (DASC/PiCom/CBDCom/CyberSciTech) (pp. 901-906). IEEE. doi:10.1109/DASC/PiCom/CBDCom/CyberSciTech.2019.00166

Cha, S. C., Chen, J. F., Su, C., & Yeh, K. H. (2018). A blockchain connected gateway for BLE-based devices in the internet of things. *IEEE Access, 6*, 24639-24649.

Chakraborty, R. B., Pandey, M., & Rautaray, S. S. (2018). Managing computation load on a blockchain–based multi–layered internet–of–things network. *Procedia Computer Science*, *132*, 469–476. doi:10.1016/j.procs.2018.05.146

Chen, Y., Chen, H., Han, M., Liu, B., Chen, Q., & Ren, T. (2020). A Novel Computing Power Allocation Algorithm for Blockchain System in Multiple Mining Pools Under Withholding Attack. *IEEE Access: Practical Innovations, Open Solutions*, *8*, 155630–155644. doi:10.1109/ACCESS.2020.3017716

Chicarino, V., Albuquerque, C., Jesus, E., & Rocha, A. (2020). On the detection of selfish mining and stalker attacks in blockchain networks. *Annales des Télécommunications*, *75*(3-4), 1–10. doi:10.100712243-019-00746-2

Da Xu, L., Lu, Y., & Li, L. (2021). Embedding blockchain technology into IoT for security: A survey. *IEEE Internet of Things Journal.*

Dorri, A., Kanhere, S. S., & Jurdak, R. (2016). *Blockchain in internet of things: challenges and solutions.* arXiv preprint arXiv:1608.05187.

Hashemi, S. H., Faghri, F., Rausch, P., & Campbell, R. H. (2016, April). World of empowered IoT users. In *2016 IEEE First International Conference on Internet-of-Things Design and Implementation (IoTDI)* (pp. 13-24). IEEE.

Hayouni, H., & Hamdi, M. (2016, April). Secure data aggregation with homomorphic primitives in wireless sensor networks: A critical survey and open research issues. In *2016 IEEE 13th International Conference on Networking, Sensing, and Control (ICNSC)* (pp. 1-6). IEEE. 10.1109/ICNSC.2016.7479039

Jain, G., Singh, H., Chaturvedi, K. R., & Rakesh, S. (2020). Blockchain in logistics industry: In fizz customer trust or not. *Journal of Enterprise Information Management*, *33*(3), 541–558. doi:10.1108/JEIM-06-2018-0142

Khan, M. A., & Salah, K. (2018). IoT security: Review, blockchain solutions, and open challenges. *Future Generation Computer Systems*, *82*, 395–411. doi:10.1016/j.future.2017.11.022

Kravitz, D. W., & Cooper, J. (2017, June). *Securing user identity and transactions symbiotically: IoT meets blockchain. In 2017 Global Internet of Things Summit (GIoTS)*. IEEE.

Kumar, N. M., & Mallick, P. K. (2018). Blockchain technology for security issues and challenges in IoT. *Procedia Computer Science*, *132*, 1815–1823. doi:10.1016/j.procs.2018.05.140

Lin, W., Huang, X., Fang, H., Wang, V., Hua, Y., Wang, J., Yin, H., Yi, D., & Yau, L. (2020). Blockchain technology in current agricultural systems: From techniques to applications. *IEEE Access: Practical Innovations, Open Solutions*, *8*, 143920–143937. doi:10.1109/ACCESS.2020.3014522

Liu, B., Yu, X. L., Chen, S., Xu, X., & Zhu, L. (2017, June). Blockchain based data integrity service framework for IoT data. In *2017 IEEE International Conference on Web Services (ICWS)* (pp. 468-475). IEEE. 10.1109/ICWS.2017.54

Liu, Z., Liu, Z., Zhang, L., & Lin, X. (2018). MARP: A distributed MAC layer attack resistant pseudonym scheme for VANET. *IEEE Transactions on Dependable and Secure Computing*, *17*(4), 869–882. doi:10.1109/TDSC.2018.2838136

Lockl, J., Schlatt, V., Schweizer, A., Urbach, N., & Harth, N. (2020). Toward trust in Internet of Things ecosystems: Design principles for blockchain-based IoT applications. *IEEE Transactions on Engineering Management*, *67*(4), 1256–1270. doi:10.1109/TEM.2020.2978014

Mazzei, D., Baldi, G., Fantoni, G., Montelisciani, G., Pitasi, A., Ricci, L., & Rizzello, L. (2020). A Blockchain Tokenizer for Industrial IOT trustless applications. *Future Generation Computer Systems*, *105*, 432–445. doi:10.1016/j.future.2019.12.020

Pinna, A., Ibba, S., Baralla, G., Tonelli, R., & Marchesi, M. (2019). A massive analysis of ethereum smart contracts empirical study and code metrics. *IEEE Access: Practical Innovations, Open Solutions*, *7*, 78194–78213. doi:10.1109/ACCESS.2019.2921936

Sayeed, S., & Marco-Gisbert, H. (2019). Assessing blockchain consensus and security mechanisms against the 51% attack. *Applied Sciences (Basel, Switzerland)*, *9*(9), 1788. doi:10.3390/app9091788

Sengupta, J., Ruj, S., & Bit, S. D. (2020). A comprehensive survey on attacks, security issues and blockchain solutions for IoT and IIoT. *Journal of Network and Computer Applications*, *149*, 102481. doi:10.1016/j.jnca.2019.102481

Shafagh, H., Burkhalter, L., Hithnawi, A., & Duquennoy, S. (2017, November). Towards blockchain-based auditable storage and sharing of iot data. In *Proceedings of the 2017 on cloud computing security workshop* (pp. 45-50). 10.1145/3140649.3140656

Szabo, N. (1997). Formalizing and securing relationships on public networks. *First Monday*, *2*(9). Advance online publication. doi:10.5210/fm.v2i9.548

Tian, Z., Zhong, R. Y., Vatankhah Barenji, A., Wang, Y. T., Li, Z., & Rong, Y. (2021). A blockchain-based evaluation approach for customer delivery satisfaction in sustainable urban logistics. *International Journal of Production Research*, *59*(7), 2229–2249. doi:10.1080/00207543.2020.1809733

Wang, Q., Zhu, X., Ni, Y., Gu, L., & Zhu, H. (2020). Blockchain for the IoT and industrial IoT: A review. *Internet of Things*, *10*, 100081. doi:10.1016/j.iot.2019.100081

Xiao, Z., Li, Z., Yang, Y., Chen, P., Liu, R. W., Jing, W., Pyrloh, Y., Sotthiwat, E., & Goh, R. S. M. (2020). Blockchain and IoT for Insurance: A Case Study and Cyberinfrastructure Solution on Fine-Grained Transportation Insurance. *IEEE Transactions on Computational Social Systems*, *7*(6), 1409–1422. doi:10.1109/TCSS.2020.3034106

Zachariadis, M., Hileman, G., & Scott, S. V. (2019). Governance and control in distributed ledgers: Understanding the challenges facing blockchain technology in financial services. *Information and Organization*, *29*(2), 105–117. doi:10.1016/j.infoandorg.2019.03.001

Zhang, Y., & Wen, J. (2017). The IoT electric business model: Using blockchain technology for the internet of things. *Peer-to-Peer Networking and Applications*, *10*(4), 983–994. doi:10.100712083-016-0456-1

Chapter 3
Role of Blockchain Technology in Building Transparent Supply Chain Management

Ram Singh
https://orcid.org/0000-0002-6565-3091
Quantum University, India

Rohit Bansal
https://orcid.org/0000-0001-7072-5005
Vaish Engineering College, India

Sachin Chauhan
Quantum University, India

ABSTRACT

The chapter's fundamental goal is to discover and feature the job of blockchain technology in inventory networks including its benefits and impediments. The idea of the examination depends on auxiliary information and data. The necessary information and data have been gathered from different sites, magazines, and media reports. Supply affixes the need to confront difficulties as far as quality, cost, and speed. These boundaries can be accomplished effectively with blockchain in the inventory network of the executives.

INTRODUCTION

"Blockchain can possibly develop to be the bedrock of the overall record-keeping frameworks yet was dispatched only 10 years prior, it was made by the obscure people behind the online money cash Bitcoin, under the pen name 'Satoshi Nakamoto' Blockchain can be the foundation of the digitized inventory network". It really helps the clients and organizations track their item from the hour of pickup to the time it arrives at the end customer. Blockchain is for all time saved computerized record, which is exceptionally protected to impart to gatherings and make exchanges. Blockchain was first brought into

DOI: 10.4018/978-1-7998-8697-6.ch003

Copyright © 2022, IGI Global. Copying or distributing in print or electronic forms without written permission of IGI Global is prohibited.

monetary administrations for proficient and secure installments, economic alliance, and so forth as of late, Manufacturing, different enterprises like shopper products and retail are analyzing how to go into blockchain applications (Paliwal, V., Chandra, S., & Sharma, S. 2020). The chapter's fundamental goal is to discover and feature the job of Blockchain Technology in inventory network the board and its benefits and impediments. The idea of the examination is engaging, which depends on auxiliary information and data. The necessary information and data have been gathered from different sites, diaries, magazines, and media reports. Endeavour blockchain innovation can change the inventory network with these three use cases: Traceability, Transparency and Tradability.

Traceability: It works on functional effectiveness by planning and imagining "Venture Supply Chains, a developing number of customers request sourcing data about the items they purchase" (Casino, F., Dasaklis, T. K., & Patsakis, C. 2019). Blockchain assists associations with understanding their inventory network and draw in buyers with genuine, unquestionable, and changeless information.

Transparency: It assembles trust by catching key information focuses, like affirmations and cases, and afterward gives open admittance to this information freely. Once enlisted on the Ethereum blockchain, its credibility can be confirmed by outsider attesters and "the data can be refreshed and approved continuously" (Chanson, M. 2019).

Tradability: It is a remarkable blockchain offering that rethinks the traditional commercial center idea. Utilizing blockchain, one may "tokenize" a resource by parting an article into shares that carefully address possession (Dwivedi, Y. K., et. 2019). Like how a stock trade permits exchanging of an organization's offers, this fragmentary proprietorship permits tokens to address the worth of an investor's stake of a given item, these tokens are tradable, and clients can move possession without the actual resource evolving hands.

BLOCKCHAIN TECHNOLOGY

Blockchain is a typical, super durable record that works with the technique engaged with recording trades and following assets in a business association (Egels-Zandén, N., Hulthén, K., & Wulff, G. 2015). An asset can be considerable "a house, vehicle, cash, and land" or hypothetical "authorized advancement, licenses, copyrights, stamping", fundamentally anything of huge worth can be followed and traded on a blockchain network, lessening risk and diminishing costs for all notwithstanding (Yang, H., & Tate, M. 2012). Business runs on information. The speedier it's gotten and exact should it is however much as could reasonably be expected. Blockchain is incredible for passing on that information since it gives speedy, shared and absolutely clear information set aside on a super durable record that can be gotten to only by approval network people, a blockchain association can follow orders, portions, records, creation, and extensively more.

ELEMENTS OF BLOCKCHAIN TECHNOLOGY

Blockchain is a game plan of recording information with the end goal that makes it problematic or hard to change, hack, or cheat the system, it is essentially an automated record of trades that is duplicated and coursed across the entire association of PC structures on the blockchain. Each square in the chain contains different trades, and each time another trade occurs on the blockchain, a record of that trade is added to every part's record (Figorilli, S., Antonucci, F., & Menesatti, P. 2018). "The decentralized data base managed by various individuals is known as 'Distributed Ledger Technology (DLT)' and the blockchain is a kind of DLT wherein trades are recorded as":

Distributed Ledger Technology: Individuals from associations approach the Distributed Ledger Technology and its constant record of trades with these normal records, trades are recorded only a solitary time, discarding the duplication of effort that is normal of standard business associations (Akter, S., Michael, K. 2020). Individuals from associations approach the Distributed Ledger Technology and its constant record of trades with these normal records, trades are recorded only a solitary time, discarding the duplication of effort that is normal of standard business associations.

Permanent Records: No part can change or adjust a trade after it's been recorded to the normal record. If a trade record consolidates a bumble, (Firdaus, A., A. B. Razak 2019) one more trade ought to be added to pivot the slip-up, and the two trades are then perceptible.

Brilliant Contracts: To speed trades, a lot of rules called a quick arrangement is taken care of on the blockchain and executed therefore. "A smart understanding can portray conditions for corporate security moves; join terms for branch out insurance to be paid and extensively more". This suggests if one square in one chain was changed, it would be rapidly clear it had been screwed with (Hackius, N., & Petersen, M. 2017). Accepting software engineers expected to demolish a blockchain system, they would have to change each square in the chain, across the whole of the scattered types of the chain. "Blockchains, for instance, Bitcoin and Ethereum are consistently and perseveringly creating as squares are being added to the chain, which in a general sense adds to the security of the record".

Figure 1. Properties of DLT

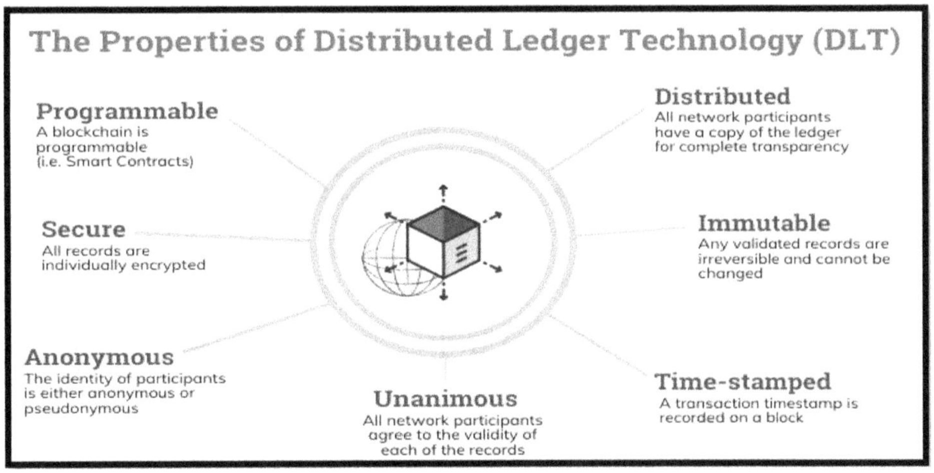

SUPPLY CHAIN MANAGEMENT

The production network fuses all of the activities, people, affiliations, information, and resources expected to move a thing from beginning to the customer, for example, in the client stock space, this most likely ranges unrefined materials, creation, packaging, dispatching, warehousing, transport, and retailing (George, R. V., Harsh, H. O., Ray, P. 2019). A definitive target is direct: meet the customer's requesting.

"By adjusting market interest across all individuals from the inventory network," Frayer says, "associations and channels cooperate to move the item." The expression "supply chain" can take on a few implications, cycles and jobs. These include: The idea of the production network, enveloping the most common way of moving a completed decent from obtainment to satisfaction in a cycle (Hughes, L., Akella, V. 2019). The business, which incorporates the transporters and guidelines that direct moving products, the capacity, which is the act of dealing with the tasks, coordinations and stock levels as a component of planning the purchasers and providers. These cycles and capacities, when progressed nicely, can enhance any industry, which is the reason inventory network the board ought to be a fundamental part of business procedure (Jia, C., Cai, Y., Yu, Y. T. 2016). Production network the executives is the most common way of incorporating the market interest the board, inside the association, yet additionally across every one of the different individuals and diverts in the production network so they cooperate most productively and adequately (Maier, D., Maier, A., Aşchilean, I. 2020). There are five essential parts in a production network the board framework: **Planning:** Wanting to fulfill customer needs, store network bosses need to get ready (Modi, D., & Zhao, L. 2020), this infers measuring demands, arranging the creation network purposely, and choosing how the affiliation will check the store organization to promise it is continuing exactly as expected the extent that capability, passing on a motivating force for customers, and helping with achieving definitive goals. "Sourcing picking suppliers who will give the product, unrefined materials, or organizations that make the thing is an essential piece of the store organization and as a part of imperative sourcing, store network chiefs ought to direct the cycles for mentioning, getting, regulating stock, and supporting receipt portions for suppliers" (Montecchi, M., Plangger, K., & Etter, M. 2019). Making store network heads moreover need to help with getting sorted out all of the means drew in with making the real thing, this fuses investigating and enduring rough materials, manufacturing the thing, quality testing, and packaging. **Returning:** Creation network chairmen in like manner need to encourage an association that supports bringing items back, on occasion, this may join dismissing or re-making a flawed thing; in others, it may basically mean returning a thing to the conveyance community (Morgan, T. R., Richey Jr, R. G., & Ellinger, A. E. 2018). This association ought to be trustworthy and versatile to help customer needs. "The foundation for all of these parts is a solid association of supporting cycles that can effectively screen the information across the stock organization and assurance adherence to laws and rules; this incorporates a wide number of divisions, including HR, IT, quality assertion, finance, thing plan, and arrangements".

APPLICATIONS OF BLOCKCHAIN IN SUPPLY CHAIN MANAGEMENT

Automotive Supply Chain

Since blockchain innovation permits the exchange of assets across the globe, it dispenses with the requirement for conventional financial exchanges that are made straightforwardly among payer and payee. Blockchain-based store network the executives framework permits exact record-keeping and provenance instructing including the item data which can be effortlessly gotten to through inserted sensors and RFID labels (Qian, X. A., & Papadonikolaki, E. 2020). Blockchain can be an optimal answer for shield their brands from copy items and in making a client centred plan of action.

Figure 2. Key areas of BC in SCM

RFID-DRIVEN CONTRACT BIDS & EXECUTION

RFID labels permit IT frameworks to peruse the labels consequently and measure them further; in this manner it would be profoundly invaluable to utilize RFID labels for savvy contracts in coordinations. RFID labels could be gainful with the utilization of the conceivable set-up (Raheem, D., Shishaev, M., & Dikovitsky, V. 2019): RFID labels for beds store data accessible on the conveyance area and date, Logistics accomplices can run the uses of these RFID labels and bid for a conveyance contact, The coordinations accomplices then, at that point offer an immaculate cost and administration gets the agreement, The brilliant contact helps in following the status and last conveyance execution of the item.

COLD CHAIN MONITORING WITH BLOCKCHAIN

Blockchain gives a solitary mark of truth in a common; alter clear record, IoT blockchain arrangement offers resource following the utilization of IoT and a blockchain network. IoT for blockchain store network arrangement engineering brings upgraded perceivability and experiences from the actual world and results in further developed coordinated effort and confidence in the business world (Sunny, J., Undralla, N., & Pillai, V. M. 2020). The common record innovation gave by the blockchain empowers members in a business organization to record the historical backdrop of deals which is sealed and can't be modified (Ramezani, J., & Camarinha-Matos, L. M. 2020). This IoT stage on blockchain arrangement permits IoT gadgets to partake in blockchain exchanges with the utilization of different IoT and resource information to approve business conditions in a trusted changeless blockchain record.

Live Tracking & Quick Processing: A blockchain-based SCM framework has been worked to work with decentralization and straightforwardness; it helps the business screen each movement progressively (Shoaib, M., Lim, M. K., & Wang, C. 2020). Despite the fact that supply chains handle huge and complex data sets, the cycle is overextended in light of middle people. Savvy Contracts have been arranged to kill their conditions on paper.

Better Traceability & Healthy CRM: Coordinating blockchain in the inventory network has diminished fake items' stockpile on the lookout (Violino, S., Pallottino, F., Sperandio, G. 2019). With better discernibility, such practices are decreased altogether. Giving the required item related data is basic with blockchain, taking client experience to another level. Besides, it permits them to really take a look at the item's validity.

Figure 3. Use of Blockchain in SCM

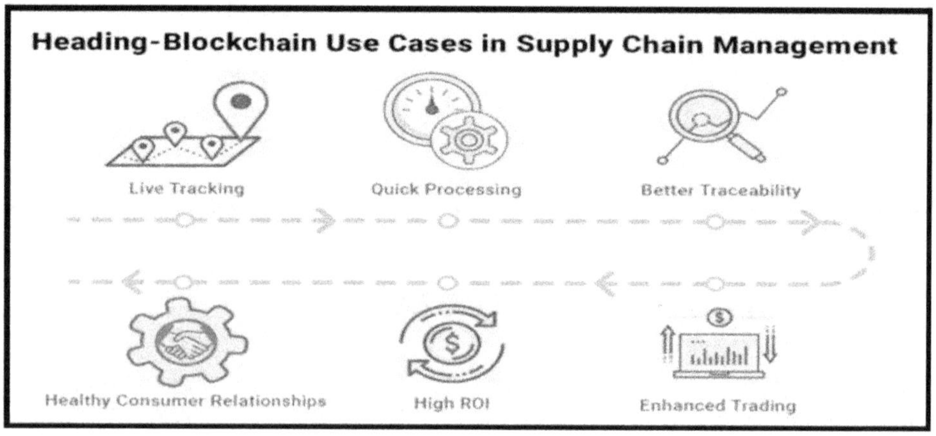

Enhanced Trading & High ROI: Possession and permitting develop a bit with the assistance of blockchain. Since each association has a comparative record rendition, they can undoubtedly screen the proprietorship records (Violino, S., Pallottino, F., Sperandio, G. 2020). With blockchain, organizations are building up premium brand distinction, bringing about a better yield on venture.

Blockchain has been arisen as a promising innovation for a detectability framework in industry (Wang, Y., Han, J. H. 2019). It can likewise be applied to many elements of a Supply Chain Management (SCM) framework, like coordinations, quality confirmation, stock administration, and estimating for the legitimate fuse of Blockchain in SCM there are some application which we are utilizing:

Stratis: Stratis, a UK-Based together stage that principally thinks with respect to utilizing Microsoft advances, is presently working with developers across the globe to give an extreme answer for inventory network the board, fueled with complete perceivability in a trustless, profoundly secure decentralized climate (Virto, L. R. 2018). This shows that software engineers worldwide will effectively create and will be focused on conveying assorted arrangements prompting exhibiting the force of the stage created by Stratis and supporting in working with Stratis Blockchain Technologies.

Treum: Treum is a cutting edge blockchain-based inventory network working framework that focuses on recognizability, straightforwardness, and exchange capacity (Yang, H., & Tate, M. 2012). It permits undertakings to construct trust with their clients via flawlessly recording on resources start to finish data, empowering makers to check if their inventory network is satisfying their item objectives.

Naturipe Farms: With the utilization of a SAP cloud stage Blockchain administration to follow blueberries from ranch to fork, Naturipe ranches place QR codes onto open boxes of products of the soil codes stay on the boxes and purchasers can check the codes with their cell phones to see where those berries were developed and what homestead rehearses were adjusted for them (Zelbst, P. J., Green, K. W., Sower, V. E., & Bond, P. L. 2019).

Tony's Chocolonely: In many regions of Africa, a large number of huge loads of cocoa beans are delivered every year by youngster workers and slaves; nonetheless, Tony's Chocolonely an Amsterdam-based chocolate organization has made a stride ahead in assisting with finishing kid work and current subjection (Zhu, S., Song, J., Hazen, B. T., Lee, K., & Cegielski, C. 2018). They are setting up a common worth chain stage called bear tracker and it incorporates a checking apparatus that can follow the area of the bean whenever and anyplace. All the rancher coops and store network entertainers are joined with the bean tracker and information is entered each week.

GlaxoSmithKline: One of the biggest drug organizations on the planet GlaxoSmithKline is working with IBM and other critical organizations to arise as a new blockchain provider organization, the association's foundation use cryptographic security and brilliant agreements and gives endeavour experiences as resources the board and spread (Kumar, N., & Ganguly, K. K. 2020) all through their whole store network. This decentralized methodology and an unchanging review trail created on blockchain disposed of the manual tedious cycles and decreased the danger of extortion and mistakes moving forward in making consistent availability across supply chains.

Luxarity: Luxarity has joined forces with critical blockchain improvement organizations to give full straightforwardness of the gift cycle by utilizing blockchain advances. They intend to foster an easy to understand gift following arrangement that can consistently incorporate with their current client travel and empower buyer cooperation with no bother. It centers on making a changeless record of how commitments are apportioned; the buyers can choose which social and instructive causes they need to help (Kumar, N., & Ganguly, K. K. 2020).

Brilliant Earth: In organization with ever record, Brilliant Earth the retailer of morally sourced jewels is following the provenance of its precious stones through blockchain. Blockchain innovation helps in following the jewel and other supporting documentation, for example, solicitations and certificate making the putting away of this chain of care data exceptionally secure.

GenuineWay: GenuineWay is a Swiss programming organization that expects to make prepared to-carry out computerized answers for little and medium-sized organizations and advance socially and harmless to the ecosystem ventures (Kumar, N., & Ganguly, K. K. 2020). The tech specialist organization is mastery in the turn of events and dispersion of blockchain incorporated answers for makers of purchaser products in the food, style, restorative and different other assorted spaces. It applies QR codes to food and alcohol things and conveys brilliant agreements for certificate of fabricate that give high quality food items to end purchasers.

BENEFITS & ADVANTAGES OF BLOCKCHAIN IN SCM

Improving Traceability

"The U.S. Medicine Supply Chain Security Act of 2013" requires drug associations to perceive and follow doctor supported meds to protect clients from phony, taken, or pernicious things. Driven by that request, a tremendous medication association in our assessment is collaborating with its store network assistants to use blockchain hence. Drug stock is marked with electronic thing codes that stick to "GS1 standards" (Héder, M. 2017). "As each unit of stock streams beginning with one firm then onto the following, its tag is separated and recorded on the blockchain, making a foundation set apart by everything completely through the creation network from its source to the end client, and some early achievement in coordinating this technique in the United States has driven the association to lead more pilots in various regions and to push toward wide execution in Europe; meanwhile", IBM is managing a near work to make a safer food creation organization. It has set up the "IBM Food Trust" and gone into a relationship with Walmart to use blockchain for new items and other food things. These sorts of utilizations require negligible sharing of data: Purchase requests, solicitations, and installments don't should be remembered for the equivalent blockchain. Subsequently, organizations that are careful about sharing cutthroat information are more able to partake on the stage. The advantages are clear, if an organization finds a defective item, the blockchain empowers the firm and its store network accomplices to follow the item, distinguish all providers engaged with it, recognize creation and shipment groups related with it, and productively review it (Modi, D., & Zhao, L. 2020). On the off chance that an item is short-lived, the blockchain allows taking part organizations to screen quality naturally: A refrigerated holder outfitted with an IoT contraption to screen the temperature can record any hazardous changes on the blockchain. Moreover, on the off chance that there are stresses over the validity of a thing that a retailer returns, the blockchain can soothe them since counterfeit product would miss the mark on a really look at history on the blockchain. Associations across ventures are subsequently examining this utilization of blockchain prodded either by rules anticipating that they should show the "provenance of their things or by downstream customers searching for the ability to follow part stock".

EXPANDING EFFICIENCY, SPEED AND REDUCING DISRUPTIONS

Emerson, an overall gathering and planning association, has a many-sided creation organization. It incorporates an enormous number of parts across various suppliers, customers, and regions. Michael Train, the head of Emerson, uncovered to us that such reserve ties every now and again need to fight with long, whimsical lead times and nonappearance of detectable quality. In like manner, a little deferral or break in any piece of the creation organization can provoke an excess of stock a ton of outs in various parts. He acknowledges that blockchain could help with beating these challenges (Zelbst, P. J., Green, K. W., Sower, V. E., & Bond, P. L. 2019).

Figure 4. Physical Supply with the help of Blockchain Technology

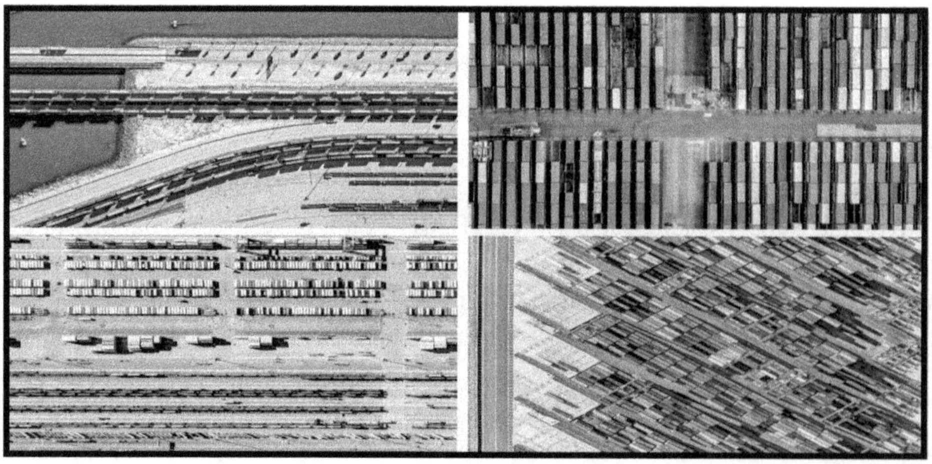

"The clear depiction of the issue and how blockchain could address it, view at thing as a, which uses parts 'C1 and C2', and thing B, which uses parts 'C1 and C3', in case the collecting of thing B is held up because of a break in the making of part C3, the ideal move is to momentarily dispense supply of C1 to thing An until the aggravation is settled". In any case, if all things and parts are made by different associations with limited detectable quality into one another's stock, what could without a doubt happen is that plenitude supply of C1 piles up at the association making thing B whether or not the maker of thing "A has a stock-out of C1". One game plan is for the associations being eluded to agree to bind together their data on the creation and stock task decisions in a regular storage facility (Kumar, N., & Ganguly, K. K. 2020). However, envision the degree of coordination that would involve: all elaborate organizations would need to trust the others with their information and acknowledge brought together choices, whether or not they are accomplices or contenders, A more functional arrangement is for taking an interest organization to share their stock streams on a blockchain and permit each organization to settle on its own choices, utilizing normal, complete data. Organizations would use a kanban framework to put orders with each other and oversee creation (Paliwal, V., Chandra, S., & Sharma, S. 2020). "Kanban cards would be assigned to the conveyed things, and the blockchain would record progressed tokens tending to the kanban cards, this would redesign the detectable quality of stock streams across associations and make lead times really obvious". Emerson isn't the solitary association that thinks blockchain could assemble the adequacy and speed of its stock organization. So does Hayward, a worldwide creator of pool equipment. "According to Don Smith, Hayward's senior VP of exercises, it is achievable to treat finished product, measure limit, work-in-measure stock, and unrefined materials like progressed cash". Blockchain makes this possible by handling the twofold spend issue the erroneous task of comparable units of breaking point or stock to two particular orders. "Walmart Canada has adequately begun using blockchain with the transportation associations that transport its stock, a typical blockchain makes it possible to synchronize collaborations data, track shipments, and automate portions without requiring basic changes to the transportation firms' internal cycles or information development structures". Part of the allure of utilizing blockchain to upgrade production network productivity and speed is that these applications, similar as those for further developing discernibility, require taking interest organizations to share just restricted information for this situation, simply stock or shipment information. Besides, these applications are valuable even inside huge associations with different ERP frameworks.

IMPROVING FINANCING, CONTRACTING & INTERNATIONAL TRANSACTIONS

At the point when stock, data, and monetary streams are divided between firms through a blockchain, critical increases in store network financing, contracting, and working together universally are conceivable, the bank that gives capital and "exchange credit" to firms deal with a notable issue of data unevenness in regards to a borrower association's business, the nature of its resources, and its liabilities. Banks plan their cycles to control such dangers, which expands exchange costs, dials back admittance to capital, and lessens the capital accessible to little firms, such gratings are adverse not exclusively to banks yet additionally to firms that need modest working capital, another movement ready for development is creditor liabilities the executives, an intricate cycle that includes invoicing, accommodating solicitations against buy orders, monitoring terms and installments, and directing surveys and endorsements at each progression (Paliwal, V., Chandra, S., & Sharma, S. 2020). Despite the fact that ERP frameworks have robotized a large number of these means, impressive manual intercession is as yet required. What's more, since neither of the executing firms has total data, clashes regularly emerged.

TRACEABILITY THROUGH BLOCKCHAIN

A third space of chance is cross boundary exchange, which includes manual cycles, actual reports, numerous mediators, and different "checks and confirmations at ports of passage and exit, exchanges are slow, exorbitant, and tormented by low perceivability into the situation with shipments". The "retailing and monetary administrations organizations we considered are directing pilot blockchain tasks or creating stages in every one of the three regions", by interfacing stock, data, and monetary streams and offering them to all executing parties, a blockchain empowers organizations to accommodate buy requests, solicitations, and installments considerably more effectively and to follow the advancement of an exchange with counterparties (Zhu, S., Song, J., Hazen, B. T., Lee, K., & Cegielski, C. 2018). Exactly when the supplier gets a solicitation, a set aside cash with induction to the "blockchain can rapidly outfit the supplier with working capital, and when item is passed on to the buyer, the bank can immediately get portions, since there is an instantly open audit trail and compromises can be mechanized, using shrewd applications that rely upon the blockchain data, conflicts between the bank and the getting firm are discarded".

CREATING A WORKABLE TECHNOLOGY

Many organizations have found that using blockchain in-store network the "board will require the arrangement of new rules, because the necessities of supply chains contrast from those of computerized monetary standards networks fundamentally, and the blockchain show for the Bitcoin network is a fantastic system" (Shoaib, M., Lim, M. K., & Wang, C. 2020) that meanwhile achieves a couple of targets, it gives an astoundingly secure, unavoidable record of financial trades; restricts the twofold spend issue, and gives affirmation of obligation regarding progressed coin. Likewise, it does as such without contingent upon a concentrated position and remembering that allowing individuals to remain puzzling and enter and leave the association wholeheartedly. To achieve this, in any case, the Bitcoin network compensations speed, consumes a ton of energy to mine "Bitcoin, and has some shortcoming to hacking, supply ties don't need to make comparable tradeoffs since they work differently and have different characteristics".

KNOWN PARTICIPANTS

"Supply chains require private Blockchains among known social events, not open Blockchains among strange customers, so people from a store organization can find the source and nature of their stock", each unit of it ought to be steadily joined with the personality of its particular owner at every movement in transit. In this way (Héder, M. 2017), just acknowledged social occasions can be allowed to look into such a blockchain, which infers that associations ought to get agree to join the structure. Furthermore, assent ought to be yielded explicitly, that is because the "open and decentralized plan of blockchain addresses a threat to data security, exactly when associations post trades on a blockchain that data can be gotten to by any part, as the volume of data extends, it may really be manhandled to collect relentless understanding, trade stocks, or predict market improvements" (Montecchi, M., Plangger, K., & Etter, M. 2019). For security reasons, thusly, the blockchain individuals ought to be thought of and supported, constructing a trusted in the get-together of associates with which to share data on a blockchain will include overcoming a couple of hardships. One is the prerequisite for an organization instrument to choose the norms of the structure, for instance, which can be free to join the association, what data is shared, how it is encoded, who draws near, how questions will be settled, and what the degree is for the use of IoT and keen arrangements (Kumar, N., & Ganguly, K. K. 2020). "Another test is figuring out some approach to address the impact that blockchain could have on assessing and stock dispersion decisions by making information about the sum or time of things in the store network more clearly". It's hard to expect wherein the creation network the costs and benefits of this straightforwardness will fall. In this way, the associations were focusing in on confined applications like the perceptibility of "meds and food things and the organization of records payable applications that are maintained by obvious use cases or authoritative requirements".

LESS COMPLEX AGREEMENT CONVENTIONS

Blockchain requires an arrangement show some instrument for keeping a lone version of the chronicled setting of trades that assented to by everyone. "Since computerized types of cash networks are shared without a central position, they use an astounding methodology called check of work and it ensures that all trades on the association are recognized by the majority of individuals, yet unfortunately, it similarly limits the speed at which new squares can be added". Subsequently, it is too postponed to even think about evening consider managing the "speed and volume of trades in supply chains". The medication business, where "4 billion attractive units enter the medicine creation network every year in the United States, the Bitcoin association, alternately, allows just around 360,000 trades each day" (Montecchi, M., Plangger, K., & Etter, M. 2019). Fortunately, if a blockchain is assent and private, the proof of-work technique isn't critical to set up understanding. Simpler systems can be used to sort out who has the advantage to add the accompanying square to the blockchain. One such procedure is an agreeable show, where the alternative to add a square turns among the individuals in a good solicitation. Since all individuals are known, a poisonous performer would be found if it used its opportunity to change the chain in a terrible or strange manner, moreover, questions can be settled viably by individuals' endorsing past blocks.

SECURITY OF ACTUAL RESOURCES

"Regardless, when a blockchain record is secure, there is at this point the danger that a dirtied or phony thing might be marked and brought into the creation organization, either in screw up or by a terrible performer". Another danger is wrong stock data coming about as a result of blunders in inspecting, naming, and data segment. Regardless, they are seriously driving real audits when things at first enter the stock organization to ensure that shipments match blockchain records, "second, they are building scattered applications, considered Apps that track things all through the store organization, really take a gander at data reliability, and talk with the blockchain to hinder bumbles and interestingness" (Dwivedi, Y. K., et. al. 2019). If a phony or a botch is recognized, it might be followed to its source using the blockchain trail of the trades for that asset, "third, associations are making the blockchain more grounded by using IoT devices and sensors to normally check things and add records to the blockchain without human mediation". If the obligation regarding assets is appended to a blockchain stage, fakes can be completely killed, for instance, schools for the most part use automated scrutinizing packs for certain, courses, working in relationship with distributers and copyright owners.

CHALLENGES IN SUPPLY CHAIN MANAGEMENT

Blockchain obviously, is as yet an arising innovation and is, thusly, not without a lot of expected issues. Ventures that need to tackle blockchain power for their store network should keep an eye out and be prepared for the accompanying difficulties (Casino, F., Dasaklis, T. K., & Patsakis, C. 2019). Supply chains are perplexing and need straightforwardness and uprightness, notwithstanding, a blockchain can help in filling this load of holes making store network tasks and the executives a lot simpler for the elaborate gatherings. Like each and every other innovation, it offers a plenty of advantages like upgraded recognizability and unwavering quality; there are as yet a few obstacles you should be prepared to manage. Thusly, here are a couple of difficulties that one should remember while executing blockchain-controlled inventory network the board arrangements.

DATA QUALITY ASSURANCE

One of the essential elements of blockchain incorporates Data changelessness; be that as it may, supply chains are as yet driven with information entered by individuals and individuals will in general make mistakes. With a blockchain, it will be more diligently to fix mistakenly entered information in contrast with a non-blockchain application; hence information entered should be liberated from blunders and slip-ups. To stay away from information spills and monetary misfortunes, it's pivotal to impart information to the ideal individuals in the right conditions. Deciding the various degrees of information secrecy makes unapproved clients distant to the data that they don't have to get to; it helps you in deciding a bunch of jobs with related admittance rights and appoints jobs to everybody under the inventory network the executive's framework. The ascent of blockchain occurred when individuals needed to decentralize applications and activities and make conditions on concentrated outsider elements like banks discretionary rather than required. Enterprises are carrying out this appropriated record innovation and utilizing it to tackle long-standing business issues. Store network the board is gradually acquiring conspicuousness in the worldwide market; however a few obstacles are in its way (Gold, S., & Heikkurinen, P. 2018). A large portion of these barriers can be killed with blockchain, and the article has revealed some insight into how.

MONITORING COLD CHAIN AND TRACING THE FOOD ITEMS

To the extent the food business, "Walmart uses blockchain to follow its thing to the end client. Walmart tracks its thing pork meat from China where blockchain tracks the piece of meat from the solicitation put to the date it is presented to the client, through this after limit, the analysts can in like manner find and dispose of the sources that give food-borne afflictions and overview out those preparing plants". Settle, Unilever, and Tyson moreover use the blockchain for the equable purposes (Zhu, S., Song, J., Hazen, B.

T., Lee, K., & Cegielski, C. 2018). Food and medication things need to put their things in cool/remarkable limit. Around here, blockchain helps in recording the tenacity, temperature, vibration, and various limits and store those characteristics on blockchain which are painstakingly planned and very strong. "Expecting the limit condition changes from what has been agreed; all the blockchain people will see it, here, a splendid arrangement comes into the edge to address the situation".

SOLAR POWER MICROGRIDS AND HEALTH INDUSTRY

"In the sun-based industry, sharp arrangements are used for the redistribution of the excess force, blockchain involves a Transactive Grid application to screen and rework the energy". Ethereum is the stage used in running this program as it helps in building a wide scope of sharp arrangements. This similarly robotizes in the purchase and arrangements of harmless to the ecosystem power energy by saving cost and defilement (Gold, S., & Heikkurinen, P. 2018). "The clinical records of patients can be gotten to from any piece of the world by the patient, by giving the key access like patient fingerprints, the entire clinical record can be seen and can alert the paramedic, who can help them with recognizing the issue suggest medication without the risk of any affectability reactions".

ECOSYSTEM STILL IN PROGRESS AND CURRENCY VOLATILITY

The primary phone was pointless until the subsequent one showed up. On schedule, the telephone spread across the world, and presently we can't manage without it. The circumstance is comparative for blockchain and organizations that need to work with explicit accomplices. Those accomplices should become tied up with blockchain too. For instance, Tomcar can at present execute Bitcoin installment for about 2 percent of the parts it purchases. Notwithstanding, specialty employments of blockchain are on the ascent. It could be simply an issue of time until organizations "join the spots" for far reaching acknowledgment. Bitcoin is a simple method to begin utilizing blockchain. The issue is that the pace of trade among Bitcoin and different monetary forms can change quickly. Installment terms should be sufficiently short or adaptable enough to have the option to trade out Bitcoin and recuperate the worth anticipated (Virto, L. R. 2018). Bitcoin and other digital currencies are likewise unpredictable in another sense. In the event that you lose the computerized key to your digital currencies save, it is basically impossible to recuperate it.

TECHNOLOGY KNOWHOW AND MINDSET

"Blockchain programming takes a blend of programming abilities; it likewise assists with getting economies and organizations, particularly your business, organizations need to prepare staff or recruit new individuals with these abilities". The most ideal decision for organization will rely upon them present circumstance and future goals (Behnke, K., & Janssen, M. F. W. H. A. 2020). Blockchain emerged when individuals started looking for an approach to decentralize applications and activities. They needed to make conditions on unified elements like banks discretionary rather than mandatory. It is another perspective, so don't be amazed on the off chance that it takes associate partners a brief period to shed your psychological shackles and get into the swing of the blockchain development.

ADVANTAGES OF BLOCKCHAIN IN SCM

Driven by organizations like Walmart and Procter and Gamble, impressive headway in store network data sharing has occurred since the 1990s, because of the utilization of "Enterprise Resource Planning (ERP) frameworks". Nonetheless, perceivability stays a test in enormous stockpile chains including complex exchanges. To represent the constraints of the current universe of monetary record sections and ERP frameworks, alongside the possible advantages of a universe of blockchain, let us portray a theoretical situation: "a basic exchange including a retailer that sources an item from a provider, and a bank that gives the functioning capital the provider needs to take care of the request". The exchange includes data streams, stock streams and monetary streams (Egels-Zandén, N., Hulthén, K., & Wulff, G. 2015). Note that a given stream doesn't bring about monetary record passages at all three gatherings included. What's more, cutting edge ERP frameworks, manual reviews, and investigations can't dependably associate the three streams, which make it difficult to dispose of execution mistakes, further develop dynamic, and resolve store network clashes.

CAPTURING DETAILS CONVENTIONAL VS. BLOCKCHAIN SYSTEMS

The monetary records and endeavour asset arranging frameworks presently utilized don't dependably permit the three gatherings engaged with a straightforward store network exchange to see every one of the important progressions of data, stock, and cash, and a blockchain framework wipes out the vulnerable sides.

"Execution blunders like mix-ups in stock information, missing shipments, and copy installments are frequently difficult to identify continuously, in any event, when an issue is found sometime later, it is troublesome and costly to pinpoint its source or fix it by following the succession of exercises recorded in accessible record sections and archives". In spite of the fact that ERP frameworks catch a wide range of streams, it tends to be hard to evaluate which diary passages, debt claims, installments, credits for returns, etc, compare to which stock exchange. This is particularly valid for organizations occupied with a huge number of exchanges every day across an enormous organization of inventory network accomplices and items (Héder, M. 2017). Exacerbating the situation, store network exercises are frequently incredibly confounded definitely more so than the show portrays, for instance, requests, shipments, and installments may not synchronize flawlessly, on the grounds that a request might be parted into a few shipments and comparing solicitations or different orders might be consolidated into a solitary shipment (Duan, J., Zhang, C., Gong, Y., Brown, S., & Li, Z. 2020). One normal way to deal with further developing inventory network execution is to confirm exchanges through reviews. Evaluating is important for guaranteeing consistence with contracts, yet it's of restricted assistance in further developing dynamic to address functional lacks. "Consider the issue a food organization faces when its items arrive at the finish of their timeframe of realistic usability in a retail location". An investigation that one of us chipped away at with a significant producer of bundled food sources tracked down that a review or an assessment of stock in a store can uncover the quantity of terminated things; however it will not clarify the causes. "Those can remember misfires for any piece of the production network, for example, wasteful stock administration upstream, problematic assignment of items to stores, powerless or irregular interest, and insufficient rack turn" (Hackius, N., & Petersen, M. 2017). A record of that load of exercises can assist with decreasing terminations. One more approach to reinforce store network tasks is mark stock with either RFID labels or electronic item codes that cling to GS1 guidelines and to then coordinate an organization's ERP frameworks with those of its providers to develop a total record of exchanges. This would wipe out execution blunders and further develop detectability; in any case, the encounters of the organizations we examined showed that incorporating ERP frameworks is costly and tedious. Huge associations might have in excess of 100 heritage ERP frameworks and after-effect of authoritative changes, consolidations, and acquisitions over the long haul. Those frameworks regularly don't effortlessly speak with each other and may even vary by the way they characterize information fields. One huge organization revealed to us it had 17 records in isolated ERP frameworks related with solitary action shipping and its providers and merchants had their own records and ERP frameworks.

Figure 5. Conventional & Blockchain Records

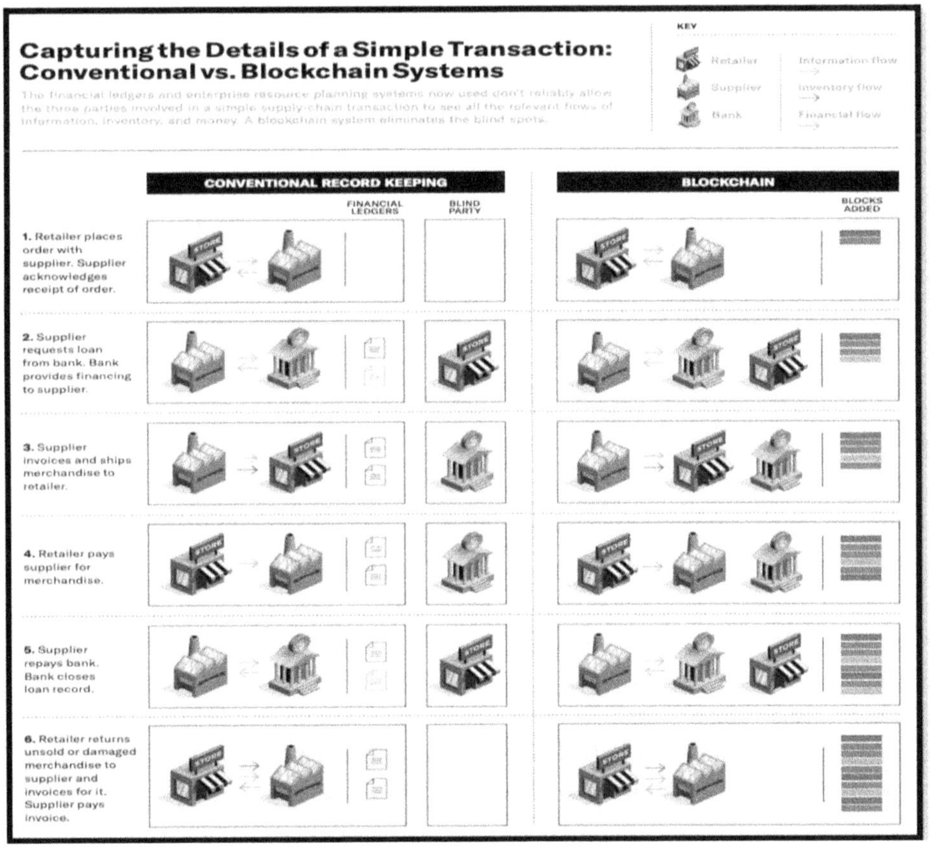

A blockchain is significant incompletely in light of the fact that it includes an ordered series of squares coordinating every one of the three sorts of streams in the exchange and catches subtleties that aren't recorded in a monetary record framework. Additionally, each square is encoded and dispersed to all members, who keep up with their own duplicates of the blockchain, because of these components, the blockchain gives a total, reliable, and carefully designed review trail of the three classes of exercises in the store network. Blockchain accordingly incredibly lessens, if not takes out, the sort of execution, recognizability, and coordination issues that we've examined. Since members have their own individual duplicates of the blockchain, each party can survey the situation with an exchange, distinguish mistakes, and consider counterparties answerable for their activities (Hackius, N., & Petersen, M. 2017). No member can overwrite past information on the grounds that doing as such would involve changing all ensuing squares on totally shared duplicates of the blockchain. The bank in our model can likewise utilize the blockchain to further develop store network financing. It can settle on better loaning choices on the grounds that by survey the blockchain, it can check the exchanges between the provider and the retailer without directing actual reviews and monetary audits, which are drawn-out and mistake inclined cycles. Furthermore, remembering loaning records for the blockchain, alongside information about invoicing, installments, and the actual development of products, can make exchanges more savvy, simpler to review, and safer for all members.

"Moreover, large numbers of these capacities can be robotized through brilliant agreements, in which lines of PC code use information from the blockchain to confirm when authoritative commitments have been met and installments can be given". Keen agreements can be modified to survey the situation with an exchange and naturally make moves like delivering an installment, recording record sections, and hailing exemptions needing manual mediation. Note that a blockchain would not supplant the wide scope of exchange preparing, bookkeeping, and the executives control capacities performed by ERP frameworks, for example, invoicing, installment, and revealing. To be sure, the encoded connected rundown or chainlike information design of a blockchain isn't appropriate for quick stockpiling and recovery or even proficient stockpiling (Zhu, et al., 2018). All things considered, the blockchain would interface with heritage frameworks across taking part firms. "Each firm would produce squares of exchanges from its inward ERP framework and add them to the blockchain; this would make it simple to coordinate different progressions of exchanges across firms".

CONCLUSION

"There is significant space to further develop supply chains as far as start to finish recognizability, speed of item conveyance, coordination, and financing, the blockchain can be a useful asset for tending to the lacks, as the organizations we examined have demonstrated". It is presently an ideal opportunity for inventory network directors who are remaining uninvolved to evaluate the capability of blockchain for their organizations (Wang, Y., Han, J. H., & Beynon-Davies, P. 2019). They need to join the endeavors to foster new principles, explore different avenues regarding various innovations, direct pilots with different blockchain stages, and construct a biological system with different firms. Indeed, this will require a responsibility of assets; however, the speculation vows to create an attractive return.

REFERENCES

Agrawal, T. K., & Pal, R. (2019). Traceability in textile and clothing supply chains: Classifying implementation factors and information sets via Delphi study. *Sustainability*, *11*(6), 1698. doi:10.3390u11061698

Akter, S., Michael, K., Uddin, M. R., McCarthy, G., & Rahman, M. (2020). Transforming business using digital innovations: The application of AI, blockchain, cloud and data analytics. *Annals of Operations Research*, •••, 1–33.

Azzi, R., Chamoun, R. K., & Sokhn, M. (2019). The power of a blockchain-based supply chain. *Computers & Industrial Engineering*, *135*, 582–592. doi:10.1016/j.cie.2019.06.042

Behnke, K., & Janssen, M. F. W. H. A. (2020). Boundary conditions for traceability in food supply chains using blockchain technology. *International Journal of Information Management*, *52*, 101969. doi:10.1016/j.ijinfomgt.2019.05.025

Carter, C. R., & Rogers, D. S. (2008). A framework of sustainable supply chain management: Moving toward new theory. *International Journal of Physical Distribution & Logistics Management*, *38*(5), 360–387. doi:10.1108/09600030810882816

Casino, F., Dasaklis, T. K., & Patsakis, C. (2019). A systematic literature review of blockchain-based applications: Current status, classification and open issues. *Telematics and Informatics*, *36*, 55–81. doi:10.1016/j.tele.2018.11.006

Chanson, M., Bogner, A., Bilgeri, D., Fleisch, E., & Wortmann, F. (2019). Blockchain for the IoT: Privacy-preserving protection of sensor data. *Journal of the Association for Information Systems*, *20*(9), 1274–1309. doi:10.17705/1jais.00567

Duan, J., Zhang, C., Gong, Y., Brown, S., & Li, Z. (2020). A content-analysis based literature review in blockchain adoption within food supply chain. *International Journal of Environmental Research and Public Health*, *17*(5), 1784. doi:10.3390/ijerph17051784 PMID:32182951

Dwivedi, Y. K., Hughes, L., Ismagilova, E., Aarts, G., Coombs, C., Crick, T., & Williams, M. D. (2019). Artificial Intelligence (AI): Multidisciplinary perspectives on emerging challenges, opportunities, and agenda for research, practice and policy. *International Journal of Information Management*, 101994.

Egels-Zandén, N., Hulthén, K., & Wulff, G. (2015). Trade-offs in supply chain transparency: The case of Nudie Jeans Co. *Journal of Cleaner Production*, *107*, 95–104. doi:10.1016/j.jclepro.2014.04.074

Figorilli, S., Antonucci, F., Costa, C., Pallottino, F., Raso, L., Castiglione, M., & Menesatti, P. (2018). A blockchain implementation prototype for the electronic open source traceability of wood along the whole supply chain. *Sensors (Basel)*, *18*(9), 3133. doi:10.339018093133 PMID:30227651

Firdaus, A., Ab Razak, M. F., Feizollah, A., Hashem, I. A. T., Hazim, M., & Anuar, N. B. (2019). The rise of "blockchain": Bibliometric analysis of blockchain study. *Scientometrics*, *120*(3), 1289–1331. doi:10.100711192-019-03170-4

George, R. V., Harsh, H. O., Ray, P., & Babu, A. K. (2019). Food quality traceability prototype for restaurants using blockchain and food quality data index. *Journal of Cleaner Production*, *240*, 118021. doi:10.1016/j.jclepro.2019.118021

Gold, S., & Heikkurinen, P. (2018). Transparency fallacy: Unintended consequences of stakeholder claims on responsibility in supply chains. *Accounting, Auditing & Accountability Journal*.

Hackius, N., & Petersen, M. (2017). Blockchain in logistics and supply chain: trick or treat? In *Digitalization in Supply Chain Management and Logistics: Smart and Digital Solutions for an Industry 4.0 Environment. Proceedings of the Hamburg International Conference of Logistics (HICL)* (vol. 23, pp. 3-18). Berlin: epubli GmbH.

Héder, M. (2017). From NASA to EU: The evolution of the TRL scale in Public Sector Innovation. *The Innovation Journal*, *22*(2), 1–23.

Hughes, L., Dwivedi, Y. K., Misra, S. K., Rana, N. P., Raghavan, V., & Akella, V. (2019). Blockchain research, practice and policy: Applications, benefits, limitations, emerging research themes and research agenda. *International Journal of Information Management*, *49*, 114–129. doi:10.1016/j.ijinfomgt.2019.02.005

Jia, C., Cai, Y., Yu, Y. T., & Tse, T. H. (2016). 5W+ 1H pattern: A perspective of systematic mapping studies and a case study on cloud software testing. *Journal of Systems and Software*, *116*, 206–219. doi:10.1016/j.jss.2015.01.058

Kumar, N., & Ganguly, K. K. (2020). External diffusion of B2B e-procurement and firm financial performance: Role of information transparency and supply chain coordination. *Journal of Enterprise Information Management*.

Maier, D., Maier, A., Aşchilean, I., Anastasiu, L., & Gavriş, O. (2020). The relationship between innovation and sustainability: A bibliometric review of the literature. *Sustainability*, *12*(10), 4083. doi:10.3390u12104083

Modi, D., & Zhao, L. (2020). Social media analysis of consumer opinion on apparel supply chain transparency. *Journal of Fashion Marketing and Management*.

Montecchi, M., Plangger, K., & Etter, M. (2019). It's real, trust me! Establishing supply chain provenance using blockchain. *Business Horizons*, *62*(3), 283–293. doi:10.1016/j.bushor.2019.01.008

Morgan, T. R., Richey, R. G. Jr, & Ellinger, A. E. (2018). Supplier transparency: Scale development and validation. *International Journal of Logistics Management*, *29*(3), 959–984. doi:10.1108/IJLM-01-2017-0018

Paliwal, V., Chandra, S., & Sharma, S. (2020). Blockchain technology for sustainable supply chain management: A systematic literature review and a classification framework. *Sustainability*, *12*(18), 7638. doi:10.3390u12187638

Qian, X. A., & Papadonikolaki, E. (2020). Shifting trust in construction supply chains through blockchain technology. *Engineering, Construction, and Architectural Management*, *28*(2), 584–602. doi:10.1108/ECAM-12-2019-0676

Raheem, D., Shishaev, M., & Dikovitsky, V. (2019). Food system digitalization as a means to promote food and nutrition security in the barents region. *Agriculture*, *9*(8), 168. doi:10.3390/agriculture9080168

Ramezani, J., & Camarinha-Matos, L. M. (2020). Approaches for resilience and antifragility in collaborative business ecosystems. *Technological Forecasting and Social Change*, *151*, 119846. doi:10.1016/j.techfore.2019.119846

Shoaib, M., Lim, M. K., & Wang, C. (2020). An integrated framework to prioritize blockchain-based supply chain success factors. *Industrial Management & Data Systems*, *120*(11), 2103–2131. doi:10.1108/IMDS-04-2020-0194

Sunny, J., Undralla, N., & Pillai, V. M. (2020). Supply chain transparency through blockchain-based traceability: An overview with demonstration. *Computers & Industrial Engineering*, *150*, 106895. doi:10.1016/j.cie.2020.106895

Violino, S., Pallottino, F., Sperandio, G., Figorilli, S., Antonucci, F., Ioannoni, V., Fappiano, D., & Costa, C. (2019). Are the innovative electronic labels for extra virgin olive oil sustainable, traceable, and accepted by consumers? *Foods*, *8*(11), 529. doi:10.3390/foods8110529 PMID:31731433

Violino, S., Pallottino, F., Sperandio, G., Figorilli, S., Ortenzi, L., Tocci, F., & Costa, C. (2020). A full technological traceability system for extra virgin olive oil. *Foods*, *9*(5), 624. doi:10.3390/foods9050624 PMID:32414115

Virto, L. R. (2018). A preliminary assessment of the indicators for Sustainable Development Goal (SDG) 14 “Conserve and sustainably use the oceans, seas and marine resources for sustainable development”. *Marine Policy*, *98*, 47–57. doi:10.1016/j.marpol.2018.08.036

Wang, Y., Han, J. H., & Beynon-Davies, P. (2019). Understanding blockchain technology for future supply chains: A systematic literature review and research agenda. *Supply Chain Management*, *24*(1), 62–84. doi:10.1108/SCM-03-2018-0148

Yang, H., & Tate, M. (2012). A descriptive literature review and classification of cloud computing research. *Communications of the Association for Information Systems*, *31*(1), 2. doi:10.17705/1CAIS.03102

Zelbst, P. J., Green, K. W., Sower, V. E., & Bond, P. L. (2019). The impact of RFID, IIoT, and Blockchain technologies on supply chain transparency. *Journal of Manufacturing Technology Management*, *31*(3), 441–457. doi:10.1108/JMTM-03-2019-0118

Zhu, S., Song, J., Hazen, B. T., Lee, K., & Cegielski, C. (2018). How supply chain analytics enables operational supply chain transparency: An organizational information processing theory perspective. *International Journal of Physical Distribution & Logistics Management*, *48*(1), 47–68. doi:10.1108/IJPDLM-11-2017-0341

Chapter 4
Studying the Adoption of Blockchain Technology in the Manufacturing Firms:
A Case Study-Based Approach

Subhodeep Mukherjee
https://orcid.org/0000-0002-6863-4881
GITAM University (Deemed), India

Manish Mohan Baral
https://orcid.org/0000-0002-9620-1872
GITAM University (Deemed), India

Venkataiah Chittipaka
https://orcid.org/0000-0002-7804-0796
Indira Gandhi National Open University, India

ABSTRACT

This chapter studies blockchain technology logistics and supply chain adoption in four manufacturing firms. Semi-structured interviews are conducted, and the results are analyzed using case study methods. Four manufacturing firms are selected for the study. First firms deal with consumer electronics manufacturing, second firms deal with auto components manufacturing, third firms deal with paint manufacturing, and fourth firms deal with consumer electronics, manufacturing, wearables manufacturing. The case study is analysed using cross-case analysis and withing case analysis.

INTRODUCTION

Blockchain technology (BCT), which has been around since bitcoins in 2009, has matured to the point where it is suitable for a wide range of applications. In the current literature, BCT is frequently referred

DOI: 10.4018/978-1-7998-8697-6.ch004

Copyright © 2022, IGI Global. Copying or distributing in print or electronic forms without written permission of IGI Global is prohibited.

to as a disruptive technology and an innovation capable of disrupting business processes, abruptly postponing opportunities for action in companies, and radically changing business models (Pavithran et al., 2020). With that in mind, BCT, a decentralized record that works with exchanges of cryptographed information in blocks, has provoked scholastic and business curiosity because of its capacity to confirm, review, and ensure communicated information and data (Bamakan et al., 2020; Gokalp et al., 2019).

BCT has excellent implementation potential in supply chain (SC) operations management because it can work with complex communications among network partners and address the issue of information irregularities (Shin, 2019). As indicated by reports, roughly 62% of SC leaders have utilized BCT, and the normal business esteem added by this Industry 4.0 constituent innovation will surpass US$3.1 trillion by 2030 (Wamba & Queiroz, 2020). The BCT is a distributed system that maintains a consistent, unchanging, and chronological chain of transactions between network participants (Mukherjee et al., 2022a). Due to the shared organization of the BCT, there are no mediators between the players; accordingly, makers or providers in a coordination's chain can manage their clients (Coita et al., 2019; Grover et al., 2019). Trust is a fundamental part of business connections among outsiders, and trust is an innate part of the BCT agreement component (Hijazi et al., 2019; S. Yadav & Singh, 2020).

Disintermediation, or the removal of intermediaries, can achieve SC management objectives such as cost, quality, speed, reliability, risk reduction, sustainability, and flexibility (Makhdoom et al., 2019; Sunny et al., 2020; Yusof et al., 2018). In any case, it is muddled what impact BCT will have on coordination's chain jobs and errands and which go-between charges BCT will cause (Pal et al., 2021a). Players in a coordination's chain should battle with new players and capacities and the deficiency of long-haul colleagues. Maintaining a functional SC necessitates comprehension and transparency regarding the shifting roles and processes caused by BCT (Beck et al., 2017; Macrinici et al., 2018; Marsal-Llacuna, 2018). To achieve this, we led an audit of the writing to record and dissect the overall errands of a go-between (Longo et al., 2019; Sheel & Nath, 2019).

Manufacturing has always been thought of as a tradition-bound industry. The Factory of the Future, however, is set to look very different as technology such as BCT, AI, and machine learning gain traction (Fosso Wamba et al., 2020; Kamble et al., 2019; Latif et al., 2021; Wong et al., 2020). As BCT develops, makers will actually want to defeat a portion of the hindrances to huge scope arrangement of other cutting edge advancements and creative plans of action (Cole et al., 2019; Vafadarnikjoo et al., 2021). Subsequently, more proficient industrial facility tasks will arise, requiring information sharing and coordinated effort across complex organizations of organizations and machines. This will be the new business standard (Chen et al., 2020; Dolgui et al., 2020; Dubey et al., 2020).

LITERATURE REVIEW

Blockchain

BCT is a disseminated, unchanging record that improves on the recording of exchanges and the following of resources in a business organization. An unmistakable resource (like a house, vehicle, money, or land) can likewise be theoretical (licensed innovation, licenses, copyrights, marking). Basically, anything of significant worth can be followed and exchanged on a BCT organization, bringing down hazard and bringing down costs for all gatherings included. A BCT is an assortment of information coordinated into individual squares put away on the entirety of clients' PCs (Bosu et al., 2019; Ikeda & Hamid, 2018;

Tönnissen & Teuteberg, 2018). This data segmentation into blocks yields a chain-like sequence that reflects the course of transactions (Kshetri, 2018; Lim et al., 2021). Cryptographic methods are used to protect the data blocks from subsequent changes, resulting in a gapless chain of linked data blocks over time (Kulkarni & Patil, 2020; Saurabh & Dey, 2021). The consensus mechanism is used to agree on the correct state of data on the BCT network among all BCT network participants (Dinh et al., 2018; Dwivedi et al., 2020; Queiroz et al., 2019).

Information is the lifeblood of business (Mukherjee et al., 2021a). The sooner and all the more exactly it is gotten, the better. BCT is great for conveying that data since it gives moment, shared, and totally straightforward information put away on an unchanging record that main organization individuals with consent can get to (Babich & Hilary, 2020; Hijazi et al., 2019; Nakamoto, 2008). A BCT organization can follow orders, instalments, records, creation, and significantly more. Since individuals share a solitary perspective on reality, you can see all subtleties of an exchange from start to finish, giving you more prominent certainty and new efficiencies and openings. Every exchange is recorded as a "block" of information as it happens (Di Vaio & Varriale, 2020; Queiroz et al., 2020; Sheel & Nath, 2019; L. W. Wong, Leong, et al., 2020).

These exchanges address the exchange of an unmistakable (an item) or immaterial resource (scholarly) (Pal et al., 2021b). The information square can store any data you need, including who, what, when, where, how much, and surprisingly a shipment's condition, like temperature. Each block is linked to the ones that came before and after it (Cole et al., 2019; Dwivedi et al., 2020; Francisco & Swanson, 2018; Verhoeven et al., 2018). These squares structure an information chain as a resource move starting with one area then onto the next or proprietorship changes hands (Mukherjee et al., 2021b). The squares affirm the exact time and grouping of exchanges and are safely connected together to keep any square from being changed or embedded between two different squares (Mathivathanan et al., 2021; Schlecht et al., 2021; Viriyasitavat et al., 2020). In a BCT, exchanges are connected in an irreversible chain. Each extra square fortifies the past square's check and consequently the whole BCT. The BCT becomes tamper-evident. As a result, they delivered immutability's critical strength (Dolgui et al., 2020; Makhdoom et al., 2019; Yadav & Singh, 2020). This wipes out the chance of malevolent entertainer altering and makes a confided in record of exchanges for yourself and other organization individuals (Treiblmaier, 2018; Wu et al., 2019). You can believe that as an individual from an individual's just organization, you will get exact and convenient information from the BCT and that your secret BCT records will be shared distinctly with network individuals to whom you have explicitly allowed admittance (Mukherjee & Chittipaka, 2021b). All organization individuals should concede to the precision of the information, and all approved exchanges are unchanging in light of the fact that they are recorded for all time (Gokalp et al., 2019; Kshetri, 2018; Wong, Tan, et al., 2020). A transaction cannot be deleted by anyone, not even the system administrator. Time-consuming record reconciliations are eliminated with a distributed ledger shared among network members (Alazab et al., 2020; S. E. Chang & Chen, 2020; Dutta et al., 2020).

A public BCT, such as Bitcoin, is one that anyone can join and participate in. Significant computational power is required, there is little or no privacy for transactions, and security is weak (Durach et al., 2020; Saberi et al., 2019; van Hoek, 2019). These are critical contemplations for BCT use cases in the venture. A private BCT network is a decentralized shared organization, like a public BCT organization. Be that as it may, the organization is administered by a solitary association, which figures out who is permitted to partake, carries out an agreement convention, and keeps up with the common record (Aslam et al., 2021; Koh et al., 2020; Tipmontian et al., 2020). Contingent upon the utilization case, this can altogether build member trust and certainty. A private BCT can be utilized in the background of an organization (Chang et al., 2018; Helo & Hao, 2019; Yadav et al., 2020).

This ensures that the data is consistent across all network nodes. Proof-of-work is the most well-known consensus mechanism in which the computer must execute a complex mathematical algorithm (Banerjee, 2018; Filimonau & Naumova, 2020; Gökalp et al., 2020). Solely after effective execution can another information block on the BCT be produced, which should be approved by different PC in the distributed organization prior to being remembered for the BCT (Mukherjee et al., 2021). Notwithstanding the information, squares comprises of a timestamp and the past square's hash esteem. To shield the squares from ensuing changes, cryptographic strategies are utilized, bringing about a nonstop chain of connected information blocks over the long haul (Clohessy et al., 2019; Korpela et al., 2017; Sheel & Nath, 2019).

Blockchain in Logistics and Supply Chain

BCT is thought to be a good fit for logistics and SC for a variety of reasons. As an item drops down the worth chain (from creation to utilization), the information produced at each progression can be archived as an exchange, making a long-lasting history of the item. BCT can successfully add to I recording each and every resource (from improvement to compartments) as it moves through the SC hubs, (ii) following requests, receipts, solicitations, instalments, and some other authority report; and (iii) following computerized resources (like guarantees, certificates, copyrights, licenses, chronic numbers, and standardized tags) in a bound together and versatile way (Clohessy et al., 2019; Durach et al., 2020).

The advantages of incorporating BCT into the SC are as per the following: expanded maintainability decreased mistakes and deferrals, lower transportation costs, quicker issue distinguishing proof, expanded trust (customer and accomplice trust), and further developed item transport and stock administration. The SC is clear with BCT (Alazab et al., 2020; Bai and Sarkis, 2020; Filimonau and Naumova, 2020). It is considered to show the development of merchandise both spatially and transiently all through different stages and cycles of the SC, starting with the state of being of the transfer at some random time and advancing through various varieties of the products (e.g., temperature deviations) and supporting coordination's dynamic. The influence of BCT is becoming more prevalent as factories worldwide become increasingly interconnected (Casino et al., 2019; Kshetri, 2017). Manufacturers face a more significant challenge than ever before in securely sharing data inside and outside the factory walls. BCT can scale transparency and trust throughout the industrial value chain (Casino et al., 2019; Grover et al., 2019; Tapscott & Kaplan, 2019).

New maintenance approaches, such as automated service agreements and shorter maintenance times, can be supported by BCT (Andoni et al., 2019; Zhao et al., 2019). These improvements are important to deal with the expanded intricacy and mechanical refinement of cutting-edge producing hardware. Users append each device's service agreements and installation documentation to the BCT record, resulting in a digital twin that facilitates outsourced maintenance. BCT can then be used to automate the execution and payment of scheduled maintenance (Onik et al., 2019; Zhang et al., 2018). At the point when a machine needs administration, it can create a help demand and a shrewd agreement for the work or a new part. When the request has been satisfied, instalment handling happens consequently. Moreover, the BCT record incorporates permanent documentation of the upkeep history. These applications, which are as yet in the beginning phases of advancement, further develop gear unwavering quality, make hardware wellbeing and steady loss checking simpler to oversee and make auditable wellbeing appraisals of apparatus (Di Vaio & Varriale, 2020; Saberi et al., 2019).

Despite BCT's positive contributions to the SC, Wamba and Queiroz (2020) show a difference in BCT acceptance in the logistics sector between the US and India, which should be considered when designing BCT-based global SC. Hughes et al. (2019) contrast the UN Sustainable Development Goals with the capabilities of BCT in their literature review to demonstrate the benefits of BCT in achieving those goals. To investigate the impact of BCT on the SC, Wang et al. (2019) conducted interviews with SC experts. Yusof et al. (2018) studied a successful BCT-enabled e-commerce platform in a conglomerate and concluded that BCT allows companies to issue cryptocurrency while protecting sensitive data (Roy & Giduturi, 2019).

Producers are trying BCT executions, which can possibly assist them with smoothing out activities, acquire more prominent perceivability into SC, and track resources with phenomenal accuracy (Behnke and Janssen, 2020; Pournader et al., 2020). BCT can upset the manner in which makers configuration, designer, assembling, and scale their items. Besides, it is reworking how organizations connect because of cultivating trust among contenders who should team up inside particular environments. BCT-based arrangements can flawlessly total the entirety of this information, offering critical benefit to modern organizations and aiding completely understanding the capability of other trend setting innovations like increased reality, IoT, and 3D printing (Dinh et al., 2018; Etemadi et al., 2021).

BCT has a lot of potential in the manufacturing industry (Mukherjee et al., 2021c). By expanding perceivability across all spaces of the cycle, from providers, key sourcing, acquirement, and provider quality, to shop floor tasks, which incorporate machine-level checking and administration, BCT can empower a totally new assembling plan of action (Casino et al., 2019; Y. Chang et al., 2020). All manufacturing businesses rely on SC (Baral & Verma, 2021). To improve efficiency, most of them can benefit from BCT's dispersed record construction and square based way to deal with collecting esteem trade exchanges. Makers will further develop request conveyance time by further developing provider request exactness, item quality, and detectability (Ivanov et al., 2019; Vafadarnikjoo et al., 2021; Zhang et al., 2018).

RESEARCH METHODOLOGY

Research Design

We carried out qualitative research using case study analysis. In information systems research, case study research is the most common type of qualitative research. It is widely used and can provide information that other methods cannot (Rowley, 2002). Empirical studies on real-world phenomena are conducted using case study research (Rose et al., 2014) instead of laboratory or experiment. The primary advantages of case study research are that phenomena are studied in their natural setting, and theories can be generated from practice. We conducted multiple case studies to ensure that our research findings were meaningful. The results become more robust as the number of cases increases (Rowley, 2002) and provide a more solid foundation for developing theories (Yin, 1994). The selection of cases for case study research is a significant challenge (Baral et al., 2021). However, it should be borne in mind that pragmatic and logistical reasons also guide the selection of topics. We selected four manufacturing firms from India. We conducted three interviews for each manufacturing firm in our sample: one with the SC manager, IT manager, and procurement manager. An open-ended questionnaire was developed for the semi-structured interview format to adjust our questions to the respondents' statements (Eisenhardt & Graebner, 2007). Table I shows the details of the respondents concerning work experience and qualification.

Table 1. Respondents details

Firm description	Respondent designation	Respondent qualification	Work Experience
Case A - Consumer Electronics firm	SC manager	B. tech and MBA	Six years
	IT manager	B. tech	Four years
	Procurement manager	BSC and MBA	Eight years
Case B - Auto components Company	SC manager	BBA and MBA	Seven years
	IT manager	B. tech	Ten years
	Procurement manager	BBA and MBA	One year
Case C- Paint manufacturing company	SC manager	BBA and MBA	Two years
	IT manager	BCA and MCA	13 years
	Procurement manager	B. tech	Eight years
Case D- Consumer Electronics, Manufacturing, Wearables	SC manager	B. tech and MBA	15 years
	IT manager	B. tech	Two years
	Procurement manager	B. tech and MBA	Seven years

Case Description

Case A - Consumer Electronics Firm

It creates connected products and solutions for automakers, consumers, and businesses worldwide, such as related car systems, audio and visual products, enterprise automation solutions, and connected services.

Case B - Auto Components Company

It operates the business in products as diverse as Wiring Harness, Electronic Sensors and Controllers, Automotive Switches, Power Cords, Automotive Cables, Connectors and Terminals, suiting to 2-Wheelers, 3-Wheelers, Commercial Vehicles, Off-Road Vehicles, Earth Movers, Farming Equipment's, Medical Equipment's & Domestic Appliances, etc.

Case C- Paint Manufacturing Company

This company is a paint manufacturing company in India. It has an employee of 3274. It manufactures and distributes paints all over India. The color manufactured is used by the automobile firms and the for-painting buildings.

Case D- Consumer Electronics, Manufacturing, Wearables

This company manufactures consumer electronics like keyboards, mice, computer hardware, watches, mobile chargers, headphones, etc. It sells its product both online as well as in offline mode.

RESULTS

In this section, we will discuss the within-case analysis and cross-case analysis.

Within Case Analysis

Table II shows the overview of the within-case analysis of the four case studies. The details of the results will be shared in the entire paper.

Case A

It had been found that the firm has not adopted BCT in their SC process, but they were very much interested in adopting the BCT and will adopt it shortly. It was found that the company employees are ready to embrace BCT in their process, and there is no change resistance among the employees. The company's employees are prepared to adopt the latest innovative technologies to make the system efficient and effective. It has been found that the employees of the firms do not have adequate knowledge about BCT and require proper training in the BCT. Top management should provide an appropriate program of training for its employees in the area of BCT. Top management is supporting BCT adoption in their firm. Top management agreed in providing adequate infrastructure facilities for the technology adoption. The top authority will also provide a good training program to its employees. Cost for the adoption of BCT was found not an issue in the firms. It was found that the company has proper adequate infrastructure for adopting BCT in the SC area. The company is already having an appropriate IT network present in the firm. It had been found that the firm had trust in the BCT and its technologies. The employees agreed that there would be an increase in process efficiency after the adoption of BCT. There will be an increase in transparency in the systems after adopting BCT in the SC area. The traceability of the products will be done in a better way.

Case B

It was found that this firm is using BCT and its related technologies in some areas as the companies are already using BCT, so there is change resistance among the employees for the latest technology. The employees are very much innovative technology adoption-friendly. The employees have knowledge and training about BCT and its technologies. It has been found that the top management is very much supporting BCT adoption in the systems. But they agreed that the cost is not an issue in adopting BCT and its related technologies. BCT adoption is an expensive process and requires lots of resources. Companies have adequate IT infrastructure for BCT. It was found that the companies trust the technology adoption of BCT, and they had no problem sharing the data on the BCT platforms. They agreed that with the implementation of BCT in SC, they could improve transparency, efficiency, and traceability.

Case C

It was found that the company has been using BCT for quite some time. They are very much habituated with it. Employees are in support of technology adoption, and they are ready to learn the technology. Some of the employees have knowledge and rest are going through training programs arranged by the company. Top management is in favour of technology adoption in their systems. But they agreed that the cost is an issue in the adoption of BCT and its related technologies. It was found that the company lacks IT infrastructure, so the development of IT infrastructure is going on in full scale and is likely to be completed by six months. It was found that the companies have trust in sharing the data. They agreed that with the implementation of BCT in SC, they could improve transparency, efficiency, and traceability.

Case D

The company had not adopted BCT and its related technologies in their systems. It was found that the employees of the company are against the usage of the latest innovative technologies. They have fear losing their jobs if the company adopts the latest technologies. So the employees are not ready for change resistance. Employees were neither having prior experience nor proper training towards the adoption of BCT. It has been found that the top management is also not very much supporting the adoption of BCT as they have some serious concerns. Also, the cost for the adoption of the BCT in the systems is going above their budget. There is a lack of proper IT infrastructure in the company. They lack trust in the information. They disagreed that with the implementation of BCT in SC, they can improve transparency, efficiency, and traceability.

Cross Case Analysis

In this section, we have a detailed cross-case analysis. Table III shows the detailed cross-analysis of the case study. The first question was whether the company had adopted BCT and its technology in their systems. Company B and C already use BCT in their plans, but companies A and D are not using BCT in their SC areas. The second question was whether the employees are ready to adopt the latest technology and there is no change resistance among the employees. It was found that the employees of company A, company B, and company C do not have any kind of change resistance and are ready to adopt the latest technologies like BCT. But on the other hand, the employees of company D are not prepared to assume any newest technology as they have fear in their mind regarding changes that will occur after the innovation adoption.

The third question was whether the employees had any prior knowledge or training about BCT and related technologies. The employees of company A and company D do not have adequate knowledge about BCT, so they require proper training about BCT to implement their learning. The employees of company B have prior knowledge and training about BCT and its related technology. The employees of company C are going through the training process in the areas of BCT. The fourth question was asked whether the top management is supporting the adoption of BCT or not. It was found that the ultimate direction of company A, company B, and company C are very much supportive of innovation adoption, especially BCT.

Table 2. Overview of the within-case analysis

No	Questions	Case A	Case B	Case C	Case D
Q1	Does the company adopt BCT technologies in their SC, and if not, when will they embrace them?	No, I will adopt shortly	Yes	Yes	No.
Q2	Are the company employees ready to adopt the latest technology, and will there be no employee resistance?	Yes. There will be no change resistance.	There is no change resistance.	There is no change resistance.	Employees are against the usage of the latest technology.
Q3	Do the employees have adequate knowledge and training about BCT?	No.	Yes	Employees are going through the training process	No.
Q4	Is top management supporting the adoption of BCT?	Yes	Yes	Yes	No.
Q5	Does the cost of the technology have an impact on the adoption?	No	No	Yes	Yes
Q6	Does the company have adequate IT infrastructure for technology adoption?	Yes	Yes	No, infrastructure development is going on.	No.
Q7	Does the company have trust in sharing the information or storing it on the BCT platform?	Yes	Yes	Yes	No.
Q8	Does the adoption of BCT in SC will increase the process efficiency?	Yes	Yes	Yes	No.
Q9	Does the adoption of BCT in SC will increase the transparency in the system?	Yes	Yes	Yes	No.
Q10	Does the adoption of BCT in SC help in better traceability of the product?	Yes	Yes	Yes	No.

On the other hand, the top management of company D is not supporting BCT adoption in their systems. The fifth question that was asked was regarding cost and its impact on BCT adoption. Company A and B agreed that the price is not an issue in adopting BCT and related technology. But The responses of company C and company D were opposite as they decided that cost would be an issue in adopting BCT and its technology. The sixth question was asked regarding IT infrastructure in the company. Company A and company B responded that there is adequate IT infrastructure in the company. Still, company D responded that the three lacks sufficient infrastructure in the company, and company C responded that the infrastructure development is going through. The seventh question that was asked is regarding the trust the company has towards BCT. Company A, B, and C responded that they trust in sharing the data in the BCT platform, but company D answered that they do not trust sharing the data in the BCT platform.

The eight questions that were asked are regarding process efficiency in the SC area after adopting BCT. Company A, B, and C responded that BCT adoption would bring process efficiency, but company D answered that they do not believe that BCT adoption will bring process efficiency. The ninth question that was asked is regarding transparency in the SC system after the adoption of BCT. Company A, B, and C responded that they believe that BCT adoption will be transparent in the system, but company D answered that they do not think there will be transparency. The last question was regarding the traceability of the product in SC through BCT. Company A, B, and C responded that they believe that BCT adoption will help better trace the product. Still, company D answered that they do not think BCT adoption will help trace the product better.

Table 3. Cross case analysis of the case study.

No.	Questions	Description
Q1	Has the company adopted BCT technologies in their SC, and if not, when they will adopt them?	Case B and C have given positive responses using BCT, but cases A and D do not use BCT in SC.
Q2	Are the company employees ready to adopt the latest technology, and will there be no employee resistance?	Case A, Case B, Case c responded that there is no change resistance among the employees, but Case D responded that there is change resistance among the employees
Q3	Do the employees have adequate knowledge and training about BCT?	Case A and Case D responded that the employees are not having adequate knowledge about BCT. Still, Case B responded that the employees have sufficient knowledge, and Case C responded that the employees are going through the training process.
Q4	Is top management supporting the adoption of BCT?	Case A, Case B, Case C responded that the top management is supportive of the latest technology adoption. Still, Case D responded that the top management is not supporting in latest technology adoption.
Q5	Does the cost of the technology have an impact on the adoption?	Case c and Case D responded that the cost would factor in BCT adoption, but Case A and B responded that the price would not factor in technology adoption.
Q6	Does the company have adequate IT infrastructure for technology adoption?	Case A and Case B responded that there is adequate IT infrastructure in the company. Still, Case D responded that the three lacks sufficient infrastructure in the company, and Case C responded that the infrastructure development is going through.
Q7	Does the company have trust in sharing the information or storing it on the BCT platform?	Case A, Case B, and Case C responded that they trust in sharing the data in the BCT platform, but Case D answered that they do not trust sharing the data in the BCT platform.
Q8	Does the adoption of BCT in SC will increase the process efficiency?	Case A, B, and C responded that BCT adoption would bring process efficiency, but Case D answered that they do not believe that BCT adoption will bring process efficiency.
Q9	Does the adoption of BCT in SC will increase the transparency in the system?	Case A, B, and C responded that they believe that BCT adoption will be transparent in the system, but Case D answered that they do not think transparency will be.
Q10	Does the adoption of BCT in SC help in better traceability of the product?	Case A, Case B, and Case C responded that they believe that BCT adoption will help better trace the product. Still, Case D answered that they do not think BCT adoption will help trace the product better.

DISCUSSION

This study will bring about the perspective of the manufacturing firms in adopting BCT adoption in logistics and SC. BCT technologies can transform manufacturing SC by eliminating the middleman, streamlining processes, improving overall security, and simplifying data management. In the SC, BCT can enhance the transparency and accuracy of end-to-end tracking. Actual resources can be digitized, and a decentralized, changeless record of all exchanges made, permitting resource following from creation to conveyance or end-client use. This expanded SC straightforwardness gives more prominent perceivability to organizations and buyers. By expanding SC straightforwardness, BCT can assist with lessening misrepresentation in high-esteem products like jewels and drug drugs (Ivanov et al., 2019; Vafadarnikjoo et al., 2021; Zhang et al., 2018). BCT could assist organizations with seeing how fixings and completed merchandise are gone through every subcontractor, decreasing benefit misfortunes from fake and dark market exchanging and expanding end-client certainty by lessening or disposing of the effect of fake items (Vafadarnikjoo et al., 2021).

A case study-based approach is used in four manufacturing firms in India. An interview was conducted using questions to the three employees of each firm. The first firm that was selected deals with consumer electronics products. The second firm that was chosen deals with auto components products and supply them to the OEM companies. The third company that was selected for the study deals with paint manufacturing. The fourth company that was chosen deals with consumer electronics. Three respondents were selected from each firm for the interview process. After the collection of the data, we had performed a within-case analysis and cross-case analysis. It was found that the companies know of BCT technologies and their benefits.

CONCLUSION

This study shows the adoption of BCT in manufacturing firms in India. Qualitative research is conducted using case study methods. Four manufacturing firms were selected for the study. Three-person were interviewed for this in each firm. The interviewed persons have prior knowledge and experience in the area of BCT. The outcome of this study will show how much the manufacturing industries are adopting BCT in the systems. It will also motivate them to adopt the technology in the near future. The company needs to know the benefits of the technologies and how it is revolutionizing the world.

REFERENCES

Alazab, M., Alhyari, S., Awajan, A., & Abdallah, A. B. (2020). Blockchain technology in supply chain management: An empirical study of the factors affecting user adoption/acceptance. *Cluster Computing*, *24*(1), 83–101. doi:10.100710586-020-03200-4

Andoni, M., Robu, V., Flynn, D., Abram, S., Geach, D., Jenkins, D., McCallum, P., & Peacock, A. (2019). Blockchain technology in the energy sector: A systematic review of challenges and opportunities. In *Renewable and Sustainable Energy Reviews* (Vol. 100, pp. 143–174). Elsevier Ltd. doi:10.1016/j.rser.2018.10.014

Aslam, J., Saleem, A., Khan, N. T., & Kim, Y. B. (2021). Factors influencing blockchain adoption in supply chain management practices: A study based on the oil industry. *Journal of Innovation & Knowledge*. doi:10.1016/j.jik.2021.01.002

Babich, V., & Hilary, G. (2020). Distributed ledgers and operations: What operations management researchers should know about blockchain technology. *Manufacturing & Service Operations Management*, *22*(2), 223–240. doi:10.1287/msom.2018.0752

Bamakan, S. M. H., Motavali, A., & Babaei Bondarti, A. (2020). A survey of blockchain consensus algorithms performance evaluation criteria. In *Expert Systems with Applications* (Vol. 154, p. 113385). Elsevier Ltd. doi:10.1016/j.eswa.2020.113385

Banerjee, A. (2018). Blockchain Technology: Supply Chain Insights from ERP. In Advances in Computers (Vol. 111, pp. 69–98). Academic Press Inc. doi:10.1016/bs.adcom.2018.03.007

Beck, R., Avital, M., Rossi, M., & Thatcher, J. B. (2017). Blockchain Technology in Business and Information Systems Research. *Business & Information Systems Engineering*, *59*(6), 381–384. doi:10.100712599-017-0505-1

Bosu, A., Iqbal, A., Shahriyar, R., & Chakraborty, P. (2019). Understanding the motivations, challenges and needs of Blockchain software developers: A survey. *Empirical Software Engineering*, *24*(4), 2636–2673. doi:10.100710664-019-09708-7

Casino, F., Dasaklis, T. K., & Patsakis, C. (2019). A systematic literature review of blockchain-based applications: Current status, classification and open issues. In *Telematics and Informatics* (Vol. 36, pp. 55–81). Elsevier Ltd., doi:10.1016/j.tele.2018.11.006

Chang, J., Katehakis, M. N., Melamed, B., & Shi, J. (Junmin). (2018). Blockchain Design for Supply Chain Management. SSRN *Electronic Journal*. doi:10.2139/ssrn.3295440

Chang, S. E., & Chen, Y. (2020). When blockchain meets supply chain: A systematic literature review on current development and potential applications. In *IEEE Access* (Vol. 8, pp. 62478–62494). Institute of Electrical and Electronics Engineers Inc. doi:10.1109/ACCESS.2020.2983601

Chang, Y., Iakovou, E., & Shi, W. (2020). Blockchain in global supply chains and cross border trade: A critical synthesis of the state-of-the-art, challenges and opportunities. *International Journal of Production Research*, *58*(7), 2082–2099. doi:10.1080/00207543.2019.1651946

Chen, J., Cai, T., He, W., Chen, L., Zhao, G., Zou, W., & Guo, L. (2020). A Blockchain-Driven Supply Chain Finance Application for Auto Retail Industry. *Entropy 2020, 22*(1), 95. doi:10.3390/e22010095

Clohessy, T., Acton, T., & Rogers, N. (2019). Blockchain Adoption: Technological, Organisational and Environmental Considerations. *Business Transformation through Blockchain*, 47–76. doi:10.1007/978-3-319-98911-2_2

Coita, D. C., Abrudan, M. M., & Matei, M. C. (2019). *Effects of the Blockchain Technology on Human Resources and Marketing: An Exploratory Study*. doi:10.1007/978-3-030-12453-3_79

Cole, R., Stevenson, M., & Aitken, J. (2019). Blockchain technology: Implications for operations and supply chain management. *Supply Chain Management*, *24*(4), 469–483. doi:10.1108/SCM-09-2018-0309

Di Vaio, A., & Varriale, L. (2020). Blockchain technology in supply chain management for sustainable performance: Evidence from the airport industry. *International Journal of Information Management*, *52*, 102014. doi:10.1016/j.ijinfomgt.2019.09.010

Dinh, T. T. A., Liu, R., Zhang, M., Chen, G., Ooi, B. C., & Wang, J. (2018). Untangling Blockchain: A Data Processing View of Blockchain Systems. *IEEE Transactions on Knowledge and Data Engineering*, *30*(7), 1366–1385. doi:10.1109/TKDE.2017.2781227

Dolgui, A., Ivanov, D., Potryasaev, S., Sokolov, B., Ivanova, M., & Werner, F. (2020). Blockchain-oriented dynamic modelling of smart contract design and execution in the supply chain. *International Journal of Production Research, 58*(7), 2184–2199. doi:10.1080/00207543.2019.1627439

Dubey, R., Gunasekaran, A., Bryde, D. J., Dwivedi, Y. K., & Papadopoulos, T. (2020). Blockchain technology for enhancing swift-trust, collaboration and resilience within a humanitarian supply chain setting. *International Journal of Production Research, 58*(11), 3381–3398. doi:10.1080/00207543.2020.1722860

Durach, C. F., Blesik, T., Düring, M., & Bick, M. (2020). Blockchain Applications in Supply Chain Transactions. *Journal of Business Logistics*. doi:10.1111/jbl.12238

Dutta, P., Choi, T. M., Somani, S., & Butala, R. (2020). Blockchain technology in supply chain operations: Applications, challenges and research opportunities. *Transportation Research Part E, Logistics and Transportation Review, 142*, 102067. doi:10.1016/j.tre.2020.102067 PMID:33013183

Dwivedi, S. K., Amin, R., & Vollala, S. (2020). Blockchain based secured information sharing protocol in supply chain management system with key distribution mechanism. *Journal of Information Security and Applications, 54*, 102554. doi:10.1016/j.jisa.2020.102554

Eisenhardt, K. M., & Graebner, M. E. (2007). Theory Building From Cases: Opportunities And Challenges. *Academy of Management Journal, 50*(1), 25–32. doi:10.5465/amj.2007.24160888

Etemadi, N., Van Gelder, P., & Strozzi, F. (2021). An ism modeling of barriers for blockchain/distributed ledger technology adoption in supply chains towards cybersecurity. *Sustainability (Switzerland), 13*(9), 4672. doi:10.3390u13094672

Filimonau, V., & Naumova, E. (2020). The blockchain technology and the scope of its application in hospitality operations. *International Journal of Hospitality Management, 87*, 102383. doi:10.1016/j.ijhm.2019.102383

Fosso Wamba, S., Kala Kamdjoug, J. R., Epie Bawack, R., & Keogh, J. G. (2020). Bitcoin, Blockchain and Fintech: A systematic review and case studies in the supply chain. *Production Planning and Control, 31*(2–3), 115–142. doi:10.1080/09537287.2019.1631460

Francisco, K., & Swanson, D. (2018). The Supply Chain Has No Clothes: Technology Adoption of Blockchain for Supply Chain Transparency. *Logistics, 2*(1), 2. doi:10.3390/logistics2010002

Gokalp, E., Coban, S., & Gokalp, M. O. (2019, November 1). Acceptance of Blockchain Based Supply Chain Management System: Research Model Proposal. *1st International Informatics and Software Engineering Conference: Innovative Technologies for Digital Transformation, IISEC 2019 - Proceedings*. 10.1109/UBMYK48245.2019.8965502

Gökalp, E., Gökalp, M. O., & Çoban, S. (2020). Blockchain-Based Supply Chain Management: Understanding the Determinants of Adoption in the Context of Organizations. *Information Systems Management*, 1–22. doi:10.1080/10580530.2020.1812014

Grover, P., Kar, A. K., Janssen, M., & Ilavarasan, P. V. (2019). Perceived usefulness, ease of use and user acceptance of blockchain technology for digital transactions–insights from user-generated content on Twitter. *Enterprise Information Systems, 13*(6), 771–800. doi:10.1080/17517575.2019.1599446

Helo, P., & Hao, Y. (2019). Blockchains in operations and supply chains: A model and reference implementation. *Computers & Industrial Engineering*, *136*, 242–251. doi:10.1016/j.cie.2019.07.023

Hijazi, A. A., Perera, S., Alashwal, A. M., Alashwal, A. M., & Calheiros, R. N. (2019). Blockchain Adoption in Construction Supply Chain: A Review of Studies Across Multiple Sectors. *CIB World Building Congress,* 17–21. https://www.researchgate.net/publication/333879452

Ikeda, K., & Hamid, M. N. (2018). Applications of Blockchain in the Financial Sector and a Peer-to-Peer Global Barter Web. In *Advances in Computers* (Vol. 111, pp. 99–120). Academic Press Inc. doi:10.1016/bs.adcom.2018.03.008

Ivanov, D., Dolgui, A., & Sokolov, B. (2019). The impact of digital technology and Industry 4.0 on the ripple effect and supply chain risk analytics. *International Journal of Production Research*, *57*(3), 829–846. doi:10.1080/00207543.2018.1488086

Kamble, S., Gunasekaran, A., & Arha, H. (2019). Understanding the Blockchain technology adoption in supply chains-Indian context. *International Journal of Production Research*, *57*(7), 2009–2033. doi:10.1080/00207543.2018.1518610

Koh, L., Dolgui, A., & Sarkis, J. (2020). Blockchain in transport and logistics – paradigms and transitions. *International Journal of Production Research*, *58*(7), 2054–2062. doi:10.1080/00207543.2020.1736428

Korpela, K., Hallikas, J., & Dahlberg, T. (2017). Digital Supply Chain Transformation toward Blockchain Integration. *Proceedings of the 50th Hawaii International Conference on System Sciences*. 10.24251/HICSS.2017.506

Kshetri, N. (2017). Blockchain's roles in strengthening cybersecurity and protecting privacy. *Telecommunications Policy*, *41*(10), 1027–1038. doi:10.1016/j.telpol.2017.09.003

Kshetri, N. (2018). 1 Blockchain's roles in meeting key supply chain management objectives. *International Journal of Information Management*, *39*, 80–89. doi:10.1016/j.ijinfomgt.2017.12.005

Kulkarni, M., & Patil, K. (2020). Block Chain Technology Adoption for Banking Services- Model based on Technology-Organization-Environment theory. SSRN *Electronic Journal*. doi:10.2139/ssrn.3563101

Latif, R. M. A., Farhan, M., Rizwan, O., Hussain, M., Jabbar, S., & Khalid, S. (2021). Retail level Blockchain transformation for product supply chain using truffle development platform. *Cluster Computing*, *24*(1), 1–16. doi:10.100710586-020-03165-4

Lim, M. K., Li, Y., Wang, C., & Tseng, M.-L. (2021). A literature review of blockchain technology applications in supply chains: A comprehensive analysis of themes, methodologies and industries. *Computers & Industrial Engineering*, *154*, 107133. doi:10.1016/j.cie.2021.107133

Longo, F., Nicoletti, L., & Padovano, A. (2019). *Blockchain-enabled supply chain: An experimental study*. Elsevier. https://www.sciencedirect.com/science/article/pii/S0360835219304139

Macrinici, D., Cartofeanu, C., & Gao, S. (2018). Smart contract applications within blockchain technology: A systematic mapping study. In Telematics and Informatics (Vol. 35, Issue 8, pp. 2337–2354). Elsevier Ltd. doi:10.1016/j.tele.2018.10.004

Makhdoom, I., Abolhasan, M., Abbas, H., & Ni, W. (2019). Blockchain's adoption in IoT: The challenges, and a way forward. In *Journal of Network and Computer Applications* (Vol. 125, pp. 251–279). Academic Press. doi:10.1016/j.jnca.2018.10.019

Marsal-Llacuna, M. L. (2018). Future living framework: Is blockchain the next enabling network? *Technological Forecasting and Social Change, 128*, 226–234. doi:10.1016/j.techfore.2017.12.005

Mathivathanan, D., Mathiyazhagan, K., Rana, N. P., Khorana, S., & Dwivedi, Y. K. (2021). Barriers to the adoption of blockchain technology in business supply chains: A total interpretive structural modelling (TISM) approach. *International Journal of Production Research, 59*(11), 3338–3359. doi:10.1080/00207543.2020.1868597

Mukherjee, S., Chittipaka, V., & Baral, M. M. (2021). Developing a Model to Highlight the Relation of Digital Trust With Privacy and Security for the Blockchain Technology. IGI Global. doi:10.4018/978-1-7998-8081-3.ch007

Nakamoto, S. (2008). Bitcoin: A peer-to-peer electronic cash system. *Decentralized Business Review, 21260.*

Onik, M. M. H., Aich, S., Yang, J., Kim, C.-S., & Kim, H.-C. (2019). Blockchain in Healthcare: Challenges and Solutions. In *Big Data Analytics for Intelligent Healthcare Management*. Elsevier Inc. doi:10.1016/B978-0-12-818146-1.00008-8

Pavithran, D., Shaalan, K., Al-Karaki, J. N., & Gawanmeh, A. (2020). Towards building a blockchain framework for IoT. *Cluster Computing, 23*(3), 2089–2103. doi:10.100710586-020-03059-5

Queiroz, M. M., Fosso Wamba, S., De Bourmont, M., & Telles, R. (2020). Blockchain adoption in operations and supply chain management: Empirical evidence from an emerging economy. *International Journal of Production Research*. Advance online publication. doi:10.1080/00207543.2020.1803511

Queiroz, M. M., Telles, R., & Bonilla, S. H. (2019). Blockchain and supply chain management integration: a systematic review of the literature. In Supply Chain Management (Vol. 25, Issue 2, pp. 241–254). Emerald Group Publishing Ltd. doi:10.1108/SCM-03-2018-0143

Rose, S., Spinks, N., & Canhoto, A. (2014). Management Research : Applying the Principles. In *Management Research*. Routledge. doi:10.4324/9781315819198

Rowley, J. (2002). Using case studies in research. *Management Research News, 25*(1), 16–27. doi:10.1108/01409170210782990

Saberi, S., Kouhizadeh, M., Sarkis, J., & Shen, L. (2019a). Blockchain technology and its relationships to sustainable supply chain management. *International Journal of Production Research, 57*(7), 2117–2135. doi:10.1080/00207543.2018.1533261

Saberi, S., Kouhizadeh, M., Sarkis, J., & Shen, L. (2019b). Blockchain technology and its relationships to sustainable supply chain management. *International Journal of Production Research, 57*(7), 2117–2135. doi:10.1080/00207543.2018.1533261

Saurabh, S., & Dey, K. (2021). Blockchain technology adoption, architecture, and sustainable agri-food supply chains. *Journal of Cleaner Production, 284*, 124731. doi:10.1016/j.jclepro.2020.124731

Schlecht, L., Schneider, S., & Buchwald, A. (2021). The prospective value creation potential of Blockchain in business models: A delphi study. *Technological Forecasting and Social Change*, *166*, 120601. doi:10.1016/j.techfore.2021.120601

Sheel, A., & Nath, V. (2019). Effect of blockchain technology adoption on supply chain adaptability, agility, alignment and performance. *Management Research Review*, *42*(12), 1353–1374. doi:10.1108/MRR-12-2018-0490

Shin, D. D. H. (2019). Blockchain: The emerging technology of digital trust. *Telematics and Informatics*, *45*(September), 101278. Advance online publication. doi:10.1016/j.tele.2019.101278

Sunny, J., Undralla, N., & Madhusudanan Pillai, V. (2020). Supply chain transparency through blockchain-based traceability: An overview with demonstration. *Computers & Industrial Engineering*, *150*, 106895. Advance online publication. doi:10.1016/j.cie.2020.106895

Surendra Yadav, V., & Singh, A. R. (n.d.). *A Systematic Literature Review of Blockchain Technology in Agriculture*. Academic Press.

Tapscott, D., & Kaplan, A. (2019). *Blockchain Revolution in Education and LifeLong Learning: Preparing for Disruption, Leading the Transformation*. www.blockchainresearchinstitute.org/contact-us

Tipmontian, Alcover, & Rajmohan. (2020). Impact of Blockchain Adoption for Safe Food Supply Chain Management through System Dynamics Approach from Management Perspectives in Thailand. *Proceedings, 39*(1), 14. doi:10.3390/proceedings2019039014

Tönnissen, S., & Teuteberg, F. (2018). Using blockchain technology for business processes in purchasing – Concept and case study-based evidence. *Lecture Notes in Business Information Processing*, *320*, 253–264. doi:10.1007/978-3-319-93931-5_18

Treiblmaier, H. (2018). The impact of the blockchain on the supply chain: A theory-based research framework and a call for action. *Supply Chain Management*, *23*(6), 545–559. doi:10.1108/SCM-01-2018-0029

Vafadarnikjoo, A., Badri Ahmadi, H., Liou, J. J. H., Botelho, T., & Chalvatzis, K. (2021). Analyzing blockchain adoption barriers in manufacturing supply chains by the neutrosophic analytic hierarchy process. *Annals of Operations Research*, 1–28. doi:10.100710479-021-04048-6

van Hoek, R. (2019). Unblocking the chain – findings from an executive workshop on blockchain in the supply chain. *Supply Chain Management*, *25*(2), 255–261. doi:10.1108/SCM-11-2018-0383

Verhoeven, P., Sinn, F., & Herden, T. (2018). Examples from Blockchain Implementations in Logistics and Supply Chain Management: Exploring the Mindful Use of a New Technology. *Logistics*, *2*(3), 20. doi:10.3390/logistics2030020

Viriyasitavat, W., Da Xu, L., Bi, Z., & Sapsomboon, A. (2020). Blockchain-based business process management (BPM) framework for service composition in industry 4.0. *Journal of Intelligent Manufacturing*, *31*(7), 1737–1748. doi:10.100710845-018-1422-y

Wamba, S. F., & Queiroz, M. M. (2020). Blockchain in the operations and supply chain management: Benefits, challenges and future research opportunities. In *International Journal of Information Management* (Vol. 52, p. 102064). Elsevier Ltd., doi:10.1016/j.ijinfomgt.2019.102064

Wong, L. W., Leong, L. Y., Hew, J. J., Tan, G. W. H., & Ooi, K. B. (2020). Time to seize the digital evolution: Adoption of blockchain in operations and supply chain management among Malaysian SMEs. *International Journal of Information Management*, *52*, 101997. doi:10.1016/j.ijinfomgt.2019.08.005

Wong, L.-W., Tan, G. W.-H., Lee, V.-H., Ooi, K.-B., & Sohal, A. (2020). Unearthing the determinants of Blockchain adoption in supply chain management. *International Journal of Production Research*, *58*(7), 2100–2123. doi:10.1080/00207543.2020.1730463

Wong, L. W., Tan, G. W. H., Lee, V. H., Ooi, K. B., & Sohal, A. (2020). Unearthing the determinants of Blockchain adoption in supply chain management. *International Journal of Production Research*, *58*(7), 2100–2123. doi:10.1080/00207543.2020.1730463

Wu, H., Cao, J., Yang, Y., Tung, C. L., Jiang, S., Tang, B., Liu, Y., Wang, X., & Deng, Y. (2019). Data management in supply chain using blockchain: challenges and a case study. *Proceedings - International Conference on Computer Communications and Networks, ICCCN*. 10.1109/ICCCN.2019.8846964

Yadav, S., & Singh, S. P. (2020). Blockchain critical success factors for sustainable supply chain. *Resources, Conservation and Recycling*, *152*, 104505. doi:10.1016/j.resconrec.2019.104505

Yadav, V. S., Singh, A. R., Raut, R. D., & Govindarajan, U. H. (2020). Blockchain technology adoption barriers in the Indian agricultural supply chain: An integrated approach. *Resources, Conservation and Recycling*, *161*, 104877. doi:10.1016/j.resconrec.2020.104877

Yusof, H., Farhana Mior Badrul Munir, M., Zolkaply, Z., Jing, L. C., Yu Hao, C., Swee Ying, D., Seang Zheng, L., Yuh Seng, L., & Kok Leong, T. (2018). Behavioral Intention to Adopt Blockchain Technology: Viewpoint of the Banking Institutions in Malaysia. *International Journal of Advanced Scientific Research and Management, 3*. www.ijasrm.com

Zhang, P., Schmidt, D. C., White, J., & Lenz, G. (2018). Blockchain Technology Use Cases in Healthcare. In *Advances in Computers* (Vol. 111, pp. 1–41). Academic Press Inc. doi:10.1016/bs.adcom.2018.03.006

Zhao, G., Liu, S., Lopez, C., Lu, H., Elgueta, S., Chen, H., & Boshkoska, B. M. (2019). Blockchain technology in agri-food value chain management: A synthesis of applications, challenges and future research directions. *Computers in Industry*, *109*, 83–99. doi:10.1016/j.compind.2019.04.002

Chapter 5
Mutual Recognition Mechanism Based on DVCS Oracle in the Blockchain Platform:
DVCS Oracle in the Global Supply Chain

Vladimir Nikolaevich Kustov
Saint Petersburg State University of Railway Transport of Emperor Alexander I, Russia

Ekaterina Sergeevna Selanteva
New Space of Trade LLC, Russia

ABSTRACT

The main purpose of this chapter is to present the need to use the mutual recognition mechanism (MRM) of electronic signatures based on the DVCS oracle in the blockchain platform for the global supply chain. The authors begin their research by comparing a single-domain traditional supply chain with a multi-domain global supply chain. In the second case, the necessity of using an MRM electronic signature based on the DVCS oracle is justified. Various options for constructing MRM are discussed. The chapter provides a comparative assessment of the electronic signature validation protocols and the rationale for using the DVCS protocol to implement the blockchain oracle. As a result, the authors propose to use a well-tested software and hardware complex of the Litoria DVCS as a DVCS oracle and illustrate its use with practical examples.

"And if blockchain technology becomes a key tool for increasing the progress of mankind, then in the future it can become an information platform on the scale of the Universe." (Swan, 2018)

DOI: 10.4018/978-1-7998-8697-6.ch005

Copyright © 2022, IGI Global. Copying or distributing in print or electronic forms without written permission of IGI Global is prohibited.

INTRODUCTION

Over the past thirteen years since the appearance of the first blockchain platform and the first Bitcoin cryptocurrency (Satoshi, 2008), many different events have occurred. Sometimes they were contradictory, from uncontrollable delight (Swan, 2018) (Kustov & Stankevich, 2019) to complete rejection and skepticism. Serious concerns have been expressed that the blockchain will kill medium and small businesses (Chris, 2017). There have also been repeated attempts to reconcile skeptics with optimists (Kustov & Stankevich, 2018).

However, despite all these contradictions, blockchain technology is dynamically developing and embracing more and more new sectors of the economy, sometimes taking on a global character. The supply chain is no exception. At the same time, along with the positive results of the widespread introduction of blockchain technology, its distinctive negative features are increasingly manifested, among which it should be mentioned:

1. The widespread use of smart contracts, developed mainly in the Solidity language (Dannen, 2018), reveals more and more vulnerabilities in smart contracts (Shapiev, 2019) that bring significant financial losses (Report, 2019). These vulnerabilities arise for two main reasons:
    a. insufficiently secure technology for developing smart contracts, which results in errors in their development;
    b. Both insufficient reliability of the source data transmitted to the smart contract from the external environment.
2. Limited supply on the market of reliable hardware and software communication tools (that is, oracles) of smart contracts operating in a closed environment, with information flows in the surrounding world.
3. Supply chains from interdepartmental trade turnover, closed within one country, everywhere acquire a global character (Kupriyanovsky et al., 2016). Electronic document flow is becoming cross-border. The widespread use of electronic signatures in the exchange of electronic documents creates many problems in verifying electronic signatures made using different cryptographic standards. There is a need to develop a secure mechanism for verifying electronic documents before writing them to the blockchain platform. In their research, the authors develop the idea of using a mutual recognition mechanism for this purpose, the core of which is the DVCS oracle.

STATEMENT OF THE RESEARCH TASK

So, the data in supply chains are not always prominent, accessible, or trusted. The use of blockchain technology helps to ensure the exchange of secure data with supply chain partners using blockchain-based solutions with restricted access rights.

Currently, this problem is becoming very relevant. Consumers want guaranteed quality, so their participation in supply chains is very demanding. The selection of suppliers becomes very careful to ensure a minimum of risks and high transparency choice.

In this chapter, the authors propose conducting a study of ways to reduce disruptions in supply chains using a mutual recognition mechanism to increase data reliability to assess the possibility of future blockchain applications.

The widespread use of blockchain in supply chains, which has begun in recent years, provides the following advantages compared to traditional supply chains:

1. The transparency of supply chain networks may end with the participants closest to you. Thanks to distributed ledger technology, which provides the only option for trusted information, blockchain-based solutions give participants a clearer picture of all operations in the supply chain.
2. Just a single small error in the operation of the blockchain platform can cause many disruptions in the functioning of the supply chain. Blockchain-based solutions for the supply chain use smart contracts automatically initiated when predefined business conditions are met. It ensures transparency of operations in almost real-time and the possibility of an earlier response to detecting an exceptional situation.
3. Also, a severe and sometimes tricky problem for the buyer and seller is always selecting a new supplier. Blockchain solutions for supply chains can speed up this process by using an immutable data record about a new supplier that business network participants can trust.

Along with the noted advantages of using blockchain-based supply chains, several problems should be noted that require solutions soon:

1. Insufficient communication of secure blockchain platforms with external sources of information using trusted communication channels. The info flows entering the blockchain consist of documents and the data's reliability, integrity, and authenticity, which is ensured through an electronic signature (ES). In this regard, there is an urgent need for trusted validation of an ES before uploading documents to the blockchain. This function can be assigned to a special oracle connector that confirms the item instance and makes a positive or negative decision based on the verification results. The electronic document and the positive receipt are recorded in the blockchain if the result of the ES verification is positive. If the result is negative, the document is returned to the source along with a negative receipt.
2. There are two classes of supply chains:
    a. A single-domain (limited by the borders of one state) supply chain (Figure 1). In such supply chains, the validation function of the ES is often assigned to the internal mechanisms of the blockchain. Practice shows insufficient reliability and universality of validation mechanisms in this case. In this case, we need a separate external secure and proven tool for validating the ES in the form of a particular connector - oracle.
    b. A multi-domain or global supply chain (Figure 2) provides for cross-border transportation of goods. The function of validating the ES under the documents, in this case, becomes much more complicated and becomes necessary. The fact is that different states use different cryptographic standards of the ES, and in general, these standards are incompatible, and the use of oracles to validate ES becomes necessary.
3. There are three main validation protocols. The authors will talk about them further. The authors were faced with the task of choosing the most effective of them. According to the results of the tests, the DVCS protocol showed the best characteristics. The authors suggest using DVCS oracle as a blockchain oracle.

Figure 1. Single-domain supply chain

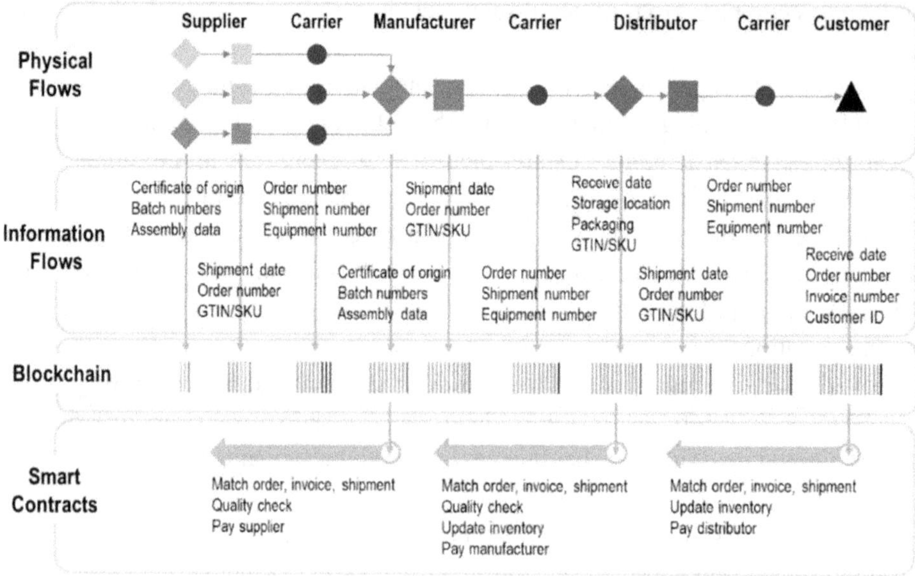

Figure 2. Multi-domain global supply chain

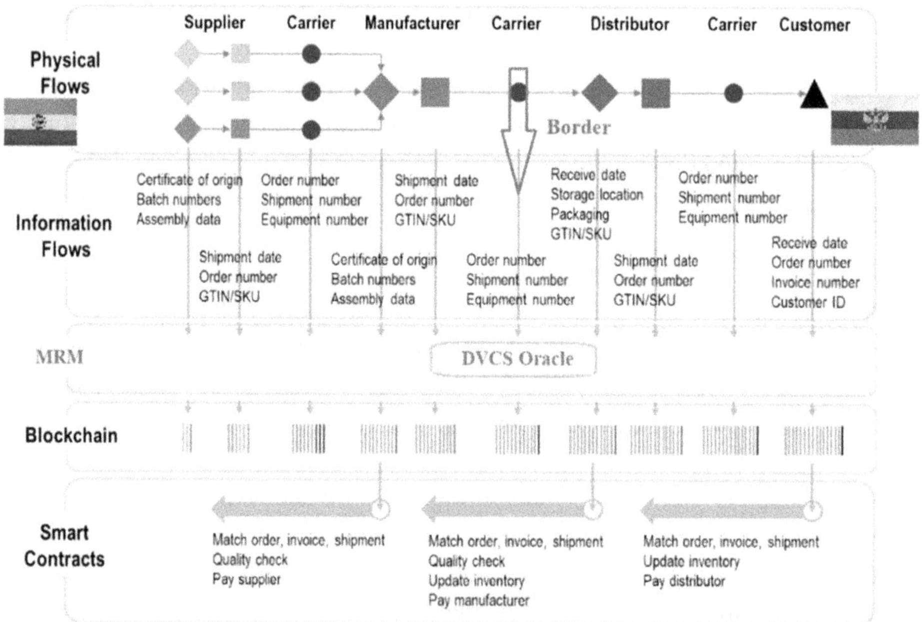

Let us take a closer look at the description of the functionality of the single-domain supply chain.

Before sending components to the manufacturer, the supplier provides them with the following information in electronic form, recorded in the blockchain in the following transactions: Certificate of origin, Batch numbers, and Assembly data. Immediately before the transfer of components to the transport organization, the supplier records and transmits to it add the following information, which is also recorded in the blockchain in the form of transactions: Shipment date, Order number, Global Trade Item Number (GTIN), and Stock Keeping Unit (SKU). The transport organization adds additional transactions to the blockchain at the delivery stage: Order number, Shipment number, Equipment number. Having received the components, the manufacturer produces the necessary products and additionally enters its transactions into the blockchain: Certificate of origin, Batch numbers, and Assembly data. Processing of all information recorded in the blockchain at the stages of component supply and production is carried out by the following smart contracts:

1. Match order, invoice, and shipment;
2. Quality check;
3. Pay supplier.

The manufacturer adds the following transactions to the blockchain before sending finished products: Shipment date, Order number, GTIN/SKU. At the stage of transportation, the transport organization transmits to the additional distributor information recorded in the blockchain: Order number, Shipment number, Equipment number.

After receiving the products, the distributor creates transactions: Receive date, Storage location, Packaging, GTIN/SKU. The distributor uses smart contracts at the stages of delivery receipt of finished products:

1. Match order, invoice, and shipment;
2. Quality check;
3. Update inventory;
4. Pay manufacturer.

Next, the distributor prepares the goods for shipment to the customer and records transactions in the blockchain: Shipment date, Order number, GTIN/SKU. At the delivery stage of the goods by the transport organization to the Customer, transactions are created: Order number, Shipment number, Equipment number. After receiving the goods, the Customer makes and writes transactions to the blockchain: Receive date, Order number, Invoice number, Customer ID. At the final stage, the following smart contracts are used:

1. Match order, invoice, shipment;
2. Update inventory;
3. Pay distributor.

Thus, the cycle of the single-domain supply chain is completed. For a multi-domain global supply chain, the sequence of recording transactions and executing the corresponding smart contracts is identical. However, introducing an additional level of mutual recognition mechanism based on the DVCS Oracle solves the problem of safe, confidential transmission of information in the cross-border electronic document flow.

Thus, the authors believe that the primary purpose of this chapter is to present the need to use the Mutual Recognition Mechanism (MRM) of ES based on the DVCS Oracle in the blockchain platform for the global supply chain.

LET'S TALK ABOUT ORACLES

Oracles play an essential role in any ecosystem based on blockchain. Oracles solve one of the most critical tasks in distributed registry systems - ensuring trusted data transfer from the outside world to smart contracts implemented by blockchain platforms. Therefore, careful development of the algorithms on which the oracles are based is now becoming necessary.

What is a Blockchain Oracle?

Any distributed registry system is always deterministic — transactions are written into blocks only in chronological order. The smart contract is executed in the blockchain in a closed, protected environment that cannot receive verified data from the outside world. Oracles are designed to translate information to a form convenient for processing in the blockchain.

In other words, the oracle provides a trusted transfer of information from the outside world to the blockchain. Oracles perform an essential role of a third trusted party for smart contracts, providing the possibility of reliable automatic fulfillment of the conditions stipulated by the smart contract. In practice, users and individual enterprises using smart contracts often have trouble because smart contracts are in a closed, trusted space, which requires high-reliability characteristics to be unblocked. That is, the work of smart contracts requires a very secure blockchain. The technical and financial costs associated with such a blockchain are becoming relatively high.

The algorithm implemented in a smart contract must be correctly and accurately implemented and consider many contradictory simulations. Developing a smart contract becomes a very time-consuming process, which naturally increases the number of critical errors. After launching, it is impossible to change the smart contract or stop its operation until all the prescribed conditions are met.

However, as far as the outside world is concerned, it is not deterministic like the blockchain. One or both parties may probably encounter data transmission errors in the blockchain, leading to incorrect execution of the smart contract. Blockchain oracle solves the problem of smart contract communication with the outside world and ensures their reliable implementation by supplying trusted information from the external environment. In this case, the oracle performs the role of an adviser who interprets individual critical events in the external environment.

How Does the Oracle Work?

When developing blockchain oracles, developers are forced to solve one fundamental question: how can information about events occurring in the environment be reliably delivered to a smart contract? The developer can use three things for this:

1. Software or hardware acts as a ***primary source of data***.
2. ***Request*** for data transfer.
3. The ***Oracle*** itself or the ***Oracle Agreement***.

The primary source of data is intended to provide the necessary information for the oracle. There are many primary sources of data in the Internet of things around us that transmit data to oracles. The primary sources of data are very diverse. For example, they can be used as:

1. Transponders of travel documents for the operational management of passenger flows in the subway.
2. All kinds of meteorological sensors transmit data for predicting emergencies as a result of worsening weather conditions.
3. Various trackers for monitoring cargo transportation and much more.

A data transfer ***request*** is a specially coded message transmitted to the primary source of data. In response to the issued request, the smart contract receives trusted information for its execution.

The ***Oracle*** or ***Oracle Agreement*** is a program (unit) or group of programs (units) using in the blockchain connections a primary source of data and converting information received from direct sources of data into a format convenient for processing in the blockchain.

Types of Oracles

Depending on their functional purpose, design, and use, oracles can have the following types:

1. ***Oracle as a program*** is executed in software format, processing information coming from the source online. This type of oracle can transmit to smart contract bets on the results of football matches or boxing matches, information from traffic cameras about violations of traffic rules for making a smart contract decision on the payment of a fine, and so on. Oracles can have many different primary data sources, including numerous websites on social networks, which oracles transmit to smart contracts.
2. ***Oracle as the unit.*** These oracles are designed to transmit information from physical devices from the outside world of the so-called Internet of things. These include various monitors for monitoring the movement of vehicles, temperature sensors, and other weather parameters. Cash tags for tracking the movement of goods to manage smart contracts for supply chains. The problems associated with such oracles' work ensure high reliability of the data flow of information extracted from them.
3. ***Oracle as an entry*** into a smart contract. This oracle is programmed as an input to a smart contract and contains its executable code directly in the smart contract. It is designed to transmit information from the external environment when certain conditions are met during the execution of a smart contract. For example, to perform an automatic purchase of bitcoins or their immediate sale, a smart contract must constantly monitor at what point in time the bitcoin rate is to the maximum or minimum. Oracle, as an entry, is always ready to provide such information to the smart contract online.
4. ***Oracle as an exit.*** Oracle, as an exit, works in reverse order and transmits data to the external environment. Thus, some external smart lock system, having received information from the smart contract about a successful (unsuccessful) payment, transmitted to it through the oracle as an exit, can connect (close) the user access to the resource. Oracle as an exit can also be an integral part of a smart contract.
5. ***Oracle Agreement.*** Many event prediction systems use an oracle to predict outcomes of situations related to specific events. In such difficult situations, it is not enough to use only one oracle. In this regard, many oracles are used, the so-called Oracle agreement, the result of their work is summed up according to the majority scheme.

6. ***DVCS Oracle.*** Its necessity for the global supply chain has already been mentioned in the introduction. Still, it deserves separate detailed consideration, and its device will be described later in a separate section.

Who Develops Blockchain Oracles?

Among the companies involved in the development and implementation of blockchain oracles, the authors can specify the following companies:

- ***Oraclize*** — offers secure and "provably honest" data allocated from the pages of websites, using the TLSNotary/pagesigner tool developed by this company. This tool is a kind of TLS oracle that creates certified cryptographic evidence of the authenticity of the data presented by the website.
- ***Chainlink*** is a decentralized, secure oracle network created by the Smart Contract company. This oracle network belongs to the oracle agreement type and solves the problem of transferring data for smart contracts from the external environment.
- ***BNC (BraveNewCoin)*** — is a company engaged in the study and analysis of cryptocurrency exchange rates. This company has put a secure network of fourteen oracles for smart contracts working in the Ethereum environment into public access for free. Oracles transmit daily updated information about quotes of fourteen major cryptocurrencies to smart contracts.
- ***DVCS Oracle*** — oracle is based on the DVCS protocol of electronic signature verification. In many cases, the input data for a smart contract is the result of checking an electronic signature or a set of electronic signatures. In this case, it is necessary to allocate a trusted third party, the risks of incorrect verification of which will be provided, and certificates confirm the correctness of the work following current legislation. Gazinformservice LLC is Russia's leading developer of DVCS oracles.

Oracle Security Issues

1. All information security problems can be divided according to the data compromise points that oracle provides to the blockchain system:
    a. The input data stream from the oracle to the blockchain is compromised
    b. , and the oracle transmission channel to the blockchain is compromised.
    c. The oracle itself is compromised:
        i. Intentionally - the attacker has learned to give out the information he needs for the oracle's information.
        ii. Not intentionally (a software error).

The oracle infrastructure is actively developing, representing a secure communication channel of the surrounding digital environment for data delivery to the blockchain. This fact makes it possible to solve data transfer problems to the blockchain for the rapid execution of smart contracts for various purposes in decentralized blockchain networks. However, one should always consider the high risks of using false data in the blockchain due to compromising oracles.

Choosing a Validation Protocol for Oracle

Currently, there are three verification protocols most commonly used in practice: XML Key Management Specification (XKMS) (XML, 2005), OASIS Digital Signature Service (DSS) (OASIS, 2007), Data Validation and Certification Server (DVCS) (Internet, 2001).

The authors compared the validation protocols XKMS, OASIS DSS, and DVCS by various functional parameters to determine the most effective of the three protocols for use as an oracle.

This assessment is of practical importance in the context of correlating the capabilities of the compared protocols to implement the functions of the TTP, enshrined in Article 18.1 of Federal Law No. 63-FZ of 06.04.2011 "On Electronic Signature":

1. A trusted third party provides services:
    a. to confirm the validity of electronic signatures used when signing an electronic document, including establishing the facts that the relevant certificates are valid at a certain point in time, created and issued by accredited certification centers, whose accreditation is right on the date of issue of these certificates;
    b. to verify the compliance of all qualified certificates used when signing an electronic document with the requirements established by this Federal Law and other regulatory legal acts adopted following it;
    c. to verify the credentials of participants in electronic interaction;
    d. to create and sign a receipt with a qualified electronic signature of a trusted third party with the result of checking a qualified electronic signature in an electronic document with trusted information about the moment of its signing;
    e. data storage, including documentation of operations performed by a trusted third party.
2. A trusted third party (TTP) ensures the confidentiality, integrity, and availability of information during its processing and storage and transmission using information and telecommunication technologies.

Based on these requirements, to analyze the validation protocols, the authors set and evaluated the following tasks:

- To check the ES under the document;
- To check the validity of the ES Verification Key certificate (SVKC);
- To submit the results of the inspection in the form of a receipt, for use it as confirmation of the commission of specific actions with an electronic document or SVKC at a fixed time;
- To meet accessibility, integrity, and confidentiality requirements of information during its processing and storage and its transmission using information and telecommunication technologies.

In addition, for the practical use of the protocol, such parameters as a variety of options for interacting with the service support for standard transport protocols and the ability to check electronic documents of various formats are essential. Therefore, authors will include additional parameters in the comparison, according to which they will conduct it:

1. The type of request to the service.

2. The types of transport protocols.
3. The types of signatures.

The interaction of legal entities and individuals with government agencies and interdepartmental cooperation within the Russian Federation and in international formats is mainly regulated by regulations of one level or another. It can be determined the following summarizing the requirements for such interaction:

- The document presentation formats - XML and PDF.
- The type of ES used - CMS, XADES, PADES, XMLDSig.
- The possibility to validate the ES without receiving the electronic document (ED) itself (by hash).
- The ability to create and verify the time stamp.
- The possibility to create more than one ES in one ED.
- The fulfilling request speed to verify one document instance.
- The development difficulty.
- The check result is legally binding.
- The protocol possibility to fulfill transboundary trust.

Let's briefly describe the main distinguishing features of the validation protocols under consideration.

XKMS Protocol

The XKMS protocol describes the methods of registration, distribution, and the ES verification keys used in the XML signature and encryption standards. XKMS also formalizes the specifications of XML services: Key Registration (X-CROSS) and Key Information (X-KISS). The XKMS protocol is compatible with any public key infrastructure, including X.509.

The X-KISS user can pass the XML signature processing tasks <ds: KeyInfo> to the XKMS service. The purpose of the protocol development was to reduce the complexity of using XML signatures in various applications. Any application that becomes a client of the XKMS service becomes free from the syntactic complexity of a basic PKI such as PGP, SPKI, or X.509/PKIX.

X-CRS is a public key information and registration management service. The user of this service can create a request to associate some information with his public key. Such information may contain the user's ID or name and other data required by a specific PKI implementation.

XKMS allows users to authenticate them and confirm ownership of the ES key if they are generating a key pair. When developing the key pair, the service ensures the transfer of the ES key to users.

XKMS provides tools for registering DSA and RSA keys and defines requirements for expanding the protocol's capabilities to use other cryptographic standards, for example, based on Elliptic Curve and Diffie-Hellman standards.

XKMS provides opportunities to use different methods of canonicalization while complicating its use in development.

XKMS provides the ability to exchange messages. In this case, the messaging session consists of a sequence of request-response pairs. Messages are presented in a standard template supported by various exchange protocols. However, to ensure higher compatibility, XKMS recommends developers to use SOAP over HTTP, although the possibility of using other protocols is not excluded.

XKMS standardizes three query templates:

- X-KISS - request to determine or confirm the location;
- X-KRSS - request for registration, revocation, restoration, or renewal;
- Connected request - can contain more than one request X-KRSS or X-KISS.

XKMS defines two types of request processing - synchronic and asynchronous:

1. Synchronic - a response to the request is issued, and the request processing ends there.
2. Asynchronous - the response is not issued immediately, a notification that the request has not yet been completed and other responses will be made later.

The disadvantages of the protocol are:

- high memory requirements when processing large ED;
- when using data represented by containers, additional work is needed;
- low performance;
- cannot create and validate ES in PDF format.

OASIS DSS Protocol

The Organization for the Advancement of Structured Information Standards (OASIS) is engaged in the development of structured information standards, contributing to the achievement of consensus in the industry and the creation of global standards in the field of information security, cloud technologies, energy, IoT, emergencies, and other developing technologies.

The Digital Signature Service (DSS) developed by OASIS contains the following components:

1. The Base Module consists of DSS Core Protocols and DSS Elements and Bindings.
2. OASIS DSS Profiles:
    a. XML Timestamp Profile;
    b. ES Gateway Profile
    c. The profile of the ES made following German law;
    d. Entity Seal Profile;
    e. Electronic PostMark (EPM) Profile;
    f. Abstract Code-Signing Profile;
    g. J2ME Code Signing Profile;
    h. Asynchronous Process Abstract Profiles;
    i. Advanced ES Profile.

The Base Module provides main elements and protocols supporting specific scenarios according to DSS profiles.

Signature and verification protocols are mainly designed to create and verify XML or CMS signatures and binary or XML timestamps. These protocols can be extended to other signatures and timestamps, for example, PGP signatures.

Optional input data for the signature protocol are the type of signature for whom belongs the key are used to sign, for whom belongs the signature is intended, which signed and non-signed data to put in the signature.

Input data for the verification protocol are: the validity of the signature at a certain point in time, additional data required for signature verification (certificates, CRLs), requests to the server to obtain information about the signer, or the time of signature creation.

Disadvantages of the protocol:

1. OASIS DSS does not allow you to get a report on a multi-signature ED;
2. It is not possible to work with PDF signatures.

DVCS Protocol

The DVCS protocol is described in the RFC 3029 "Internet X.509 Public Key Infrastructure Data Validation and Certification Server Protocols", published by the Internet Engineering Task Force (IETF).

The document describes the DVCS protocols used for data exchanging. The DVCS is the server, so-called a TTP, that can be used to build reliable, trusted verification services.

RFC3029 uses four classes of certification and validation services:

- Certificate of Possession of Data (cpd);
- Certificate of Claim of Possession of Data without providing it to the service (ccpd);
- Verification of Signed Document (vsd);
- Verification of Public Key Certificates (vpkc).

CPD is a confirmation service that the data submitted for verification belonged to their owner before the time of their verification.

CCPD is a service for confirming claims to data ownership, identical to CPD, but provided that the owner does not represent the actual data but their hash.

VSD is an ES of ED verification service used to confirm the validity of an ES document. This service verifies all ES's of ED by checking the information it collects about the certificates of the ES verification keys and their statuses. The service checks the algorithmic correctness of all ES's attached to the ED. It also verifies the trust of the ED signers by verifying the entire certificates chain from the sign holder to the certification authority that released the certificate to the DVCS server or the senior root certification authority in the hierarchy. Verification of the validity of certificates can be carried out both according to the certificate revocation list (CRL) or according to more up-to-date data - according to the online certificate status protocol (OCSP) in real-time (Network, 2013) or by accessing a trusted cervices list (TCL) or another trusted DVCS service. Failure to check one ES does not necessarily lead to loss of the check as a whole and vice versa. If all ESs are successfully checked, a global error may occur if there are not enough ESs in the ED.

A CMS ES can use as a usual ES and a PDF ES because it is founded on a CMS ES.

VPKC is the service intended for verifying the validity of certificates of ES verification keys. It is described in RFC 2459 and is used to check the validity of certificates at a given time. When checking the certificate of the ES verification key, the DVCS checked that the certificate specified in the request is valid and defines its revocation status at the indicated time. DVCS validates the entire certification path from the certificate issuer to the root certification authority. It is also possible to use external information (CRL, OCSP, and DVCS) when checking. DVCS employs the default ASN1 coding.

The benefit of the DVCS protocols is that they may be capsulated in one message the services for verifying the certificate's validity, the validity of the ES, and the time stamp.

The disadvantage is that a user cannot open the verification results with a text editor to view and copy information and verify XML signatures.

The downside is that the validation outcomes cannot be open with a word processor to look at and backup the information and the impossibility of validating XML ES.

As a successfully implemented project, it should be mentioned that the TTP service of the Eurasian Economic Commission is efficiently functioning based on the DVCS oracle.

Comparative Analysis of Validation Protocols

A comparative overview of the validation protocols DVCS, OASIS DSS, and XKMS is given in Table 1. For visualization, each position is assigned a rating on a five-point scale. The significance of "1" is a value that does not allow solving problems, and the significance of "5" is a value that will enable solving problems.

Table 1. Comparison overview of validation protocols

Nº	Comparative Settings	XKMS	OASIS DSS	DVCS
1	Type of request	— verification of XML ES; — key couple registration by the key couple holder	— creating an ES; — verification of the validity ES of ED; — provision of timestamp services	— cpd; — ccpd; — vsd; — vpkc
	Rating	3	4	5
2	The transport protocol used	Protocol SOAP via HTTP	— protocol SOAP; — protocol HTTP POST; — protocol TLS	— protocol HTTP POST — protocol TLS; — protocol S/MIME
	Rating	2	5	5
3	The kind of ES that may be checked	XML ES	— XML ES; — CMS ES — Binary Time Stamp ES; — XML time stamp ES; — XADES and CADES; — PGP ES	— CMS ES; — PDF ES based on a CMS ES
	Rating	3	5	4
4	The ability to verify the ES of ED by hash	Absent	Present	Present
	Rating	1	5	5
5	The ability to check and generate a timestamp	Absent	Present	Present
	Rating	1	5	5

Table 1. Continued

Nº	Comparative Settings	XKMS	OASIS DSS	DVCS
6	The possibility to process more than one ES in a single ED	Present and an account is given for every ES	Present, but an account is not given for every ES	Present and an account is given for every ES
	Rating	5	4	5
7	The processing speed of the request for verification of the item instance	— Small, XML-format accommodates an abundance of excess data; — it is hard to deal with big files	Depends on the kind of ES (XML or CMS)	Extremely high, you may employ an individual ES
	Rating	3	4	5
8	Difficulty of realization	Medium	Medium	Minima
	Rating	4	4	5
9	The juridical power of the check's results	The ES can sign the check's results.	The ES can sign the check's results.	The ES can sign the check's results.
	Rating	5	5	5
10	The relevance of the protocol to ensuring cross-border credibility	Possibly	Possibly	Present
	Rating	4	4	5
	Shortcomings	— a high volume of storage is needed to parse big ED; — requires more handling in the way of the data containers; — lowly; — doesn't accept PDF ES	— it is not possible to report for each signature in an ED with several signatures; — doesn't accept PDF ES	— it can't be open with a word processor to see and back up the info
Medium rating:		3,1	4,5	4,9

So, according to those results obtained during the comparison analysis of validation protocols, the XKMS turned out to be the most inconvenient to use as an oracle. This protocol has a vast number of limitations. The most significant limitation is the lack of the possibility of forming a timestamp, and there is also no possibility of checking the improved ES. In addition, XKMS is the lowest-performing protocol.

A little more practical for solving ES validation tasks is the OASIS protocol. However, the DVCS protocol turned out to be the optimal solution for implementing the Oracle prototype. It has the highest performance, higher content of ES validation results. Based on this protocol, a global TTP chain can be easily built by somebody for their cross-border use. The Russian Federation successfully uses the DVCS protocol in both interdepartmental and cross-border electronic interaction. Some pilot projects in international formats in cross-border B2B processes have been carried out based on the DVCS protocol.

So, according to the results of the expert estimate, it could be concluded the DVCS protocol possesses the best characterizations for the solution of the stated tasks of creating DVCS oracle.

Technological Solutions to MRM Based on DVCS Oracle

There can be various technological options for cross-border electronic document exchange (Kustov & Domrachev, 2011). However, according to the Buy-Ship-Pay model (White, 2017), it is proposed to use data that is usually necessary during the document's legal function fulfillment to provide interoperability to trade-related electronic documents (Table 2).

Table 2. Able e-documents attributes used for cross-border paperless trade exchange

N°	Attribute type	Description/comments
1	Content	An aggregate of at least one of the following attributes is the content, the informational essence of a document, which is to be irrespective to an expression form – whether paper or electronic one: 1) document type, 2) document classification, 3) document title.
2	Document issuer legal status	An aggregate of the following attributes is the document issuer legal status: 1) logotype, 2) name of an issuer, 3) issuer reference data (address, contacts, etc.), 4) seal impression.
3	Signatory status (powers)or signatory position	A brief description of signatory powers with their duration is stated.
4	Signature	An aggregate of the following attributes is the signature: 1) issuer's signature, 2) signature stamp of confirmation, 3) signature stamp of approval, 4) visa (clearance / endorsement stamp), 5) copy certification stamp, 6) seal of issuing organization.
5	Time	A statement of the time point of signing is attached based on a trusted time source (the validity aspect).
6	Place	A signing statement (where the signatory expressed their will to sign by triggering signing) is optional. If this type of service is not available, the attribute place can be considered one of the content attributes.

Data models should be built based on international standards and recommendations to ensure compatibility with other global systems and applications.

Standardization and applications of data elements are observed in the following documents:

- Trade data element Directory UN (UNITED, ISO 7372) (Trade, 2005);
- The core component is Library UN/CEFACT (CCL) and the technical specifications of UN/CEFACT (CCTS) (TBG17, 2020).

The Essence of Mutual Recognition

Mutual recognition is the mutual acknowledgment of the truth of trade-related information and EDs that are exchanged over borders between a couple of other countries (UN, 2016).

The conformity of the subject of electronic communication with the appropriate legislative, organization, and technology demands and/or guidelines and regulations and/or proceedings is provided by an institutional mechanism that ensures fulfillment of the righthand and lawful interest of the subjects of the electronic interoperation. (Silanteva & Kustov, 2020).

Following article 8 of the Framework Agreement on the Facilitation of Cross-Border Paperless Trade in the Asia-Pacific Region (FA-CPT, 2016) and the Explanatory Note to the Framework Agreement on Assistance from One Country to Another, depending on national laws, a widely used and legally recognized form of ES is digital signatures based on public-key cryptography. The document is signed with an ES using a secret key, which is in the exceptional ownership of the signatory and is checked using the relevant open key. After carrying out necessary verification, the certifying authority issues a DSC (Digital Signature Certificate) and acts to confirm the public key as a trust binding. In most countries, papers signed with the application of DSC, issued by a licensed certifying authority, are legitimately accepted. Nevertheless, a certifying authority acknowledged in one country may not be recognized in the other, which causes difficulties in a cross-border paperless transaction. Consequently, the certifying authorities must guarantee *an essentially equal degree of safety*.

The test of *an essentially equal degree of safety* is taken from article 12, paragraph 3, of the UNCITRAL Model Law on Electronic Signatures (UNCITRAL, 2001). It indicates for parties that information and papers will be acknowledged when they ensure a *degree of safety* identical to, though not similar to, the *degree of security* of the recognizers. The *parties should mutually agree upon an essentially equal degree of* protection. Let's define the factors that could be taken into account when evaluating the degree of safety (Methodology, 2017):

1. Availability of financial and man resources and funds of trusted services provider;
2. Reliability of used equipment and program systems;
3. Security and vulnerability of the algorithm and/or mechanism used for the ES;
4. Procedures for handling ES certificate, certificate request, and storing corresponding records;
5. The ability of subscribers and/or relied upon parties to access the information;
6. The regularity and scope of inspections conducted by an autonomous authority;
7. Needs, benefits, and challenges of mutual recognition.

Green Corridor Project between Russia and the EU

Green Corridor Project is based on the use of Trusted Third Party (ITU-T, 2002). The customs authorities of the EU countries want to be sure that the goods exported from the EAEU be imported into the EU in the same form in which they left the territory of the EAEU. An available option is to send an export declaration with a note on the export of goods from the EAEU.

The customs representative receives the relevant export declarations from the customers and sends them in electronic form (XML format) through the information integrator to the customs office before the vehicle arrives at the point where the cargo will carry out the customs clearance cargo be carried out.

When checking the import declaration, the customs inspector contains the information in the import declaration with the data from the export declaration. In case of their compliance, customs clearance and release of goods take place in a simplified form for a minimum period.

To realize the project is used customs control tower (CCT) (Figure 3).

Figure 3. Customs control tower (CCT)

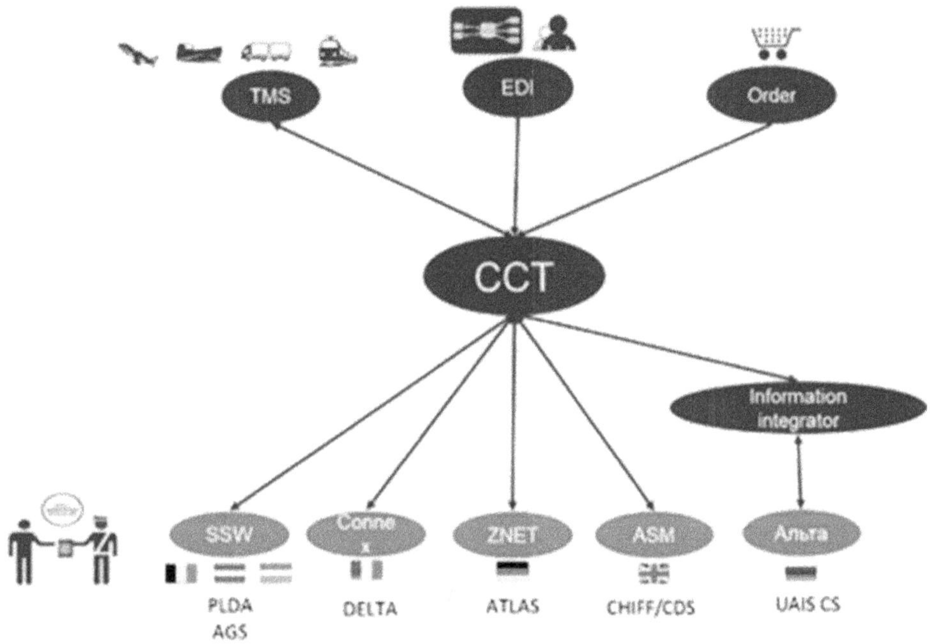

CCT is designed to integrate customs systems of different countries to monitor customs operations and use data to process import, export, and transit procedures. It is a highly automated system for exchanging data and documents on a blockchain platform between all participants in the supply chain, including government and supervisory authorities. The DVCS oracle mechanism verifies all data entering the blockchain. Integration of data received from participants of foreign economic activity with data of transport management systems (TMS) and warehouse complexes is carried out only after verification of electronic signatures by DVCS oracle. Thus, trusted CCT data allows you to control the supply chain using all modes of transport entirely. The system can be connected to other platforms using Application Programming Interface (API), Electronic Data Interchange (EDI), and two-way automation and control. CCT will provide direct interaction with local customs software in all European countries and around the world. Figure 4 presents an existing process of document exchange.

The proposed scheme of interaction (Figure 5) supports the one-time provision of information and documents. This MRM provides smooth and transparent cross-border electronic data and e-documents exchange.

The following way should conduct realization of mutual recognition mechanism:

1. Creation and submission to the customs authorities of the Russian Federation of a transit/export declaration by the sender or his customs representative in the Russian Federation.
2. Transfer the export declaration in XML format to the information integrator to verify the integrity of the digital signature, thereby DVCS oracle. If necessary, transfer other formalized documents for verification and confirmation of the EDS.
3. Verification of the validity of the ES of the customs authority of the Russian Federation by the information integrator.

4. Transfer data to the EU customs authorities (set "export declaration in XML + receipt with the results of the ES check" issued by DVCS oracle).
5. Transfer the export declaration in XML to the Customs Control Tower for subsequent transmission to the customs representative in the EU.
6. If necessary, add to the information exchange data about the electronic navigation seal placed on the container or cargo compartment of the vehicle.
7. Processing information in the Customs Control Tower and transferring it to the EU unit for import/transit declaration.
8. Submission of the import/transit declaration by the recipient or their customs representative in the EU.
9. The EU Customs Authority compares the information specified in the export declaration and the import/transit declaration.
10. The EU Customs authority decides on the release/transit of goods; the Customs Control Tower and the customs representative receive this information.
11. In case of refusal to release/transit – standard forms of control are applied (request additional documents, inspection, and sampling).

Figure 4. The Standard scheme of interaction

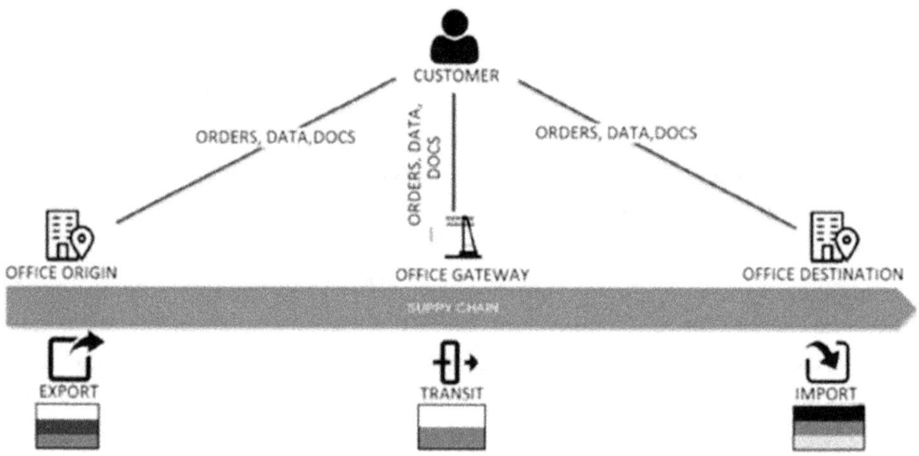

This MRM allows minimizing customs risks and simplified customs clearance. The green corridor project is based on the principle of one-time information provision about products and provides transparency for the entire supply chain and traceability of goods.

Software Package Litoria DVCS Oracle

The software package Litoria DVCS Oracle (SP Litoria DVCS Oracle) (Software, 2017) checks the ES and the validity of the ES verification key certificate. SP Litoria DVCS Oracle enables the user to make a check request, parse such a request, and create an answer containing the check result.

Figure 5. Proposed MRM based on DVCS oracle for interaction

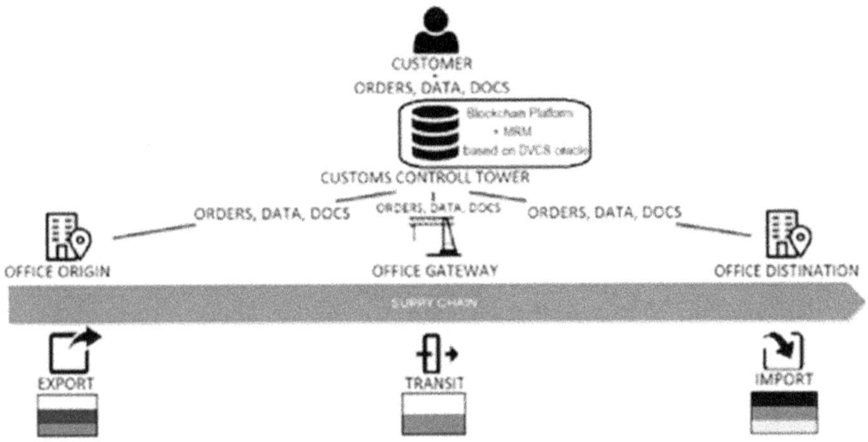

The main task of SP Litoria DVCS Oracle is to offer ES check service for interagency and international data exchange of participants in the conditions of ensuring the integrity and reliability of ED's and their ES's. (Software, 2013).

The following functions are implemented in the SP Litoria DVCS Oracle:

1. Creation of all DVCS requests (following RFC3029) To perform this task:
    a. Certification of Possession of Data (cpd);
    b. Certification of Claim of Possession of Data without providing it to the service (ccpd);
    c. Verification of Signed Document (vsd);
    d. Verification of Public Key Certificates (vpkc).
2. Verification of every contained information in the query.
3. Creation:
    a. timestamps,
    b. DVC answers and their analyses conform to the RFC 3029.
4. Archive and store in memory:
    a. user's data,
    b. serial numbers creation to DVC-receipts,
    c. audit of log file events on the SP Litoria DOCS Oracle authentication server includes the event's kind, time, and date.
5. Providing the designer with program tools that ease the creation of customer apps, such as:
    a. customer service SDK DVCS is a program component, including libraries (C# and C++) that are used when creating apps using the functionality of the service DVCS;
    b. Customer service SDK TSP is a program component including libraries (C# and C++) used to create apps using the timestamps following RFC3161.

During the development of the SP, the following regulatory documents were used:

1. RFC3029 "Internet X.509 Public Key Infrastructure Data Validation and Certification Server Protocols (DVCS)";
2. RFC3161 "Internet X.509 Public Key Infrastructure Time-Stamp Protocol (TSP) ";
3. RFC6960 "Internet X.509 Public Key Infrastructure Online Certificate Status Protocol – OCSP".

The following components are included in the PC:

4. Authentication Service (DVCS);
5. Time Stamp Service (TSP);
6. SDK client for DVCS service;
7. SDK client for TSP service;
8. Administrator automated workplace.

The block diagram of the interaction of the SP Litoria DVCS Oracle components is illustrated in Figure 6.

Figure 6. The block diagram of the interaction of the SP Litoria DVCS oracle components

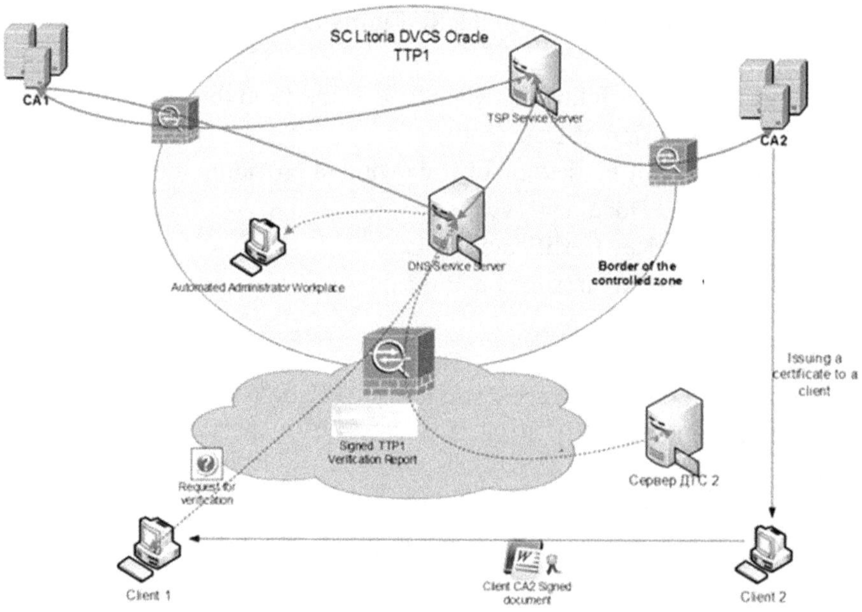

The main component of the SP Litoria DVCS Oracle is the web authentication service, which operates on the authentication server platform, and performs:

1. Processing DVCS requests following RFC 3029 (VSD, VPKC, CPD, CPD).
2. Formation of DVCS responses based on the results obtained during authentication.
3. Construction of DVC receipts using electronically signed DVCS responses.

4. Search and issue of DVC receipts generated for previously received DVCS requests.
5. Forming and sending a request to the time stamp server.

CONCLUSION

The chapter begins with a review of the principles of building traditional supply chains using blockchain technology. These supply chains are built according to a four-level scheme, including the following levels: physical flows, information flows, a blockchain platform, and the level of smart contracts. The authors substantiate the need for an additional MRM to ensure secure cross-border interchange of lawfully relevant ED's. The authors propose a theoretical model for the design of the MRM based on the DVCS Oracle.

Mutual recognition based on the principles proposed by the authors will provide an uninterrupted, transparent, and trusted environment for the cross-border interchange of information and papers in e-form. The introduction of MRM will assist in easing interaction and ensuring confidence between parties involved in ED-interchange in global supply chains.

Mutual acknowledgment considering the varying technological, legislative, and administrative circumstances in different countries poses considerable challenges that could be surmounted by establishing confidence that would guarantee the cross-border interchange of information and paper in e-form between countries. A TTP whose role is performed by a DVCS oracle creates this trust. MRM based on DVCS oracle allows you to verify electronic data interchanged among countries whenever the PKI uses various, conflicting cryptographic standards.

The paramount need for mutual recognition is to develop an opportunity to interchange trade-related information and paper in e-form over borders among various countries with varying technological approaches and within other jurisdictions. MRM, presented by the Green Corridor project, allows you to overcome all obstacles and provide uninterrupted data exchange.

REFERENCES

Chris, J. S. (2017). *Who will be killed by blockchain: 4 small business areas that will soon disappear.* https://incrussia.ru/understand/kogo-ubet-blokchejn-4-sfery-malogo-biznesa-kotorye-skoro-ischeznut/

Dannen, K. (2018). *Introduction to Ethereum and Solidity.* Samizdat.

Framework Agreement on Facilitation of Cross-Border Paperless Trade in Asia and the Pacific (FA-CPT). (2016). Economic and Social Commission for Asia and the Pacific, E/ESCAP/RES/72/4.

Internet, X. (2001). *509 Public Key Infrastructure. Data Validation and Certification Server Protocols.* Network Working Group Request for Comments: 3029. https://www.ipa.go.jp/security/rfc/RFC3029EN.html

ITU-T. (2002). *Recommendation X.842 information technology security techniques guidelines for the use and management of trusted third party services.* https://www.itu.int/rec/T-REC-X.842

Kupriyanovsky, V., Namiot, D., & Sinyagov, S. (2016). Cyber-physical systems as a base for the digital economy. International Journal of Open Information Technologies, 4(2), 18-25.

Kustov, V. N., & Domrachev, A. A. (2011). Transboundary Trust Space as a Component of an International E-Commerce Soft-Infrastructure. *APEC PROJECT Supply Chain Connectivity: e-Commerce as the Main Driver and Integration Too,* 85-96.

Kustov, V. N., & Silanteva, E. S. (2020). Mutual recognition mechanism of legally significant e-documents and data in the cross-border document flow. *Journal of Physics: Conference Series*, *1703*(1), 012011. doi:10.1088/1742-6596/1703/1/012011

Kustov, V. N., & Stankevich, T. L. (2018). Once Again, about Blockchain Technology. *J. Intellectual Technologies on Transport*, (3), 38–46.

Kustov, V. N., & Stankevich, T. L. (2018). Blockchain Prospects: a Dialogue between a Skeptic and an Optimist. *Bulletin of Scientific Conferences, 1*(37), 77-84.

Kustov, V. N., & Stankevich, T. L. (2019). Blockchain Technology: a Story of Ingenious Simplicity or Enlightened Thinking. How to protect yourself from blockchain? *J. Information Protection, 2*(86), 11-18.

Methodology of formation of transboundary trust environment and the requirements for its creation, functioning and development. (2017). *XXIII International Conference on Soft Computing and Measurement (SCM'2020) Journal of Physics: Conference Series*. https://www.unescap.org/resources/methodology-formation-transboundary-trustenvironment-and-requirements-its-creation-0/

Network Working Group. (2013). *Request for Comments 6960 Internet X.509 Public Key Infrastructure Online Certificate Status Protocol – OCSP*. https://tools.ietf.org/html/rfc6960/

OASIS Digital Signature Services eXtended (DSS-X) TC. (2007). https://www.oasis-open.org/committees/tc_home.php?wg_abbrev=dss-x

Report of the company Positive Technologies. (2019). *Initial Coin Offering. Threats to information security*. https://www.ptsecurity.com/upload/corporate/ru-ru/analytics/ICO-Threats-rus.pdf

Satoshi, N. (2008). *Bitcoin. A Peer-to-Peer Electronic Cash System*. https://bitcoin.org/bitcoin.pdf

Shapiev, M. M. (2019). Vulnerabilities of smart contracts and ways of their exploitation. *Scientific Electronic Journal "Meridian", 10*(28), 1-5.

Silanteva, E. S., & Kustov, V. N. (2020). Technological aspects of the trust in the cross-border paperless exchange. *Journal of Physics: Conference Series*, *1703*(1), 012049. doi:10.1088/1742-6596/1703/1/012049

Software Electronic Signatures and Infrastructures (ESI) Policy requirements for certification authorities issuing public-key certificates. (2013). https://www.etsi.org/deliver/etsi_ts/102000_102099/102042/02.04.01_60/ts_102042v020401 p.pdf

Swan, M. (2018). Blockchain: The scheme of a new economy. Olymp-Business Publishing House.

TBG17 CCL (Core Component Library). (2020). *Submission Guidelines and Procedures*. UN/CEFACT/TBG17/N004 Draft Version 3.0.

The software package "Trusted Third Party Services "Litoria DVCS." (2017). Program Description, 72410666.00044-01 13 01, 36 p.

Trade data element Directory (TDED) UNTDED. (2005). ISO 7372:2005, Vol. 1 Data Elements.

UN ESCAP. (2016). *Framework Agreement on Facilitation of Cross-border Paperless Trade in Asia and the Pacific*. https://treaties.un.org/doc/source/docs/ESCAP_RES_72_4-E.pdf

UNCITRAL. (2001). *Model Law on Electronic Signatures*. https://uncitral.un.org/en/texts/ecommerce/modellaw/electronic_signatures/

White Paper on a Reference Data Model. (2017). Centre for Trade Facilitation and Electronic Business, Twenty-third session.

XML Key Management Specification (XKMS 2.0). (2005). *Version 2.0 W3C Recommendation*. https://www.w3.org/TR/xkms2/

Chapter 6
Blockchain in Logistics and Supply Chain Monitoring

Krati Reja
Vellore Institute of Technology, VIT Bhopal University, India

Gaurav Choudhary
Technical University of Denmark, Denmark

Shishir Kumar Shandilya
https://orcid.org/0000-0002-3308-4445
VIT Bhopal University, India

Durgesh M. Sharma
https://orcid.org/0000-0002-9378-3061
G.H. Raisoni College of Engineering, Nagpur, India

Ashish K. Sharma
https://orcid.org/0000-0002-9117-4481
G.H. Raisoni College of Engineering, Nagpur, India

ABSTRACT

Supply chain management (SCM) is a system to manage the flow of goods and services, and from transforming the raw into finished products, it has challenges that are needed to be achieved like good quality services to the consumer, reducing labor cost, etc. Industries need to digitize real assets and make distributed, immutable transactions possible to trace assets from manufacture to supply. To overcome the lack of transparency and traceability of the products in the enterprise resource planning system in supply chain (SC) and logistics issues, there is a solid need to employ a method that can efficiently track assets from production to supply decentralized, immutable records of all transactions. A blockchain (BC) is a decentralized software network that follows a digital ledger to exchange entities digitally and a way through which it makes secure transactions. Thus, this chapter proposes integrating BC in logistics and SC monitoring by giving a template on how Python and Flask can be used for BC with the SCM system to improve traceability without involving any intermediary.

DOI: 10.4018/978-1-7998-8697-6.ch006

Copyright © 2022, IGI Global. Copying or distributing in print or electronic forms without written permission of IGI Global is prohibited.

INTRODUCTION

The use of digital technology has rapid growth in the whole world. The rapid growth and use of the internet have made business development and processes more efficient than ever. Digitalization has helped to solve many business Challenges (Tsiulin et al., 2020). Supply Chain Management (SCM) is a system that connects the primary roots of the company to its customers to manage the flow of goods and services, and it comprises whole operations from transforming the raw into finished products. It is the method through which supply chain (SC) operations are supervised to benefit rivals and enhance the value of their consumers.

Supply Chain Management (SCM) is a system to manage the flow of goods and services, and from transforming the raw into finished products but it has challenges that are needed to be achieved like good quality services to the consumer, reducing labor cost, etc. Industries need to digitize real assets and make distributed, immutable transactions, possible to trace assets from manufacture to supply. To overcome the

lack of transparency and traceability of the products in the Enterprise Resource Planning system in Supply Chain (SC) and logistics issues, there is a solid need to employ a method that can efficiently track assets from production to supply decentralized, immutable records of all transactions.

The Supply Chain and logistic monitoring comprise of challenges that are needed to be achieved like lack of trust, good quality services to the consumer, visibility, fast-evolving in the markets due to this it becomes inevitable, increased amount of fraudulent activities, reducing labor cost, raw materials, and energy, unexpected delays in the deliveries, improving the relationship between traders by delivering product timely, lack of traceability, reduces the risk by making up the consumer demand with product delivery time due to the continuous variation in the market, trained staff for serving their consumer timely.

These challenges in the supply chain compromise in every stage of the supply chain. These challenges occur from phases like Plan, Source, Make, Deliver and Return. The Supply Chain Management (SCM) process has already been facing such situations, and meanwhile, a new challenge has been introduced in the name of Pandemic, i.e., COVID-19. To protect lives from this Pandemic, the whole countries have been locked down completely, and due to this, the supply chain processes have been affected badly, the consumers' basic needs could not have been delivered timely, and in many countries, people died of hunger. The COVID-19 remains in the countries and disturbing the economies around the world. Moreover, despite the burden to acquire the economy regain and running, ongoing unpredictability, lack of customer belief, and supply chain challenges pursue bear a pressure. Organizations need to digitize physical assets and make a distributed, immutable record of all transactions, making it feasible to trace assets from manufacture to supply or consumer usage.

However, there is a lack of transparency and traceability of the products in the Enterprise Resource Planning (ERP) system in supply chain and logistics. To overcome the issue, there is a solid need to employ some technique or a model that can efficiently trace assets from manufacture to supply or consumer usage decentralized, immutable record of all transactions. The integration of blockchain with logistics and supply chain monitoring can provide a solution that will help solve all these challenges faced by the supply chain.

A blockchain is a decentralized software network that follows a digital ledger and a way through which it makes secure transactions without an arbitrator. Blockchain differs from the central database by the way blockchain stores the data (Tijan et al., 2019). A blockchain is a fixed time-framed chain record of data dispersed and controlled by nodes of the computer network. It is a method to exchange entities digitally.

Entities like sale deeds to currencies to votes can be encoded by tokenizing, storing, and exchanging on a blockchain network. Blockchain technology has many applications in Healthcare, the Educational sector, voting mechanisms, the automobile industry, personal identity security, and Supply chain monitoring (Sharma et al., 2021). Different types of data can be stored in a blockchain. The most common type is the records of transactions for supply chain monitoring. The blockchain will store the product data that will help in tracing the product. As the data is immutable and decentralized, it builds trust between different parties. A blockchain collects the data in groups known as blocks, and blockchain has a particular space to store the data or information; when it is filled, it chains itself with a previous block (chain is the hash to the previous block), and when any new data needs to be added, it is then added in the new block, every block in the blockchain comprises timestamp stating when the block is connected to the chain. It is difficult to go back and alter any content once stored in the blockchain, especially those already agreed by the majority by general agreement (consensus). As the block contains its hash, previous blocks hash, and a timestamp (a mathematical function calculates hash), if any participant in the blockchain changes their copy of data, then the hash will change, and it will not match with other copies, and thus all other participants will know that the data has been modified. Blockchain can be applied to many fields which require transparency, security, traceability, etc.

Blockchain can greatly improve supply chains by enabling faster and more cost-efficient delivery of products, enhancing products' traceability, improving coordination between partners, and aiding access to financing. Blockchain is a leading-edge technology that is being implemented universally nowadays. It enforces application in a secure and distributed way and therefore reassures some amount of reliability. Due to these reasons, blockchain technology has been adopting in a distrustful society. The supply chain connects the primary roots of the company to its customers. It involves transforming raw material into a finished good that will serve its purpose to the customers. However, this process encounter several difficulties that must be resolved using technology as the usage of the technology and internet has a great expansion around the world; resolving these difficulties with technology will be favorable to customers as it will be simply manageable to customers worldwide. Any changes made to the data will be visible to every participant in the blockchain, and hence it will improve the visibility. Moreover, Blockchain enhances the ability to quickly pinpoint potential sources of contamination to efficiently prevent, contain or rectify outbreaks. Blockchain can enable more transparent and accurate end-to-end tracking in the supply chain: Organizations can digitize physical assets and create a decentralized immutable record of all transactions, making it possible to track assets from production to delivery or use by end user. In this way Blockchain can improve traceability in supply chain.

Integrating blockchain technology with supply chain monitoring will help overcome the challenges tackled by the supply chain industry. It provides all the participants within the blockchain visibility to the same. Using a centrally authorized database decreases the trust within the parties; participants in a supply chain always need to depend on the third party for managing the information stored on the database. Using blockchain, some researchers have proposed a model for improving trust, visibility, and traceability in business processes. However, some model in the literature survey has given only a theoretical explanation and shortfall to explain its practical implementations (Jabbar et al., 2021), whereas some models were not cost-effective (Mao et al., 2018). Integrating blockchain with the supply chain can be a cure (Issaoui et al., 2019). But due to a lack of knowledge of people and many other factors, many supply chain organizations are not adopting blockchain in this field. The help of a centrally controlled database reduces the reliance within the parties; members in a supply chain always need to trust the third party to handle the information kept on the database. Some research workers proposed prototypes for improving faith, transparency, and traceability in commercial practices using blockchain. Many multinational organizations like IBM, Oracle, and Microsoft have given good examples for adopting blockchain and tracking their products through the supply chain know as BaaS (Blockchain as a Service), and soon this technology will proliferate in every field. Integrating blockchain with different technology like the IoT will take blockchain technology to new heights. Various organizations have started many new initiatives like the pilot project, Everledger for integrating the supply chain with blockchain.

Thus, this study proposes integrating blockchain in SCM and Logistics using a Logical Model in Python. The objective is to define how blockchain makes better traceability and transparency of supply chain and logistics with the help of suggestions to implement a method for the creation of blockchain for performing an essential function like adding a new block to the chain, performing transactions, implementing and validating Proof of Work, methods for using Flask framework for new transactions, mining a new block, etc. and suggested a template code for proceeding the above-discussed processes for the implementation. Thus, the study will boost the confidence of organizations in supply chain management and assist the blockchain developers by giving them a template on how we can use Python and Flask for blockchain with the Supply Chain Management system in improving traceability without involving any intermediary. Finally, this study discusses the challenges- processing speed of a transaction gets degrade due to decentralized control when Blockchain with Supply chain integrate when compared to centralized control, incompatible issue due to different blockchain platforms have different protocols, blockchain with less number of nodes has a higher risk of attacks into the network, and this gap motivates the research workers to make this proposed prototype model, a safe and secured one. It is expected that a proper solution will be set up to resolve the technical shortcomings that are pointed out in the chapter, and proper practical implementation will be introduced, and as future direction this leaves a broader scope in the integration of Blockchain with Logistics and Supply Chain Monitoring model.

This chapter is organized into the following sections. The first section covers the blockchain and supply chain management models. The next section discusses the problem statement on the supply chain. The third section analyzes the surveys of various research workers who work on blockchains with the management of the supply chain process. The fourth section discusses the Blockchain and Supply Chain management background. The following section proposes the solution and results on the integration of Blockchain with Supply Chain management and finally challenges along with its future direction and then concludes the whole survey in summarized form.

RELATED WORK

Blockchain is a recent technology that exponentially improves transparency, traceability, scalability, and security in business, supply chain, banking, and other transaction networks, creating new opportunities for growth and innovation, reducing the risk of related business operations and cost. Krings, et.al enlightened on the prospective offered by Blockchain Technology for equipping SC to the usual well (Krings, K., & Schwab, 2021). Numerous research has been published to brief out the challenges, design issues, and various future research in supply chain management, also discussed in Table 1. Song et al. research paper mainly focus the influence of Blockchain in SC traceability through the present business application, i.e., logistics, quality affirmation, inventory control, and predicting. This paper elaborates on how features of Blockchain can be helpful in the SC and how Blockchain is beneficial for supply chain management. It also has thrown light on how more opportunities. Blockchain gives SC traceability over conventional centralized systems. However, it lacked in elaborating on how the Blockchain can be implemented for better traceability of the SCM (Song et al., 2019).

Hellani, et al. focused the necessities and difficulties of SC transparency. Afterwards examined a set of SC projects that handle data transparency problems by applying Blockchain in their core platform in diverse ways. Moreover, they studied the projects' methods and the tools applied to modify transparency. As a result of the projects' examined, they recognized that further improvements are desirable to set a stability in between the data transparency and process opacity required by several associates, to confirm the privacy of their procedures and to control access to sensitive data (Hellani et al.,2021). Paliwal et al. have found the role of blockchain technology in SCM which is sustainable. To response the research query, the study has created a model that uses: who, where, what, when, and how (5w+1H) pattern. The paper has proposed a model which is a reusable classification framework (ETLCL) based on grounded theory and the technology willingness level for doing literature surveys in several focus domains of developing technology. The results of the study prove traceability and visibility as the main interest of adopting blockchain technology. The limitation of this research is that this field has been drawing more attention to academics and organizational, and in the future, the literature is expected to double as more and more companies adopt Blockchain (Paliwal et al., 2020).

Perboli et al. have defined a typical methodology for preparing a plan to evolve and authenticate the complete Blockchain solution and incorporate it into the Corporate Plan. The paper deliberates how the Blockchain will aid to reduce logistics expenditures and optimize the processes and the study challenges. The GUEST approach is expressed in five phases (GO, UNIFORM, EVALUATE, SOLVE, and TEST). In this approach classifying the important actors associated in the supply chain procedure, their works, and efforts need to be adequately defined; otherwise, this method will not be efficient and cost-effective (Perboli et al., 2018).

Weber et al. has suggested a Blockchain model for resolving trust in a collaborative business where two or more companies need to run a business process. The study was focused on the demonstration of the Business Process Model (BPM). A case or prototype is taken on how to increase trust between 2 parties was implemented using Ethereum for the Blockchain and Solidity for the Smart Contracts, was verified by employing it to business model taken from the literature part (Weber et al., 2016).

Guerreiro et al. proposed on the BPM, giving a perfect model for making safe and protected transactions using Blockchain and the company's operating system (enterprise). The study aims to solve the potential risk involved in executing business transactions, making faith, visibility, and traceability against any fraudulent activity, and increasing authenticity (Guerreiro et al., 2013).

Leng et al. suggested a public Blockchain of the agronomic SC system based on dual chain design to increase the productivity of Blockchain in the agriculture SC. Their study stated that their proposed way offers flexible rent-seeking and matching mechanisms for public service platforms. Furthermore, the solution ensures the visibility, safety, and security of transaction information and provides privacy to organizational information. Therefore, the model makes a better public service platform and the altogether effectiveness of the system. The major limitation is the blockchain network size and the slow performance due to the extensive network (Leng et al., 2018).

Mao et al. has suggested a credit evaluation system using blockchain technology for regulating and managing of the SC in the food industry. The model collected credit evaluation texts from the buyers by smart contracts in blockchain technology, and then those collected texts are evaluated by a deep learning technique Long Short Term Memory (LSTM). The study aimed to show the efficiency of their model but did not study the complete system cost and the profits clearly (Mao et al., 2018).

Sripathi has examined and researched to answer - what are the risk involved in early adoption, size of the organization, how is the IT investment of the company, and the number of shareholders in the SC can affect the implementation of Blockchain technology by a food companies?" The research in this paper aims to understand how the above features influence the use of blockchain technology in the food companies' SC. The study also elaborated on how Blockchain can be used in the SC to track food worldwide and make sure that the food supplied by the company is safe and hygienic by the companies like Walmart, Nestle, Fijian, etc. The research developed three hypotheses that can analyze and answer the research question. This paper does not elaborate on how RFID, NFC tags can be used for tracing the product. The hypothesis needed to be tested statistically, and a survey is needed to support the hypothesis (Sripathi, 2019).

Aliyu et al. has discussed how supply chain management can use one of the blockchain technology application to improve and integrate the process of their transactions and activities by connecting to an extensive smartphone application that will connect all participants or actors or people associated in the process of the SC to insert, recover, store, manage or distinguish information across the network in the blockchain technology. The paper has also given an overview of how Walmart plans to use blockchain hyperledger to track or trace the origin of goods. Finally, this paper has provided certain challenges faced by the SC and how blockchain technology, precisely hyperledger, could be used to eliminate those challenges (Aliyu et al., 2018).

Table 1. Authors' contributions in blockchain technology analysis table

Related Work	Key Contribution	Cost Effective	Methodology	Use Cases	Traceability and Transparency
Song et al., 2019	It emphases on the effect of blockchain in SC traceability by the present industry application	--	No	No	Yes
Sripathi, 2019	The possibility of the research in this paper is to comprehend and suggest how some variables affect the adoption of blockchain in the Food SC.	--	No	Yes	Yes
Paliwal et al., 2020	It investigates the role of blockchain technology in sustainable SCM	--	Yes	No	Yes
Mao et al., 2018	It proposes a Blockchain-based credit evaluation system to build up the efficiency of regulation and administration in the food SC.	No	Yes	No	Yes
Leng et al., 2018	It proposes a public Blockchain of the agricultural SC system based on dual chain design to improve the effectiveness of Blockchain in the agricultural SC.	Yes	Yes	No	Yes
Guerreiro et al., 2013	It presents an Enterprise Operating System with the integration of Blockchain for performing a safe business transactions	Yes	Yes	No	Yes
Weber et al., 2016	It proposes a Blockchain way to solve the lack of trust issue in joint methods	Yes	Yes	No	No
Aliyu et al., 2018	It discusses how supply chain management can use one of the blockchain technology application	--	No	Yes	--
Perboli et al., 2018	It defines a typical methodology for preparing a plan to evolve and authenticate the complete Blockchain solution and incorporate it into the Corporate Plan	Yes	Yes	Yes	--

BACKGROUND

Blockchain and Supply Chain

Blockchain can be defined as a distributed and decentralized database that can store transaction records and ensures transparency, traceability, security, and immutability. It is also called a chain of blocks storing transactional data not controlled by any single authority. The transactional records stored in a blockchain are timestamped, which means that the time at which any transaction was added to a block will also be a part of that block (Chang & Chen, 2020). Blockchain is a system of multiple computers or peers connected in a network that performs as a decentralized network over the internet (Abeyratne & Monfared, 2016). Every node in the blockchain network has the power to create a transaction, validate a transaction, accept a transaction, and make a block. Blockchain is a sequence of blocks (set of records) linked with each other cryptographically. Due to immutability in blockchain, when we insert a transactions set in a blockchain, inserted blocks become blockchain network part, and then no one can contradict it or modify it. Every node in a network of blockchain has an individual reproduction of the database that stores the transactions. Anyone in the blockchain network, an authorized participant can check or use the transaction history from the database whenever they want and receive revised data each time a node attaches any fresh transactions (block) into the chain. The private, consortium, or hybrid blockchain can be used by an organization that does not want to share every little detail with others. In these types of blockchain, an organization can control and restrict who can be a part of that blockchain. However, private blockchains are less secure, and trust-building is a little complicated than public blockchain. However, it is entirely dependent on the organization's type of blockchain network (public, private) they want to work on. While comparing blockchain with a traditional centralized solution provides immutability, transparency, traceability, trust, and more security. Figure 1 has demonstrated the utilization of Blockchain technology in the SC and Logistics, manufacturers, retailers, growers, healthcare, secure voting, financial, educational, and many more sectors.

The supply chain is the connection or network between the company and its supplier to manufacture and deliver the finished product or goods to the customer. Supply chain management represents that how the final product reaches the buyer safely and serves its purpose. Logistics is the subsection of the supply chain as logistics move goods from place to place (Dobrovnik et al., 2018), so tracking the products is essential whether the final good reaches the customer. Quality Function Deployment (QFD) methodology is the most reliable and proved method to identify customer-based strategy. QFD can help determine critical customer requirements and prioritize them to determine the critical supply chain factors to improve supply chain performances. The use of QFD has been reported by many in varied sectors. The usefulness of QFD especially in forecasting and website design was discussed by (Sharma and Khandait, 2016), (Purohit and Sharma, 2015), (Sharma and Khandait, 2017), (Sharma et. al., 2009). However, supply chain and logistics are facing difficulties and challenges concerning the security, visibility, transparency of various operations, transactional issues, manual errors, delay in processing, updating, or sharing data and information, speed in delivering goods and services, difficulties in tracking and tracing the origin of their goods and services. One of the technologies that can overcome these shortcomings can be the application of blockchain in SCM.

Role of Blockchain in Supply Chain Monitoring (SCM)

Blockchain has a significant role to play in SCM. Blockchain builds communication between partners. This builds a streamlined process with shorter lead times, reduced redundancy, fewer delays, and ultimately a leaner supply chain. It also ensures that quality standards are met, giving the seller more control of the production of the product from A to Z. Blockchain can leverage traceability for improving operational efficiency through mapping and visualization of enterprise supply chains. The continuously increasing demand for sourcing information about products is also a notable factor for emphasizing the need for blockchain traceability. Blockchain can enable more transparent and accurate end-to-end tracking in the supply chain: Organizations can digitize physical assets and create a decentralized immutable record of all transactions, making it possible to track assets from production to delivery or use by end user.

The challenges faced by SC and logistics domain like security, visibility, transparency of various operations, transactional issues, manual errors, delay in processing, updating or sharing data and information, speed in delivering goods and services, can be solved by blockchain as it provides transparency, traceability, immutability, trust, and security. SCM has three different categories of flows: material flow, data flow, and money flow. Material flow involves moving products and goods from one point to another, data flow is the transmission process that happens from the producing point until the point of the utilization of those goods, and money flow includes the charges of each product or goods produced during the process. Blockchain technology will be handling all these basic flows of the supply chain process. In addition, blockchain technology has several applications that will help change how supply chain processes do their management and other business activities (Aliyu, 2018).

Integration of Blockchain with IoT

The first blockchain platform was Bitcoin proposed in the form of cryptocurrencies. It offers a technique to store transactions in a rapid, inexpensive, and straightforward means, which may be employed in applications as a safe payment system within the IoT area; autonomous devices will use Bitcoins to make micro-payments, operating in the main as wallets (Villegas-Ch, 2020). However, once the utilization of blockchain is restricted to micro-payments, applications are connected to the currency, which may be a disadvantage because it is expressed using smart contracts is a standard answer when integration blockchain with IoT.

The number of platforms have been proposed in the integration of blockchain with IoT also discussed in Table 2.

Ethereum was one among the well-settled blockchains together within smart contracts. Ethereum is represented as a blockchain with an inbuilt programing language (Solidity) and as a consensus-based (general agreement) virtual machine running globally (Ethereum Virtual Machine EVM). In presence of intelligent contracts moves the blockchain far from currencies and enables the combination of this technology in novel domains.

Hyperledger is a publicly accessible platform on which several projects associated to blockchain have already been introduced (Kamath, 2018). Fabric is a permissioned blockchain network, and without cryptocurrency, many business applications based on Blockchain platform such as IBM. Using the IBM Watson IoT platform, integration of IoT units with Fabric provides data to the blockchain which regulates devices and permits data cleaning and analysis.

The multichain platform creates private blockchains deploys as a proof of concept of an IoT- blockchain application and Arduino board, one of them.

Litecoin is like Bitcoin but has characteristics like quick transaction validation times, better storage efficiency, reduction of time to generate blocks (from 10 min to 2.5), and the Proof of Work (PoW) based on scrypt, a memory concentrated password-based essential derivation function. In addition, the computational requirement of nodes is lesser, thus it is more appropriate in IoT.

Lisk is a decentralized application provides a blockchain platform comprises sub-blockchains and a way out to use cryptocurrencies and it is used by javascript developers. It works with Chain of Things to discover whether blockchain technology could be useful in gaining security in IoT (Reyna, 2018).

Figure 1. Application of blockchain in supply chain.

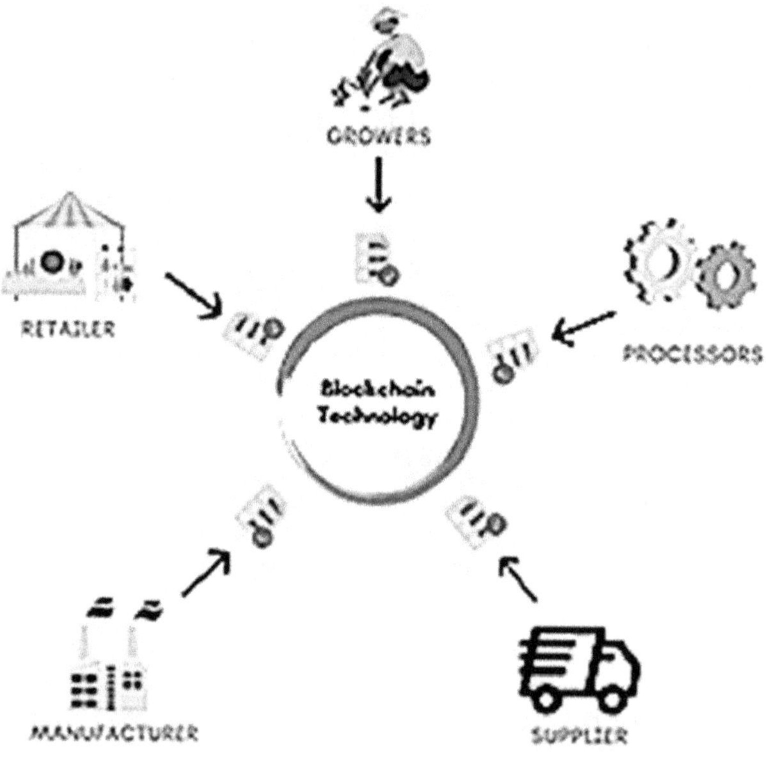

Table 2. Integration of blockchain with IOT

Platform	Blockchain	Cryptocurrency	Smart Contracts
Ethereum	Public and Permission- based	Ether	Yes
Hyperledger Fabric	Permission-based	None	Yes
Multichain	Permission-based	Multi-currency	Yes
Litecoin	Public	Litecoins	No
Lisk	Public and Permission- based	LSK	Yes

Everledger

Everledger is an independent platform created for providing a safe and stable digital data of any object's origin, characteristics, and rights in all directions. Diamonds, wines, luxury goods, art, and much more provide traceability and authenticity to the products. Everledger uses blockchain technology which develops trust in what everyone buys. Using the everledger platform, producers, buyers, makers, and sellers can trace their products' source, rights, and features. This platform is trusted by Tencent, blockchain Australia, reverse logistics, Moyo gems, and many more.

Pilot Project

Blockchain technology will be used as pilot to track and recognize the prescribed medicine in the collaboration with KPMG, Walmart, IBM, etc. (Aliyu, 2018; Kamath, 2018). The businesses will form a joint permissioned blockchain network that will use to observe the products instantaneously. The blockchain network is needed to decrease the period of detailed list tracing and provide easy retrieval of trustworthy distributed information. Through blockchain technology, the project will also improve the efficiency of data collaborated among different network associates and helps to regulate the reliability of products in the distribution chain. Every business will be expertise in the project.

PROPOSED SOLUTION

System Model

Blockchain has diverse application areas like healthcare, education system, voting system, supply chain, and management. To support the integration of blockchain in SCM, we propose a model with the help of Figure 2, which can be treated as a logical model for a blockchain supporting supply chain management:

- Every organization dealing with supply chain management needs proper traceability of its product. So an organization that decides to take on blockchain for the traceability of their manufactured products requests a track and trace service for their supply chain.
- An ID (unique identity number) will be generated based on the number of items entered into the system. The id will be generated through the mining process, such as PoW (Proof of Work).
- The miners who are successful in generating the ID will be rewarded with a token.
- There will be two different types of tokens will be introduced - one for the smart payment currency for any financial and business activity (let's say this token as X) and another for the working of smart contracts and for running the apps on the blockchain (let's say this token as Y). The Y token will be used for rewarding the miners.
- The generated ID will be encoded to the IoT items (RFID trackers, NFS chips, QR codes, etc.) built within the organization to track the item throughout their life cycle.
- The organization will use these IoT items encoded with the ID on their manufactured products.
- As the product moves to different places or departments like production factories, warehouses, distribution centers, logistics, wholesale or retail shops, etc., all the related records that will denote the track of the product will be updated to the blockchain service.

- All the programming logic related to the transaction among the stakeholders will be encoded inside the smart contract, which will require the token for processing.
- If the tokens are insufficient for processing any transaction, they can be purchased.
- X is the smart currency for this blockchain. For example, FIAT currency (which is not backed up by any precious metal) can be exchanged through Gemini or GDAX (these are cryptocurrency exchange that allows people to buy, sell, and trade digital coins) into bitcoin that can be further exchanged into X.
- To run any business activities using this blockchain, the smart cryptocurrency X will be used, and any insufficiency in tokens can be resolved through its purchase and exchanging FIAT currency into bitcoin and then to the X.

Figure 2. Working of system model.

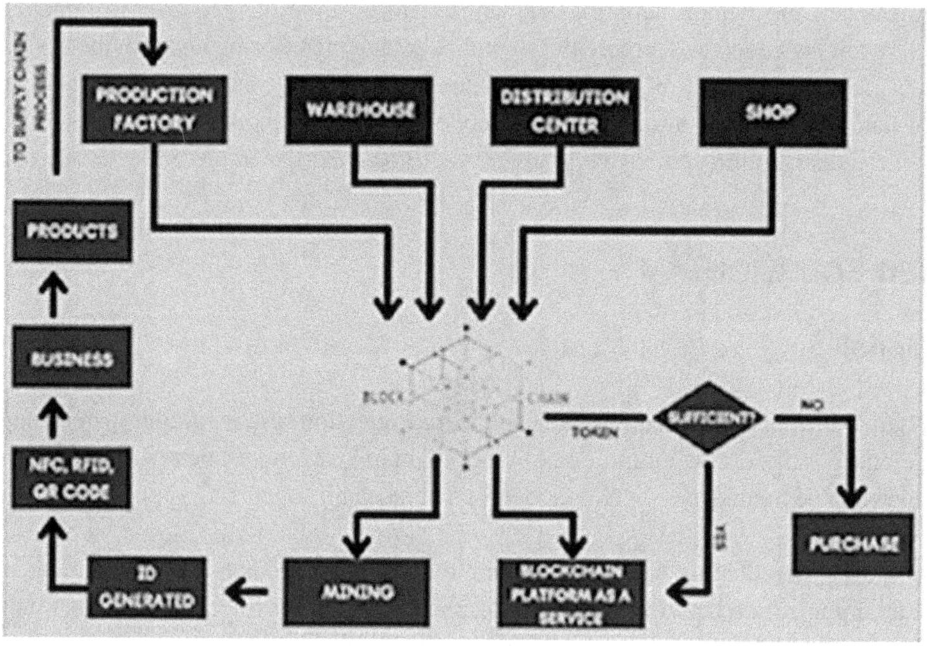

Implementation

For creating a blockchain, we can always use open-source platforms already built and tested in the market, such as Hyperlegder Fabric, BigchainDB, Multichain, open-chain, etc. However, suppose any organization aims to create a blockchain that solely serves the purpose of that particular organization. In that case, we can use Python for creating the blockchain, which performs essential functions of blockchain-like adding a new block to the chain, performing transactions, and adding it to the list of the transaction, a function for calculating hash value, a function that will return the last block of the chain, implementing proof o of work and a function for validating proof of work (PoW) and then we will be using Flask for representing our blockchain as an API. By this chapter, a blueprint of how a blockchain can be created and perform essential functions using Python as follows with the help of Algorithm:

- The blockchain class will maintain the chain as it will store the transactions, and other methods will be used to attach a new block in the chain.
- Any block in the chain will consist of an index (denote the particular no. of that block), a timestamp (UNIX time), transaction list, PoW, and the previous block's hash.
- Now for adding any transaction to the block, the method NewTransaction() and this method will take sender(string: sender's address), receiver(string: receiver's address), amount(int) and will finally return the particular block's index that will have this new transaction then it will append the details like sender, receiver, the amount in the list of CurrentTransaction[].
- Firstly we will create a genesis block (first block of the chain) by calling the method NewBlock (PreviousHash=1, proof=100) here; we will define the parameters/arguments of the block so based on the given parameters, it will create the genesis block of the chain.
- For the NewBlock() method, this method will create the new block in the chain; this method will take the proof, PreviousHash, as an argument that the proof will be given by the PoW algorithm used in the code. This will finally return a new block as a dictionary where the block variable will be defined and as a dictionary which will contain keys as an index (calculated by len(chain)+1), timestamp, transactions (fetch the list of CurrentTransaction declared in the code), proof, PreviousHash(calculated using hash (chain[-1] this will be hashing the last element in the list with variable name chain).
- After creating a new block, reset the CurrentTransaction list by defining it as an empty list.
- Append the block in the list defined in the program with the variable name chain.
- The method the rear block will return the real block in the list chain.
- The hash method will create the hash of the last block using the SHA-256 hashing algorithm. This method will contain the argument as a block in the form of a dictionary. Using hexdigest() present in Hashlib, we will get the hash of the block.
- A Proof of Work (PoW) method will be created that will be used for mining the block here; we will be defining the algorithm such that miners need to search a number n, when hashed with the preceding block's hash will generate a hash with four leading 0s.
- A ValidProof() method will also be created to validate whether the proof of work is valid or not, which means whether the proof has four leading 0s or not according to the defined algorithm. If we want to make it more difficult for the miners to find the value of n, we can increase the leading zero in the algorithm. The addition of a single leading zero will make it difficult, and the time required for finding a solution will also be increased.
- For making our blockchain an API, we will be using the Flask framework.
- In flask we will create 3 methods: NewTransaction (to make a new transaction to a block), mining (to mine a new block), FullChain (it will return the full blockchain)
- Now we will import the Flask, request library in the code. Firstly we will instantiate our blockchain class.
- For NewTransaction method, we will take the input from the user, so it will be a POST method. When a user sends all the data for a transaction like a sender, receiver, and amount, the transaction will be attached to the block.
- For the mining method, which will be a GET request, it will perform three tasks: calculating the PoW, rewarding the miner, and attaching the new block to the chain.
- For creating blockchain as decentralized, there is a need for one node to know about its neighboring nodes. Each node in the network should contain a list of additional nodes. So for this, two

methods /NodeRegistry (it will accept the list of new nodes) and NodeSettle (it will ensure that a node has the correct chain) will be created.

- Set() will be used for carrying the new node list as we know that set allows unique values, so it does not matter how many times it has been added a node; only a single entry will be considered.
- Whenever a single node has no identical chain than another, our longest chain will be authentic to resolve this.
- The function ValidChain() will loop through every block and verify both hash and the proof.
- For resolving conflict, we will check if there exists a good chain with a length greater than ours then we will replace it with the longest chain.

Proposed Algorithm. A template of code is given below:

```
Class BC(object):
defi ___initialize___(self):
defi ___initialize___(self):
    self.chain = []
    self.CurrentTransactions = []
defi   NewBlock(self)  :
       #Create a fresh Block and attach it to the chain
      : parameter proof: <int> The proof calculated using POW algorithm
      : parameter PreviousHash:<str> Hash of preceding Block
      : return <dict> Fresh Block       // key value pair
" " "
defi TransactionNew(self):
     # Attach a fresh transaction to the transaction list
" " "
     Makes a new transaction to go into the later mined Block
      : parameter source: <stri> Sender Address
      : parameter receiver: <stri> Address of the Recipient
      : parameter amount: <int> Amount
      : return <int> The directory of the Block that will preserve the trans-
actions
" " "
@static method
defi hash(block):
       # Hashing the Block
" " "
       Makes a SHA -256 hash of a Block
      : parameter block: <dict> Block
      : return: <str>
" " "
@property
defi LastBlock (self):
```

```
# Returns the previous Block in the chain
Return self.chain[-1]
```

Result

The result presents the blockchain model for improving traceability and transparency. The purpose is to evaluate a model that can help organizations overcome the problems in supply chain monitoring. The model defines how the products manufactured by the organization will be linked to the blockchain using sensors like RFID, QR codes, etc. The model suggests creating a blockchain with its smart currency for transactions and a digital currency for rewarding the miners. Any FIAT currency can be exchanged into bitcoin and later converted into the currency used by the blockchain as suggested in the model. The id that the model will generate will be used to track the product. The implementation of how a blockchain can be built using python and flask is shown.

A proper algorithm is given showing how python and flask will be used with a code template to understand the concept properly. Later in the future, it can help produce a better blockchain solution with other aspects of technology. Compared with a centralized database, it has options like create, update, and delete options, whereas the solution given in the model is that once the product is added to the block, it cannot be deleted or changed. This model will provide more transparency in the supply chain when compared with any centralized database software. For improving traceability and transparency in SCM, blockchain technology will be a significant help. Many companies dealing with the supply chain are adopting blockchain compared to centralized ERP software like Oracle SCM, E2open, SAP SCM, logility, etc. The model suggested in this chapter will help the organization to track the bills and payments.

Organizations are switching from centralized software to blockchain as it is hard for an attacker to take over the whole blockchain. If any of the nodes in the blockchain is attacked and the data of that particular block is lost will not affect much as blockchain is a decentralized ledger all the records or transactions are shared to every node/peer of the network so data will not be lost but using a centralized software if attacked all the data will be lost if no backup of that particular data has been made. The blockchain market is estimated to increase from 82 million USD in 2017 to 3486 million USD by 2023. The model suggested in the research paper will add more efficiency and transparency (visibility) to the supply chain monitoring and establish confidence among stakeholders. The main objective of the model is to eliminate the middle party and aims to develop a decentralized system with higher availability.

DISCUSSION

The integration of blockchain with supply chain monitoring will improve the traceability and transparency of the whole system (Abeyratne & Monfared, 2016). It will develop trust and deliver high value to the customers. Integration of blockchain with IoT has helped organizations load their product to the blockchain using RFID cards, sensors for tracking the location of the products, etc.

Traceability: The system model of blockchain discussed is a distributed shared ledger technology. It will assist to improve traceability and transparency by its general agreement (which is known as consensus) mechanism and distributed ledger. Each node contributing on a blockchain platform preserves and authenticates transaction records in the distributed ledger. The primary role in the supply chain involves manufacturers, suppliers, transporters, suppliers, and consumers, have a transactional record as it is distributed to each node in the network, and have permission to monitor the product's life cycle.

Trust: The model will provide a trustworthy environment without depending on or trusting any single entity (Weber et al., 2016). In any traditional model in which stakeholders who do not trust each other need to depend upon a third party that is trusted by all. Blockchain eliminates the need to trust any third party. The model discussed in the paper will allow stakeholders or any participant in the blockchain to build trustworthy collaboration as any single entity will not handle it. Every detail about the product loaded in the blockchain using the RFID card, QR codes sensors, etc., will be shared among all participants so there will be complete visibility.

Privacy: Data privacy is not available in Public blockchain. In a public blockchain, anyone can join the network as no prior permission is needed to add the blockchain network, and all the information shared in the network is public. So the organizations can opt for permissioned blockchain, which will include the parties trusted by the organization and who are involved in the supply chain process for that organization's product. Furthermore, even the organization can encrypt the data payload, the status of any publicly available process.

CONCLUSION

The adoption of blockchain technology has already demonstrated to be a helpful supply chain traceability system. The integration of blockchain with other new technologies will improve its transparency, traceability for tracking the material flow in the Supply Chain. The paper aimed to review how blockchain can improve traceability in the supply chain without involving any intermediary. This paper provides a model for blockchain that will help decode how blockchain could be used for tracking the product. The paper also gives a template on how we can use python and flask to create a blockchain that can be improved in the future and provide more blockchain technology features. The application of blockchain has several technical limitations addressed in the paper that include storage capacity, scalability, interoperability, and security (51% attack), which are expected to be improved when applied in the field of SCM. The implementation of blockchain in supply chain and logistics is average due to the presence of technical issues and some organizational issues (lack of awareness and understanding, less cooperation, etc.); nevertheless, it will soon gain the confidence of the majority of organizations in supply chain management. As for future result opportunities, it is expected that a proper solution will be set up to resolve the technical shortcomings that are pointed out in the chapter, and proper practical implementation will be introduced. Many multinational organizations have started taking steps towards utilizing blockchain in supply chain monitoring with inspiring results.

Challenges and Future Work

A rising number of companies have shown their interest to accept blockchain technology due to its advantages like decentralization, distributed ledger, visibility, traceability, etc., but now many companies are addressing technical challenges in blockchain like storage capacity, scalability, interoperability, 51%attack (Reyna et al., 2018; Aliyu et al., 2018).

- **Storage capacity and scalability:** The speed of processing a transaction in a blockchain network is slow compared to centralized software (Reyna et al., 2018). For example, Visa can process 2000 transactions per second, whereas it has found that compared with the bitcoin blockchain, it can process only 3 to 7 transactions per second, and Ethereum can approximately process 20 transactions. When integrating blockchain with an IoT device that produces gigabytes (GB) of data in a real-time, blockchain is not proposed to store a huge amount of data as an IoT device produces it in real-time. Some researchers have proposed distinct techniques to clean the data and compressing IoT data.
- **Interoperability:** Different blockchain platforms have protocols, consensus mechanisms, programming language, security, and privacy measures. Due to the lack of universal standardization, it is difficult for different networks to communicate. Such uniformity across blockchain platforms makes it difficult for the mass adoption of this technology. Now there are some platforms like Ark that use Smart Bridges architecture to resolve this challenge. There is a need for more research and future work that will allow resolving this challenge.
- **Security (51% attack):** The current blockchain technology has the possibility of a 51% attack. In this attack, a collection of miners tries to regulate more than 50% of a network's mining power, calculating power, or hash rate and have the capacity to control the blockchain. Blockchain with a small number of nodes has a high chance of a 51% attack (Aliyu et al., 2018). To resolve these challenges, more research and future works are needed.

REFERENCES

Abeyratne, S. A., & Monfared, R. P. (2016). Blockchain ready manufacturing supply chain using distributed ledger. *International Journal of Research in Engineering and Technology*, *5*(9), 1–10. doi:10.15623/ijret.2016.0509001

Aliyu, S., Tom, A. M., Haruna, I., Taiye, M. A., & Barakat, M. M. (2018). The Role of Blockchain Technology Applications in Supply Chain Management. *International Journal of Computer Mathematics*, 1.

Chang, S. E., & Chen, Y. (2020). When blockchain meets supply chain: A systematic literature review on current development and potential applications. *IEEE Access: Practical Innovations, Open Solutions*, *8*, 62478–62494. doi:10.1109/ACCESS.2020.2983601

Dobrovnik, M., Herold, D. M., Fürst, E., & Kummer, S. (2018). Blockchain for and in Logistics: What to Adopt and Where to Start. *Logistics*, *2*(3), 18. doi:10.3390/logistics2030018

Guerreiro, S., van Kervel, S. J., & Babkin, E. (2013, July). Towards Devising an Architectural Framework for Enterprise Operating Systems. In ICSOFT (pp. 578-585). Academic Press.

Hellani, H., Sliman, L., Samhat, A. E., & Exposito, E. (2021). On Blockchain Integration with Supply Chain: Overview on Data Transparency. *Logistics*, *5*(3), 46. doi:10.3390/logistics5030046

Issaoui, Y., Khiat, A., Bahnasse, A., & Ouajji, H. (2019). Smart logistics: Study of the application of blockchain technology. *Procedia Computer Science*, *160*, 266–271. doi:10.1016/j.procs.2019.09.467

Jabbar, S., Lloyd, H., Hammoudeh, M., Adebisi, B., & Raza, U. (2021). Blockchain-enabled supply chain: Analysis, challenges, and future directions. *Multimedia Systems*, *27*(4), 787–806. doi:10.100700530-020-00687-0

Kamath, R. (2018). Food traceability on blockchain: Walmart's pork and mango pilots with IBM. *The Journal of the British Blockchain Association*, *1*(1), 3712. doi:10.31585/jbba-1-1-(10)2018

Krings, K., & Schwab, J. (2021). *Blockchain technology in supply chains: What are the opportunities for sustainable development? (No. 2/2021)*. Briefing Paper.

Leng, K., Bi, Y., Jing, L., Fu, H. C., & Van Nieuwenhuyse, I. (2018). Research on agricultural supply chain system with double chain architecture based on blockchain technology. *Future Generation Computer Systems*, *86*, 641–649. doi:10.1016/j.future.2018.04.061

Mao, D., Wang, F., Hao, Z., & Li, H. (2018). Credit evaluation system based on blockchain for multiple stakeholders in the food supply chain. *International Journal of Environmental Research and Public Health*, *15*(8), 1627. doi:10.3390/ijerph15081627 PMID:30071695

Paliwal, V., Chandra, S., & Sharma, S. (2020). Blockchain technology for sustainable supply chain management: A systematic literature review and a classification framework. *Sustainability*, *12*(18), 7638. doi:10.3390u12187638

Perboli, G., Musso, S., & Rosano, M. (2018). Blockchain in logistics and supply chain: A lean approach for designing real-world use cases. *IEEE Access: Practical Innovations, Open Solutions*, *6*, 62018–62028. doi:10.1109/ACCESS.2018.2875782

Purohit, S. K., & Sharma, A. K. (2015). Database Design for Data Mining driven Forecasting Software Tool for Quality Function Deployment. *International Journal of Information and Electronic Business*, *7*(4), 39–50.

Reyna, A., Martín, C., Chen, J., Soler, E., & Díaz, M. (2018). On blockchain and its integration with IoT. Challenges and opportunities. *Future Generation Computer Systems*, *88*, 173–190. doi:10.1016/j.future.2018.05.046

Sharma, A., Tiwari, S., Arora, N., & Sharma, S. C. (2021). Introduction to Blockchain. In *Blockchain Applications in IoT Ecosystem* (pp. 1–14). Springer. doi:10.1007/978-3-030-65691-1_1

Sharma, A. K., & Khandait, S. P. (2016). A Novel Software Tool to Generate Customer Needs tor Effective Design of Online Shopping Websites. *International Journal of Information Technology and Computer Science*, *83*(3), 85–92. doi:10.5815/ijitcs.2016.03.10

Sharma, A. K., & Khandait, S. P. (2017). A Novel Fuzzy Integrated Customer Needs Prioritization Software Tool for Effective Design of Online Shopping Websites. *International Journal of Operations Research and Information Systems (IJORIS)*, *8*(4), 23–38.

Sharma, A. K., Mehta, I. C., & Sharma, J. R. (2009). Development of Fuzzy Integrated Quality Function Deployment Software - A Conceptual Analysis. *I-Manager's Journal on Software Engineering*, *3*(3), 16–24. doi:10.26634/jse.3.3.190

Song, J. M., Sung, J., & Park, T. (2019). Applications of blockchain to improve supply chain traceability. *Procedia Computer Science*, *162*, 119–122. doi:10.1016/j.procs.2019.11.266

Sripathi, L. (2019). *Adoption of Blockchain technology in food supply chain management*. Academic Press.

Tijan, E., Aksentijević, S., Ivanić, K., & Jardas, M. (2019). Blockchain technology implementation in logistics. *Sustainability*, *11*(4), 1185. doi:10.3390u11041185

Tsiulin, S., Reinau, K. H., Hilmola, O. P., Goryaev, N., & Karam, A. (2020). Blockchain-based applications in shipping and port management: a literature review towards defining key conceptual frameworks. *Review of International Business and Strategy*.

Villegas-Ch, W., Palacios-Pacheco, X., & Román-Cañizares, M. (2020). Integration of IoT and Blockchain to in the Processes of a University Campus. *Sustainability*, *12*(12), 4970. doi:10.3390u12124970

Weber, I., Xu, X., Riveret, R., Governatori, G., Ponomarev, A., & Mendling, J. (2016, September). Untrusted business process monitoring and execution using blockchain. In *International Conference on Business Process Management* (pp. 329-347). Springer. 10.1007/978-3-319-45348-4_19

Chapter 7
Logistics Management Using Blockchain:
A Review of Literature and Research Agenda

Nwosu Anthony Ugochukwu
City University, Malaysia

S. B. Goyal
https://orcid.org/0000-0002-8411-7630
City University, Malaysia

ABSTRACT

As logistics companies continue to expand due to the revolution of Logistics 4.0, the complexity of the multiple connected organizations makes it impossible for a clear view of logistics operation. Since customer information is shared between companies, unauthorized access to personal information is inevitable, and it poses several threats to customers. To address this challenge, blockchain with some fascinating properties like enhanced security and transparency will be deployed. Blockchain is a technology that can be used to improve efficiency, visibility, and security in logistics management. This chapter will explore the current applications of blockchain in logistics management based on an analysis of the findings of several scholars. The change from traditional logistics to digital logistics, digital logistics issues, as well as blockchain principles, this study also provides useful insights into how blockchain can disrupt conventional operations in logistics management. It also lays the groundwork for future study into blockchain's applicability in digital fleet management.

DOI: 10.4018/978-1-7998-8697-6.ch007

Copyright © 2022, IGI Global. Copying or distributing in print or electronic forms without written permission of IGI Global is prohibited.

INTRODUCTION

Due to the industry 4.0 revolution (Kshetri, N, 2017), modern logistics operations keep expanding but a lot of challenges confront its operations such as a lack of operation visibility from beginning to end due to enormous multiple agents involved within the logistics management framework, Increasing complexity in supply chains has made it difficult for logistics companies to identify the root cause of problems, thereby hindering the organization from taking fast and reliable decision. Traditional logistics management information systems have flaws like lack of openness, security issues, and unreliable ((Wang, Y., Hugh Han, 2019), unauthorized disclosure of personal information is the order of the day as information are shared and transferred between the logistics enterprises thereby resulting in to increase in frauds and other social vices during the operational process. The engagement of Blockchain which is innovation will offer solutions to these problems.

Blockchain is a p2p (peer-to-peer) network designed to run a decentralized ledger (S. Nakamoto, 2008) and is not under the direction of a centralized authority. Participants in the Blockchain network have complete transparency and can view and check the ledger at any moment. Blockchain is quickly becoming one of the most popular academic topics. Studies have recently focused on Blockchain from a variety of perspectives, comprising the design of systems, theoretical investigations, and frameworks for making decisions.

Bitcoin, a kind of crypto (digital) currency, was first presented in 2008. To complete a transaction on the internet between two parties, Bitcoin uses cryptographic evidence. It is regarded as the ignitor of Blockchain, allowing transactions to be completed without the use of a third party (Casino, F, Dasaklis, T., 2019).

From (FINTECH), Financial Technology to Supply Chain and Logistics Management, Blockchain innovation is embracing a variety of sectors. Blockchain can alter existing systems, streamline procedures, and increase operational efficiency. According to a survey by PwC, 84 of 600 executives from a range of industries stated that their company has been working with Blockchain technology since 2018. The financial sector, supply chains, and energy industry are the top three businesses embracing this innovation, according to the survey (Davies, S., & Likens, S, 2018). The management of supply chains and logistics with Blockchain will enable the creation of traceable supply chain systems while maintaining the immutability of any data recorded in the ledger (Rao, J. J., & Kumara, V, 2017) Through the development of trust models between supply stakeholders, protection of asset transactions, enabling real-time communication, improving quality management, and improving forecasting and inventory management are all ways to improve supply chain management, Blockchain has the potential to add economic value to solve critical Supply chain concerns (Mohanta, B. K., Jena, 2019).

Blockchain uses a consensus process to safeguard and store data in a shared database. Block networks are built by representing the data owners and data sources with an information grid.

Several pilot-size projects based on Blockchain adoption in the management of logistics and supply chains have recently attempted to capitalize on the technology's usefulness. Big industry leaders like IBM (International Business Machines) have some famous successful cases.

IBM was one of the first companies to develop Blockchain innovation. Recently, IBM launched the first Blockchain-based system for tracking and tracing vaccines along the distribution chain, from production to administration. This solution helps manufacturer's monitor the supply chain to improve recall management and build trust between the government and the private sector. The system provides preemptive detection and notification of supply chain problems, fraud, and storage conditions (IBM, 2020).

Following the Blockchain pilot trials, the next stage is for the industry to evaluate the best Blockchain depending on performance, technical attributes, and deployment cost. In research and practice, to assist decision-makers, only a few technology evaluation models are available. (Bai, C & Sarkis, J, 2020). Many scholars believe that Blockchain has considerable promise, a conceptual analysis and decision-making framework, however, are needed to scale the costs which are advantages of deploying this technology.

The goals of this research are to gain a general understanding of Blockchain principles and their prospects for enhancing security; improving efficiency in logistics management frameworks and recommending future research that may be beneficial to logistics management through the use of Blockchain.

OVERVIEW OF LOGISTICS MANAGEMENT

Logistics Management

Logistics is generally defined as activities influenced by demand. It defines the requirements for the objects, the people, physical products, as well as for services, information, and energy. (Wannenwetsch, H. (Ed.), 2014) Objects must be delivered at the right time, at the right quantity, at the right cost, and in the right place. Alternatively, logistics management can be defined as establishing an organized and methodical network between a company and its suppliers to produce and sell a specific product to the end-user (CSCMP, 2018), to lower costs, and remain competitive. There is an interaction among processes, data, and information flows, as well as people, entities, and other resources. Simply put, the logistics management process involves all stages of bringing a product from its initial state to its final destination beginning with the transformation of raw materials into manufactured products, warehouse storage, market movement, and distribution to the final customer as shown in fig 1.

Figure 1. Simplified structure of logistics management

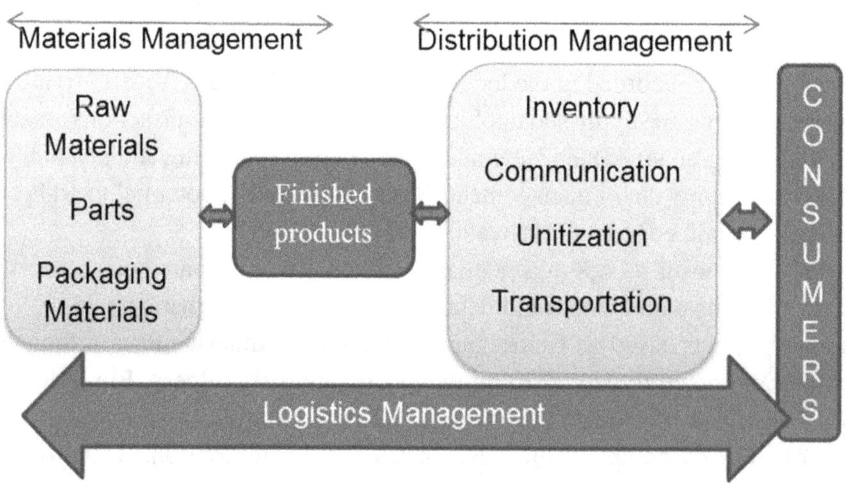

The logistics management process includes activities such as sourcing, procurement, conversion, and other related activities. The need to coordinate and collaborate with channel partners, such as suppliers, intermediaries, third-party service providers, and customers, is also crucial. In essence, logistics management combines supply chain and demand management within and between businesses (CSCMP, 2018).

The logistics management ecosystem is composed of five major components: planning, packing, inventory control, transportation, and control of information.

Planning (warehousing, storage material handling): Planning in logistics is essential for strong supply chain connectivity because by constantly synchronizing the entire supply chain, interfaces and links the entire supply chain. The market is usually dynamic, and a demand-supply mismatch isn't uncommon. Logistics management ensures that manufacturers supply goods on a consistent and continuous basis. Great planning is needed to actualize this that is the reason the process has now become a vital aspect of logistics management. Despite the need for manufacturers to operate efficiently, the demand for the product is not equal to the supply because of the same imbalance that has previously been discussed. In such cases, storing extra items produced requires additional storage units and warehouses. Material handling equipment is needed to move materials around inside a warehouse as well as to load and unload items into and out of delivery vehicles, as well as sophisticated storage equipment like racks or shelving. Materials handling is a process that includes utilizing manual, semi-automated, and computerized equipment and frameworks to assist logistics and keep supply chain operations running smoothly. By doing so, forecasting, resource allocation, production planning, inventory reduction, customer service, and support are improved. Planning is a key component of logistics management, as it helps synchronize the various operations and processes. Management of logistics involves the timely delivery of goods and services at each level, and efficient management is impossible without comprehensive Logistics Planning.

There may be an insufficient supply of commodities during demand-supply variations or imbalances, or storage facilities may be required to hold excess items. It is impossible to accomplish all of this without meticulous planning.

Packaging or Unitization: Packaging and unitizing of products or items are essential to long-term product maintenance. A product's packaging protects it not only during transit from the producer to the retailer but as well as during storage and display. The packaging of an item may lure a buyer to consider buying it. As a result, many businesses perform considerable study into the color schemes, patterns, and types of packaging that their potential customers find most appealing. For easier handling, the unitization process groups multiple distinct things into a single large delivery unit. It's also important because it helps with storage and transit.

Typically, packaging coupled with unitization aid in packing products in a cuboidal form or shape because makes them easy to handle, transport, and store.

Essentially, packaging serves two purposes: it protects an item or good during transport and it keeps the product in good condition while it is stored in a warehouse. Cuboidal packing can also be called unitization because it involves merging many things into a single entity. In general, cubes are useful for storing and moving since they can be easily transported.

Inventory Management: The goal of inventory control is to ensure that a business maintains adequate stock levels to meet client needs as quickly as possible while keeping storage costs low. Maintaining information on stock situations, warehouse availability, and market demand and supply research, as well as projecting demand and managing stocks accordingly, are all important components of inventory management. Since demand is variable, inventory control is a particularly helpful technique for managing the flow of commodities in a supply chain. Inventory management benefits include.

- Correct Order Fulfillment
- Effective Inventory Planning and Organization
- It offers a well-organized warehouse
- It saves both time and money
- It Improves Productivity
- It promotes Customer Satisfaction

The decisions regarding what stocks should be stored, where the stocks should be stored, and how much of the inventory should be stored are among the most crucial duties of inventory control.

Transportation: Logistics companies use transportation to link their various activities. Transport plays a crucial role in the entire product manufacturing process, from production to delivery (and vice versa). It comprises successfully and efficiently designing, implementing, and controlling the forward and reverse movement of commodities in a supply chain. Modes of transportation include automobiles, cargo trains, freight shipping, and air travel. An effective transportation management system should be able to automate loads, track shipments, increase performance and efficiency, and assist with inventory control.

A good Transportation Management System (TMS) is required for proper transportation because it automatically tenders loads, tracks shipments, and retains and analyzes past information. Since transportation entails maintaining direct contact with customers, timely delivery management is critical. TMS may help keep inventory small, which keeps the supply chain process going smoothly. Consistently delivering items will have a negative impression on the client. Customer satisfaction rises as a result of improved performance.

Control of Information: This system aids in the business management process. A smooth operation of various operational processes and procedures requires information and control. The system involves real-time delivery tracking, which tells a truck driver where to park and deliver the next cargo. The process incorporates management operations such as sales, distribution, marketing, manufacture, and supply with value chains, which combine customer and market needs with company potential to meet financial goals.

Additionally, it affects other inventory control processes by determining how much inventory should be stored in warehouses. Sustainable logistics aims to reduce and eliminate waste while improving business efficiency. Therefore, logistics management is inextricably linked to information and control. The logistics industry has advanced in the last few years due to the integration of new technology that digitalizes logistics management operations.

Digital Logistic Management Concept

Digital logistics refers to digitizing traditional data collection in logistics management, which is often manual and prone to human error. Digital logistics helps optimize and accelerate logistics operations, strategies, and systems. In other words, it automates the logistics chain's routine-like components that can be automated. This digital strategy not only allows your company to save money on operational expenditures, lost productivity, and correct order fulfillment, but it also improves data transparency for all vendors and partners involved in logistics management and operations. All stakeholders have access to the knowledge they need to make agile, educated decisions even in the face of the unexpected by utilizing thoughtfully-integrated business logistics tools that collaborate and communicate through a single information system.

Digital logistics management (DLM) has had a significant impact on logistics management operations, and it is clear that this improvement is a competitive advantage that firms can capitalize on for years to come. Logistics management is undergoing digital transformation due to the power of driven data insights (Chung, G, 2018).

Key Technology Enablers of Digital Logistics Management

Digital transformation in the logistics industry can be attributed to the internet of things (IoT), big data, robotics, automation, cloud, artificial intelligence, and Blockchain innovation (Kersten, W., M. Schroder, 2015) as shown in fig 2.

Figure 2. Digital logistics management technology enablers.

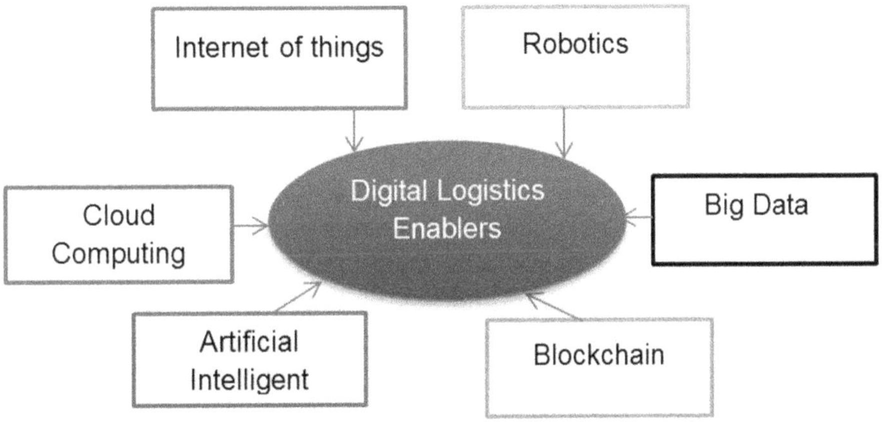

IoT Digital Logistic Management Enabler: In IoT technologies, sensors allow physical objects to be connected to receive, store, and transmit data, which can be used to make decisions. IoT can be deployed in the management of logistics To improve the vehicles, infrastructure, and services of transportation systems while benefiting both operators and customers (Lyons, G, 2017).

The global connected logistics market is estimated to reach $27 billion by 2023, according to Allied Market Research (Allied Market Research, 2018) IoT can improve service quality and control in logistics operations by enabling real-time connectivity. However, overall implementation costs are still considerable, and challenges such as segregation persist.

Cloud Digital Logistics Management Enabler: Cloud logistics as a term refers to an innovative business model known as Logistics as a Service (LaaS). Smart storage is been deployed in cloud logistics to store Logistics data. Logistics enterprises can use innovative IT solutions linking to the logistics business by utilizing LaaS. Logistics management information communication is becoming easier and more viable because of LaaS (Ilin, V, Simić, 2013). Logistics as a service also makes it easier to set up efficient and effective logistical procedures, which saves time and money. For logistics enterprises or companies to compete favorably on the market, a pay-per-use policy and scalability may be beneficial. More than half of logistics companies now employ cloud-based services, with another 20% expecting to do so soon (Brandl, N, 2016).

Robotic and Automated Digital Logistics Management Enabler: Robotics is a branch of science that is intimately linked to AI, as well as cloud computing, IoT, and big data. Robotics are automating the logistics management practices like production and warehousing. According to a DHL study, 80 percent of warehouses are still handled manually today (Bonkenburg, T., 2016), indicating that there is plenty of room for automation. Autonomous vehicles are deployed to transport goods in highly automated warehouses. In terms of speed, precision, safety, and tracking, autonomous vehicles outperform traditional forklifts, hand pallet trucks, and high rack pallets. (GU, J, 2007). Autonomous cars can also be reconfigured, remain operational indefinitely without the need for human involvement, and can be integrated with other robots and equipment easily. Compared to traditional warehouses, fully digitalized warehouses offer greater flexibility and eliminate the requirement for fixed infrastructure installation (Vis, I. F. A, 2006). The implementation, on the other hand, will necessitate a large investment of resources. Nonetheless, technological advancements may reduce the number of resources necessary soon.

Big Data Digital Logistics Management Enabler: Big data is defined as data that has Volume, velocity, variety, and veracity. Big data is digitalizing the logistics business by converting large amounts of unstructured data into useful information for logistics managers for fast and effective decision-making processes (Simi ć, 2017).

Turning underutilized data into a competitive advantage on the market has enormous potential. The implementation of big data in logistics has led to better market demand (Tan, K.H, 2015) forecasting, and new business models tailored to client needs, to name a few benefits. Big data analytics combined with artificial intelligence will enable real-time route optimization, holistic forecasting of fleet capacity and demand for goods, and risk reduction across the logistics partners' network.

Artificial Intelligence Digital Logistics Management Enabler: Artificial intelligence (AI) can be defined as a collection of technologies that work together to tackle complex issues and it gradually becomes part of every IT system. It's linked to IoT technology, which allows sensors to collect data, cloud computing technology, and the big data paradigm. AI technology is made up of three parts: sensing, processing, and learning. Sensing components are devices that collect data from the physical world (sensors). Processing components are a collection of data-handling algorithms found in many software solutions. Learning components are patterns captured in structured and unstructured data. AI is digitalizing the management of Logistics by providing optimal truck routing solutions, resulting in cost savings, accurate demand forecasting, quick decision making, and higher customer satisfaction through the personalization of logistics services.

Blockchain Digital Logistics Management Enabler: Blockchain is a digital ledger that is decentralized, distributed, and opens. It records transactions across many computers in such a way that any record that is changed retrospectively affects all subsequent blocks. (Economist, 2015). A centralized database can be converted into a distributed, decentralized system using Blockchain technology. In a logistics environment, distributed storage systems can store and manage large amounts of data generated by internet of things applications. Blockchain application in logistics has digitalized the logistics industry, with the greatest promise in global commerce; with its solutions that reduce supply chain trade barriers and can boost global GDP and global trade by 15% (Moavenzadeh, J, 2013). Increased transparency, traceability, and speed of products delivery are just a few of the ways Blockchain digitalized logistics operation (Pilkington, M, 2016).

Challenges of Digital Logistics Management

As the logistics enterprise is expanding due to the revolution of logistics 4.0 (Hofmann, E, & Rüsch, M, 2017) which bring about the transformation and digitalization of logistics management operations, digital logistics management have been facing a lot of issues such as Data Security and privacy issues, Inefficient logistics system, Lack of visibility in end-to-end operations, transparency and so on.

Data Security and Privacy Issue*:* In a digital logistics environment, digitalization and technology have increased the challenges and risks associated with data integrity, privacy, and data security. However, IoT and cloud computing are technologies that are digitizing the management of the logistics ecosystem but they are centralized and have drawbacks in terms of data security, privacy, and network maintenance costs. An organization with a highly fragmented and complex logistics process must share data continuously to keep logistics processes optimized. One advantage is that the stock level is kept to a minimum and be in competitive advantage. The digital logistics industry is still far from being able to guarantee the security of the information being exchanged between players (PTI Blog, 2019). In recent years, cyber-attacks on Maersk group and Dohme (Holland, M, 2017) have made it clear that there is more than can be done to strengthen cyber-security or risk-bearing operations, which can have serious logistical repercussions. Security, on the other hand, is a major concern for policymakers. With the use of the sensor in collecting data in case of internet of thing digitalized logistics, the data and information stored are prone to attack; Access to sensitive enterprise data by unauthorized entities can have serious consequences from a variety of perspectives. For instance, the production plan may need to be updated, and trading partners' confidence in investment may dwindle. (Williams, Z, Lueg, 2008). Since a security breach is an event in which a logistics company loses sensitive data, security standards and norms are also required to achieve a large number of network partners. Data leaks endanger not only end-users but also providers, stifling the digital revolution.

Inefficient Logistics Management System*:* Efficiency is critical to every organization's long-term survival. Warehouse capacity, shipping length, order accuracy, timely delivery, transportation, cost, the number of damaged products, and inventory turnover are some of the major efficiency measures in logistics management. The use of obsolete systems for sharing documents like (Boison & Antwi-Boampong, 2019) Bills of Lading, Letters of Credit, Customs Declarations, and Dangerous Goods Notifications (Dubovec, 2005) Yang (2019a). also presents issues such as an increase in completion times, a significant risk of document manipulation, and the potential for inaccurate data (Liu, 2020).

In digitalized logistics, paperwork processing accounts for 50% of costs (Hackius, N, 2019). Large are data are being captured in big data digitalized logistics, the majority of them are processed manually. Multiple parties communicate via e-mail or phone call rather than using an electronic format like electronic data exchange (EDI). Each logistics provider has its management platforms and data, with just the most minimal interconnection between them thereby making the logistics management inefficient.

Visibility and Transparency Issue*:* In logistic management, the term visibility refers to activities such as in-transit goods movement and in-plant activities and deliveries by trucks from warehouses and hubs to customers' doorsteps that are transparent, traceable, and readily traceable to all stakeholders within the supply chain. With digitalized logistics management, in transit, an order moving from a warehouse to a central hub for ultimate distribution to customers has little to no visibility. This is because warehouse management systems and third-party logistics systems are not compatible. In the same way, a transport management system (TMS) and an inventory management system (IMS) cannot be linked. And a transport management system cannot be integrated with an order management system. Lack of end-to-end visibility and transparency among the stakeholders are the major problem for the effective administration of logistics management operations. The use of Blockchain will be providing solutions to these issues. The next session will discuss Blockchain and its characteristics and basic principles.

INTRODUCTION TO BLOCKCHAIN

Distributed ledger technology (DLT) (S. Nakamoto, 2008) often known as Blockchain is a decentralized, ever-growing collection of data known as "blocks" that are linked and secured via encryption across a peer-to-peer network. To build a network or chain, each block typically contains information from all previous blocks and transactions, as well as a cryptographic hash of the previous block, a timestamp, and transaction data. After the Blockchain has processed the data, each computer in the network locks in at the same time, creating a permanent, hard-to-change digital record. Each Blockchain system determines who can add new blocks to the chain, as well as how the technique is carried out.

After the Blockchain has processed the data, each computer in the network locks in at the same time, creating a permanent, hard-to-change digital record. Each Blockchain system outlines who is permitted and how new blocks are added to the chain. As shown in Fig, Blockchain (Lee Kuo Chuen D, 2015) has a unique attribute that makes it superior to traditional databases. One of the most important aspects of a Blockchain is that it is impervious to data manipulation. It's a decentralized, distributed ledger system for recording transactions between two parties in an efficient and verifiable manner. Blockchain is generally managed via a peer-to-peer network, and it is verifiable using a consensus-based approach to keep the ledger correct. The nature of the transaction is immediately accessible throughout the Blockchain.

Cryptographic protocols (Pilkington, M, 2016) are used in transactions to ensure that the data recorded in any given block cannot be modified once it has been recorded without affecting all following blocks, which necessitates network majority cooperation. As a result Blockchain's most unique property is that it cannot be altered (Chang J, 2017). On the Blockchain, it is impossible to modify any unit of data. (Zheng Z, Xie S, 2017).

Figure 3. Blockchain unique properties

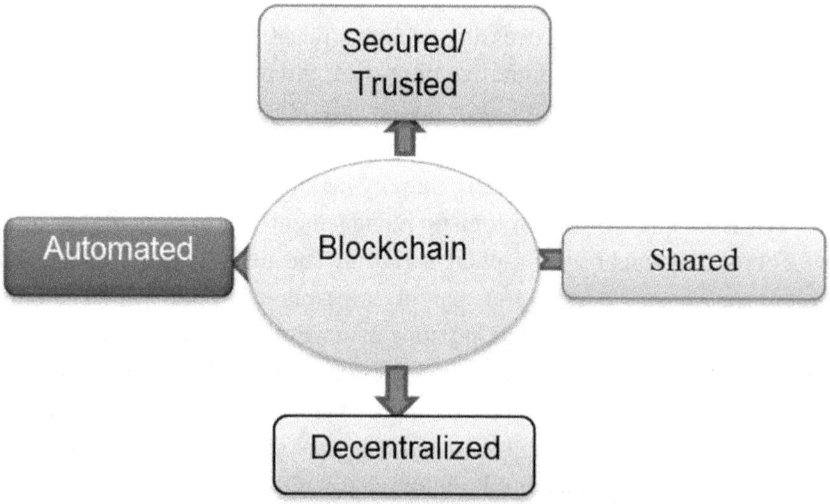

Bases of Blockchain Operations

Systems based on Blockchain comprised of these three conceptual components namely, distributed ledger, digital signature, and consensus procedures.

Distributed Ledger

An Individual or organization can join the network and a copy of the distributed ledger to be shared All of the transactions are in chronological order on this copy. A peer-to-peer network node is used to carry out transactions. A set of digital data or transactions is represented by a "hash" identifier in each block of the ledger. The initial block in the chain is called the genesis block. A miner is a person who creates and validates blocks in the Bitcoin network. After being validated by miners, the digital transaction is added to the distributed ledger. As fresh blocks are added to the chain's end, the digital ledger continues to grow (Fang, W, Chen, 2020).

The type of Blockchain determines the data recorded within the block. For example, Bitcoin makes use of Blockchain innovation to keep track of transaction details like the sender, receiver, and amount transacted. Fig 4 shows the data format and stored information in Blockchain.

Figure 4. Structure of blockchain

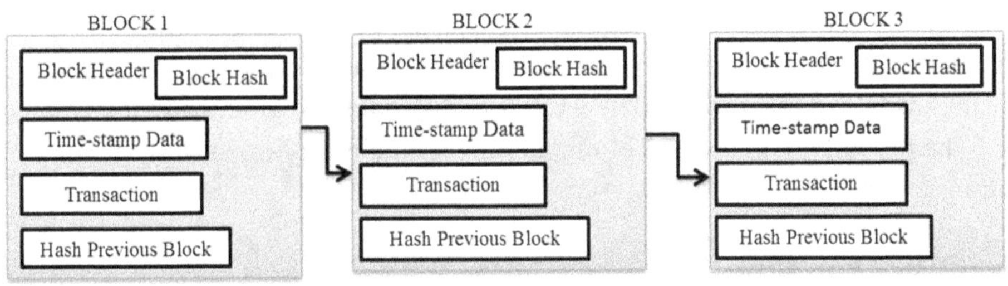

Digital Signature

Control nodes validate data using a cryptographic mechanism. Key generation, signing, and confirming a digital signature is the three steps involved in creating one.

1. **Algorithm for key generation:** During this phase, two keys are generated: private and public. The private key is used to sign messages, while the public key is made public to ensure that the message was signed with the correct private key.
2. **Verification algorithm**: The receiving node verifies the transacted data by compressing the decrypted signature using a public key and the hash value generated from the incoming data, and the node authenticates and validates data at this phase. The changed ledger is then broadcast to the network as a last confirmed version after providing the signature and recording the data in a block. Fig.5 is a diagram showing how a digital signature is created.

Figure 5. Creation of digital signature

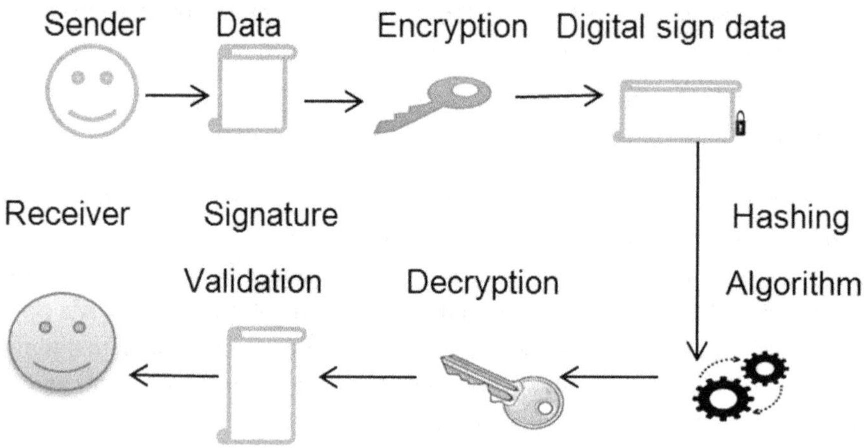

Consensus Procedure

By using the consensus procedure, a new transaction can be added to the ledger. In each link in the chain, the terms and conditions for executing a data transaction are specified. This protocol is exemplified by Proof of Work (PoW) (Janssen, M, 2020). Proof of work security gives the Blockchain a high level of security, as well as making re-mining of current blocks with fraudulent data impossible.

By increasing the time it takes to add a new block to the chain, the process inhibits manipulation and cyber-attacks. The property of consensus eliminates the risk of a single centralized entity manipulating information transactions.

Principles of Blockchain

In a recent paper published in Harvard Business Review (Iansiti M, Lakhani K, 2017), five key concepts underlying Blockchain principles were proposed: distributed database, peer to peer transmission, transparency with pseudonymity, irreversibility of record, and conceptual logic.

Distributed Database: The ledger is duplicated in a plethora of databases that are all identical. Each participant in a Blockchain has complete access to the database, and no single participant has control over the data or information. A partner's transaction records can be verified directly without the involvement of third-party middlemen.

Peer to Peer Transmission: Without the requirement for central coordination, communication occurs directly amongst peers. At the same time, peer nodes serve as both clients and servers to other nodes on the network.

Transparency with Pseudonymity: Transactions are made between Blockchain addresses, which are visible to anybody with access to the system. When changes are made to one copy, they are updated in all other copies at the same time. Each user on the Blockchain is recognized by a unique alphanumeric address. Users can choose to stay anonymous or reveal their real identities to others.

Irreversibility of Record*:* The records in the database cannot be changed once a transaction has been entered. To ensure that the database recording is permanent and accessible to everyone on the network, a variety of computational approaches are applied.

Conceptual Logic*:* Because the ledger is digital, users can create algorithms and rules that automatically activate transactions between nodes.

Types of Blockchain

Different types of Blockchain exist depending on the networks (J. d. Kruijff and H., 2017), and the network designs differ depending on how transactions are carried out and how quickly users can access data. Blockchain networks are classified in general based on the model and consensus employed. Different kinds of Blockchain that exist are namely public, private, and hybrid Blockchain.

Public Blockchain: Designed to eliminate the middleman, this kind of Blockchain is accessible to anyone with a computer and Internet connection. Where a completely decentralized transaction is required, public Blockchain is the best option. The Bitcoin Blockchain, as well as others such as Ethereum, IOTA, and others, are examples of some public Blockchain only allow for reading and writing. Bitcoin, for instance, employs an open-source methodology that allows anybody to contribute. The computation power and capacity required to carry out such a task duplicate transactions make this public Blockchain slow and resource-intensive, but they are extremely secure (Pinto R, 2019).

Private Blockchain: A corporation establishes a permission network in which all participants are recognized and trusted. In a private Blockchain, the networking system is password-protected. Participants must receive an invitation or authorization before they can participate. Administrators can selectively allow nodes to verify. When the Blockchain is used amongst organizations that are part of the same legal entity, this is advantageous. Faster transaction speeds, data/content privacy, and centralized control over who has access to the Blockchain are just a few of the benefits of adopting a private Blockchain. local business and governance frameworks are better suited to the private Blockchain. Governments may use a private Blockchain to conduct vote polls, saving billions of dollars in the process since these mechanisms make voting entirely secure and resistant to corruption (Thompson C, 2016). The financial services sector is home to a large number of private Blockchain-based applications for instance private Blockchain technology is being tested by Bank of America, JPMorgan Chase, the New York Stock Exchange, and Fidelity Investments as an alternative to paper-based and manual transaction processing (Iansiti M, Lakhani K, 2017).

Hybrid Blockchain: The benefits of both public and private Blockchains are combined in this Blockchain. Hybrid Blockchain combines a public Blockchain (in which all participants are included) with a private network (permission-based or invitation-only) that limits participation. A hybrid Blockchain can help highly regulated businesses and governments. This innovation gives users more freedom and control over which data is kept private and which data is published publicly. In the real world, there are numerous examples of hybrid Blockchain. For example, Xin-Fin is a hybrid Blockchain that combines Ethereum (a public Blockchain) and Quorum (a private Blockchain) (a private Blockchain). More than a dozen pilot projects in supply chain logistics, aviation, international trade, and financial settlements have been completed by XinFin. Ramco Systems, a multibillion-dollar software company, provides Xin-Fin hybrid Blockchain solutions to its clients for deploying Blockchain-based supply chain logistic solutions (Freuden, D, 2018).

Blockchain Platforms

There are a variety of Blockchain platforms available, some of which are open-source, allowing companies and developers to speed up development while cutting initial expenses. Table 1 outlines the most popular Blockchain platforms along with their applications (Sharma TK, 2019). Due to Bitcoin's success, organizations are now considering other Blockchain platforms that are open source.

Table 1. Different types of blockchain platforms

Blockchain Platform	Blockchain Network	Background
Ethereum	Public	It is an open platform for developing and using decentralized applications. No one owns or controls the platform. Adaptable and flexible, it is used in smart contracts
Hyperledger	Hybrid	Open-source collaborative effort formed to advance Blockchain technology across various industries. Provides a variety of commercial Blockchain technology products, such as edger frameworks, smart contracts engines, and utility libraries.
MutliChain	Private	A platform for developing and deploying private chains within and between organizations. A more advanced version of Bitcoin's core software is designed to support private financial transactions.
HydraChain	Private chain	This is an extension of the Ethereum platform that aids in the creation of permissioned distributed ledgers.
IBM Blockchain	P2P lending via bitcoin	Developed on top of Hyperledger, it provides organizations with additional security and infrastructure features.
IOTA	Private /public	The Tangle concept is used to create a distributed ledger. An essential component of machine economy, allowing small, free nano payments.
Factom	Private / public	A platform for Blockchain-as-a-service (BaaS) designed to allow Blockchain functionality to be incorporated into applications without using bitcoin or infrastructure; provides full settings for research, development, and production usage.

Blockchain Applications

Generally, Blockchain technology is utilized in many ways, from public ledgers to private ledgers, depending on specific needs. Many of them even use smart contracts. Here are some areas where the benefits of introducing Blockchain have been investigated.

Education Blockchain*:* Sensitive documents like education transcripts and certificates are validated and recorded in the same way as they are in a notary.

Insurance Blockchain*:* Smart contracts, which must adhere to certain rules in a certain way, are an ideal risk-management tool. In this way, insurance claims could be processed faster and with fewer errors if certain conditions are met.

Healthcare Blockchain*:* Medical records are easily accessible from anywhere. This might be combined with other applications, such as smart contracts and sensors, to automatically monitor patient status. Blockchain is also transforming cyber-attacks in healthcare industry (Nwosu A.U & Goyal S.B, 2020).

Cloud Blockchain*:* Instead of traditional centralized clouds, distributed cloud storage may become a reality in the future.

E-Voting Blockchain: Digital voting might become a reality using Blockchain. It provides a secure and anonymous way to conduct e-voting, and security concerns have been the most significant barrier to e-voting.

IoT Blockchain*:* The Blockchain allows any object connected to the Internet to upload data, which can then be stored or processed. Devices with sensors, for example, can be programmed to send their values to a Blockchain, which can then be queried by others to verify their value. The smart contracts may even be programmed with events that are triggered based on what's happening and the data sent from the devices.

Logistics Blockchain*:* Following is a list of some of the applications of logistics management with Blockchain. (a) Easier Documentation: Transportation by container involves a significant amount of paperwork, which takes time and money. A bill of lading or other paper-based freight document is vulnerable to forgery, theft, and fraud. (b)Identify and prevent counterfeit products.

EXISTING LOGISTICS MANAGEMENT SYSTEM ISSUES AND TECHNOLOGIES (LMS)

There exist some issues and challenges confronting the Logistics management system, it is summarized in table 2.

Table 2. Exiting issues in logistics management system

Authors	Existing Logistics management system issues
(Hasan et al, 2019)	It is difficult to have a transparent exchange of information.
(Korpela, Hallikas, & Dahlberg, 2017)	With several stockholders, there is a lack of real-time access to information.
(Wu et al, 2017)	It is impossible to validate a logistics management system.
(Seo et al, 2014)	Lack of efficiency
(Czachorowski et al, 2019)	There is a low level of automation due to the high degree of homogeneity in data transmission among logistics service providers in the horizontal and vertical value chains.
(Kum Fai & Vinh, 2016)	Lack of privacy, trust, and commitment

Existing technologies such as (ICT), (IoT), RFID, and drones have been deployed in logistics management systems to solve the problems as shown In Table 3.

Methodology/Algorithm to Handle Logistics Management System Issues with Blockchain

This involves the steps the logistics management system based in Blockchain innovation will resolve the issues such as lack of security, inefficiency, and lack of end-to-end visibility and so on confronting the system. Fig 6 demonstrates the mechanism to handle LMS issues by Blockchain.

Table 3. Summary of existing technologies utilized in solving logistics management systems issues.

Authors/Year	Technology	Uses in Logistics
(Anwar., 2019)	Information Communication Technology(ICT)	Improved tracking and tracing logistics process with a monitor.
(Aziz, M, 2019) (Tadejko, 2015) (Lee et al, 2017) (Ben-Daya, 2017)	Internet of things (IoT) Internet of thing and Logistics Management	• It uses sensors to collect logistics data and information • Enhanced visibility, warehouse management, and fleet management
(Feng Tian, 2016) (Semunab et al, 2016)	Radio Frequency Identification(RFID)	• Enhances traceability in the logistics management system • Inventory and warehouse management activities are being improved. • Improve reverse logistics.
(iThink Logistics Blog, 2019)	Logistics Drones	The use of unmanned Arial vehicles to transport goods from one place to another
(Li et al, 2013) ((Yang et al, 2017)	Cloud Logistics	• virtualization of logistics resources in a cloud logistics • for intelligent logistics management • Smart storage
((Zheng,Wu, 2017)) (Zhong et al, 2016b) (AddoTenkorang, 2016) (Lamba and, 2017) (Wang et a, 2016)	Big Data, Big Data and Logistics Management, Big Data/ Operation and Logistics Management, Big Data Logistics and SCM	Smart inventory management system for order picking

Figure 6. The mechanism to handle issues in LMS

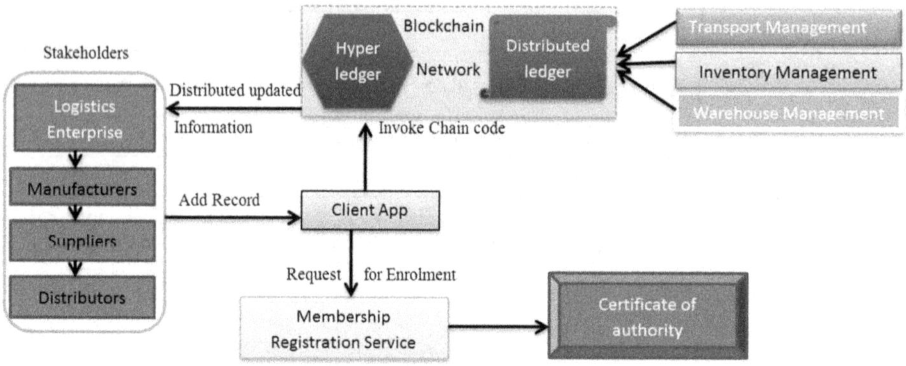

The stakeholders (logistics enterprise, the Manufacturers, suppliers, distributors) can add their details by registering through the client application interface and they can request for certificate of authority via the membership registration service. This certificate of authority will verify and authorize all the stakeholders and clients to be connected to the Blockchain network.

Hyperledger Blockchain will provide privacy and security for customers or client information by invoking chain code and the information stored in the decentralized Blockchain will not be altered or manipulated with the use of encryption. For easy automation the transportation, inventory, and warehouse system will be connected to the distributed Blockchain network, the logistic enterprise can easily access the warehouse, track parcels and manage the inventory. For enhanced efficiency and visibility, the logistic enterprise can communicate with manufacturers, suppliers, and distributors they can view updated information over the distributed Blockchain network

DISCUSSION

This section of the research discussed the advantages of Blockchain in logistics management, the contribution of Blockchain to resolve the issues challenging logistics management systems, and the difficulties in implementing Blockchain in the logistics industry

Blockchain Benefits in Logistics Management

By using Blockchain technology in the logistics business, offers transparency, builds confidence, and promotes cooperation and teamwork.

Improved Transparency: A platform based on Blockchain can provide associated stakeholders with reliable, consistent, and unchanging data. Data from the Blockchain network can be accessible in real-time. unlike traditional data exchange approaches. Thus, end-users have access to data about the logistics process.

Establishing Trust*:* Establishing trust between two parties is tough, but the adoption of Blockchain in conjunction with a distributed ledger system will ensure stakeholder trust. Utilizing Blockchain, The success of logistics companies can be assessed based on their past performance, such as on-time deliveries and pickups. Furthermore, customers' performance can be monitored by logistics companies including contract fulfillment. The payment and pricing process can also be simplified using smart contracts. Automating payment processes is possible if all prerequisites are met.

Increased Collaboration and Cooperation: After trust has been established, stakeholders will be more willing to work together. Through real-time data sharing, players in the logistics industry can seek worldwide solutions to lower overall costs and boost profitability. Stakeholder plans and timelines can be adjusted in response to changing conditions. Even though the stakeholders are competitors, they can benefit by collaborating. Competitors, for example, might lower costs and increase capacity utilization by using collaborative logistics.

Improve Security of Logistics Documents: Through the use of smart contracts and immutable data provenance, Blockchain can effectively handle the privacy of logistics documents such as a letter of credit, customs declaration, notification of dangerous products, and bill of lading.

Blockchain contribution to solving the issues of logistics management systems is summarized in table 4.

Challenges of Adoption of Blockchain in Logistics

There are various barriers to Blockchain adoption in the logistics industry, including data storage and transmission, incentive systems, and implementation costs.

Data Storage and Transmission*:* Every day, the logistics business collects and stores a vast amount of data. Because data is repeatedly saved in each node in the Blockchain network as additional data is collected, the Blockchain application is threatened; each node in the network demands a considerable amount of storage capacity, so In the end, this will lead to a waste of storage. Second, IoT devices deployed in large numbers can cause network congestion, which lowers service quality. Consequently, Blockchain stability cannot be guaranteed. As a result, the logistics industry has a huge difficulty in data transfer.

Incentive Mechanism*:* In cryptographic systems, miners are rewarded for participating in Blockchain networks. The logistics business reaps few benefits when logistics companies record data on the logistical process. This prevents them from being motivated to do so. Logistics companies are essential to the development of Blockchain, and In no manner can Blockchain applications and services be used to help with logistics operations. In this situation, incentive mechanisms are essential.

Implementation Cost: The logistics industry faces a cost and risk dilemma with Blockchain-based logistics management systems. Logistics companies face high costs. Device costs, training costs, operation costs, and maintenance costs are the four sorts of costs. Even though prospective benefits have been discovered, the majority have yet to be realized. Blockchain adoption may not be a wise investment for companies. Furthermore, the excessive risk is a burden. The potential applications of Blockchain are currently being researched. Consequently, logistics organizations' activities may be disrupted when technical problems occur.

Table 4. Contribution of blockchain to logistics management system ***issues***

Authors	Blockchain deployment Area	Description
(Chen, S, 2017)	Maintain Data Integrity (Tamper-proof transaction)	The cryptography of public and private keys is used in Blockchain. This enables product source authentication and traceability in real-time, as well as greater confidence and trust among logistical players.
(Fu, Y, 2019)	Synchronization and enhanced information sharing	Blockchain deployed the distributed system to enhance information across the logistics managers
(Hao, Y, 2019)	Logistics management Smart contract	A Blockchain-based logistic contract manages digital assets and automates the exchange of agreements, assets, and digital data. Contract negotiation, payment conditions, participant obligations, and contract fulfillment verification are all made easier. This strategy lowers third-party expenditures while also streamlining shipping operations..
(Cleland-Huang, J, 2012)	Logistics tracking and tracing	The distributed ledger makes the data always accessible to authorized users because It's a shared and distributed resource. The availability of data allows stakeholders in the logistics supply chain to make better informed decisions during container transit.
(Kshetri, N, 2017)	Logistics management system security and privacy	.Private channels and Orion nodes for the Hyperledger Fabric and Besu networks, respectively, enable security for transactions between participating organizations in the logistics supply chain.

CONCLUSION AND FUTURE DIRECTION

Logistic services are expanding globally and the complexities in logistics operations are increasingly rising, with these challenges, organizations cannot make fast and effective decisions when needed thereby leading to the long delivery time and incurring more expenses. Blockchain as a disruptive technology can transform current logistics industries. The technical enablers of digital logistics management, as well as the obstacles of digital logistics management, were discussed in this study, which also highlighted Blockchain features and the Blockchain concept. The numerous types of Blockchain networks and a description of different Blockchain platforms were emphasized, as well as the current difficulties in logistics management and the existing technology that contributes to logistics management. This study concludes that Blockchain can innovate the management of logistics functions.

Future study will examine the following questions, how to use Blockchain to properly track and trace the GPS location of logistics drivers. Secondly, to figure out how to set up a fleet management framework based on Blockchain. Thirdly, we need to determine how to deal with storage concerns while implementing Blockchain technology.

REFERENCES

Addo-Tenkorang, R., & Helo, P. T. (2016). Big Data Applications in Operations/Supply-chain Management: A Literature Review. *Computers & Industrial Engineering*, *101*, 528–543. doi:10.1016/j.cie.2016.09.023

Allied Market Research. (2018). *Global Connected Logistics Market Expected to Reach $27,722 Million by 2023*. https://www.alliedmarketresearch.com

Anwar. (2019). *Connect2Smallports project: South Baltic small ports – Gateway to the integrated and sustainable European transport system*. Accessed on 10th November 2021. Available: http://bth.diva-portal.org/smash/record.jsf?pid=diva2%3A1361852&dswid=7361.M

Aziz, M. F., Khan, A. N., Shuja, J., Khan, I. A., Khan, F. G., & Khan, A. R. (2019). A lightweight and compromise-resilient authentication scheme for IoTs. *Transactions on Emerging Telecommunications Technologies*, 3813. doi:10.1002/ett.3813

Bai, C., & Sarkis, J. (2020). A supply chain transparency and sustainability technology appraisal model for blockchain technology. *International Journal of Production Research*, *58*(7), 2–7. doi:10.1080/00207543.2019.1708989

Ben-Daya, M., Hassini, E., & Bahroun, Z. (2017). Internet of Things and Supply Chain Management: A Literature Review. *International Journal of Production Research*. Advance online publication. doi:10.1080/00207543.2017.1402140

Boison, D. K., & Antwi-Boampong, A. (2019). Blockchain ready port supply chain using a distributed ledger. In NB! ICT Innovation, Regulation, Multi Business Model Innovation, and Technology (pp. 1–32). Multi-agent.

Bonkenburg, T. (2016). *Robotics in logistics*. DHL Customer Solutions & Innovation, Troisdorf.

Brandl, N. (2016). *Siegeszug der Cloud*. https://logistik-heute.de

Casino, F., Dasaklis, T. K., & Patsakis, C. (2019). A systematic literature review of Blockchain-based applications: Current status, classification, and open issues. *Telematics and Informatics*, *36*, 55–81. doi:10.1016/j.tele.2018.11.006

Chang, J. (2017). *Blockchain: The immutable ledger of transparency in healthcare technology*. Accessed on November 4th, 2021, Available: https://medium.com/@sidebench/blockchainthe-immutable-ledger-of-transparency-in-healthcare-technology-a4a64b1d5594

Chen, S., Shi, R., Ren, Z., Yan, J., Shi, Y., & Zhang, J. (2017). A blockchain-based supply chain quality management framework. In *2017 IEEE 14th International Conference on e-Business Engineering (ICEBE)* (pp. 172–176). 10.1109/ICEBE.2017.34

Chung, G., Gesing, B., Chaturvedi, K., & Bodenbenner, P. (2018). *Logistics trend radar*. DHL Customer Solutions & Innovation.

Cleland-Huang, J., Hayes, J. H., Zisman, A., Egyed, A., Grünbacher, P., & M¨ader, P. (2012). Traceability fundamentals. In *Software and Systems Traceability* (pp. 3–22). Springer. doi:10.1007/978-1-4471-2239-5

Council of Supply Chain Management Professionals (CSCMP). (2018). *CSCMP's definition of supply chain management*. Author.

Davies, S., & Likens, S. (2018). *PwC's global Blockchain survey*. Accessed on October 8, 2021. Available: https://www.pwc.com/jg/en/publications/blockchain-is-here-next-move.pdf

Dubovec, M. (2005). The problems and possibilities for using electronic bills of lading as collateral. *Ariz. J. Int'l & Comp. L.*, *23*, 437.

Economist. (2015). *Blockchain: The great chain of being sure about things*. Accessed 05.11.2021, Available: https://www.economist.com

Fang, W., Chen, W., Zhang, W., Pei, J., Gao, W., & Wang, G. (2020). Digital signature scheme for information non-repudiation in the Blockchain: A state of the art review. *EURASIP Journal on Wireless Communications and Networking*.

Feng, T. (2016). An agri-food supply chain traceability system for China based on RFID. *13th International Conference on Service Systems and Service Management (ICSSSM),* 1-6.

Freuden, D. (2018) Hybrid Blockchain: the best of both public and private. *BRAVE NEW Coin*. https://bravenewcoin.com/insights/hybrid-blockchains-the-best-of-both-public-and-private

Fu, Y., & Zhu, J. (2019). Big production enterprise supply chain endogenous risk management based on blockchain. *IEEE Access: Practical Innovations, Open Solutions*, *7*, 15310–15319. doi:10.1109/ACCESS.2019.2895327

Goudos, S. K., Dallas, P. I., Chatziefthymiou, S., & Kyriazakos, S. (2017). A Survey of IoT Key Enabling and Future Technologies: 5G, Mobile IoT, Semantic Web, and Applications. *Wireless Personal Communications*, *97*(2), 1645–1675. doi:10.100711277-017-4647-8

Gu, J., Goetschalckx, M., & McGinnis, L. F. (2007). Research on warehouse operation: A comprehensive review. *European Journal of Operational Research*, *177*(1), 1–21. doi:10.1016/j.ejor.2006.02.025

Hackius, N., Reimers, S., & Kersten, W. (2019). *The Privacy Barrier for Blockchain in Logistics: First Lessons from the Port of Hamburg. Logistics Management*. Springer.

Hao, Y. (2019). Blockchain in operations and supply chains: A model and reference implementation. *Computers & Industrial Engineering*, *136*, 242–251. doi:10.1016/j.cie.2019.07.023

Hasan, H., AlHadhrami, E., AlDhaheri, A., Salah, K., & Jayaraman, R. (2019). Smart contract-based approach for efficient shipment management. *Computers & Industrial Engineering*, *136*, 149–159. doi:10.1016/j.cie.2019.07.022

Hofmann, E., & Rüsch, M. (2017). Industry 4.0 and the current status as well as prospects on logistics. *Computers in Industry*, *89*, 23–34. doi:10.1016/j.compind.2017.04.002

Holland, M. (2017). *Rückkehr von Petya – Kryptotrojaner legt weltweit Firmen und Behörden lahm*. Academic Press.

Iansiti, M., & Lakhani, K. (2017). The truth about blockchain. *Harvard Business Review*. Available on https://hbr.org/2017/01/the-truthaboutblockchain?utm_source=datafloq&utm_medium=ref&utm_campaign=datafloq

IBM. (2020). *Vaccine distribution on Blockchain*. Accessed on October 27, 2021. Available: https://www.ibm.com/blockchain/solutions/vaccine-distribution

Ilin, V., & Simić, D. (2013). From traditional ICT solutions towards cloud computing in logistics. *Proceedings of the 1st Logistics International Conference*, 78-83.

iThink Logistics Blog. (2019). *11 Major Innovations in the Logistics Industry*. Accessed on 11th November 2012.Available: https://ithinklogistics.com/blog/11-major-innovations-done-to-transform-the-logistics-industry/

Janssen, M., Weerakkody, V., Ismagilova, E., Sivarajah, U., & Irani, Z. (2020). A framework for analyzing Blockchain technology adoption: Integrating institutional, market, and technical factors. *International Journal of Information Management*, *50*, 302–309. doi:10.1016/j.ijinfomgt.2019.08.012

Kersten, W., & Schroder, M. (2015). Supply Chain Risk management for Industries 4.0. Industry 4.0 Management, 31(3), 36–40.

Korpela, K., Hallikas, J., & Dahlberg, T. (2017). Digital supply chain transformation toward blockchain integration. *Proceedings of the 50th Hawaii international conference on system sciences*. 10.24251/HICSS.2017.506

Kruijff, J., & Weygand, H. (2017, June). Using Enterprise Ontology to Gain a Better Understanding of the Blockchain Advances in Information Technology Engineering. *Lecture Notes in Computer Science*, 29–43. doi:10.1007/978-3-319-59536-8_3

Kshetri, N. (2017). Blockchain's roles in strengthening cybersecurity and protecting privacy. *Telecommunications Policy, 41*(10), 1027-1038.

Lamba, K., & Singh, S. P. (2017). Big Data in Operations and Supply Chain Management: Current Trends and Future Perspectives. *Production Planning and Control*, *28*(11–12), 877–890. doi:10.1080/09537287.2017.1336787

Larson, P. D., & Halldorsson, A. (2004). Logistics versus Supply Chain Management: An International Survey. *International Journal of Logistics: Research and Applications, 7*(1).

Lee, C. K. M., & Yaqiong Lv, K. K. H. (2018, April 18). Design and Application of Internet of Things-based Warehouse Management System for Smart Logistics. *International Journal of Production Research, 56*(8), 2753–2768. Advance online publication. doi:10.1080/00207543.2017.1394592

Lee Kuo Chuen, D. (2015). *Handbook of digital currency* (1st ed.). Elsevier. Available http://EconPapers.repec.org/RePEc:eee:monogr:9780128021170

Li, W., Zhong, Y., Wang, X., & Cao, Y. (2013). Resource Virtualization and Service Selection in Cloud Logistics. *Journal of Network and Computer Applications, 36*(6), 1696–1704. doi:10.1016/j.jnca.2013.02.019

Liu, H. (2020). Blockchain and bills of lading: Legal issues in perspective. In *Maritime Law in Motion* (pp. 413–435). Springer. doi:10.1007/978-3-030-31749-2_19

Lyons, G. (2017). Getting smart about urban mobility – Aligning the paradigms of smart and sustainable. *Transportation Research Part A, Policy and Practice, 115*, 4–14. doi:10.1016/j.tra.2016.12.001

Moavenzadeh, J. (2013). *How can supply chains drive growth?* Accessed on 02.11.2021. Available https://www.weforum.org

Mohanta, B. K., Jena, D., Panda, S. S., & Sobhanayak, S. (2019). Blockchain technology: A survey on applications and security privacy challenges. *Internet of Things, 8*.

Nakamoto. (2008). *Blockchain, "A peer-to-peer distributed ledger System" (electronic cash system).* Academic Press.

Nwosu, A. U., & Goyal, S. B. (2020). Blockchain Transforming Cyber-attacks in Healthcare Industry. *World Congress on Information and Communication Technologies.*

Pilkington, M. (2016). Blockchain Technology: Principles and Applications. In *Research Handbook on Digital Transformations*. Edward Elgar Publishing.

Pinto, R. (2019). *What role will Blockchain play in cybersecurity?* Forbes Technology Council. Accessed on 9th November 2021 Available: https://www.forbes.com/sites/forbestechcouncil/2019/04/03/what-role-will-blockchains-play-in-cybersecurity/#4c84e231295c

Popper & Lohr. (2017). *Blockchain: A Better Way to Track Pork Chops, Bonds, Bad PeanutButter?* Academic Press.

PTI Blog. (2019). *5 Big Challenges for Digital Logistics*. PIT's Container Terminal Automation Conference (CTAC). Accessed on 9th November 2021, Available: https://www.porttechnology.org/news/pti_blog_5_big_challenges_for_digital_logistics/

Rao, J. J., & Kumara, V. (2017). Review of supply chain management in manufacturing systems. In *International Conference on Innovative Mechanisms for Industry Applications (ICIMIA) Bangalore* (pp. 759–762). 10.1109/ICIMIA.2017.7975567

Semunab, S. N., & Noor, N. M. (2016). Implementation of Wireless Mobile RFID Reader in Real-World Industry Environment. *Journal Technology, 78*(5–10), 74–82.

Seo, Y.-J., Dinwoodie, J., & Roe, M. (2014). Measures of supply chain collaboration in container logistics. *Maritime Economics & Logistics*. Advance online publication. doi:10.1057/mel.2014.26

Sharma, T. K. (2017). *List of best open source Blockchain platforms*. Blockchain Council. Available: https://www.blockchain-council.org/blockchain/list-of-best-open-source-blockchain-platforms/

Simi, Ć., & Ilin, V. (2017). Utilizing big data for safety and sustainable mobility. *Proceedings of the 6th International Conference "Towards a Humane City"*, 317-323.

Tadejko, P. (2015). Application of Internet of Things in Logistics – Current Challenges. *Economics and Management*, *7*(4), 54–64.

Tan, K. H., Zhan, Y. Z., Ji, G., Ye, F., & Chang, C. (2015). Harvesting Big Data to enhance supply chain innovation capabilities: An analytic infrastructure based on deduction graph. *International Journal of Production Economics*, *165*, 223–233. doi:10.1016/j.ijpe.2014.12.034

Thompson, C. (2016). *How does the Blockchain work? The Blockchain review by intrepid*. Accessed on 9th November 2021, Available: https://medium.com/blockchain-review/the-difference-between-a-privatepublic-consortium-blockchain-799ae7f022bc

Vis, I. F. A. (2006). Survey of research in the design and control of automated guided vehicle systems. *European Journal of Operational Research*, *170*(3), 677–709. doi:10.1016/j.ejor.2004.09.020

Wang, G., Gunasekaran, A., Ngai, E. W. T., & Papadopoulos, T. (2016). Big Data Analytics in Logistics and Supply Chain Management: Certain Investigations for Research and Applications. *International Journal of Production Economics*, *176*, 98–110. doi:10.1016/j.ijpe.2016.03.014

Wang, Y., Hugh Han, J., & Beynon-Davies, P. (2019). Understanding Blockchain technology for future supply chains: A systematic literature review and research agenda. *Supply Chain Management*, *24*(1), 62–84. doi:10.1108/SCM-03-2018-0148

Wannenwetsch, H. (Ed.). (2014). *Integrierte Materialwirtschaft, Logistik und Beschaffung* (5th ed.). Springer. doi:10.1007/978-3-642-45023-5

Williams, Z., Lueg, J. E., & LeMay, S. A. (2008). Supply chain security: An overview and research agenda. *International Journal of Logistics Management*, *19*(2), 254–281. doi:10.1108/09574090810895988

Wu, H., Li, Z., King, B., Miled, Z. B., Wassick, J., & Tazelaar, J. (2017). A distributed ledger for supply chain physical distribution visibility. *Information (Basel)*, *8*(4), 137. doi:10.3390/info8040137

Yang, C. S. (2019a). Maritime shipping digitalization: Blockchain-based technology applications, future improvements, and intention to use. *Transportation Research Part E, Logistics and Transportation Review*, *131*, 108–117. doi:10.1016/j.tre.2019.09.020

Zheng, Z., Xie, S., Dai, H., Chen, X., & Wang, H. (2017). An overview of Blockchain technology: architecture, consensus, and future trends. *IEEE 6th international congress on big data*. Accessed on 5th November 2021. Avalaible:https://www.researchgate.net/publication/318131748_An_Overview_of_Blockchain_Technology_Architecture_Consensus_and_Future_Trends

Zhong, R. Y., Newman, S. T., Huang, G. Q., & Lan, S. (2016b). Big Data for Supply Chain Management in the Service and Manufacturing Sectors: Challenges, Opportunities, and Future Perspectives. *Computers & Industrial Engineering*, *101*, 572–591. doi:10.1016/j.cie.2016.07.013

Chapter 8
IoT and Blockchain for Secured Supply Chain Management

Jayashree K.
Rajalakshmi Engineering College, India

Srinivasan S. P.
Rajalakshmi Engineering College, India

Babu R.
https://orcid.org/0000-0003-0891-7190
Rajalakshmi Engineering College, India

ABSTRACT

As supply chains become more dynamic, incorporate a scope of partners, and intensely depend on an assortment of outside counterparties, blockchain has arisen as a feasible possibility to de-tangle all information, archives, correspondence exchanges that exist inside the production network organization. Each production network will have enormous measure of information being traded between different stages in a supply chain network. To deal with colossal of measure of information and guarantee its security, supply chain can consolidate IoT and blockchain. This will help in further developing security, usefulness, proficiency, and benefit of the production network. This chapter examines the foundation of blockchain, IoT, and a portion of the issues confronting present day supply chain. The significant advantages for supply chains utilizing IoT and blockchain are analyzed, and future examination heading for Integration of IoT and blockchain for supply chain management are discussed.

INTRODUCTION

As of late, inventory Supply Chain Management (SCM) and logistic have seen colossal perspective changes. The expanding revenue in SCM and logistic has been driven by aggressive tension and has prompted its possible height to transform into a basic piece of organization tasks and methodology. The job of these hierarchical capacities has reasonably, turn into further articulated, and organizations want

DOI: 10.4018/978-1-7998-8697-6.ch008

Copyright © 2022, IGI Global. Copying or distributing in print or electronic forms without written permission of IGI Global is prohibited.

to proficiently deal with their supply chain and logistic exercises to support its serious situation in an inexorably unique commercial climate.

A supply chain network remains an association so as to contact a commerce as well as its providers to make and convey a particular element to customers. Different jobs, people, associations, information, and assets together structure this organization. SCM is a critical interaction and organizations make progressed and inventive stockpile chains to lessen costs and empower a speedier assembling cycle to contend successfully in the commercial centre. In an effective production network, the use of supply chain can be limited to the accompanying basic essential fields in particular buying, sourcing, asset following, demand preparing, inventory control, logistic, and customer relations. Despite the fact that they appear to be autonomous constructions, they are profoundly reliant upon one another (Reet Tuteja & Prabu Shankar, 2021).

SCM includes arranging and executing all cycles engaged with securing last wares. It's a snare of individuals, organizations, associations, innovation, and instruments incorporated into item creation. Design as well as usage obtainment, as it devours advantages like great productivity as well as effectiveness, limited item obscuration, satisfying deals need, and so forth. Trend setting innovations, for example, Artificial Intelligence are being utilized in SCM to assist organizations with addressing certain setbacks. In any case, within administration of a production network that involves enlistment in addition to checking, blockchain innovation can possibly change the manner in handling the supply chain. In its framework, an item comprises of numerous parts that are given by the various makers (Dwivedi et al., 2021). In the whole cycle, if any producer or some other substance presents the bad quality parts, then, at that point, it is very costly to identify the inferior quality parts.

The rest of this chapter is systematized such as: Section 2 delivers a broad overview of IoT and Block chain; related works are discussed in section 3. Section 4 discusses various challenges of IoT in BioT in SCM. The future research directions are discussed in Section 5 and Section 6 provides the conclusion of the chapter.

BACKGROUND

Improvements in Information Technology have presumed a vital part in upgrading, implementing, and controlling the streams in addition capability of commodities, organizations, and information from the beginning abode to the blot of operation on the way to expand consumer loyalty. The speed of progress brought by new advancements has changed the manner by which organizations make and convey an incentive for customers.

The supply chains apprehended improved intricacy in latest times because of the expanded size of the organizations, differentiated item portfolio, upgraded client inclinations, questionable interest conditions, want to collaborate with numerous providers, a huge quantity of geographic locations to be served, and range of mediators (Kamble et al., 2018).

Role of IoT in SCM

The IoT presents bountiful advantages to customers, and can possibly change the manners in which the consumers communicate with innovation in basic ways. The inescapability and correspondences involved in IoT can give various facilities for accommodating organizations and individuals, yet moreover make various opportunities to handle security. (Jayashree & Babu., 2018)

There remain five significant IoT advances mainly utilized in supply chains and logistics. They incorporate Radio-Frequency IDentification (RFID), Wireless Sensor Networks (WSN), middleware, distributed computing, and IoT application programming.

Features of IoT System

The features as discussed by (Hany F.Atlam, 2020) are as follows

- Sensing abilities: The primary innovation that advances improvements in different IoT areas is the remote sensor organization. WSN is commonly an organization of sensors that nous data about the environmental elements and direct the data above a correspondence vehicle for preparation. Sensors are the structure squares of the IoT that empower gathering of all constant and context oriented data about the environmental elements which permit the leaders to settle on exact choices on schedule.
- Connectivity: Connectivity is unique of the critical qualities of the IoT framework. Connectivity empowers billions of gadgets towards remain open distantly.
- Large Scale Network: The enormous number of gadgets and articles make a huge scope network that can't be overseen by conventional or old style techniques.
- Dynamic framework: The IoT is a powerful framework in nature. It can interface different items in various areas. also, with sensors that gather different ongoing and logical data about environmental elements, IoT gadgets can be progressively adjusted to changing situation and conditions.
- Intelligent capabilities: With cutting edge equipment, programming and detecting abilities that empower the gathering of an immense volume of context oriented information, IoT gadgets can settle on shrewd choices in a few conditions and coordinate keenly with other teaming up objects.
- Unique Identity: Having the capacity to associate with the Internet can be ensured, provided that every gadget can have an exceptional character or identifier. In IoT framework, makers provide an identification for every gadget that permits it on the way to keep informed gadgets towards suitable stages particularly on the off chance that there was a security break.
- Autonomous choice: Numerous sensors in the IoT framework, so that empower gathering of colossal relevant and constant information about the general climate. This unique information, permit IoT gadgets to create perspective responsive plus independent choices.
- Heterogeneity: IoT framework permits various gadgets and things to be addressable and communicate with one another.

Role of Blockchain in SCM

A blockchain is a determined digital record that is warehoused on different PCs in a public or private organization. As every exchange happens, it is placed into a block. Each block is associated with the any previous block as well as a block next. Respectively block is added to the following in an irrevocable sequence and exchanges are obstructed organized. When these blocks stay gathered in a sequence, they can't be altered by means of a particular person. As a replacement for, it is checked as well as maintain utilizing administrative conventions (Cheng et al., 2017).

Block chain has been perceived by other monetary or non-monetary areas, for example, banking, Supply chain and logistics, the pharmaceutical business, shrewd agreements and network protection. There have been numerous applications in various areas and enterprises like money, medical services, utilities, farming, land, and SCM (Neha Jain 2019). In a supply chain, the block chain will help with following the item journey from a raw substance provider to a consumer.

Key Characteristics of Blockchain (Zibin Zheng et al., 2018)

- Decentralization: In traditional transaction frameworks, each contract must be approved from side to side chief trustworthy partner organization, unavoidably coming about the expense and the presentation blockages at the dominant servers. In an unexpected way, an exchange in the blockchain organization can be led among two peers devoid of the confirmation by way of the significant partner. Thus, blockchain can essentially lessen the server costs and relieve the performance holdups by the chief server.
- Persistency: From the time when every one of the transactions thinning out through the organization should remain affirmed as well as documented in blocks dispersed in the entire system, it remains almost difficult towards alter. Moreover, respectively communicated block must remain approved by means of different hubs and transactions would remain checked. Therefore, some distortion may possibly be recognized without any problem.
- Anonymity: Every client can collaborate with the block chain system by means of a produced address. Additionally, a client might produce numerous locations in the direction of stay away from distinctiveness openness. There could be as of now not any focal party keeping client's hidden data. This instrument protects a specific measure of security on the exchanges remembered for the block chain. Block chain can't ensure the ideal protection safeguarding because of the characteristic imperativeness.
- Auditability: Subsequently each one based on exchanges on the block chain stays correct and verified by means of the timing information, clients can follow the past records without verification and receiving in the direction of some hub in the distributed network.

There are three distinct kinds of block chain characterized. They are given as follows (Pawade et al., 2021)

1. Public blockchain:
   A public blockchain implies the data and admission to the framework are accessible to each and every individual who is keen in participating, for example, bitcoin, ethereum, etc.

2. Private blockchain:
   Explicit clients and private associations utilize the private kind of blockchain. The login subtleties are furnished uniquely to the approved clients with credible data.

3. Federated blockchain:
   In a federated blockchain network, different elements utilize the network. A unified blockchain permits different associations to utilize the network. Federated blockchain types are typically utilized in the financial area and monetary applications

There are some basic qualities among blockchain and supply chain netwoks (Wang et al., 2021). First and foremost, in cooperation the blockchain and supply chain remain an organization arrangement, both include various clients, hubs, inner or potentially outside partners. Secondly, the blockchain is a decentralized organization, and most colleagues/organizations generally settle on decentralized choices in a traditional supply chain. Thirdly, in cooperation blockchain and supply chain networks intensely depend on the associations otherwise connections between the hubs. Fourthly, in cooperation blockchain and production network involve a specific degree regarding joint effort as well as logistic.

There are three significant fields of blockchain that empowers supply chains, in particular, Recognizability, Smart Contracts and Secure exchanges (Shivam Bajaj, 2018). Recognizability can be computerized and rearranged by effective utilization of blockchain innovation and comparing electronic tracking innovation. Smart Contracts is an electronic agreements dependent on mechanized activities that are set off through predefined occasions for instance computerized execution of instalments if there should be an occurrence of an in-quality and on-time conveyance. Secure Transactions are the ability of information approval in blockchain innovation which guarantees safe exchange of secret business archives, move of delivery reports or orders and request affirmations. Blockchain innovation can offer a public cloud administration as a mix stage which can be incorporated with IoT.

Integration of Blockchain and IoT

SCM is a critical means of transportation aimed at assisting with addressing food uncertainty plus add towards general medical problems. Inside a compound food supply chain, the effective recognizability framework be able to create huge commitment in food review as well as general wellbeing. It be able to assist with detaching specific items and fixings from the base of the issue in a quicker speed to forestall further misfortune. Generally, the detectability framework to a great extent depended upon paper-based frameworks or inward PC frameworks (Aung & Chang, 2014).

The reconciliation of Blockchain innovation by means of IoT resolve stay an impetus aimed at expanded isolated machine diagnostics, reciprocal information analytics, then machine-to-provider associations occasioning in further developed added parts substitution plus general conservation procedures (Dogo et al. 2019). By joining Blockchain innovation and IoT, trade partners gain innovative and ideal bits of knowledge interested in their supply chain progressively by means of further exact as well as dependable data around basic cycles, occasions, and item credits, for example, quality, execution and accessibility. This combination innovation be able to assist with improving end-to-end traceability plus empower fast review capacities of hazardous merchandise (Fosso Wamba et al, 2018).

IoT works in the supply chain over the four fundamental parts (Gohil & Thakker, 2021) such as Sensors plus actuators, Internet passages, Edge IT examination and Data centre maintenance. Combination of blockchain and IOT expands the expectation among every one of the partners and individuals associated with the total supply chain since they gain admittance to the actual continuous information. Everybody in the chain be able to follow the phase of the item plus accept the provision period. Combination like this comforts in the stock administration, request anticipating, monetary and functional administration of the multitude of individual associations engaged with the chain. Asset tracing is the furthermost critical component of BIoT in supply chain. Totally the logistics suppliers' exercises be able to be followed altogether by means of the assistance of IoT, plus the aforementioned stands open towards altogether the individuals from the chain through the assistance of a distributed blockchain server (Pureswaran, 2015).

The pertinence regarding Blockchain in IoT network relies upon a few factors (Kamran et al., 2020)

- Blockchain be able to decide protection as well as security concern if an IoT application requires a distributed peer to peer ecological system.
- Blockchain may possibly stay as a capable security arrangement if IoT application needs toward keep up with pricing measure for its offered types of assistance without the control of outside parties.
- On the off chance that IoT applications request towards safeguard records plus detectability of successive businesses, the blockchain be able to be perhaps the best solution.

Executing blockchain in the IoT framework remains certainly not a simple assignment. The foremost plus significant advance stands toward the preference of blockchain stage that will be taken on to blend the IoT with blockchain technology (Panarello, et al., 2018).

Ethereum, Hyperledger and IOTA remain the furthermost widely recognized stages that be able to be used in carrying out blockchain with IoT.

Figure 1. Difficulties while dealing with IoT data on the blockchain

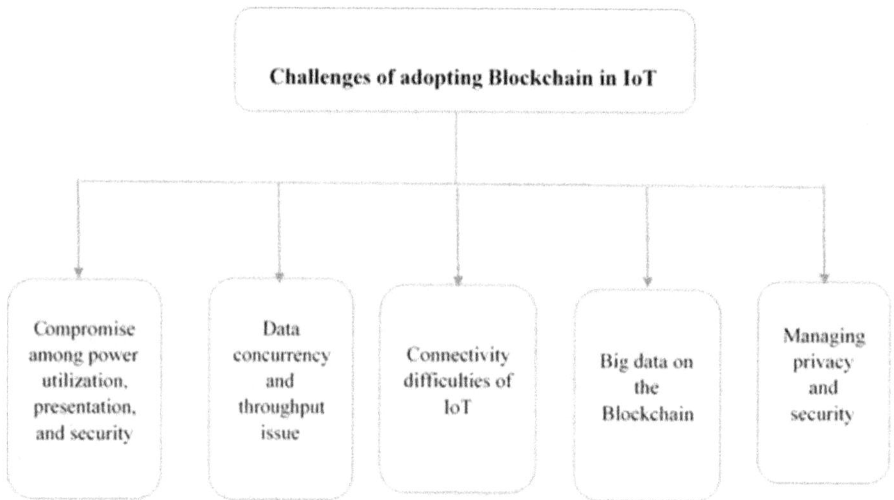

The difficulties while dealing with IoT data on the Blockchain is as shown in Figure 1. and it is explained as below

- The compromise among power utilization, presentation, and security: The extraordinary computational force needed in the direction of track Blockchain calculations devises dialed back the headway of these innovation put together applications with respect to resource controlled strategies.
- Data concurrency and throughput issue (Alfonso Panarello et al, 2018): In IoT frameworks, the IoT gadgets persistently stream information which brings about high concurrency (Pradip Kumar Sharma et al, 2020). The Blockchain throughput is restricted because of its compound cryptographic security convention and agreement systems. The fast bringing together of different blocks

in the midst of BC hubs in a chain-structured record have need of a greater volume of data transmission, which be able to further develop BC output.

- Connectivity difficulties of IoT (Hany F Atlam & Gary B Wills, 2019): The IoT gadgets are relied upon to be associated with high processing storage and system resources to impart IoT information to possible partners. The IoT has restricted abilities to interface them with BC innovation to give novel business freedoms to the execution of new applications and administrations in different areas.
- Big data on the Blockchain: In the Blockchain organization, each member keeps a duplicate of the total dispersed record. Consequent to the affirmation of another block, the block is communicated all through the distributed organization of peers, and each hub affixes the affirmed Block in the direction of belonging to the neighbourhood record. Whereas the decentralized memory arrangement further develops proficiency, takes care of the bottleneck issue and eliminates the requirement for third party trust (Elena Karafiloski & Anastas Mishev, 2017), the administration regarding IoT information operating the Blockchain locates a weight continuously in members' storing space.
- Challenges inside managing privacy and security: Blockchain can ensure straightforwardness of exchanges, which is fundamental in certain applications like finance. Be that as it may, client's secrecy might be antagonistically influenced while storing and analyzing IoT information from specific IoT frameworks like eHealth on the BC (Tianqi Yu et al, 2019). To keep a reasonable level of pellucidity as well as protection, the improvement of economical right to use mechanism aimed at IoT utilizing Blockchain remains essential.
- Difficulties of changeable BC trendy IoT: Even though a few BC innovative elements as well as transference, secrecy, immutability as well as mechanization remain likely security answers aimed at different IoT applications, the aforesaid components consolidated posture different new administrative challenges (Joshua Ellul et al., 2020). The permanence highlight infers that information is for all time distributed in DTL on the peer-to-peer organization as well as can't remain erased or else altered. Likewise, because of the shortfall of administration, records can't be separated for keeping up with protection prior to distributing them on the BC.

RELATED WORK

With regards to world-wide commercial run through, various collaborating-partners centered supply chains, IoT-based applications improve in the direction of work with the distribution of further exact as well as ideal data pertinent towards creation, feature mechanism, dispersion as well as logistics. (Ing-Ray Chen et al., 2014). Abderahman Rejeb et al, (2019) have discussed the primary examination regions at the crossing point among IoT and Blockchain technology are adaptability, security, unchanging nature and inspecting, adequacy and productivity of data stream, detectability and interoperability, and quality. Rahul Raman et al., (2021) proposed a framework for following dairy items from rancher to buyer. The Hyperledger Fabric structure, that takes a particular engineering plus provisions capable of agreement conventions, remains utilized towards fabricating the framework. The Hyperledger Fabric possess eight significant contemplations for building Hyperledger texture Blockchain Developer, Blockchain Regulator, Blockchain Operator, Blockchain Architect, Blockchain User, Legacy Data Coordinator, Conventional Processing Platform and Participation Services.

Algan Tezel et al., (2020) introduced a blockchain organization aimed at supply chains in the commercial dependent taking place essential and optional information then necessitates thorough thought plus advancement of correlative functional cycles. The proposed structure gives greater dependability of data assortment and recuperation, just as information checking. In any case, the shortcoming remains that private blockchains remain helpless against hacking plus basic far reaching information verification components. Besides, private blockchains can't interface with each other. To address the apparent difficulties and specialized restrictions, more review is needed to additionally perceive the capacities and commitments of participants. Antonios Litke et al., (2019) discussed a thorough analysis of the blockchain fitting in the supply chain industry. Thus they described the precise elements of blockchain that affect supply chain such as scalability, performance, consensus mechanism, privacy considerations, location proof and cost.

Nakasumi looks at blockchain-based keys to address a portion of the supply chain issues, for example, double marginalization and data asymmetry and so on. This exploration tends to the significance of building effective supply chain. To create it, the review suggests that the knowledge is one of the main devices for makers in the supply chains. Due to the gigantic measure of information created and traded that is required for the production exercises, the study indicates that perceive the most significant ones and focus just on the "strategic transaction" prompting future changes at the supply chain level. Blockchains be able to remain designed for encode purpose and store on-chain information plus record timestamped exchanges. Besides, they be able to computerize covenants over and done with the usage of canny protocols towards track techniques dependent on a bunch of circumstances, relations, plus conventions that members trendy the framework devise settled upon. Tandon et al., (2019) gave a survey of blockchain innovation and the way it gives a definitive answer towards handling security plus protection tasks related by means of the IoT framework. Authors have deliberated about the advantages plus difficulties of incorporating blockchain with IoT. Sohail Jabbar et al., (2021) have proposed MOHBSChain, a novel structure for Blockchain-empowered inventory chains. In view of exact information from German-and English-talking experts, a calculated model for the capability of blockchain in SCM was created utilizing the Grounded Theory procedure (Härtinga et al., 2020). This information raises the effectiveness, trust, control, versatility, security and expenses as significant impacting factors which have been referenced more than once and accentuated by a few specialists and are consequently considered as the reason for the model. Besides, the examination of the information showed that the capability of the blockchain technology directs the distinctive affecting components through the utilization case, the joint effort, the information just as the regulatory system.

Hedge et al., (2020) proposed the standard execution of blockchain in farming supply chain. Modern farming supply chain comprises various blemishes, for example, go-betweens and agents who hooked on promoting stations towards value and give misfortunes towards makers. Manufacturers need admittance to convenient, precise data on market patterns, occasional vacillations, evaluating, quality, and amount needs. Information missing, misinterpretations, and an absence of certainty among various levels can be survived if blockchain can be used to convey reliable data about the supply chain. Makers can settle on all around educated choices, bringing about additional benefits and lesser misfortunes. Fotiou et al., (2018) proposed solution empowered transference for right of entry mechanism, confirmation as well as installments relying upon blockchain innovation. Zhang, (2016) have executed a pervasive social network based medical services framework. Security is safeguarded as soon as the information remains being divided among pervasive social network hubs by means of utilizing blockchain.

Qu et al., (2019), in request to deal with the retailers' orders safely and proficiently, the study recommends a Consumer Ordering Consensus Protocol in place of Business-to-Consumer available trade organizations. The convention remains carried out utilizing canny agreements as well as blockchain innovation. The purchaser presents a request demand by means of smart agreement in this framework and the smart agreement is then shipped off the Ethereum blockchain network. The entreaty demand is kept in a block by way of exchange information. The entreaty demand remains shipped off all organization members, containing the yard plus transporter and the request data got by means of every hub remains at that time confirmed. In case there is a special case or a request demand that is invalid, a reject cautioning is given to client's dependent on the agreement instrument. The client would then be able to choose whether to put in another request. The strategy will proceed until the following stage where the solicitation for request is prepared. After all hubs have permitted a request demand, the items will then, at that point, be provided from the broker to the customer.

PetriHelo, & Shamsuzzoha, (2020) proposed an entryway worked by means of RFID, IoT, and blockchain techniques joined trendy a timely interpretation. Momentary data is given through RFID and IoT, even though an arrangement of dependable organized registers is given through Blockchain innovation. The framework devises definitive administration by way of nearby remains steady information plus straightforwardness, confidence because of expanded perceivability of exchange and false disclosure, and an unmatched common organization. While blockchain and smart agreement innovations have enormous guarantee, the real solution recurrence towards content-related inquiries remains reduced, in addition to neighbourhood reminiscence is frantically necessary. Impending examinations have to focus on expanding uprightness plus effectiveness in circumstances that join ERP and transportation checking programming interested in a multi-bunch blockchain-based organization.

Seyed Mojtaba Hosseini Bamakan (2021) introduced an exhibition assessment framework for the Service Supply Chain (SSC). Firstly, to analyze the base of issues, a progressive system for SSC execution assessment models was introduced. This system comprises of three levels: measurements, models, and key performance areas. The Adaptive Network-based Fuzzy Inference Systems (ANFIS) archetypal remained proposed by way of a wisdom as well as prescient archetypal aimed at execution assessment in the subsequent stage. The researchers also offered Di-ANFIS structure by means of coordinating blockchain innovation, IoT, and canny agreements towards accomplish a protected, trustable, plus savvy execution assessment framework. The Di-ANFIS design comprises six layers such as the information, association, blockchain, savvy, ANFIS, and application. The above structure is able to track as well as move data plus gathered information inside a solid in addition to carefully designed climate through the supply chain.

Sun et al., (2018) suggested Ethereum blockchain-based rich-meager customers IoT key for handling concerns of resource-constrained IoT while chipping away at the excavating of blockchain in IoT. The plan of IoT-specific agreement conventions would help the coordination of a Blockchain in an IoT-based supply chain plus set out open doors for creating content-situated agreement protocols. By and large, these headways will upgrade the trustworthiness of sensitive information through the cross-approval with the tangible information from other IoT hubs and chronicled information.

Pongnumkul et al., (2017) have done an enactment examination towards the survey of presentation plus restrictions of Ethereum and Hyperledger. The above outcomes showed particularly Hyperledger Fabric reliably beat Ethereum as far as propagation time, performance and throughput. Blockchain is feeble beside substantial assaults for taking attention regarding elliptic curve digital logarithm problem.

Aforementioned issue stands utilized aimed at confirming the exchanges in blockchain. Anti-quantum exchange verification methodology stays introduced inside blockchain (Yin et al., 2015).

The researchers provide experiences about the significance of the blockchain technology for different savvy applications in which security stays vital (Umesh Bodkhe et al.,2020). The work is discussed in four parts. The initial segment examines the conventional security frameworks, foundation, and history of the blockchains. The subsequent part depicts the essential engineering of the blockchain technology, remembering the confirmation of every exchange for the disseminated network which makes a long-lasting, checked and unalterable nature of record for the data or information. Additionally, the blockchain reference design which comprises of three unique networks like public, cloud and enterprise. The third part centers around the ongoing deployment of the blockchain for different applications like smart medical care, smart cultivation, supply-chain and logistics, business, tourism and friendliness, energy, horticulture, computerized content appropriation, smart city, IoT, and assembling. The fourth part concentrates on the open issues and difficulties in Industry 4.0 based savvy applications and proposed some blockchain based answers for those applications.

Feng Tian (2016) exhibits a global positioning framework aimed at food supply dependent on RFID and blockchain innovation. The framework incorporates gathering, move, and dissemination of valid information and information maintenance in all current connects to the arrangement of horticultural food that gets observing, following, and tracking. This framework wipes out the requirement for a dependable, medium-sized association and gives a stage to receptiveness, straightforwardness, lack of bias, trustworthiness, and security. There are a couple of deterrents, as technology advances, the blockchain is as yet now the aforementioned outset plus a few disadvantages towards with practice and great RFID price. Later on, the aforementioned will work on the superiority plus security of rural items.

IOTA can be characterized as a distributed stage that works with and measures different exchanges between imparting gadgets over the Internet. Essentially, IOTA executes a planned non-cyclic outline of exchanges rather than tied blocks of various exchanges. This gives few advantages, for example, it gives a lightweight arrangement as agreement doesn't need most of conveying hubs to support distinctive increased exchanges, all things considered, two exchanges can be checked by single hubs presenting an exchange themselves. This lessens exchange time and overhead (Raschendorfer et al., 2019).

Al-Rakhami, & Al-Mashari, (2021) introduces a trust model that uses a lightweight way to deal with advance an open and detectable framework utilizing blockchain innovation. Capacity, idleness, and computational prerequisites can be diminished utilizing the proposed model. At the point when AI stages and innovation are incorporated with blockchain, can distinguish information designs and prescient investigation which incorporates foreseeing future interest, catch information from the retail location frameworks, history of purchase data, foreseeing deals designs, distinguishing expected issues ahead of time, improving courses to arrive at the objective and dealing with system movement in the general supply chain (Salah et al., 2019).

CHALLANGES OF IOT AND BLOCKCHAIN IN SCM

Conventional supply chain measures, particularly worldwide commerce, there remain enormous amount regarding correspondences plus archives, thus necessitate loads concerning endeavors plus period towards finish. The above incorporate authoritative reports plus agreements thus organizations will bring about expenses toward give what's more. Blockchain could give an answer by means of individually archive or document can stay transferred plus united towards distinct office or commercial, consequently altogether decreasing the endeavors aimed at correspondences or moving documents as well as further developing the data partaking in a supply chain (Benton et al., 2018, Wollschlaeger et al., 2017).

The advantages of utilizing Blockchain which marks appropriate aimed at Industrial IoTs are Scalable, Secure, Distributed and suspicious, Resilient and Auditable features. (Bahga et al., 2016). The difficulties while taking care of IoT information on the Blockchain are the compromise between power utilization, execution, and security data simultaneousness and throughput issue, handling big data on the blockchain, challenges in keeping up with both straightforwardness and protection, regulating difficulties of blockchain in IoT (Ashraf Uddin et al., 2021). The challenges that the industry is presently facing to whilst the incorporation of blockchain into the current SCM are Performance, Scalability and Privacy, (Mark H. Meng & Yaou Qian, 2018)

The central point that influence the improvement of the Blockchain IoT (BIoT) application are (Aggarwal et al., 2021)

- Energy Efficiency
  Blockchains devour bunches of force in view of mining and peer to peer correspondence. On account of consensus procedure, blockchains like bitcoin obliterates widespread power in the mining system. Around remains part of energy waste in light of the fact that peer to peer correspondence burns-through persistent force.

- Privacy
  Privacy remains the principle attention in the IoT conditions then IoT applications facades certificate issue. Towards conquer the protection issue Zero information confirmation comes hooked on an activity thus don't count personalities regarding client for the period of some exchange in addition to stock preferred degree of verification.

- Throughput and latency
  Design which is similar the blockchain ought to be required for controlling enormous measure of exchanges per unit time at the time of situating of an IoT. Additionally, this will become testing factor for such networks, for example, bitcoin which supports up to seven exchanges each second.

FUTURE RESEARCH DIRECTIONS

Kamalendu pal & Ansar-UL-Haque Yasar, (2020) have discussed about the incorporation based on blockchain and IoT, business data trade accomplices acquire new and convenient experiences hooked on the supply chain continuously by means of further exact as well as solid data around significant cycles, occasions, as well as item credits such as quality, execution and accessibility. This IoT and blockchain combination can assist with upgrading end to end detectability plus empower fast review abilities of perilous merchandise. Subsequently, trade accomplices will be educated with regards to the items, likely dangers, and the deterrent and remedial activities required for supporting the enough progression of safe items to the consumers.

Clement Nartey et al., (2021) have discussed that to upgrade BIoT applications and arrangements, further exploration and examination should occur in certain spaces to make organizations protected, secure, and adaptable. These regions incorporate the accompanying:

- Machine Learning-Based Solutions for Privacy and Security of BIoT Applications: About artificial intelligent executions aimed at BIoT protection plus security devise be there conversed, however it is savvy to evaluate other AI calculations like K-NN as well as further deep learning plus grouping methods towards making improved interruption recognition and security conservation.
- Technical Challenges with Decentralization: Because of concerns regarding adaptability, security, plus protection, the vast majority of the BIoT applications that have been suggested are needed in the direction of enhance about type of control towards the blockchain. Examinations as well as exploration should remain done so require to assist with diminishing inclination aimed at control plus change toward genuinely decentralized designs so remain versatile aimed at BIoT applications.
- Blockchain Infrastructure: Trust remains a fundamental piece of utilizing IoTs on blockchains; subsequently, the aforementioned remains fundamental to have a blockchain framework that genuinely settles the concern of confidence inside BIoT executions, subsequently IoT gadgets yield exceptionally critical information. Various methodologies devise stayed specified towards this concern, however they form the most part rely upon interdomain approaches and control frameworks.
- Governance, Regulations, and Legal Aspects: The blockchain world, because of the aforementioned undeniable degree regarding decentralization, remains realized through numerous individuals by means of “no-mans land”. Around remain no significant guidelines as well as legitimate aspects that tight spot the utilization of blockchains plus their execution. IoT actuality further to a framework so comes up short on this form of administration can be exceptionally risky.

CONCLUSION

The IoT saves time and enriches the value of life to an abundant extent (Babu & Jayashree, 2016.) Integration of blockchain and IoT in supply chain assists supply chain individuals towards diminishing their representatives answerable aimed at customary SCM and protect their huge measure based on income. Industrialists be able to lessen staff regarding feature confirmation plus looking after group by means of that undertaking be able to remain effectively through sensors on the apparatus, plus constant information remain transferred over IOT on blockchain server. The assigned manager be able to monitor completely the creation through sensor plus change the necessary location according to information and information on blockchain server. The aforementioned remains vital aimed at some association towards making a decent crucial presentation marker towards building proficiency of cycles; blockchain-IOT can assist organizations with boosting their key performance framework on constant premise which is apparent to all partners. An outline of IoT, Blockchain and the integration of Blockchain and IoT in SCM has been presented.

REFERENCES

Aggarwal, V., Sharma, K., Kaushik, N., Bhushan, B., & Himanshu. (2021). Integration of Blockchain and IoT (B-IoT): Architecture, Solutions, & Future Research Direction. *IOP Conf. Series: Materials Science and Engineering, 1022*. 10.1088/1757-899X/1022/1/012103

Al-Rakhami, M. S., & Al-Mashari, M. A. (2021). Blockchain-Based Trust Model for the Internet of Things Supply Chain Management. *Sensors (Basel)*, *21*(5), 1759. doi:10.339021051759 PMID:33806319

Atlam, H. F., Azad, M. A., Alzahrani, A. G., & Wills, G. (2020). A Review of Blockchain in Internet of Things and AI Big Data. *Cognitive Computation*, *4*, 28.

Atlam & Wills. (2019). Technical aspects of blockchain and iot. In *Advances in Computers* (Vol. 115, pp. 1–39). Elsevier.

Aung, M. M., & Chang, Y. S. (2014). Traceability in a food supply chain: Safety and quality perspective. *Food Control*, *39*, 172–184. doi:10.1016/j.foodcont.2013.11.007

Babu, R., & Jayashree, K. (2016). *Prominence of IoT and Cloud in Health Care. International Journal of Advanced Research in Computer Engineering & Technology*, *5*(2), 420–424.

Bahga, A., & Madisetti, V. K. (2016). Blockchain Platform for Industrial Internet of Things. *Journal of Software Engineering and Applications*, *9*(10), 533–546. doi:10.4236/jsea.2016.910036

Bajaj. (2018). Blockchain and IoT based Smart Container Management for Global Supply Chain Traceability. *IJARIIE*, *4*(4).

Bamakan, S. M. H., Faregh, N., & ZareRavasan, A. (2021). Di-ANFIS: An integrated blockchain–IoT–big data-enabled framework for evaluating service supply chain performance. *Journal of Computational Design and Engineering*, *8*(2), 676–690. doi:10.1093/jcde/qwab007

Bodkhe, U., Tanwar, S., Parekhi, K., Khanpara, P., Tyagi, S., Kumar, N., & Alazab, M. (2020). Blockchain for Industry 4.0: A Comprehensive Review Special Section on Deep Learning Algorithms for Internet of Medical Things. *IEEE Access: Practical Innovations, Open Solutions*, *8*, 79764–79800. doi:10.1109/ACCESS.2020.2988579

Chen, I.-R., Guo, J., & Bao, F. (2014). Trust management for service composition in SOA-based IoT systems. *Proceedings of the IEEE Wireless Communications and Networking Conference (WCNC)*, 3444-3449. 10.1109/WCNC.2014.6953138

Cheng, S., Zeng, B., & Huang, Y. Z. (2017). Research on application model of blockchain techonology in distributed electricity market. *IOP Conference Series: Earth and Enviornmental Sciene*, 93.

Dogo, E. M., Salami, A. F., Aigbavboa, C. O., & Nkonyana, T. (2019). Taking Cloud Computing to the Extreme Edge: A Review of Mist Computing for Smart Cities and Industry 4.0 in Africa. Edge Computing, 107–132.

Dwivedi, Roy, Karda, Agrawal, & Amin. (2021). Blockchain-Based Internet of Things and Industrial IoT: A Comprehensive Survey. Hindawi Security and Communication Networks.

Ellul, Galea, Ganado, Mccarthy, & Pace. (2020). Regulating blockchain, dlt and smart contracts: a technology regulator's perspective. *ERA Forum*, *21*, 209–220.

Fosso Wamba, S., Kamdjoug, K., Robert, J., Bawack, R. G., & Keogh, J. (2018). Bitcoin, Blockchain, and FinTech: A Systematic Review and Case Studies in the Supply Chain. *Prod. Plan. Control.*

Fotiou, N., Siris, V. A., & Polyzos, G. C. (2018). Interacting with the Internet of Things Using Smart Contracts and Blockchain Technologies. In *Lecture Notes in Computer Science* (Vol. 11342, pp. 443–452). Springer.

Gohil & Thakker. (2021). Blockchain-integrated technologies for solving supply chain challenges. *Modern Supply Chain Research and Applications*, *3*(2), 78-97. doi:10.1108/MSCRA-10-2020-002

Härtinga, R., Sprengela, A., Wottlea, K., & Rettenmaiera, J. (2020). Potentials of Blockchain Technologies in Supply Chain Management – A Conceptual Model 24th International Conference on Knowledge-Based and Intelligent Information & Engineering Systems. *Procedia Computer Science*, *176*, 1950–1959. doi:10.1016/j.procs.2020.09.334

Hegde, B., Ravishankar, B., & Appaiah, M. (2020). Agricultural Supply Chain Management Using Blockchain Technology. *International Conference on Mainstreaming Block Chain Implementation*, 1-4. 10.23919/ICOMBI48604.2020.9203259

Helo, P., & Shamsuzzoha, A. H. M. (2020, June). Real-time supply chain—A blockchain architecture for project deliveries. *Robotics and Computer-integrated Manufacturing*, *63*, 101909. Advance online publication. doi:10.1016/j.rcim.2019.101909

Jabbar, S., Lloyd, H., Hammoudeh, M., Adebisi, B., & Raza, U. (2021). Blockchain-enabled supply chain: Analysis, challenges, and future directions. *Multimedia Systems*, *27*(4), 787–806. doi:10.100700530-020-00687-0

Jain. (2019). Security Issues in Blockchain based Applications. *International Journal of Engineering and Advanced Technology, 8*(6S).

Jayashree, K., & Babu, R. (2018). Privacy in the Internet of Things. *The Internet of Things in the Modern Business Environment.* doi:10.4018/978-1-5225-2104-4.ch005

Kamble, S., Gunasekaran, A., & Arha, H. (2018). Understanding the blockchain technology adoption in supply chains-Indian context. *International Journal of Production Research, 25.*

Kamran, M., Khan, H. U., Nisar, W., Farooq, M., & Rehman, S.-U. (2020). Blockchain and internet of things: A bibliometric study. *Computers & Electrical Engineering*, *81*, 106525. doi:10.1016/j.compeleceng.2019.106525

Karafiloski & Mishev. (2017). Blockchain solutions for big data challenges: A literature review. In *IEEE EUROCON 2017-17th International Conference on Smart Technologies* (pp. 763–768). IEEE.

Litke, A., Anagnostopoulos, D., & Varvarigou, T. (2019). Blockchains for Supply Chain Management: Architectural Elements and Challenges Towards a Global Scale Deployment. *Logistics*, *3*(1), 5. doi:10.3390/logistics3010005

Meng & Qian. (2018). The Blockchain Application in Supply Chain Management: Opportunities, Challenges and Outlook. *The 3rd Symposium on Distributed Ledger Technology.*

Nakasumi, M. (2017). Information Sharing for Supply Chain Management based on Block Chain Technology. *IEEE 19th Conference on Business Informatics.*

Nartey, C., Tchao, E. T., Gadze, J. D., Keelson, E., Klogo, G. S., Kommey, B., & Diawuo, K. (2021). On Blockchain and IoT Integration Platforms: Current Implementation Challenges and Future Perspectives Hindawi. *Wireless Communications and Mobile Computing, 2021*, 6672482. doi:10.1155/2021/6672482

Pal & Yasar. (2020). Internet of Things and Blockchain Technology in Apparel Manufacturing Supply Chain Data Management. *Procedia Computer Science, 170*, 450–457.

Panarello, A., Tapas, N., Merlino, G., Longo, F., & Puliafito, A. (2018). Blockchain and iot integration: A systematic survey. *Sensors (Basel), 18*(8), 2575. doi:10.339018082575 PMID:30082633

Panarello, A., Tapas, N., Merlino, G., Longo, F., & Puliafito, A. (2018). Blockchain and IoT Integration: A Systematic Survey. *Sensors (Basel), 18*(8), 2575. doi:10.339018082575 PMID:30082633

Pawade, R., Biradar, S., Rakshita, S., Ramegowda, S., & Rumma, S. S. (2021). A Comprehensive Review on Blockchain Technology for Interactive Healthcare Systems. *International Journal of Engineering Research & Technology.*

Pongnumkul, S., Siripanpornchana, C., & Thajchayapong, S. (2017). Performance Analysis of Private Blockchain Platforms in Varying Workloads. *Proceedings of the 2017 26th International Conference on Computer Communication and Networks (ICCCN)*, 1–6. 10.1109/ICCCN.2017.8038517

Pureswaran, V. (2015). *Empowering the edge-practical insights on a decentralized Internet of Things.* IBM Institute for Business Value.

Qu, F., Haddad, H., & Shahriar, H. (2019). Smart Contract-Based Secured Business-to-Consumer Supply Chain Systems. *IEEE International Conference on Blockchain*, 580-585. 10.1109/Blockchain.2019.00084

Rahul Raman, Sushmitha, & Nalini. (2021). A Survey Paper on Blockchain Technologies in Supply Chain Management. *International Journal of Research in Engineering and Science, 9*(6), 79-86.

Raschendorfer, A., Mörzinger, B., Steinberger, E., Pelzmann, P., Oswald, R., Stadler, M., & Bleicher, F. (2019). On IOTA as a potential enabler for an M2M economy in manufacturing. *Procedia CIRP, 79*, 379–384. doi:10.1016/j.procir.2019.02.096

Rejeb, A., Keogh, J. G., & Treiblmaier, H. (2019). *Leveraging the Internet of Things and Blockchain Technology in Supply Chain Management Future Internet.* Academic Press.

Salah, K., Rehman, M. H. U., Nizamuddin, N., & Al-Fuqaha, A. (2019). Blockchain for AI: Review and open research challenges. *IEEE Access: Practical Innovations, Open Solutions, 7*, 10127–10149. doi:10.1109/ACCESS.2018.2890507

Sharma, P. K., Kumar, N., & Park, J. H. (2020). Blockchain technology toward green iot: Opportunities and challenges. *IEEE Network, 34*(4), 263–269. doi:10.1109/MNET.001.1900526

Sun, H., Hua, S., Zhou, E., Pi, B., Sun, J., & Yamashita, K. (2018). Using Ethereum Blockchain in Internet of Things:A Solution for Electric Vehicle Battery Refueling. In *Lecture Notes in Computer Science* (Vol. 10974, pp. 3–17). Springer.

Tandon, A. (2019). An empirical analysis of using blockchain technology with internet of things and its application. *International Journal of Innovative Technology and Exploring Engineering*, *8*, 1470–1475.

Tian, F. (2016). An agri-food supply chain traceability system for China based on RFID & blockchain technology. *13th International Conference on Service Systems and Service Management (ICSSSM),* 1-6. 10.1109/ICSSSM.2016.7538424

Tuteja & Shankar. (2021). A Novel Technique for Securing Supply Chain Management using Blockchain. *Turkish Journal of Physiotherapy and Rehabilitation*, *32*(2), 3467–3487.

Uddin, M. A., Stranieri, A., Gondal, L., & Balasubramanian, V. (2021). *A Survey on the Adoption of Blockchain in IoT: Challenges and Solutions. Blockchain, Research and Applications*. doi:10.1016/j.bcra.2021.100006

Wang, M., Wu, Y., Chen, B., & Evans, M. (2021). Blockchain and Supply Chain Management: A New Paradigm for Supply Chain Integration and Collaboration. *Operations and Supply Chain Management*, *14*(1), 111 – 122.

Wollschlaeger, M., Sauter, T., & Jasperneite, J. (2017). The Future of Industrial Communication: Automation Networks in the Era of the Internet of Things and Industry 4.0. *IEEE Industrial Electronics Magazine*, *11*(1), 17–27. doi:10.1109/MIE.2017.2649104

Yin, W., Wen, Q., Lin, W., Zhang, H., & Jin, Z. (2015). An Anti-quantum Transaction Authentication Approach in Blockchain. *IEEE Access: Practical Innovations, Open Solutions*, *14*.

Yu, Wang, & Zhu. (2019). Blockchain technology for the 5g-enabled internet of things systems: Principle, applications and challenges. *5G-Enabled Internet of Things*.

Zhang. (2016). A Secure System for Pervasive Social Network-Based Healthcare. *Special Section on Trust Management in Pervasive Social Networking (TruPSN)*.

Zheng, Z., & Shaoan, X. (2018). Blockchain challenges and opportunities: A survey. *International Journal of Web and Grid Services*, *14*(4), 352. doi:10.1504/IJWGS.2018.095647

Chapter 9
Transformation of Asset Management Systems Through Blockchain

Ankur Agrawal
Sharda University, India

Swati Bansal
https://orcid.org/0000-0001-8557-0114
Sharda University, India

Monica Agarwal
Sharda University, India

Reema Agarwal
Lloyd Institute of Management and Technology, India

Mohammad Rumzi Tausif
Prince Sattam Bin Abdulaziz University, Saudi Arabia

ABSTRACT

The concept of blockchain is prevalent globally in today's times. It has shown remarkable growth and has shown a lot of achievement by executing systems of peer-to-peer cryptocurrency. The cryptocurrency was introduced in 2009 but created hype about digital currency around the world in 2017. Blockchain works on the concept of a "distributed ledger/database." The transactions are recorded and replicated to all the participating parties chronologically. Blockchain has verified to be immutable and provides accountability, integrity, and quite a lot of confidentiality through a pair of private and public keys. Various sectors have started using blockchain due to its salient features. Asset management is also one of the areas where blockchain can reduce transaction costs, approval waiting time, and increase transparency. The complicated processes of asset management can be automated by unifying permissioned and permissionless blockchain. This chapter discusses how asset management firms can use blockchain opportunities to harness its benefits.

DOI: 10.4018/978-1-7998-8697-6.ch009

Copyright © 2022, IGI Global. Copying or distributing in print or electronic forms without written permission of IGI Global is prohibited.

INTRODUCTION

A blockchain can be defined as a "distributed ledger/database" to record the transactions in a chronological manner without the intervention of any central authority. The blockchain concept was first introduced around 2008 and used in a cryptocurrency named Bitcoin in 2009. This Bitcoin created hype in the cryptocurrency market in 2017. Bitcoin and blockchain are used as synonyms in the cryptocurrency literature, but the earlier one is an application, whereas the latter is a concept or framework. Conceptually a blockchain is a sequential chain of blocks, and these blocks are analogous to pages in a manual ledger. As a transaction take place, it is transmitted to the entire blockchain network in the form of the coded language known as cryptography.

In a traditional transaction management system, a trusted third party is required to authenticate a transaction. At the same time, a blockchain work on a peer to a peer network system, no centralized or trusted third party is required to authenticate a transaction. Any specific party/ node in the network act as a miner. Miners act as transaction validating agents in a blockchain network. The only requirement is miner has to solve a highly coded puzzle attached with a transaction to ensure no double-spending and other parameters of an authentic transaction. Once the miner validates a transaction, it is updated to all the network nodes.

Although blockchain is synonyms to Bitcoin and crypto-currencies, the application of the concept is continuously increasing in other areas such as Global payment, Insurance Claim processing, Internet of Battle-Field Things (IoBT) and Internet of Things (IoT). The glaring features of Blockchain technology, like its anatomy, immutability, decentralization and integrity, are making it a feasible choice for financial services applications. With the help of this technology, financial transactions can occur without any financial institutions like banks or any other intermediaries.

From the application point of view, blockchain systems can be bifurcated as:

1. Permissionless blockchain systems are formulated mainly for cryptocurrency assets, like Bitcoin. This blockchain is public; that is why any node can be a party in maintaining a blockchain without the permission of any designated authority (Nakamoto,2008). Permissionless blockchains are used for cryptocurrency transactions among private identities. Through the mining process, new currency units are created.
2. Whereas a network of priory known parties is available, a permissioned blockchain network is maintained to manage the blockchain. A consensus protocol is used to a mutual agreement for validating a transaction among the trusted parties.

There are several challenges to assets like cars and houses on the blockchain. First, we have to check the physical existence of the asset, its registration and its actual owner. Second, it is also to ensure that the asset is not sold two or more times or two or more people simultaneously. Finally, it is also essential to know whether the transfer of the asset is allowed in the law of the land or not.

The main objective of this chapter is to discuss how assets management can be improved by the application of the blockchain mechanism. For this purpose combination of permissioned and permissionless blockchains is required. We will also discuss the complete concept and model for unifying the permissioned and permissionless blockchains with a suitable theoretical and feasible technical framework.

Before diving deeper into the topic, we need to understand the following essential components of blockchain:

1. Business networks: A business network is a group of persons having joint or commercial interests to create wealth by exchanging goods and services.
2. Participants: Participants have common interests such as suppliers, customers, suppliers, partners and third-party vendors. For permissionless blockchain, participants may be anonymous, whereas participants should be known for the permissioned blockchain business networks.
3. Assets: Assets can be defined as "Anything capable of being owned or controlled to produce value." Assets are generally classified as tangible and intangible. Transactions of both kinds of assets are performed over business networks to create economic value for the participating entities.
4. Transactions: A transaction can be defined as the exchange of anything having economic value known as assets. Participants are unknown in permissionless (bitcoin) transactions, whereas known in business transactions for permissioned blockchains.
5. Contracts: Blockchain contracts are automated functions that perform a specific task for which they have been created. A smart contract is triggered automatically as the conditions are matched.
6. Ledger: the ledger is a chronological record of a business transaction. In the blockchain, ledgers are shared and replicated across blockchain nodes; once validate

ASSET MANAGEMENT

Asset Management can be defined as "a process managing the transfer of assets from one entity to another". An asset management framework manages valuable things, whether tangible or intangible, from an entity or group. There can be various examples of assets like commodities, bonds, debentures, stocks, real estate, and private equity, and many intermediaries are involved in traditional asset management frameworks like brokers, auditors, asset managers, approvers and custodians. These intermediaries increase the time and cost and certain loopholes in the asset management system.

The manual trade processes for asset management are time-consuming and error-prone as it involves many mediators. Moreover, every party has to keep a record of theirs. Therefore, it takes time to settle any deal. Let us take an example of the conventional trading process of an asset. To find trustful investors, a car seller looks out for a physical or electronic platform to sell a car—the owner contract to a broker for seeking an appropriate buyer and give the owner a good deal. The second option may be that the owner chooses an electronic platform for the same. Since the broker of e-broker (electronic platform) acts as a linkage between the buyer and the seller, the broker has to do the due diligence of the seller-buyer and the asset, i.e., the car. It is also the duty of the broker or booking agency to take care of the sale deed and proper registration of the car in the name of the buyer and transfer the money to the seller's account after taking his commission from one/ both parties.

BLOCKCHAIN AND ITS ARCHITECTURE

1. Permissionless Blockchain

These blockchains are used in Bitcoin and the network of Permissionless as it is open for all. A permissionless blockchains asset is represented as an asset type. It represents ownership and monetary value measured in currency units. Transactions stand to transfer the ownership of assets and currency units from one party to another party. Party stands for an identity in the transaction represented by a digital signature. The Consensus protocol is used to validate ownership, and it is the storage layer where the assets ownership information is stored. Identities are used to determine the owner of an asset, and then the public keys are used to implement further (Nakamoto,2008).

A permissionless blockchain system (Alladi et al.,2020) mainly comprises three layers namely: (i) an application layer (ii) a consensus layer and (iii) a storage layer. These are shown in Figure 1.

Figure 1. Architecture of permissionless blockchain (Zakhary et al., 2019)

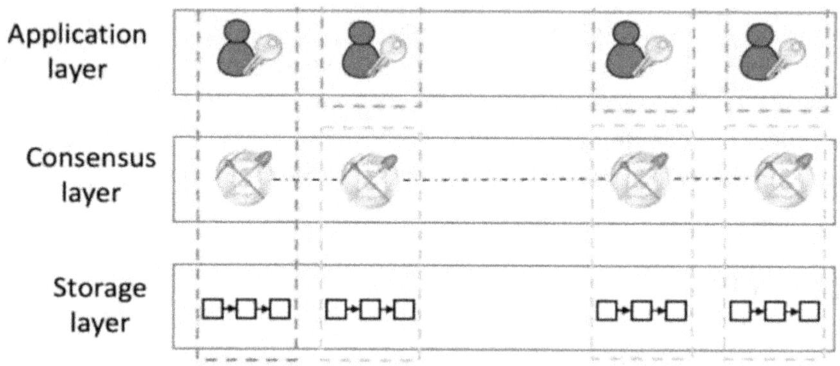

a. The application layers

Transactions are the first layer through which end-users initiate the transaction. Identities of end-users are defined by public keys, whereas their private keys generate signatures. Thus, transactions are generated through digital signatures. Once transactions are developed, it is replicated on all the nodes of the network.

b. The Consensus Layer

In permissionless blockchains, mining is the means to establish consensus. Mining is simply a transaction validation process. The node that validates the transactions is known as the mining node. A cryptographic puzzle is attached to every transaction. Minor receives put the valid transactions into a block by solving the attached puzzle. After validation, the nodes are updated by the block. The transactions blocks are received by the minor to make up the blockchain progress. Only after the solution of the puzzle, a transaction gets authenticated and added to the blockchain as a block.

c. The storage Layer

It contains a copy of a tamper-proof ledger. The ledger updates every block of the chain. The mining node then maintains this ledger. The storage layer contains a distributed ledger which is generally decentralized. A network of open nodes then manages this ledger. Every ledger comprises valid transactions of an asset transfer among end-users

2. Permissioned Blockchains

In permissioned blockchain, nodes are known and identified. However, although all the nodes are known, they lack trust in each other. The blockchain was originated from Bitcoin- Cryptocurrency. However, recently, it has focused on its salient features such as security, provenance, authenticity, and transparency. Moreover, since it caters to most of the desired features for a transaction, it can also be applied to other areas such as healthcare, insurance, SCM, and IoT (Nakamoto, 2008).

The permissioned blockchain is almost similar to the permissionless blockchain, with a bit different in Conesus procedure. It is comprised of (i) the application layer, (ii) the Consensus layer, and (iii) the Storage layer.

a. The application layer

The application layers of a permissioned blockchain, end-user use their public key to submit their transaction on the network. The process and function of the application layer are identical for both permissionless blockchain and permissioned blockchain.

b. The consensus layer

The consensus layer in permissioned blockchain is different from permissionless blockchains. Here mining is replaced with consensus protocol (Cachin, 2016). Ordering and validating the transaction is taken care of by the consensus layer in the same manner as for permissionless blockchain.

c. The storage layer

The storage layer in permissioned blockchain is similar to permissionless blockchains. The ledger, which is updated after every valid transaction, is maintained and manages by this layer.

Figure 2. Architecture of permissioned blockchain (Zakhary et al., 2019)

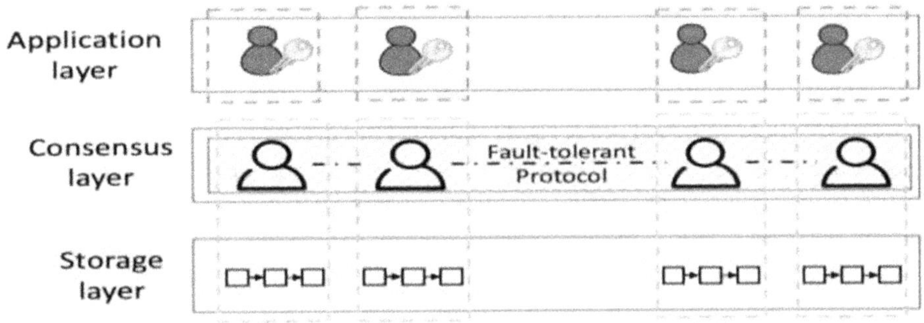

APPLICATION FRAMEWORK OF BLOCKCHAIN FOR ASSETS MANAGEMENT

This asset management system can be developed by unifying the permissionless and permissioned blockchain network. All the agencies' offices and offices are required to set up their own permissioned blockchains network. To register their assets, end-users can request

the government office to register their assets through a smart contract of some permissionless blockchain. For this registration, the end-user must be charged a specific fee. Now it will be the duty of the government office to check the registration of the asset only after make sure that it is registered in only one unique permissionless blockchain.

This is a must check to ensure that the asset should not be sold or trying to sell by the end-users through several smart contracts. This is technically known as double-spending. If the government office is satisfied with no double-spending, it should issue an authenticated smart contract. Then, the governmental office checks double-spending and encodes the law of the land in the smart contract. After all these checks and validation, the governmental office can deploy the smart contract, included in the registration request of the end-user on the permissionless blockchain.

The asset registered only through smart contract, and governmental office identity is allowed to trade in the permissionless blockchain. The end-user can trade using the private identity of end-users. All this process also ensures the abidance of the law of the land.

For example, we created a scenario for asset management (Car); the RTO-Delhi set up a permissioned blockchains network for car registration. Anurag wants to register his car on the network, which he requests through a smart contract. The RTO office also issues a smart contract to the manufacturing company, stating the transfer of ownership of this car and payment of governmental tax. After ensuring double-spending and validating, information about registration of Anurag's exists on all nodes of permissioned blockchain.

Now, if a valid party, say Manoj, is willing to purchase Anurag's car. Manoj first ensures whether the RTO office identity authenticates the car; for this, he initiates a smart contract to check the validity of the car registration in the name of Anurag. If it turns out to be correct, Manoj can purchase the car only after invoking a "Buy function" application/request. This function is attached to the mining nodes of the network. This application/request is executed along with the offer of currency units. The currency should be in the denomination that Manoj's wants to reimburse for the car. If the Buy function call succeeds, Anurag gets paid the amount, the tax is credited to the government account, and the car ownership is transferred to Manoj (Notheisen et al., 2017).

The government offices will do the asset registration through their trusted asset registration and database management systems. A permissioned blockchains network will be created among interrelated governmental officials who will work as validators. The governmental officials (validators) run a "Byzantine fault-tolerant", e.g., PBFT (Castro & Liskov, 1999) or a "crash fault-tolerant", e.g., Paxos (Lamport, 2019) consensus protocol to approve on the registered assets.

For asset registration, the end-user has to send a request to the permission blockchain. Validators have to route a consensus protocol to confirm that the asset is not registered earlier. Once it is ensured, the validator executes a predetermined smart contract, generating another smart contract by which the asset is registered. After the registration of the asset on the permissioned blockchain, they authenticate the resulting smart contract deployment in a permissionless blockchain. This smart contract contains multi-signature of the validators as well as the end-user identity.

Figure 3. Demonstrates the architecture for unifying the permissioned and permissionless blockchain (Zakhary et al., 2019)

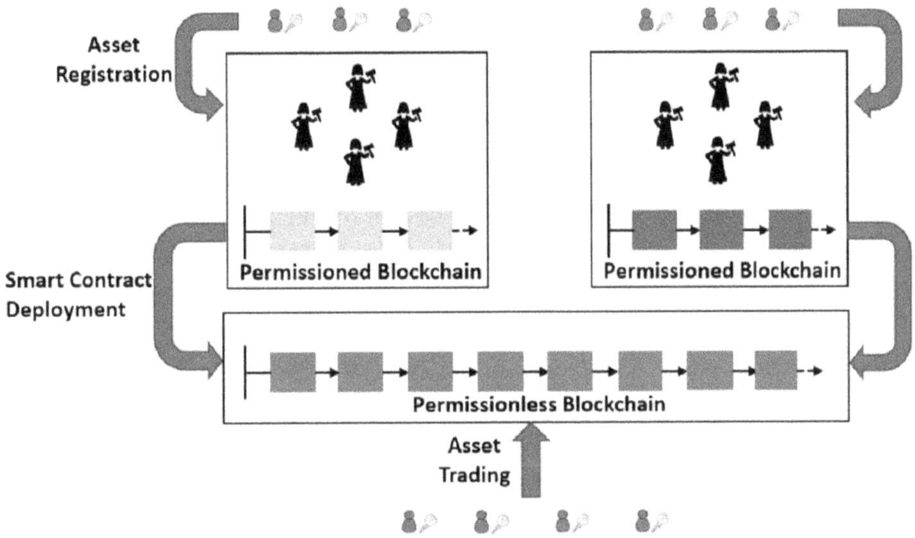

Different government offices can utilize the similar or different permissionless blockchains to organize their smart contracts. These contracts are used for asset registration. For instance, both register (for the house) and RTO (for car) offices can go for the identical blockchain (Ethereum) to register houses and cars.

After registration of an asset in a permissionless blockchain, end-users can do a transaction for these assets. The transaction took place in four folds. Currency units transactions: permit end-users to exchange the ownership and rights of units of currency among end-user by using personal identities. These are the essential built-in function to support a transaction. Complex asset to currency units: These transactions occur on the identical blockchain where registration of complex block chain takes place. The complex assets are traded for currency units by the end-users by using the smart contract, i.e., call function. For example, Manoj wants to buy a car. He has to calls a smart contract the "Buy function" of the car. The call of the Buy function is complemented with currency units offered by Manoj. This Buy function will transfer the currency units to the seller of the car (Anurag). In this way, the car's owner will be transferred to Manoj (caller of the "Buy function").

Complex asset to currency unit's transactions: When seller and buyer are registered on a different blockchain, Complex asset to currency unit's transactions comes into the picture. For example, Seller (Anurag) registered in the Bitcoin blockchain, and buyer (Manoj) registered in the Ethereum blockchain. An atomic cross-chain transaction will take place between them.A commitment protocol of atomic cross chain ensures that Anurag's car is transferred to Manoj and Manoj's currency units to Anurag in the other blockchain take place.

Complex asset to complex asset transactions: Swapping of complex assets registered in the same or different blockchain is possible because of a complex asset to complex asset transactions process. This can happen either by using the call function for the identical blockchain. For the different blockchain network, an atomic cross-chain commitment protocol is used for performing the transaction.

BENEFITS OF BLOCKCHAIN IN ASSETS MANAGEMENT

This would include benefits Quick process: By using the smart contracts, which execute automatically, intermediaries and central authority between buyers and sellers can be removed. This then leads to transactions been done effectively and efficiently. In addition, asset management, which is done with the help of blockchain, helps in reducing the turnaround time of the overall process.

Ownership of Control: People generally are required to visit different organizations to verify the authenticity of their data. However, with the help of blockchain technology, the data can be replicated on various nodes across the network. The users involved in blockchain-based assets management can then control the data by managing the access. This also ensures that manipulation of data is not done.

Traceability: Blockchain helps trace back the data at any time by maintaining the records of transactions in chronological order. With this feature, the probability of frauds like money laundering and handling the missing data can be reduced to a large extent. Further, each and every member of the network has the facility of tracing the old transactions as and when required. Audit of blockchain transactions is also possible on a real-time basis.

Regulatory Compliance: With the help of Blockchain technology, an environment can be created where both market players and regulators can access the trusted, auditable and immutable data. The firms can rely on compliance and duties using blockchain.

Eliminating intermediaries: By using smart contracts, the intermediaries in the transaction can be eliminated. As discussed earlier, a particular software program executes automatically when all the pre-specified conditions are filled. Thus, the use of smart contracts reduces the cost of asset management and saves the time and energy of human beings.

CHALLENGES OF BLOCKCHAIN IMPLEMENTATION

Though the blockchain technology has unlimited potential but it also has certain risks involved. For instance the term "decentralized" is misleading in some cases. Smart contracts can have scalability and security issues. It may allow for inadvertent users similarly the number of users can be restricted due to scalability issues. For asset management system number of external application data sources and different protocols are used. Sometimes, emergency shutdowns are also used to upgrade smart contract (Schär, 2021). These challenges need to be addressed to tap the full potential of blockchain for solutions.

Some challenges are almost standard for all blockchain networks, and there are some specific challenges for asset management applications, including the following.

1. General Challenges
    a. Throughput and bandwidth Challenge: The current network bandwidth is sufficient for the transactions of the blockchain. Every authenticated transaction has to be updated on every node of the network on a real-time basis. Therefore, it requires comparatively more bandwidth. It is a challenge to calculate the suitable throughput and bandwidth for a specific purpose blockchain network.

b. Latency/delay in blockchain network: There are two contradictory objectives as far as the frequency of updates in the network is concerned. Ideally, a ledger needs to be restructured in the blockchain as soon as it is upended. However, it takes some time due to the network traffic, and the challenger can prolong a block of the miner from accomplishing all other miners. Therefore, addressing these types of attacks is a real challenge.

c. Energy consumption in the blockchain: measuring the ideal energy consumption for multifaceted computation in the blockchain is necessary to make operational setups. It is a cumbersome process as the depth of the network is not known, and it is dynamic.

2. Specific Challenges for asset management application

To create an asset management system, we have to unify permissioned and permissionless blockchain. Unifying permissioned and permissionless is not an easy task. We have to face various challenges.

First and foremost, the asset management system and its scalability depends upon the scalability that the network possess. As far as permissionless blockchain is concerned, it is not scalable. The other challenge is what if the identity of the validator is misused or stolen. The stolen identity of validators in the permissioned block- can be used to destroy the existing smart contracts. It can also be misused for authenticating a smart contract for non-existing assets. Finally, there should be flexibility for registration assets in multiple permissionless blockchain challenges. At present, registration of an asset occurs in only a single permissionless blockchain, with one at a time. We will discuss all the issues mentioned above in the subsequent discussion.

Tokenization

Unpermissioned blockchains allows participants of the network, to share an immutable database in the form of a ledger. Generally, it is used to track the innate protocol asset of the respective blockchain. However, with the increasing popularity and utility of unpermissioned blockchain, additional assets are being added in these ledgers. Adding the new asset in to the ledger of a blockchain, is known as tokenization and the asset so added are known as tokens.

Tokenization makes a transaction more effectual and the assets more manageable. A tokenized asset takes no time to transfer around the globe from one party to another. Tokens can be embedded with smart contract and used for numerous public applications. Tokens are one of the important ingredients of asset management in blockchain ecosystem.

As far as technical aspect is concern, there are numerous of ways by which creation of tokens can happen (Roth, Schär, and Schöpfer, 2019). However, with the help of smart contract prototype referred as the "ERC-20 token standard", Ethereum blockchain issues maximum of tokens for most of the unpermissioned blockchain so other options may be dropped as far as financial applications are concern (Vogelsteller and Buterin, 2015).

OTHER APPLICATIONS OF BLOCKCHAIN

Figure 4. Other Application of Blockchain

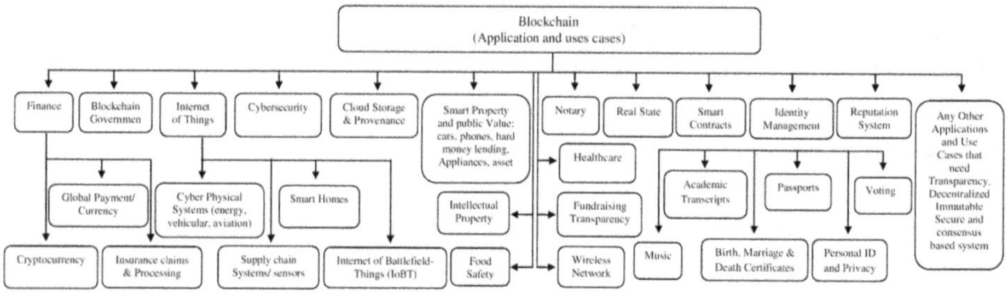

Finance

Conventionally, a bank is an intermediary which verifies the financial transactions between two parties. Intermediaries are overloaded with immense work in a centralized system. Moreover, there are chances of errors and fraud as things are centralized. Furthermore, the process is time- costly and consuming. The blockchain provides a feasible solution for such a complicated process by introducing the concept of distributed public ledger system, where miners work as a validator for "proof-of-work" (Morris, 2017). Each and every node in the blockchain is replicated with a copy which is a duplicate of the reorganized transaction. In this way, transparency and immutable of the process can be maintained.

Cryptocurrency

Cryptography is a technique that allows the money transaction securely and genuinely between two parties without any trustworthy third party, like a financial institution or a fin-tech platform Paytm. Cryptocurrency is the main application of Cryptography, a technique. Bitcoin is the most famous cryptocurrency given by Satoshi Nakamoto, who is a programmer.

All Bitcoin users other than sender and recipient and those are available online do the following things (a) check about the money sent by exploiting6 the mathematical relationship between its private and public keys; (2) to make sure that the Bitcoin are available with the sender a public transaction log is stored for every Bitcoin available. This storage is done on the computer. According to (Nakamoto, 2008) in this condition, it is almost impossible to have malicious transactions where a person can spend another person's Bitcoins.

Insurance Claims and Processing

There are several parties involved in an Insurance claim. The traditional way of managing it is a lengthy, time taking and in-transparent process. However, with permissioned Blockchain technology, the procedure can be made faster, transparent, and smooth as distributed ledger effectively and efficiently in a secured manner updated to all the network nodes. Moreover, any fictitious claims can be easily identified and removed as trustworthy multiple participants/miners need to validate it through consensus protocol.

Blockchain Government

A permissioned blockchain network is beneficial for government operations. A trustworthy, effective, collaborative and transparent network can be established between different government organizations and their branches with its use. The salient features of this technology will help to provide transparency, accountability, and trust among stakeholders (Rawat & Ghafoor,2018). Good governance can be invoked by making the Government affairs transparent by ensuring accountability of its various bodies. It will also decrease illegitimate doings. The public can get transparent food supplies and healthcare quality with a fair system (Manyika et al., 2013).

Internet of Things (IoT)

The IoT is transforming the lifestyle of human beings by using various devices connected through the Internet, like smart homes. In IoT, numerous heterogeneous devices connected through the Internet create privacy of data and cyber security. The blockchain can be a vital technology and solution to cyber security and privacy in IoT.

Energy Cyber-Physical System

A combination of a Permissioned and permissionless blockchain network can be a feasible and accountable solution for Smart energy grid systems. In a cyber-physical system (CPS), a complex interaction among power generation stations, transmission companies, sub-power station utility offices, and end occurs (Rawat et al., 2015). Therefore, prominent features of Blockchain technology can be a solution for a secure, verifiable and congenial environment to sustain bilateral communications among energy CPS stakeholders (Dong et al., 2018).

Vehicular Cyber-Physical System

Traffic efficiency and road safety can be improved with the help of autonomous driving (Rawat & Bajracharya, 2017), unmanned aerial vehicle (UAV) (Alladi et al., 2020) networks and intelligent transportation systems. The vehicular cyber-physical system is significant technology used in these systems. Since much private information of the driver or owner is involved, security in a vehicular cyber-physical system is always the main issue. The role of blockchain becomes a lot crucial here. The central features of immutability, decentralization and anonymity help build an autonomous intelligent transportation system (Sharma et al., 2017). This system can be made secure and smart with the help of private and public keys.

Blockchain in Aviation Systems

In this aviation industry, blockchain can help in providing solid partnerships with various products and services. This partnership will help provide products and travel services in a secure and distributed way.

Smart contracts could rationalize the relations between businesses and various sub-units in the industry (Akmeemana, 2017).

Supply Chain Systems/Sensors

Companies use smart sensors to collect information concerning the supply chain when products are moved and transported across the countries. These sensors help track the supplies. The use and, therefore, the requirement of such sensors is multiplying. These sensors are distributed massively and have enormous data to be studied, collected and analyzed within them. The penetration of blockchain here can be beneficial. It can be further used for disruptive transformation. This transformation is for secure and efficient networks of supply chains (Korpela et al., 2017).

Smart Homes

Blockchain and IoT devices can go a long way to build secure, reliable and sustainable smart home solutions and operations. However, there is a high resource demand required, the capacity of storage is limited, scalability is low. Therefore, the implementation is not straightforward (Dorri et al., 2017).

Internet of Battle-Field Things (IoBT)

Internet-of-Battle-field Things (IoBT) is considered the primary support for smart warfare and defence applications. Today, battlefield equipment such as unnamed aerial vehicles, combat equipment, ground vehicles, and fighters with sensors are used to acquire intelligent and suitable information to enable real-time informed decisions in an immutable and secure manner. However, IoBT is varied as it consists of diverse devices (unnamed aerial vehicles, combat equipment, ground vehicles, and fighters), networks, platforms, and connectivity. This diversity often poses privacy, security, and reliable battlefield operations such as computing and communication. Therefore, the role of blockchain technology becomes essential here. It supports reliable and secure operations for IoBT (Tosh et al., 2018).

Cybersecurity

Blockchain can be used in cybersecurity to fight future attacks. The participants/organizations can be shared information about the future cyberattack with the help of blockchain (Adebayo et al.,2019). For example, different countries or organizations are generally reluctant to share the advantage for their benefits. However, with the help of blockchain and private/ public key pairs, this sharing of information can be done without disclosing any information but for public keys. This safeguards interests of both the organizations and countries. They do not have to worry about their competitors misusing the information that has been shared. However, blockchain does not solve everything, but its characteristics and features can help leverage the systems against multiple cyber threats.

Smart Property and Public Value

Blockchain can be effectively used in managing entities/property like land, house, stocks and automobiles. It can keep track of the property records and operations presented in the form of ledger technology.

These records can then be viewed and shared by all the participating parties or concerned parties. These parties can then create contracts and verify the documents. Thus, a decentralized ledger can recover any lost record from the network (Crosby et al., 2016).

Hard Money Lending

Hard money lending is lending where the financial burdens of people are moderated for a short period. Here the borrower is required to put collateral which can be any property, for example real estate. This collateral should be trustworthy and legit. The lender's money can be lost if the collateral is found to be not redeemable. Similarly, the borrower's property can be lost if, during the agreement, the lender uses fraudulent policies. Blockchain can help in encoding property and the policies together among the users. This is done among the distributed ledger. This creates a transparent and secure environment setting where trading can be done with strangers. Smart contracts could also be deployed with the help of blockchain in these conditions.

Cars and Phones

Phones and cars that fall under personal devices are protected and taken care of by using authentication keys. These cars have smart keys that are accessible only to their owners using. The technology used here is cryptography. However, this process can be a failure if the authentication key is copied, transferred or stolen. Blockchain ledger can solve such problems where users/miners can replicate and replace credentials that were lost earlier.

Smart Appliances

Smart appliances are those electronic devices that can communicate information about the device and its environment with the help of a cyber system. It is an idea like a "talking toaster" in which it provides information to its users pertinent to its use. Similarly, the concept of a smart home comes in where there are smart appliances where the functions of smart devices are optimized with the help of a cyber-physical system. As many devices are involved, these devices can be encoded into a blockchain. The overall process then becomes secure and straightforward.

Cloud Storage and Provenance

Metadata, where records of many operations are kept, including file/data accessing activities, becomes easy and secure if kept and saved in the blockchain. This can then be shared with all the concerned stakeholders. Furthermore, blockchain also provides forensics and accountability (Liang et al., 2017). For example, if different and diverse users access google drive and edit collaborative documents, these changes are saved and stored within the blockchain. Similarly, if multiple users in the cloud make the changes, the same can be saved with the help of blockchain. Thus, accountability and integrity in the data stored in the cloud are made.

Intellectual Property

Managing the Intellectual Property can leverage Blockchain technology to provide and implement verifiable intellectual property rights (Zeilinger, 2018) where immutable, verifiable, and secure blockchain operations can resolve many disputes.

Food Safety

Around over 0.6 billion people in the world fall sick every year after consuming food that is unhealthy. Blockchain technology can be a solution to this. It can provide information across the food supply chain and support providing information related to food composition, origins, and expiry date in seconds. The related stakeholders can then better control food safety. They will have access to information that is accurate and transparent (Galvin, 2017).

Blockchain Notary

The trusted third parties like a notary can be replaced by blockchain, distributed ledger technology and cryptography. Further, blockchain even helps execute the complete notary process by making it transparent, secure and cost-effective automatically (Nofer et al., 2017).

Blockchain Health-Care

Personal health care records have information that is pretty sensitive and needs to be kept in a secure environment. Blockchain can help here. Records need to be encoded and then stored. In this case, the individuals who have the private key would only access the record. The exact process and protocol can be used for Health Insurance Portability and Accountability Act (HIPAA) laws to protect the confidentiality and security of the data. The records of the patients can then be sent to the doctor or insurance providers through the blockchain, and the health records of the patients are kept safe and secure (Mettler, 2016).

Fundraising and Transparency

During fundraising, transparency becomes an issue that needs to be taken care of. Blockchain, when used as a distributed ledger technology, can help to provide a secure, transparent, and secure environment. Its features of verifiability, security and immutability help in creating this environment. Blockchain can help fundraising in a long way (Zhu & Zhou, 2016).

Wireless Networks and Virtualization

The growth and development of CPS and IoT applications have put much pressure on wireless technology. With the help of "network service providers" and mobile virtual network operators (MVNOs), Blockchain could provide a solution. This will help in improving the service quality provided to the users. This will also help prevent the same wireless being double-spend/sublease to multiple parties in a distributed manner (Rawat et al., 2017).

Real State

Blockchain technology as a distributed ledger database system can also be used in the real estate industry. For example, blocks can be used to record property titles with transactions instead of recording via a current/traditional system of record-keeping (Spielman, 2016).

Smart Contracts

Ethereum Virtual Machine (EVM) bytecode, a turing-complete byte language, is used to write smart contracts digital entity (Buterin, 2014). The function in it is a sequence of steps of instruction. The contracts are implanted with the statements made conditional, which allows them to execute on their own. Therefore, smart contracts could be standby for the intermediaries. These intermediaries generally make all the parties come to a common platform and agree on all the terms. Therefore, the blockchain makes these intermediaries or regulatory bodies redundant.

Blockchain ensures that the participant gets the contract details with the help of intelligent contracts, and then the agreements are implemented automatically once all the conditions are fulfilled.

Academic Records

A permissoned blockchain can provide a secure, verifiable, tamper-proof, and immutable solution for faculty members and institutions via decentralized ledgers (Sharples & Domingue,2016).

Blockchain Music

One big challenge for the music industry is to own products with ownership rights. Another challenge is of getting proper and fair royalty distribution. These challenges can be mitigated via blockchain and smart contracts technology and create an accurate, comprehensive and decentralized database of music rights and royalty distribution. In addition, the distributed ledger system can provide transparent information to the artist about the use of the product and royalties received on a real-time basis.

Birth, Marriage, and Death Certificates

Public ledger such as blockchain can be a good solution for issuing birth certificates, marriage certificates and death certificates. Since these are the essential documents of a citizen to be used as proof of citizenship and getting rights like work permits and voting rights, these documents are prone to be forged. The blockchain, through encrypting, can make these records more reliable (Sullivan & Burger, 2017).

Passports

Digital passport has been in existence since 2014 (Rawat et al.,2021). By using Blockchain technology, the owners can be identified online and offline. Moreover, the picture can be shared via cryptographic communication to verify the digital signature of the users. The passports are generally stored in the distributed ledger when the blockchain passport system is used.

Voting

The current voting system has flaws as costly, cumbersome, nontransparent and challenging to verify genuine and ingénue voters. However, blockchain could offer a verifiable and secure voting system very soon. Blockchain can help in providing a voting system that is immutable and verifiable. In this system, a voter can cast his vote with the highest confidentiality from any geographical location in the world (Ernest et al., 2017).

CONCLUSION

There are certain advantages and disadvantages of permissioned and permissionless blockchain networks. The permissionless blockchain network is ideal for cryptocurrency, whereas the permissioned blockchain can work only for trusted and well-known transactions. We have proposed an asset management system that pulls features from both permissioned and permissionless blockchains. Governmental offices have the potential to maintain trusted permissioned blockchains for safety and security purposes. Permissioned blockchains are used for the registration of end-user assets and to authenticate the assets transactions through smart contracts. Permissioned blockchains inhibit the users from double-spending of assets by taking care that every asset is registered only once. This registration is done in only one smart contract, which is authenticated and also only in a single permissionless blockchain. Finally, the permissioned blockchain ensures the legitimacy of assets trading. In this, the smart contract is used where land laws are encoded. Permissionless blockchains are used in the marketplaces where registered assets are used for trading. Identical or other permissionless blockchains can be used for trading registered assets in exchange for currency units. This extension of the transaction model has been made possible through single and cross-chain transactions.

REFERENCES

Adebayo, A., Rawat, D. B., Njilla, L., & Kamhoua, C. A. (2019). Blockchain-enabled information sharing framework for cybersecurity. *Blockchain for Distributed Systems Security*, 143-158.

Akmeemana, C. (2017). *Blockchain Takes Off: How Distributed Ledger Technology Will Transform Airlines*. Academic Press.

Alladi, T., Chamola, V., Sahu, N., & Guizani, M. (2020). Applications of blockchain in unmanned aerial vehicles: A review. *Vehicular Communications*, *23*, 100249. doi:10.1016/j.vehcom.2020.100249

Buterin, V. (2014). A next-generation smart contract and decentralized application platform. *White Paper, 3*(37).

Cachin, C. (2016, July). Architecture of the hyperledger blockchain fabric. In *Workshop on distributed cryptocurrencies and consensus ledgers* (*Vol. 310*, No. 4). Academic Press.

Castro, M., & Liskov, B. (1999, February). Practical byzantine fault tolerance. In OSDI (Vol. 99, No. 1999, pp. 173-186). Academic Press.

Crosby, M., & Nachiappan, P. (2016). Blockchain technology: Beyond bitcoin. *Applied Innovation Review*, *2*(6-10), 71.

Dong, Z., Luo, F., & Liang, G. (2018). Blockchain: A secure, decentralized, trusted cyberinfrastructure solution for future energy systems. *Journal of Modern Power Systems and Clean Energy*, *6*(5), 958–967. doi:10.100740565-018-0418-0

Dorri, A., Kanhere, S. S., Jurdak, R., & Gauravaram, P. (2017, March). Blockchain for IoT security and privacy: The case study of a smart home. In *2017 IEEE international conference on pervasive computing and communications workshops (PerCom workshops)* (pp. 618-623). IEEE.

Ernest, A., Hourt, N., & Larimer, D. (2017). *U.S. Patent Application No. 15/298,177*. US Patent Office.

Galvin, D. (2017). *IBM and Walmart: Blockchain for food safety*. PowerPoint Presentation.

Korpela, K., Hallikas, J., & Dahlberg, T. (2017, January). Digital supply chain transformation toward blockchain integration. *Proceedings of the 50th Hawaii international conference on system sciences*. 10.24251/HICSS.2017.506

Lamport, L. (2019). A new solution of Dijkstra's concurrent programming problem. In Concurrency: the Works of Leslie Lamport (pp. 171-178). doi:10.1145/3335772.3335782

Liang, X., Shetty, S., Tosh, D., Kamhoua, C., Kwiat, K., & Njilla, L. (2017, May). Provchain: A blockchain-based data provenance architecture in a cloud environment with enhanced privacy and availability. In *2017 17th IEEE/ACM International Symposium on Cluster, Cloud and Grid Computing (CCGRID)* (pp. 468-477). IEEE. 10.1109/CCGRID.2017.8

Manyika, J., Chui, M., Groves, P., Farrell, D., Van Kuiken, S., & Doshi, E. A. (2013). Open data: Unlocking innovation and performance with liquid information. *McKinsey Global Institute*, *21*, 116.

Mettler, M. (2016, September). Blockchain technology in healthcare: The revolution starts here. In *2016 IEEE 18th international conference on e-health networking, applications and services (Healthcom)* (pp. 1-3). IEEE.

Morris, D. Z. (2017). *Bitcoin hits a new record high, but stops short of $20,000*. Fortune.com.

Nakamoto, S. (2008). Bitcoin: A peer-to-peer electronic cash system. *Decentralized Business Review*, 21260.

Nofer, M., Gomber, P., Hinz, O., & Schiereck, D. (2017). Blockchain. *Business & Information Systems Engineering, 59*(3), 183–187. . doi:10.1007/s12599-017-0467-3

Notheisen, B., Cholewa, J. B., & Shanmugam, A. P. (2017). Trading real-world assets on blockchain. *Business & Information Systems Engineering*, *59*(6), 425–440. doi:10.100712599-017-0499-8

Rawat, D., Chaudhary, V., & Doku, R. (2021). Blockchain technology: Emerging applications and use cases for secure and trustworthy smart systems. *Journal of Cybersecurity and Privacy*, *1*(1), 4–18. doi:10.3390/jcp1010002

Rawat, D. B., & Bajracharya, C. (2017). *Vehicular cyber-physical systems*. Springer. doi:10.1007/978-3-319-44494-9

Rawat, D. B., & Ghafoor, K. Z. (Eds.). (2018). *Smart cities cybersecurity and privacy*. Elsevier.

Rawat, D. B., Parwez, M. S., & Alshammari, A. (2017, October). Edge computing enabled resilient wireless network virtualization for the Internet of Things. In *2017 IEEE 3rd International Conference on Collaboration and Internet Computing (CIC)* (pp. 155-162). IEEE. 10.1109/CIC.2017.00030

Rawat, D. B., Rodrigues, J. J., & Stojmenovic, I. (Eds.). (2015). *Cyber-physical systems: from theory to practice*. CRC Press. doi:10.1201/b19290

RothJ.SchärF.SchöpferA. (2019). The Tokenization of assets: using blockchains for equity crowdfunding. Available at SSRN 3443382. doi:10.2139/ssrn.3443382

Schär, F. (2021). Decentralized finance: On blockchain-and smart contract-based financial markets. *FRB of St. Louis Review*.

Sharma, P. K., Moon, S. Y., & Park, J. H. (2017). Block-VN: A distributed blockchain-based vehicular network architecture in smart city. *Journal of Information Processing Systems, 13*(1), 184-195.

Sharples, M., & Domingue, J. (2016, September). The blockchain and kudos: A distributed system for educational record, reputation and reward. In *European conference on technology enhanced learning* (pp. 490-496). Springer. 10.1007/978-3-319-45153-4_48

Sullivan, C., & Burger, E. (2017). E-residency and blockchain. *Computer Law & Security Review, 33*(4), 470-481.

Tosh, D. K., Shetty, S., Foytik, P., Njilla, L., & Kamhoua, C. A. (2018, October). Blockchain-empowered secure internet-of-battlefield things (iobt) architecture. In MILCOM 2018-2018 IEEE Military Communications Conference (MILCOM) (pp. 593-598). IEEE.

Vogelsteller, F., & Buterin, V. (2015). *ERC-20 token standard. Ethereum Foundation*. Stiftung Ethereum.

Zakhary, V., Amiri, M. J., Maiyya, S., Agrawal, D., & Abbadi, A. E. (2019). *Towards global asset management in blockchain systems*. arXiv preprint arXiv:1905.09359.

Zeilinger, M. (2018). Digital art as 'monetized graphics': Enforcing intellectual property on the blockchain. *Philosophy & Technology, 31*(1), 15–41. doi:10.100713347-016-0243-1

Zhu, H., & Zhou, Z. Z. (2016). Analysis and outlook of applications of blockchain technology to equity crowdfunding in China. *Financial Innovation, 2*(1), 1-11.

Chapter 10
Integration of IoT and Blockchain for Smart and Secured Supply Chain Management:
Case Studies of China

Poshan Yu
https://orcid.org/0000-0003-1069-3675
Soochow University, China & Krirk University, Thailand

Zhiruo Liu
Independent Researcher, China

Emanuela Hanes
Independent Researcher, Austria

Jabir Mumtaz
Capital University of Science and Technology, Pakistan

ABSTRACT

This chapter will focus on the combination of supply chain management and digital technology. Starting from the popular digital terms in the current market, the authors examine the current environment of the development, including Chinese government policies and the industry situation, and then compare the different characteristics of Industry 4.0 before and after digitization by combining the two digital technologies (i.e., blockchain and internet of things [IoT]). Moreover, the advantages of the integration of internet of things and blockchain in supply chain management will be highlighted. At the same time, according to the changes brought by digitization, the added value of IoT and blockchain integration will be analyzed from the perspective of different stakeholders. In addition, some Chinese case studies will be introduced to show the innovative performance of and benefits for enterprises, to provide references for enterprises, and to implement IoT for smart economic growth.

DOI: 10.4018/978-1-7998-8697-6.ch010

Copyright © 2022, IGI Global. Copying or distributing in print or electronic forms without written permission of IGI Global is prohibited.

INTRODUCTION

Since the 2008 financial crisis, many countries began to study digital technologies in order to cope with the complex financial environment. This led to changes in finance technology innovation and advancement in the technology; thus, created a fast-paced, technology-led finance environment. As a trading power, e-commerce has become a major factor in China which cannot be neglected. The earliest history of e-commerce in the world began in 1970s, when electronic trading was conducted mailing financial institution. As a result, the electronic data interchange (EDI) expanded the forms of transaction. In the 1990s, the World Wide Web (the "Web") allowed the companies to send and receive texts and photos, and the term E-commerce was introduced. Afterward, the E-commerce has reformed from B2C to B2B, as in the Chinese case of Alibaba, and then to B2E, and will continue to develop in the future (Turban et al., 2018). With the economic development and the improvement of people's living standards, technology expanded China's commerce from the traditional offline to online commerce and expanded the national as well as the international market. In 2015, payment services, online loans, data analytics and automated investment have developed into the fastest-growing areas for big data in finance (Monaco, 2019).

The data on industry e-procurement in China from2013 to 2019 published by the National Bureau of Statistics show a clear tendency. 2013, national e-procurement amounted only to 34662.9 billion Yuan. However, 6 years later that number more than tripled to 101275.1 billion Yuan, (National Bureau of Statistics, 2020). In Figure.1, the x-axis represents the years, while the y-axis represents e-procurement quantities in different years and the different colors on each column represent enterprises from different industries. All of the numbers are recorded in units of 10 billion yuan to show the yearly changes in the industry shares. As an important part of supply chain management (Chartered Institute of Procurement and Supply (CIPS), no date), the amount of e-procurement in different industries is gradually increasing in recent years.

Figure 1. E-procurement amount from 2013-2019
Data source: National Bureau of Statistics

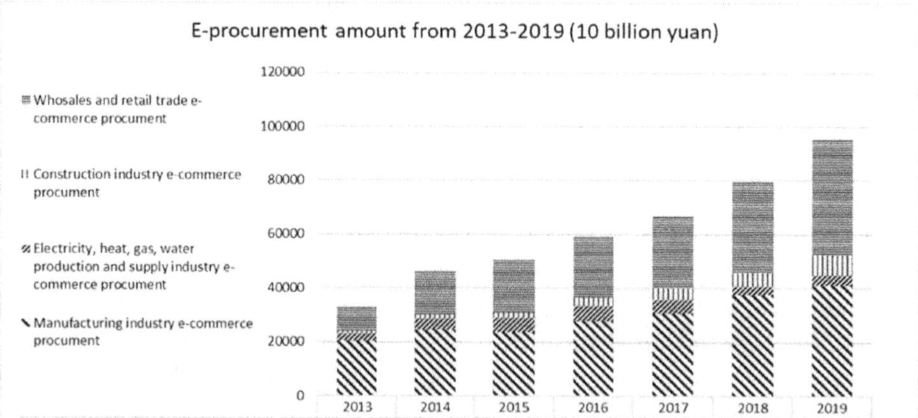

	2013	2014	2015	2016	2017	2018	2019
Whosales and retail trade e-commerce procument	8968.6	15795	19396.7	22293.3	26855.5	33508.1	42730.2
Construction industry e-commerce procument	735.1	1521.4	2172.2	3467	4370	5440.8	7673.3
Electricity, heat, gas, water production and supply industry e-commerce procument	2640.3	4303.5	5124.1	5529.5	4809.3	2691.5	3693.4
Manufacturing industry e-commerce procument	20521.7	24455.6	23805.9	27691.1	30767.2	37842.7	41302.3

With the advent and development of Industry 4.0, improved communication provides more choice to the customers and increased risks and uncertainties, an issue that modern enterprises need to consider (Scholten & Fynes, 2017). The strategic and technical choice of supply chain management is particularly important when an enterprise is faced with many suppliers and different projects, which are related to whether the enterprise can realize the potential benefits of the project and then reap the profit (Wei et al., 2021). In order to solve similar problems, the application of digital technology in supply chain management has become the focus of many enterprises. A survey on blockchain in China published by Weilian and Puhuayongdao shows that respondents think that logistics is the most valuable field for this application, accounting for 63.3% of the statistics of application ranked first. Meanwhile, 20% of the enterprises are using blockchain for supply chain management, and the majority of respondents are optimistic about the use of the technology (Weilian & Puhuayongdao, 2018). This shows that the application of digital technologies such as blockchain in supply chain management in China has a good mass base and the support of enterprises. In fact, with the policy support of Chinese leaders and the drive of leading figures from various industries, many enterprises have applied digital technologies such as internet of things (IoT) and blockchain in supply chain management and benefitted by combining them.

There have been many chapters on the theory and model of the application of digital technology in supply chain management, but there are few practical implementation cases in China (Zorzini M. et al. 2012). This chapter will give a more detailed analysis of the benefits of IoT and blockchain integration in the supply chain management from the perspective of China, and contribute to the discussion by exemplifying some recent cases in China. This chapter aims to investigate how institutional change would drive the development & promotion of blockchain-based technology integrating with supply chain business settings by analyzing the police changes set by the Chinese government. Several case studies have been used to demonstrate how the business sector responds to this institutional change. By understanding the logics of institutional change, this chapter will enable readers to interpret the future roadmap of integrating IoT and Blockchain for smart and secured supply chain management in China.

The chapter will successively be carried out from six aspects. The following section will specifically analyze the existing literature of the current popular terms related to the topic, such as IoT, blockchain, supply chain management, innovation, smart devices and Industry 4.0. The third section will focus on policies and influences of the Chinese government to promote the smart economy. The fourth section will compare the futures of Industry 4.0 before and after digitalization by connecting IoT and blockchain according to the data, to highlight the benefits brought by the integration of the IoT and blockchain. The fifth section will analyze the value-added integration of IoT and blockchain from different perspectives based on the fourth section. Section six will provide some real-life examples of the above concepts in China and analyze them. The last section will make a simple conclusion and provide some recommendations, and explain the need for further research.

LITERATURE REVIEW

In this section, the authors referred to the literature on IoT, blockchain, supply chain management and some of the terms used in the current digital environment.

Related Digital Technologies

In recent years, many industries such as agriculture, transportation, and energy have been shifting their operations and services into digital ones, and they have achieved results such as improved efficiency, enterprise performance and agility (Balci, 2021). The most important digital technologies used in digitalization include cloud computing, artificial intelligence (AI), IoT and blockchain. This chapter mainly focuses on IoT and blockchain.

IoT can connect billions of things, allowing people and things anywhere to be connected at any time (Wang et al., 2015). It collects data from the environment through sensors and devices (Karale, 2021). Compared with traditional network systems, IoT can operate in a secure and stable manner without human interference for a long time (Gulati et al., 2021). The features of IoT can be used across global supply chain management, facilitating the flow of information in real time and the tracking of business processes across different platforms (Wang et al., 2015). At present, the IoT is still an emerging and underdeveloped technology, and its privacy and security issues are still under research, but many industries can apply it to innovate and bring about better enterprise forms, while eliminating some of the manual operations and processing (Babun et al., 2021).

The blockchain technology is a technology that processes and validates data transactions on the basis of a distributed peer-to-peer network (Dietrich et al., 2021). It is an emerging technology characterized by transparency, automation and trust, providing the necessary infrastructure for financial systems, and is currently in the mass deployment phase (Wang et al., 2021b). By digitizing transactions, the readability and accessibility will be improved, so as to improve the coordination and security of information exchange (Černý et al., 2021). This distributed technology avoids intermediary transactions, potentially increasing product and service benefits and reducing capital costs. At the same time, this greatly helps small and medium enterprises to innovate by giving companies clear access to patents. As supply chains are a long-term dynamic structure, they need to constantly meet the changing needs of customers, so this is a general direction of blockchain application (Javaid et al., 2021).

The Current Digital Environment

Although many people confuse supply chain management with logistics, it's actually much more than logistics (Cooper et al., 1997). According to the Council of Supply Chain Management Professionals, supply chain management is "the planning and management of all activities involved in sourcing and procurement, conversion, and all logistics management activities. However, due to complex changes in the environment, this definition is constantly updated (Council of Supply Chain Management Professionals (CSCMP), 2013). Nowadays, it is the concept of a number of sections in the form of a network of agents to achieve a common goal, which consists of material venders, suppliers, manufacturers, distributors, retailers and customers (Terrada et al., 2020). If the supply chain has a concept of sustainability, resource efficiency, social responsibility and financial performance need to be taken into account to maintain competitiveness (Dai et al., 2021).

As a result, continuous innovation in the supply chain is needed to improve competitiveness. Innovation now also means commercializing a new idea in the marketplace (Shaikh et al., 2020). In order to improve the competitiveness of a country or industry in the era of Big data, it is necessary to accumulate knowledge and resources in different markets and fields to promote innovation (Xie et al., 2021). In the past two decades, the financial industry has seen continuous innovation with improving resource allocation rates and new innovative opportunities for many other industries. However, the social requirements for innovation are becoming more pronounced, requiring enterprises to innovate not only in terms of resources and efficiency, but also in terms of environmental protection (Yuan et al., 2021). This is a major reason why digital technology is booming.

In fact, with the development of science and technology, there are more and more smart device users in China. Smart devices are physical devices with microphones and virtual assistants, such as smartphones and smart speakers (Frick et al., 2021).They are being massively integrated into daily life on the basis of IoT (Nespoli et al., 2021). It is very common and popular to have multiple smart devices such as tablet, smartphone, laptop, even smart TV for work or communication (Zhang et al., 2013). These devices not only bring convenience to users, but also facilitate the digital transformation of industry 4.0, which is a new era of information and communications technology (ICT) where information about real products is linked to web-based applications and integrated into the production process (Ali et al., 2021). The concept was first proposed by the German government in 2011 as a critical strategy for industrial production (Bonilla et al., 2018). Because of the integration of information and communication technology and the end-to-end engineering across the entire product life cycle as its basic concept and important innovation, it is expected to meet new challenges and enhance the competitiveness of industries in Germany via the digital interconnection (Birkel & Müller, 2021), and push toward full digitalization as required by Industry 5.0.

Digital technologies such as artificial intelligence, big data and cloud computing are constantly influencing the financial industry. Facing the pressure of shortening time and changing customer groups in the digital era, some enterprises begin to innovate and promote the digitalization of their organizations (Zhou et al., 2021). As digitalization is important, especially for developing countries; digital inequalities arise if a nation cannot keep up with pace of digitalization (Jamil, 2021). There are already many non-tech industries, such as agriculture, transportation. These non-technical industries and our society will enjoy the benefits of digitalization in different forms in the future including enterprise efficiency and agility.

(Balci, 2021). As a result, the Chinese government has taken on the role of legal leadership and regulation, and some companies are using digital technology to blaze new trails.

In today's rapidly changing social and economic environment, companies face unexpected and rapid disruptive competition and new challenges, forcing enterprises to adjust their business design models to improve their performance (Guo et al., 2021). Due to the rapid changes in customer needs and the improvement of corporate efficiency requirements, the trend of future business activities is to unite, share, and emphasize the coordination of partners.

However, the necessity is difficult to be realized in the current integrated supply chain management, because of the lack of communication and complex coordination among enterprises, business integration is essential along the way to a sustainable supply chain (Ni & Sun, 2019). The integration of financial and business information requires increased communication and trust (Huang et al., 2020), and this is why the integration of IoT and blockchain is gaining a lot of attention.

GOVERNMENT ROLES IN SHAPING SMART ECONOMY FROM INSTITUTIONAL PERSPECTIVE IN CHINA (RULES AND REGULATIONS)

This chapter interprets the logics of integrating IoT and blockchain for smart and secured supply chain management in China via examining the changes of institutional settings. Institutional settings affect the direction of economic development. As pinpointed by Yu et al. (2018), "Institutions can be defined by commonly known rules used to structure recurrent interaction situations that are endowed with a sanctioning mechanism. Institutional theory looks at the deeper aspects of social structures with a high level of resilience (Scott, 2008). North (1990) defined institutions as 'the humanly devised constraints that shape interaction' and distinguished formal institutions created by entities such as the government and public services from informal institutions such as social convention or customs and implicit constraints. Economic activities are conducted under a certain institutional setting that define the interest of each member in the marketplace and how they can be achieved and protected." By comparing and analyzing the interlinked relationship between the application and the implications of blockchain-based IoTs in supply chain system, this section helps readers to better capture the changing dynamics of the rapid development of blockchain IoTs in the sector (Yu et al. 2021).

For a country, the influence of government policy and management is fundamental. Taking blockchain as an example, a survey of pwccn (Figure 2.) on the impact on blockchain development as section of the smart economy shows that policy norms have the most impact. In other words, once the national policy is issued, there will be a large number of companies to seize the opportunity to respond (Weilian & Puhuayongdao, 2018).

Figure 2. Concerns that influence the development of blockchain technology in China (Weilian & Puhuayongdao, 2018)
Source: www.pwccn.com

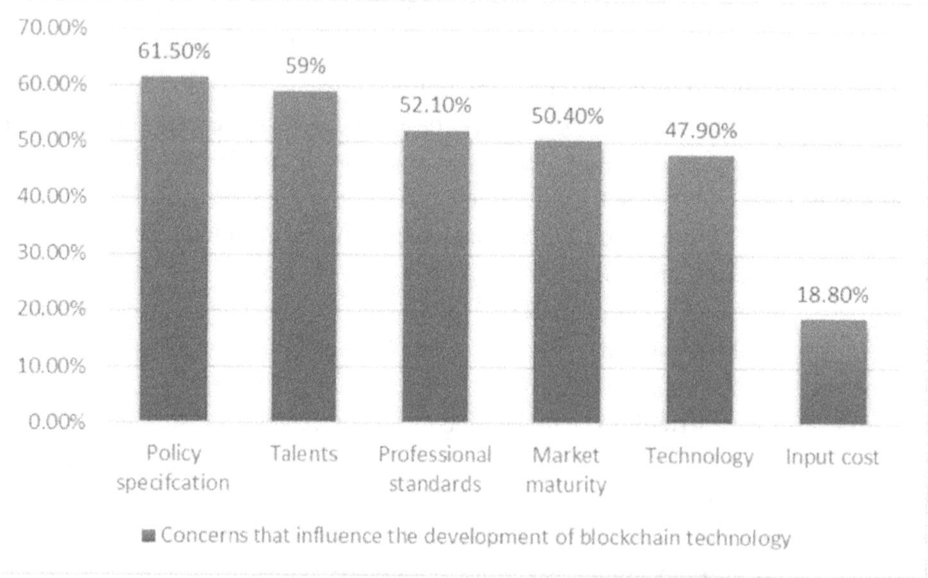

The Chinese government was quick to lead the way, as early as 2015. After seeing the development trend of digitalization, the thirteenth Five-Year Plan suggested that the economy should be guided to the direction of smart change (Xinhua, 2015). The government proposed accelerating the construction of smart economy in all aspects, streamlining administration and delegating power, encouraging traditional enterprises to transform into smart economy, and focusing on the integration of technology brands and channel resources related to smart economy (Ya, 2016). In 2017, eight cities in Shenyang signed a strategic cooperation agreement on the construction of Shenyang Economic city group, and it is expected that the cloud computing, big data and other basic platforms in each city will be built and shared by 2020 (Ying, 2017). In 2018, the Chinese government has released news from Economic Daily, hoping to lead the people in developing digital economy and smart life (Han, 2018). Then in 2019, the second session of the 13th National People's Congress put forward to expand "smart" and build industrial Internet platform (Hu, 2019). The year 2020 was the culmination of promoting the smart economy. In September 2021, Zhejiang province launched the 2020 World Digital Economy Conference showing the full convenience and infinite potential of the smart economy (Ying, 2020). China Development Research Foundation and Baidu also jointly issued New Infrastructure, New Opportunities: The White Paper on The Development of China's Smart Economy on December 15, 2020. This white paper analyzed the current patterns and trends in China and made suggestions for the next step (Foundation & Baidu, 2020). Zhejiang province has launched a digital platform economy monitoring system to prevent illegal activities and monitor risks in the smart economy (Xinhua, 2021b). These measures have created a good atmosphere to China's digital economy market and provided further guidance for industrial development.

At the same time, the government has also issued some relevant regulations according to the development trend and existing conditions. In China the guidelines tend to be tested in one place first after the proposal and then spread, the country adjusts and formulates policies in a timely manner to promote the development of the national economy. Under the leadership of the government, the digital economy of China has grown rapidly from 22 trillion yuan in 2016 (Xinhua, 2017) to 35.8 trillion yuan in 2019 (Xinhua, 2021a), and the annual growth rate exceeded 16.6% (People's Daily, 2021).

Figure 3. The digital economy in China
Data source: www.gov.cn

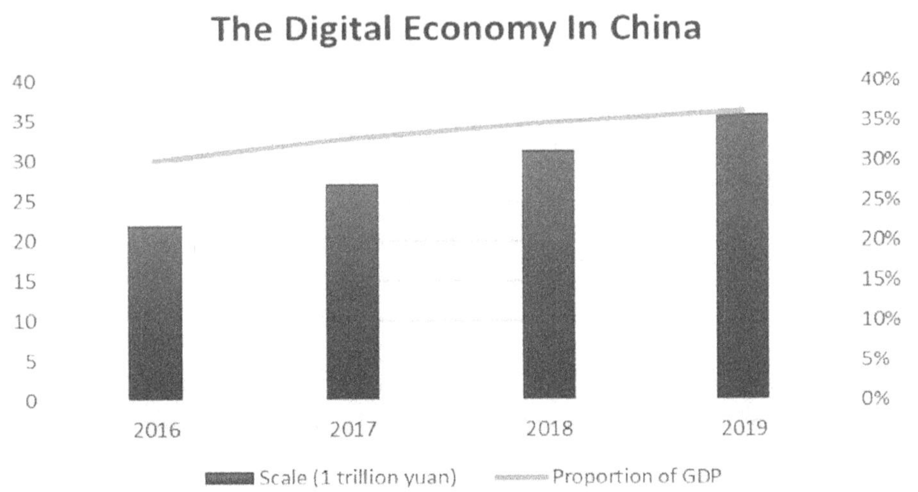

Table 1. Some regulations related to smart economy

Prohibition Field	REGULATIONS	Authority	Issue Date	Main Contents
Smart Economy	Government work report	State Council	March 5, 2017	·Accelerate the development of emerging industries ·Accelerate the research, development and transformation of new materials, artificial intelligence, integrated circuits, biopharmaceuticals and fifth-generation mobile communication technologies commercialization. ·Strengthen industrial clusters. ·Take action to develop big data, strengthen research and development and application of new-generation artificial intelligence. Promote "Internet+" in various fields ·Develop smart industries, expand smart living and build a smart society ·Use new technologies to upgrade traditional industries ·Promote smart manufacturing and develop industrial Internet platforms
	Guidelines on developing a stable digital economy and expanding employment	National Development Reform Commission; Ministry of Education; Ministry of Science and Technology; Ministry of Industry and Information Technology	September 27,2018	·Vigorously develop and stabilize the digital economy ·Job enlargement ·Promote economic transformation and upgrading ·Raise the quality of employment
	Government work report	State Council	March 5, 2019	·Build industrial Internet platforms, expand "smart+", empower the transformation and upgrading of the manufacturing industry
	Support the healthy development of new forms and models of business and activate the consumer market to create more jobs	National Development Reform Commission; Ministry of Industry and Information Technology	July 16, 2020	·Activate new consumer markets, foster new forms of online services such as digital governance ·Strengthen new drivers of growth in the real economy, enhance public service capabilities for digital transformation, speed up the digitalization of private vehicles for enterprises

Data source: www.gov.cn

THE INDUSTRY 4.0 CHARACTERISTICS BEFORE AND AFTER DIGITALIZATION AND WITH OR WITH IOT AND BLOCKCHAIN

The key topic of industry 4.0 is the Cyber-physical production systems (CPPS). With the rapid evolution of the Internet and connected systems, CPPS connects machines, production plants and workers with each other to meet the need of mass production.

In the complex and dynamic supply chain, multiple businesses work together to meet customer needs by adding value from raw materials to the final product (Javaid et al., 2021). Getting the right sections at the right time requires transparent and efficient data transmission. With shared information, cooperation between suppliers and customers can improve the competitiveness of the supply chain. Cooperation enables enterprises to reduce costs, share risks, meet customer needs and use various resources (Müller et al., 2020). Therefore, a number of digital technologies are also evolving in the middle and late part of this period, with IoT having remarkable impact in business and blockchain (Mehta & Senn-Kalb, 2021). IoT is all about connecting items for real-time data transmission, improving the efficiency of the supply chain (Rejeb et al., 2020). At the same time, blockchain is used to protect data transmission and prevent data from being tampered with and eventually, to improve the sense of trust between different industries. In addition, there are AI, cloud computing, big data and other digital technologies to promote the digitalization of the industry 4.0 (Aheleroff et al., 2020).

There are many changes in the characteristics of industry 4.0 after digitalization (Laksch & Borsato, 2019). The industrial ecosystem can get real-time data from the data center to meet the needs of all parties against industry 4.0 before the digital era, such as:

1. Before digitalization, the enterprises always have to explore the development of new products. The failure of products is accompanied by the lack of various resources and costs (Zweber et al., 2017). Therefore, it is difficult for them to calculate the best solution to develop products with existing resources and costs. As a result of advanced digital production technologies, enterprises can reduce operational costs while improving energy efficiency after enterprises computing configuration (Prümmer et al., 2019).
2. Pre-digital enterprises were afraid of waste cost and could only produce large quantities of products suitable for a critical majority of people, which could not meet people's personalized needs (O'Sullivan & Sheahan, 2019); but now the production can be shifted from mass production to mass product customization with the support of a large amount of information, so as to meet the changing personalized needs of customers and improve the competitiveness of enterprises (Aheleroff et al., 2020).
3. In the past, customers were far away from the industry (Mehta & Senn-Kalb, 2021), and they could only buy according to what the enterprise produced, but in many cases those things have long failed to meet their needs. Now the customers can be closer to the industry through e-commerce resources and get personalized psychological satisfaction and their constant feedback and suggestions drive the upgrading of the company's products (Zhou et al., 2021). Thus, the consumption structure of customers is virtually changing.
4. For the whole society, the previous occlusion between enterprises, the lack of information circulation, and the running in between enterprises and customers' needs have caused big waste in both the economy and environment (Kumar & Bhatia, 2021). Through the use of IoT, blockchain and other digital technologies, the Industry 4.0 has made a great contribution to sustainability, the economic and environment (Li et al., 2020).

THE VALUE-ADDED INTEGRATION OF IOT AND BLOCKCHAIN FROM STAKEHOLDERS (INCLUDING REGULATORS, MANAGEMENT AND INVESTORS) PERSPECTIVE

IoT is characterized by large amounts of data, openness, and lankness, but there are many challenges in terms of security, including privacy protection, resource constraints, and resistance to attacks. To make up for these deficiencies of IoT, many businesses are combining it with blockchain, which is characterized by transparency and decentralization (Saxena et al., 2021). The integration of blockchain and IoT can not only reduce the cost of developing and maintaining centralized data centers, but can also help to eliminate security issues such as a single point of failure (Daim et al., 2020). In this section, the authors will sort out the added value of integrating IoT and blockchain from 3 perspectives: regulators, management, and investors.

As Fintech moves from digitizing money to monetizing data in the digital age, regulators need to rebuild the regulatory framework. The current regulators believe that companies should be classified according to their risk level and size, which also requires close co-operation to understand the market, balance risk and potential value, while preventing regulatory arbitrage. Blockchain is assumed to replace settlement methods of the 19th century (Arner et al., 2016). So, the question is; how to understand the market? To regulators, all actions performed by IoT devices are recorded (Šarac et al., 2021). They can clearly check the actions when there is something wrong. IoT is used to handle the huge data record, and blockchain is used to ensure the security and authenticity of the data. The integration of these two can help regulators to monitor the situation.

Management needs to have a long-term plan for the structure and objectives of the company's operation, which also requires a lot of data analysis support. While IoT can help collect data, its centralized nature can lead to single points of failure and targeted cyber-attacks. At the same time, the ubiquity of IoT connectivity makes the attack range more extensive. Decision making and crisis prevention is thus more difficult for management. At such times, the combination of decentralized and interoperable blockchain and IoT is a good solution. The immutability of blockchain strengthens the trust of cooperation between enterprises, and its high elasticity can effectively prevent information attacks (Bandara et al., 2021). Management can utilize blockchains for security policy prosecution and maintaining an openly inspectable ledger of IoT interactions, excluding the third-party security dependence (Saxena et al., 2021). The security is ensured while the efficiency is improved.

China's market is characterized by serious information inequality, and only the investors with high learning ability can persevere. Facing the market with the rapid development of digital technology, investors need to learn rationally, but more importantly, they need transparent market information, risk and return information, rather than capital concentration and risk guidance (Li et al., 2021). IoT devices with blockchain have built trust and allow devices to retain current data flow while improving security and privacy (Šarac et al., 2021). They can securely and quickly track transactions and verify the condition so that the parties to the transaction are seamlessly connected, ensuring the visibility of the process (Nicoletti, 2018). This helps investors improve their investment ability through rational learning and then make better comparisons and choices to reduce financial losses.

CASES

Although many reports show that the average use of smart devices such as mobile phones and televisions is high, the smart environment in the traditional industrial sector is different. Smart devices bring users convenient and smooth experience instead of productive efficiency and safety. At the same time, the intelligent environment is not as closely connected in time and space as traditional industry, and not completely independent (Zhang et al., 2013). With the use of smart devices, especially those industries involved in supply chain management will need to innovate to solve these problems. The digitalization of industry 4.0 can facilitate solving this problem.

Businesses can integrate other smart devices into their supply chains to improve operations, reduce costs and help companies better understand what was once a fragmented landscape. In fact, IoT technology is now mature, and many companies already have installed the required sensors and devices (Cong et al., 2021). In Hangzhou, Zhejiang Province, one of the first cities to implement the policy in China, the digital economy value reached 1,129.5 billion Yuan in 2019, an increase of 379.5 billion Yuan, with the Internet of Things industry reaching 2,014 billion Yuan with the growth rate of 14.1% (Hangzhou Bureau of Statistics, 2020). This shows the vitality of the digital economy industry led by the Internet of Things.

In fact, IoT has many drawbacks in data collection, which need to be remedied by blockchain (Kumar & Sharma, 2021). Public blockchain networks are direct participants and trusted data sources for contracts due to constrained IoT devices. So, on the basis of Internet of Things data, this section will mainly focus on blockchain in digital technologies, showing its trends and effects through some data and enterprise cases.

Data

In 2017, the most frequent use of blockchain technologies by Chinese companies was anti-counterfeiting tracing, which was 50%, followed by distributed storage and authentication. In addition, data sharing and applications as well as supply chain management were also above 20% (Figure 4). The data shows that enterprises are paying attention to the application of data storage and security issues according to the characteristics of blockchain, and supply chain management. It is a major application direction of this technology due to the complex process and the need for information security. Figure 5 shows the ways of applying blockchain in these companies. More than half of the enterprises interviewed installed their own blockchain teams, and a third of them cooperated with specialized blockchain companies, but few were willing to cooperate with the blockchain departments of other enterprises. Both data were collected by PwC, VeChain Foundation through face-to-face interviews and online surveys in relevant businesses. Since blockchain itself is employed to solve the security and trust problem, their own research and development and specialized blockchain companies were to protect their own information security.

Cases

This part collects some cases of the integration and innovation of digital technology and supply chain related projects, and results achieved in social and economic benefits. The three cases are Zhongqi Anlian enterprises, Suzhou Black Cloud Intelligent Technology Co., Ltd., and Tianjin TBC Blockchain Cross-border Trade Through train. Among them, Zhongqi Anlian enterprises provides a platform with digital technology, which is easy to adjust from the macro framework and facilitate some small and micro enterprises with insufficient capital and innovation ability to carry out digital transformation. They also have made some achievements in the agricultural seed industry and energy enterprises.

Figure 4. Frequently applied blockchain techniques in enterprises in China 2017
Source: PwC; VeChain Foundation

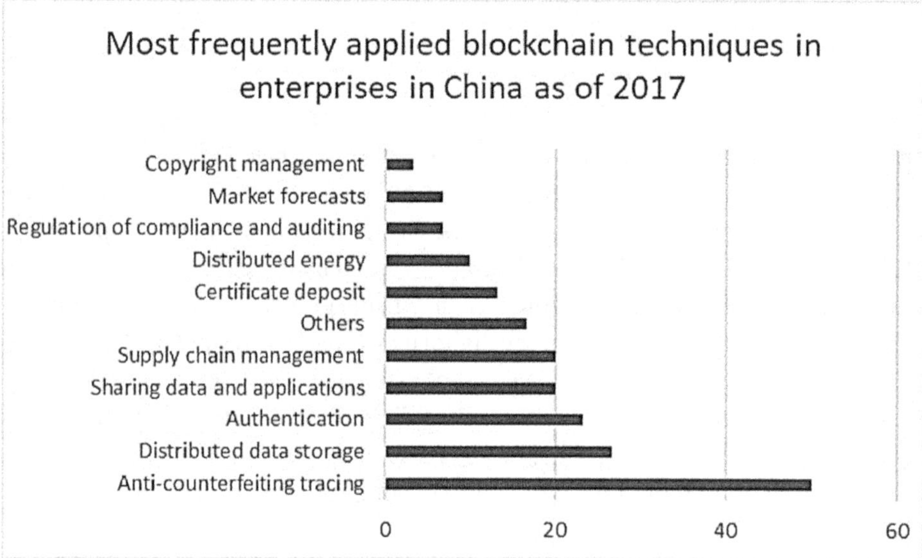

Figure 5. Ways of blockchain technology application in enterprises in China 2017
Source: PwC; VeChain Foundation

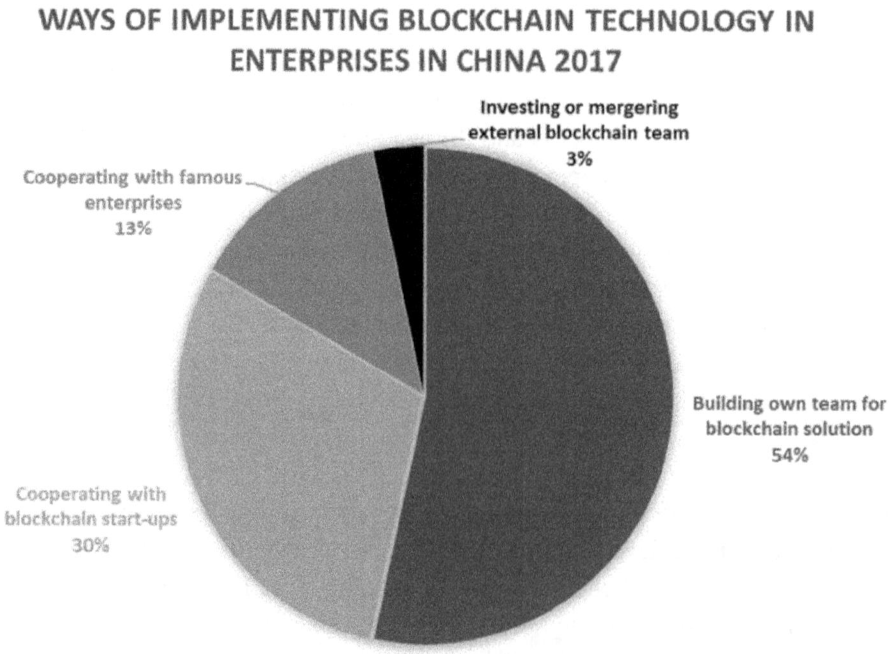

The Case of Zhongqi Anlian Enterprises

The Zhongqi Anlian chain enterprises set up a platform based on blockchain at the bottom of the supply chain finance process. With advanced infrastructure agreements, such as the internet technology, they integrated blockchain into supply chain and chain blocks in order to improve logistics. Besides, the platform includes other industries at the core of the enterprise, thus enabling upstream and downstream enterprises to provide technical services. This helps the core enterprise to optimize supply chain management and to accurate risk identification- This is an example of how, small and micro enterprises can solve financing problems for the supply chain (Jua, 2021).

Figure 6. Zhongqi Anlian enterprises
Source: www.djyanbao.com

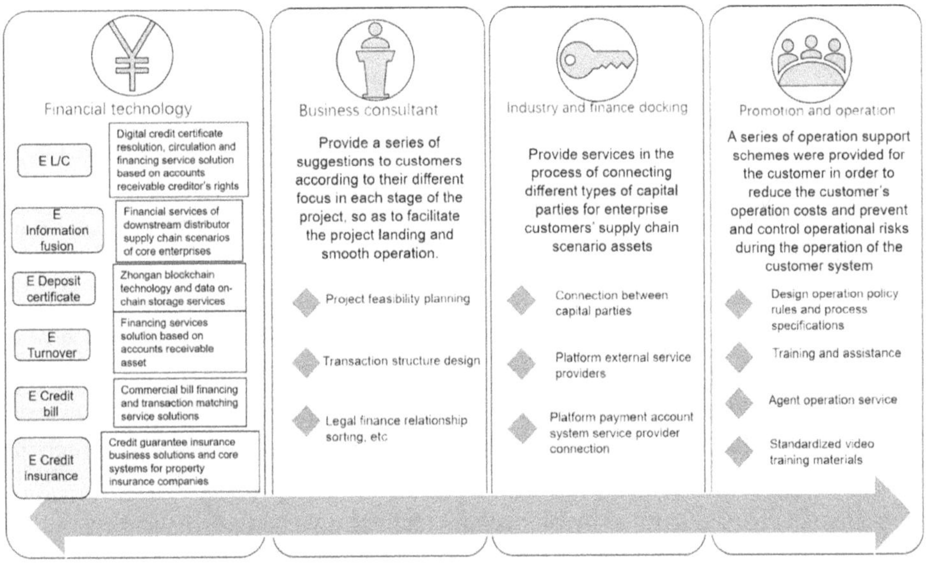

The solution will deploy blockchain nodes for each major player involved in the supply chain, forming an alliance chain so that the business data in the daily operation of the core enterprise can be quickly uploaded to the blockchain platform, ensuring the traceability of business data (China Financial Information Industry Association (CFIIA), 2021). The capital party carries out artificial risk control on the core enterprises which can issue tokens of corresponding amount to responding suppliers according to payable accounts and apply for financing by retaining tokens or applying to the capital. In addition, with the introduction of enterprise identity authentication, and the use of the online electronic signing function, signing records are stored in the blockchain network, to ensure user data security, non-tampering and permanent traceability.

Innovations in the project:

Figure 7. Business process of Zhongqi Anlian enterprises
Source: www.zqalink.com

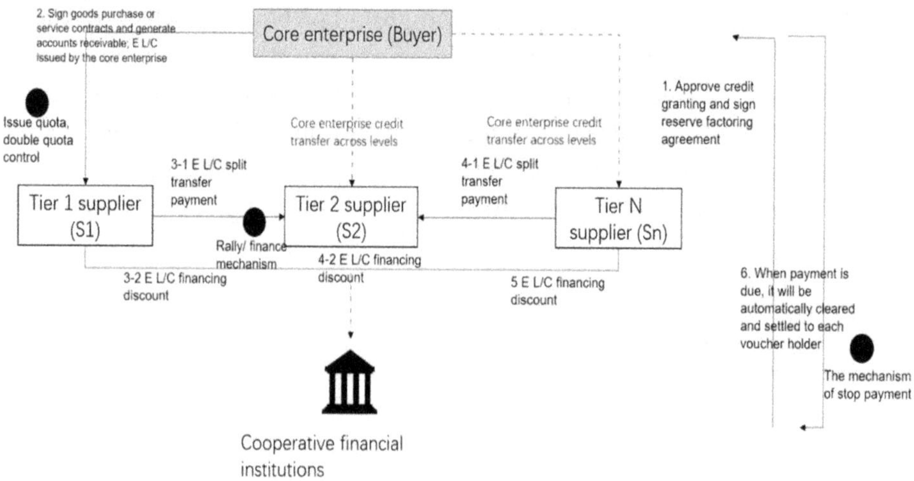

1. Through the immutable nature of supply chain trade data, the IoT technology can be used to monitor the flow of goods dynamically, record transaction, transportation and other node information, and reduce the cost (Anitha et al., 2021).
2. Through the generation of blockchain smart contracts, Anlian enterprises can solidify the path of capital settlement and cooperate with the payment system to reduce the incidence of capital consumption and default behaviors significantly (Kshetri, 2021).
3. In the case of reliable data, Anlian can break data islands, protect privacy and data security, effectively promote the integration of four streams in the supply chain system, and reduce the difficulty of risk control (Al-Talib et al., 2020).
4. The electronic vouchers generated by blockchain technology can realize flexible multi-level splitting, circulation and financing, transfer the core enterprise credit to the end supply chain, and solve the financing difficulties of small and micro suppliers (Smart City Of China, 2021).

This led to following impacts (Table 2):

The Case of Suzhou Black Cloud Intelligent Technology Co., Ltd

Suzhou Black Cloud Intelligent Technology Co. Ltd., takes artificial intelligence, blockchain, privacy computing and other cutting-edge technology research as the company's core research and development direction. They have formed an integrated intelligent technology research and exploration system converting intelligent government, industrial intelligent manufacturing, financial technology and other intelligent aspects. They have achieved a high rank in international technology assessment with the world's leading results, and number of research achievements have gained international attention (Black Cloud, 2021).

The annual shipbuilding completion in China has steadily ranked first in the world, but due to the rising costs of labor and materials and the lack of independent research and development capacity and other factors, the competitive advantage has ceased to exist. At the same time, the shipyards' blind expansion and the exaggerated profits from their previous performance have led to a disregard for supply chain management. The traditional supply chain model cannot meet the needs of modern shipping enterprises (Steuer et al., 2021). Now the profit margin of shipbuilding enterprises is declining and their survival is very difficult.

Table 2. Impact of the implementation

Project	Introduction	Impact
Agricultural Seed Industry-Longping Data Department supply chain financial service platform	Based on Longping's own seed industry chain and agricultural supply chain, it adopts the supply chain financial service mode of "N+1+N" to create its own industry and finance platform "Longping Chain" for Longping to achieve upstream suppliers' receivables financing and advance payment financing heart.	1. "Longping Chain" strengthens supply chain management, improves the collaborative efficiency of supply chain members, reduces the overall cost of the supply chain, and improves the comprehensive competitiveness of the supply chain. 2. "Longping Tong" generated on Longping Chain financial service platform is an electronic debt certificate based on blockchain technology. The holder can directly purchase and pay in "Longping Mall", and Longping Finance and its partners promise confirmation and discount.
Hainan International Energy Exchange Center based on supply chain financial services platform built on blockchain	The supply chain financial service platform based on Zhongqi Anlian blockchain technology meets the needs of financing product design for different enterprises in various scenarios of Hainan International Energy Exchange Center.	1.The "token" generated on the platform is an electronic debt certificate based on blockchain technology, supporting multi-level splitting and circulation, supporting 1~N level suppliers to hold the "token" financing, and confirming and discounting commitment of the partners of Hainan International Energy Exchange Center. 2. The platform supports multi-core enterprises to enter, and the data of suppliers and transactions are isolated from each other. After the completion of accounts receivable asset grade, support core enterprises to confirm the right of creditor's rights online; The platform connects with 10+ external interfaces and data services to assist business risk control audit, connects with bank capital account opening and online fund sorting of suppliers by combining online manual process audit.

Source: (Smart City Of China, 2021)

Figure 8. Agricultural seed industry-longping data department supply chain financial service platform
Source: www.zqalink.com

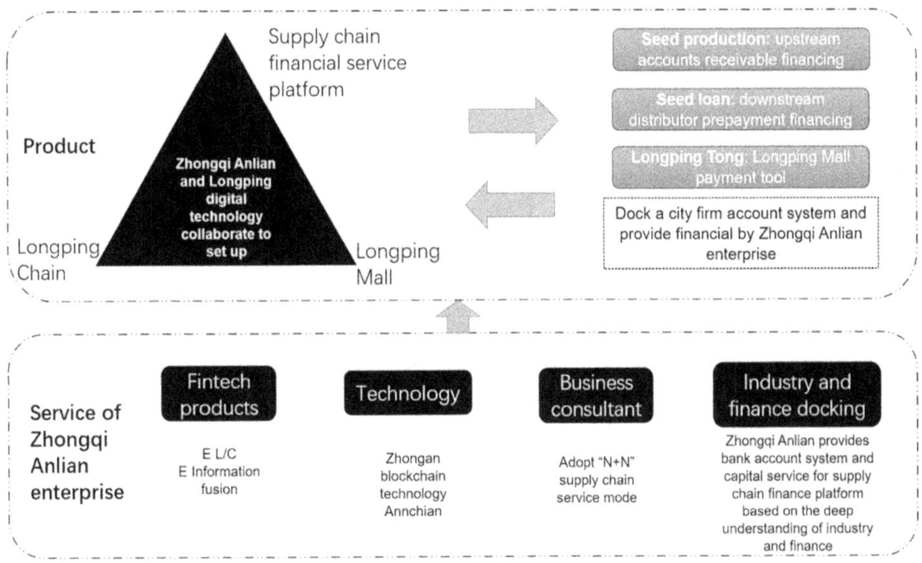

This project starts from the dissemination of supply chain management in the shipbuilding industry and the needs of collaborative design and manufacturing, and uses technologies such as smart contracts and encryption algorithms of the blockchain mechanism. This opened up the process nodes of the shipbuilding industry supply chain, and realized functions such as alliance construction, distributed member management, supply chain management, and quality management (Sairui Assesment, 2021).

Figure 9. The case of Suzhou Black Cloud Intelligent Technology Co., Ltd
Source: www.heiyunworld.com

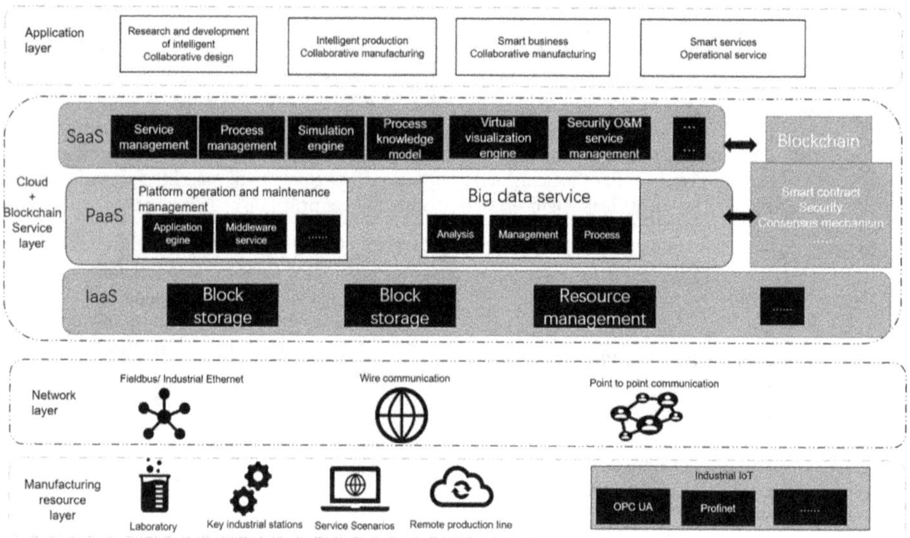

In order to keep pace with the times these enterprises have to innovate, this case provides four areas of improvement related to blockchain, including contract, data, device and traceability.

1. Contract

In the shipping industry, any link related to the transaction requires the signing of a contract, but the current offline contract signing causes a waste of paper, economic and time costs (Fiorentino & Bartolucci, 2021). To solve this problem, the enterprise uses smart contracts with blockchain systems. Information will be uploaded to blockchain to apply the business technology in the contract, through the intelligent processing to ensure authentication of all parties which are involved in the signing of the contract. The information is open, transparent and non-tampering. It ensures data information on the chain covering all contents of the contract, and can be carried out for authentication of the contract signing party. Moreover, the directly generated electronic contract reduces offline interviews and mailing and saves the time and operating cost of an offline contract (Zhang et al., 2021c).

2. Data

At present, every unit involved in the ship manufacturing supply chain saves its own data and keeps it centrally. The disadvantage of centralized preservation lies in the loss of files difficult or even impossible to retrieve, and cannot avoid the interference of human factors. To remedy this, the company uses the distributed storage and consensus mechanisms of the blockchain management to ensure information security (Zhang et al., 2021a). When the data of one node is damaged or inaccurate, the data can be recovered and compared with other nodes in time.

3. Device

With the increase of numbers of shipyard devices, the unified identification, authenticity and management between people and devices and among the devices becomes more important. The current workflow has many intermediate links, resulting in low resource utilization and efficiency of devices (Zhang et al., 2021b). Joining the cooperative manufacturing alliance and using smart devices as nodes to transmit data between different devices in each link, encryption protocols are used to achieve secure and efficient point-to-point communication between devices and ensure the security of data information (Sairui Assesment, 2021).

Figure 10. The device is connected to the alliance chain as a node
Source: Sairui Assessment

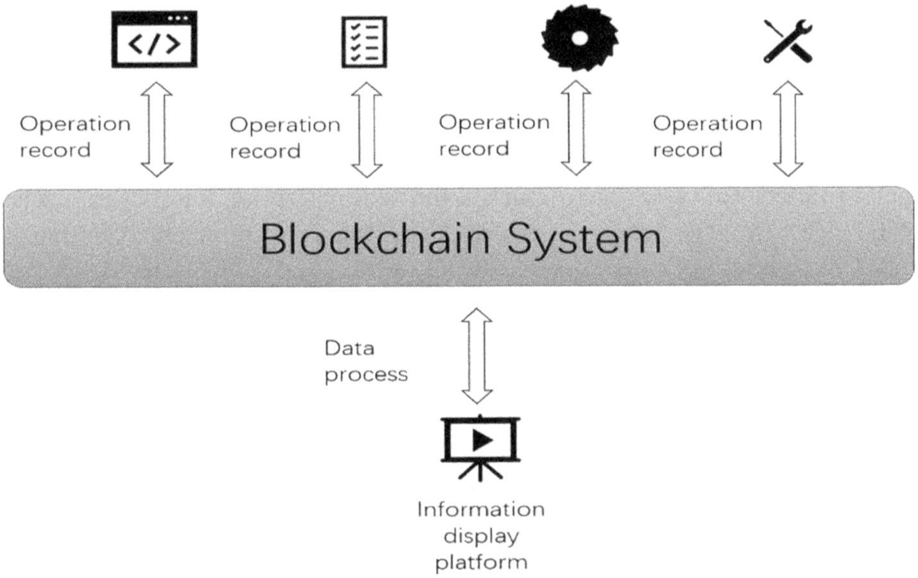

4. Traceability

At present, supply chain management is facing the problem of insufficient traceability. Loose procedures make it impossible to determine the problem at first. Without open and transparent process management and evidence management, problems in the traceability process cannot be found immediately. Blockchain can guarantee the authenticity and uniqueness of data at the technical level and provide support for process traceability (Centobelli et al., 2021). In terms of supply chain logistics, data owned by shipyards cover material device production, transportation, customs clearance, inspection, as well as port of loading and unloading, mode of transportation and other information of the whole process of production and manufacturing, providing physical paths for traceability (Sairui Assesment, 2021).

Figure 11. CSIC ship manufacturing chain management platform
Source: www.heiyunworld.com

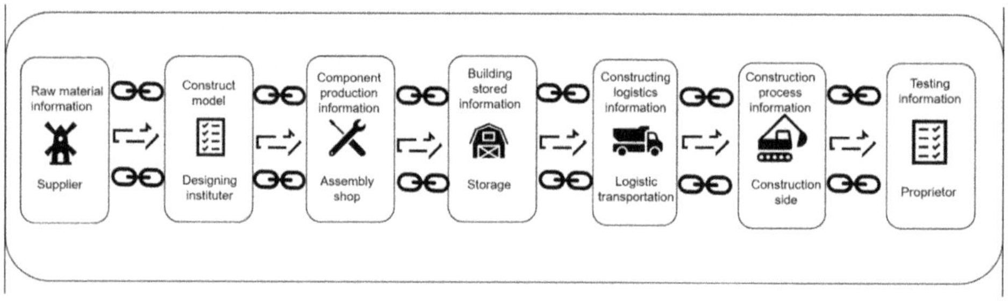

Tianjin TBC Blockchain Cross-Border Trade "Through Train" (i.e., Direct Market Access)

The "TBC blockchain Cross-border Trade Through Train" platform is designed for parallel import, customized in four varieties of value service, such as the trade enterprise, logistics enterprise, financial machine and the pipe body. The platform establishes the data standard of on-chain trade, allows the information of on-chain trade to be cross-compared and verified, and confirms the right of goods on the chain (Weiguan Tech, 2019). The digital asset system of enterprises is established, and the trustworthy traceability system of the whole permissible process of cross-competitive trade is created.

As there are many participants and the process of trade across borders is complex, it is difficult to determine the relationship of mutual trust. Characteristics of blockchain are highly consistent with the pain points of cross-border trade. Through the cross-comparison of data information of participating roles, it forms a reliable data storage chain, breaks the information island in cross-border trade, and thus solves the dilemma in the traditional process (Chen, 2019).

This overall technical module of this case is divided into four sections: the alliance blockchain basic platform, the trade through train application technology ecosystem, the IoT basic system and the artificial intelligence system. The "TBC blockchain Cross-border Trade Through Train" platform adopts the form of an alliance chain and introduces the real-name authentication system to meet the need for traceability in cross-border trade.

Figure 12. TBC blockchain cross-border trade through train
Source: www.zhiding.cn

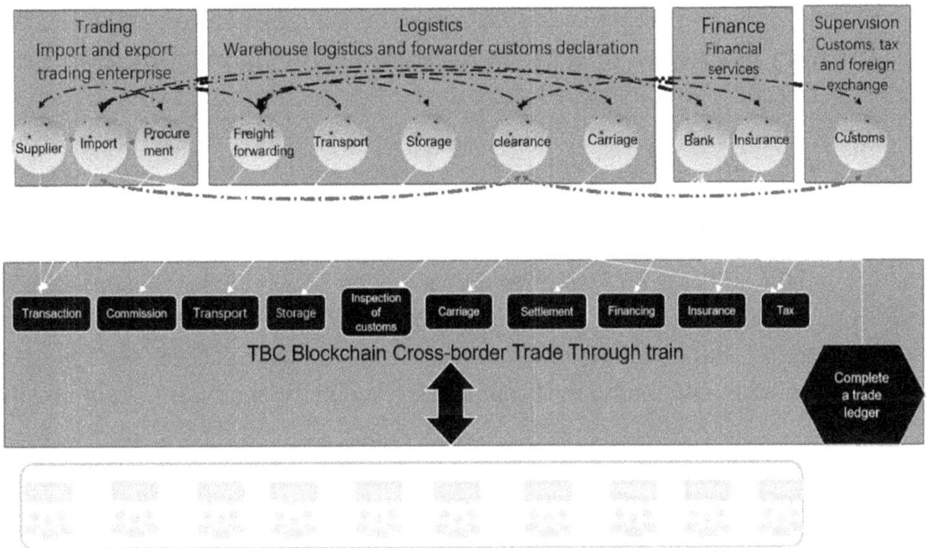

The project uses four advanced technologies: super ledger bottom layer, state secret business secret double-layer protection, blockchain identity and access control, and smart contract, and then completes the following innovations:

1. Ten business models of cross-border trade

Based on the United Nations "one buy one pay" model and combined with the actual cross-border trade business, the project refined ten business models of cross-border trade business models. This is the technical standard of its alliance chain and data collection architecture, including storage, governance and sharing, which is also the biggest innovation in the project design (Zutshi et al., 2021).

2. Single window docking with General Administration of customs

This feature realizes the connection between blockchain and single window docking, providing the customs personnel with the preset marks and inconsistent data of blockchain platform (Dabbagh et al., 2021). It forms the warning and results required by the internal customs departments such as classification, price review, anti-smuggling, tariffs and supervision, and sends them to the relevant departments for further business.

3. Set up a customs auxiliary document examination system based on blockchain data

It is set up based on the data blockchain customs auxiliary system, the examination of documents for different business roles to provide various business data for data inspection through the exploration of an practical application scenario and an application form in line with the industry and business classified scientific contribution value assessment system. This facilitates the customs internal orientation and support.

The environment created by the project has also brought commercial value. It has realized the cost reduction and efficiency increase of all roles in the industrial chain, greatly improved the synergistic ability of the industrial chain, and enhanced the competitiveness of China's industrial chain globally (Wang et al., 2021a).

Through platform enterprises, trading enterprises can accumulate credible data assets, so as to enjoy fast customs clearance, compliance cost reduction, low threshold, low interest financing products, and promote the development of honest trading enterprises. Logistics enterprises can obtain accurate high-quality customers and the authenticity data proved by many parties in the logistics process to solve the original dilemma of loss and damage of goods and unable to clarify the scope of responsibility (Jiang et al., 2021). Financial institutions can realize risk control in the whole process of capital, improve the safety of financial products, and develop new sources of revenue for financial institution.

Figure 13. Business process of TBC blockchain cross-border trade through train
Source: www.jinse.com

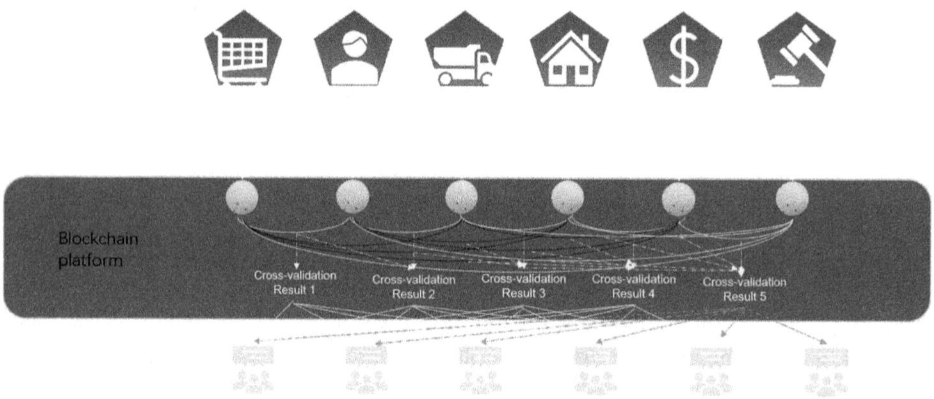

In the case the application scenario is recognized by many parties, it can make the overall ecological development of cross-border trade sound and promote the digital transformation and upgrading of traditional cross-border trade.

Tianjin "TBC Blockchain Cross-border Trade Through train" has been written into whitepapers and cases related to cross-border trade blockchain application by the General Administration of Customs of China and the World Customs Organization. It is a clear and effective implementation experience and path setting a benchmark for the application of blockchain model and technology in the field of cross-border trade by domestic government agencies, enterprises and various subsectors (Smart City Of China, 2021).

The Challenges of the Integration of IoT and Blockchain

While the integration of IoT and blockchain can bring many benefits, there are some challenges to integrate them at this stage.

Table 3. The challenges of the integration of IoT and blockchain

	Challenges	Introduction
The challenges of the integration of IoT and blockchain	TPS performance	IoT has a large amount of data and a strong real-time performance, which directly affects the network throughput
	Trusted upper chain data	The data could have been tampered with when more than half the nodes are hacked, so the upper chain data need to be trusted and secure
	Future-oriented digital economy society	IoT devices have been a mass, blockchain needs to consider how to communicate with it
	Complex hardware adaptation capability of IoT	Blockchain has to consider how to fit with IoT hardware with different capabilities

Source: www.chainnews.com

On the basis of these challenges, Wanxiang blockchain has put forward counter measures, namely RISC-V blockchain, and is being implemented in biological assets supervision, new energy vehicle battery life cycle management and the petrochemical industry trusted warehouse receipt (Wanxiang Blockchain, 2021), but the specific implementation ability remains to be tested.

CONCLUSION AND RECOMMENDATIONS

The economic environment of the supply chain is complex and changeable, and the smart economy requires the efficiency and security of all parties on the chain to be improved, which needs real-time, accurate and true information. The added value of the integration of IoT and blockchain can well meet the condition. IoT can collect data, but the accessibility, transparency and traceability of the system raises concerns about data privacy and security (Kayikci et al., 2021), and these deficiencies can be resolved with blockchain features. The management and decision-making layer of companies can quickly collect a wide range of data and make reasonable decisions through calculation. Investors can make better comparisons to reduce losses and crises. Regulators can also monitor abnormal phenomena in the industrial chain in an all-round and real-time way to carry out control. Technology is a necessary condition for the realization of the smart economy, and the above supply chain practices cannot be successfully implemented if there are technological constraints in terms of capacity and resources. At the same time, the strengthening of links between upstream and downstream enterprises meets the collaborative sharing of future smart economy and creates good conditions for sustainable development.

In fact, the sustainability of smart economy mainly reflects the ecological and industrial environment. Due to the timely circulation of information, effective design and decision-making of enterprises can greatly reduce the wasting of resources and improve waste recycling. Regulators will also be able to monitor emissions of production pollution, which is beneficial for the green economy now. In addition, enterprises strengthen communication and contact, and break down barriers, thereby promoting healthy competition between enterprises, and constantly promoting industrial innovation.

As the data shows, government policies and regulations have the greatest impact on the public, smart and secured supply chain management. The government needs to first set an example, and the supervision departments are to be arranged properly. Secondly, some large enterprises need to play a leading role in the supply chain management. Social relations are extremely important in the supply chain, which affects the sustainability concerns of upstream and downstream enterprises, thus driving the participation of small and medium-sized enterprises. Most importantly, some small and medium-sized enterprises, temporarily lagging behind, need to change the concept of supply chain management in order to keep up with the pace of smart economy, and need to be willing to innovate and transform. The ability of these three parties to make changes in the industry plays a significant role in the stability of the supply chain in society as a whole.

In this chapter, the authors reviewed the development environment of digital economy in China, sorted out the innovation and development of supply chain management under industry 4.0, and showed the rules and regulations of Chinese government for shaping smart economy. The chapter focused on the digital changes brought by the integration of Internet of Things and blockchain after industry 4.0, and summarized the value addition of the integration from several perspectives. In addition, the authors also collected Chinese cases of supply chain in terms of platform connecting various enterprises and cross-border trade for reference and discussion.

However, there are some limitations to this chapter. Due to the late development of digital economy policy, some specific data are difficult to collect. At the same time, after summarizing the benefits of IoT and blockchain integration in the supply chain management, the actual business case for IoT is not detailed enough compared to blockchain. Future studies can continue to collect the data to fill in the gaps.

ACKNOWLEDGMENT

We thank our colleagues from Soochow University, the Australian Studies Centre of Shanghai University and Krirk University as well as the independent research colleagues who provided insight and expertise that greatly assisted the research, although they may not agree with all of the interpretations/conclusions of this paper. In addition, we thank China Knowledge for supporting our research.

REFERENCES

Aheleroff, S., Zhong, R. Y., & Xu, X. (2020). A Digital Twin Reference for Mass Personalization in Industry 4.0. *Procedia CIRP*, *93*, 228–233. doi:10.1016/j.procir.2020.04.023

Al-Talib, M., Melhem, W. Y., Anosike, A. I., Garza Reyes, J. A., Nadeem, S. P., & kumar, A. (2020). Achieving resilience in the supply chain by applying IoT technology. *Procedia CIRP*, *91*, 752–757. doi:10.1016/j.procir.2020.02.231

Ali, M. H., Chung, L., Kumar, A., Zailani, S., & Tan, K. H. (2021). A sustainable Blockchain framework for the halal food supply chain: Lessons from Malaysia. *Technological Forecasting and Social Change*, *170*, 120870. Advance online publication. doi:10.1016/j.techfore.2021.120870

Anitha, K., Palaksha Reddy, K., Krishnamoorthy, N., & Jaiswal, S. (2021). IoT's in enabling the supply chain visibility and connectivity and optimization of performance. *Materials Today: Proceedings*. Advance online publication. doi:10.1016/j.matpr.2020.12.343

Arner, D. W. (2016). FinTech, RegTech and the Reconceptualization of Financial Regulation. Academic Press.

Babun, L., Denney, K., Celik, Z. B., McDaniel, P., & Uluagac, A. S. (2021). A survey on IoT platforms: Communication, security, and privacy perspectives. *Computer Networks*, *192*, 108040. Advance online publication. doi:10.1016/j.comnet.2021.108040

Balci, G. (2021). Digitalization in container shipping: Do perception and satisfaction regarding digital products in a non-technology industry affect overall customer loyalty? *Technological Forecasting and Social Change*, *172*, 121016. Advance online publication. doi:10.1016/j.techfore.2021.121016

Bandara, E., Tosh, D., Foytik, P., Shetty, S., Ranasinghe, N., & De Zoysa, K. (2021). Tikiri—Towards a lightweight blockchain for IoT. *Future Generation Computer Systems*, *119*, 154–165. doi:10.1016/j.future.2021.02.006

Birkel, H., & Müller, J. M. (2021). Potentials of industry 4.0 for supply chain management within the triple bottom line of sustainability – A systematic literature review. *Journal of Cleaner Production*, *289*, 125612. Advance online publication. doi:10.1016/j.jclepro.2020.125612

Bonilla, S., Silva, H., Terra da Silva, M., Franco Gonçalves, R., & Sacomano, J. (2018). Industry 4.0 and Sustainability Implications: A Scenario-Based Analysis of the Impacts and Challenges. *Sustainability*, *10*(10), 3740. Advance online publication. doi:10.3390u10103740

Centobelli, P., Cerchione, R., Vecchio, P. D., Oropallo, E., & Secundo, G. (2021). Blockchain technology for bridging trust, traceability and transparency in circular supply chain. *Information & Management*, 103508. Advance online publication. doi:10.1016/j.im.2021.103508

Černý, M., Gogola, M., Kubaľák, S., & Ondruš, J. (2021). Blockchain technology as a new driver in supply chain. *Transportation Research Procedia*, *55*, 299–306. doi:10.1016/j.trpro.2021.06.034

Chartered Institute of Procurement and Supply (CIPS). (n.d.). *What Is Procurement and Supply?* CIPS.

Chen, X. (2019). *Cross-border trade blockchain white paper*. Academic Press.

China Financial Information Industry Association (CFIIA). (2021). *2021 Global Blockchain Innovative Application Demonstration Case Set*. Author.

CloudB. (2021). http://www.heiyunworld.com/

Cong, L. W. (2021). Internet of Things: Business Economics and Applications. In M. Pompella (Ed.), *Review of Review of BusinessBusiness* (Vol. 41, pp. 15–30). University of Siena.

Cooper, M. C., Lambert, D. M., & Pagh, J. D. (1997). Supply Chain Management: More Than a New Name for Logistics. *International Journal of Logistics Management*, *8*(1), 1–14. doi:10.1108/09574099710805556

Council of Supply Chain Management Professionals (CSCMP). (2013). *SCM Definitions and Glossary of Terms*. https://cscmp.org/CSCMP/Academia/SCM_Definitions_and_Glossary_of_Terms/CSCMP/Educate/SCM_Definitions_and_Glossary_of_Terms.aspx?hkey=60879588-f65f-4ab5-8c4b-6878815ef921

Dabbagh, M., Choo, K.-K. R., Beheshti, A., Tahir, M., & Safa, N. S. (2021). A survey of empirical performance evaluation of permissioned blockchain platforms: Challenges and opportunities. *Computers & Security*, *100*, 102078. Advance online publication. doi:10.1016/j.cose.2020.102078

Dai, J., Xie, L., & Chu, Z. (2021). Developing sustainable supply chain management: The interplay of institutional pressures and sustainability capabilities. *Sustainable Production and Consumption, 28*, 254–268. doi:10.1016/j.spc.2021.04.017

Daim, T., Lai, K. K., Yalcin, H., Alsoubie, F., & Kumar, V. (2020). Forecasting technological positioning through technology knowledge redundancy: Patent citation analysis of IoT, cybersecurity, and Blockchain. *Technological Forecasting and Social Change, 161*, 120329. Advance online publication. doi:10.1016/j.techfore.2020.120329

Dietrich, F., Ge, Y., Turgut, A., Louw, L., & Palm, D. (2021). Review and analysis of blockchain projects in supply chain management. *Procedia Computer Science, 180*, 724–733. doi:10.1016/j.procs.2021.01.295

Fiorentino, S., & Bartolucci, S. (2021). Blockchain-based smart contracts as new governance tools for the sharing economy. *Cities (London, England), 117*, 103325. Advance online publication. doi:10.1016/j.cities.2021.103325

Infrastructure, N., & Opportunities, N. (2020). *The White Paper on The Development of China's Smart Economy*. https://www.cdrf.org.cn/jjhdt/5455.htm

Frick, N. R. J., Wilms, K. L., Brachten, F., Hetjens, T., Stieglitz, S., & Ross, B. (2021). The perceived surveillance of conversations through smart devices. *Electronic Commerce Research and Applications, 47*, 101046. Advance online publication. doi:10.1016/j.elerap.2021.101046

Gulati, K., Kumar Boddu, R. S., Kapila, D., Bangare, S. L., Chandnani, N., & Saravanan, G. (2021). A review paper on wireless sensor network techniques in Internet of Things (IoT). *Materials Today: Proceedings*. Advance online publication. doi:10.1016/j.matpr.2021.05.067

Guo, J., Zhou, S., Chen, J., & Chen, Q. (2021). How information technology capability and knowledge integration capability interact to affect business model design: A polynomial regression with response surface analysis. *Technological Forecasting and Social Change, 170*, 120935. Advance online publication. doi:10.1016/j.techfore.2021.120935

Han, H. (2018). Upgrading informaion consumption and expanding the digital economy Electronic information consumption adds luster to smart life. *Economic Daily*. http://www.gov.cn/xinwen/2018-04/17/content_5283099.htm

Hangzhou Bureau of Statistics. (2020). Hangzhou Statistical Yearbook.

Hu, Q. (2019). *Two Session Observation Smart in action*. http://www.eeo.com.cn/2019/0306/349511.shtml

Huang, J., Mei, Z., & Li, Z. (2020). Business and financial information integration and voluntary management earnings forecasts. *China Journal of Accounting Research, 13*(3), 291–307. doi:10.1016/j.cjar.2020.07.002

Jamil, S. (2021). From digital divide to digital inclusion: Challenges for wide-ranging digitalization in Pakistan. *Telecommunications Policy, 45*(8), 102206. Advance online publication. doi:10.1016/j.telpol.2021.102206

Javaid, M. (2021). Blockchain technology applications for Industry 4.0: A literature-based review. *Blockchain: Research and Applications*. doi:10.1016/j.bcra.2021.100027

Jiang, S. (2021). Blockchain competition: The tradeoff between platform stability and efficiency. *European Journal of Operational Research*. Advance online publication. doi:10.1016/j.ejor.2021.05.031

Jua. (2021). *Zhongqi Anlian- the best supply chain finance solution providers*. https://mp.weixin.qq.com/s?__biz=MzI0NTExMjc1Nw==&mid=2247484946&idx=1&sn=4094f4e4b0c4610be3517005a5c2bb13&chksm=e952ccc8de2545de4d0cc309eb0ad5db70784a645f6f006ec7c1a453b0ea664923127d6dba8e&token=510349077&lang=zh_CN#rd

Karale, A. (2021). The Challenges of IoT Addressing Security, Ethics, Privacy, and Laws. *Internet of Things*, *15*, 100420. Advance online publication. doi:10.1016/j.iot.2021.100420

Kayikci, Y., Kazancoglu, Y., Lafci, C., & Gozacan, N. (2021). Exploring barriers to smart and sustainable circular economy: The case of an automotive eco-cluster. *Journal of Cleaner Production*, *314*, 127920. Advance online publication. doi:10.1016/j.jclepro.2021.127920

Kshetri, N. (2021). Blockchain and sustainable supply chain management in developing countries. *International Journal of Information Management*, *60*, 102376. Advance online publication. doi:10.1016/j.ijinfomgt.2021.102376

Kumar, R., & Sharma, R. (2021). Leveraging Blockchain for Ensuring Trust in IoT: A Survey. *Journal of King Saud University - Computer and Information Sciences*. doi:10.1016/j.jksuci.2021.09.004

Kumar, S., & Bhatia, M. S. (2021). Environmental dynamism, industry 4.0 and performance: Mediating role of organizational and technological factors. *Industrial Marketing Management*, *95*, 54–64. doi:10.1016/j.indmarman.2021.03.010

Laksch, J. S., & Borsato, M. (2019). Method for digital evaluation of existing production systems adequacy to changes in product engineering in the context of the automotive industry. *Advanced Engineering Informatics*, *42*, 100942. Advance online publication. doi:10.1016/j.aei.2019.100942

Li, Y., Dai, J., & Cui, L. (2020). The impact of digital technologies on economic and environmental performance in the context of industry 4.0: A moderated mediation model. *International Journal of Production Economics*, *229*, 107777. Advance online publication. doi:10.1016/j.ijpe.2020.107777

Li, Z., Ge, R. Y., Guo, X. S., & Cai, L. (2021). Can individual investors learn from experience in online P2P lending? Evidence from China. *The North American Journal of Economics and Finance*, *58*, 101524. Advance online publication. doi:10.1016/j.najef.2021.101524

Mehta, D., & Senn-Kalb, L. (2021). *In-depth: Industry 4.0 2021*. Academic Press.

Monaco, E. (2019). What FinTech Can Learn from High-Frequency Trading: Economic Consequences, Open Issues and Future of Corporate Disclosure. In T. Lynn, J. G. Mooney, P. Rosati, & M. Cummins (Eds.), *Disrupting Finance* (pp. 51–70). Springer Nature Switzerland AG. doi:10.1007/978-3-030-02330-0_4

Müller, J. M., Veile, J. W., & Voigt, K.-I. (2020). Prerequisites and incentives for digital information sharing in Industry 4.0 – An international comparison across data types. *Computers & Industrial Engineering*, *148*, 106733. Advance online publication. doi:10.1016/j.cie.2020.106733

National Bureau of Statistics. (2020). *E-procurement amount (10 billion yuan)*. Author.

Nespoli, P., Díaz-López, D., & Gómez Mármol, F. (2021). Cyberprotection in IoT environments: A dynamic rule-based solution to defend smart devices. *Journal of Information Security and Applications*, *60*, 102878. Advance online publication. doi:10.1016/j.jisa.2021.102878

Ni, W., & Sun, H. (2019). The effect of sustainable supply chain management on business performance: Implications for integrating the entire supply chain in the Chinese manufacturing sector. *Journal of Cleaner Production*, *232*, 1176–1186. doi:10.1016/j.jclepro.2019.05.384

Nicoletti, B. (2018). Fintech and Procurement Finance 4.0. In Procurement Finance (pp. 155-248). doi:10.1007/978-3-030-02140-5_6

North, D. (1990). *Institutions, Institutional Change and Economic Performance*. Cambridge University. doi:10.1017/CBO9780511808678

O'Sullivan, M., & Sheahan, C. (2019). Using Serious Games to Inform Mass Customization Production Methods from the Fuzzy Front-End of New Product Development. *Procedia Manufacturing*, *38*, 478–487. doi:10.1016/j.promfg.2020.01.061

People's Daily. (2021). *China's digital economy has become more dynamic*. http://www.gov.cn/xinwen/2021-03/22/content_5594357.htm

Prümmer, M., Bergs, T., Arntz, K., & Lürken, C. (2019). Periphery evaluation for interlinked manufacturing systems in industrial tooling. *Procedia CIRP*, *81*, 470–475. doi:10.1016/j.procir.2019.03.120

Rejeb, A., Simske, S., Rejeb, K., Treiblmaier, H., & Zailani, S. (2020). Internet of Things research in supply chain management and logistics: A bibliometric analysis. *Internet of Things*, *12*, 100318. Advance online publication. doi:10.1016/j.iot.2020.100318

Assesment, S. (2021). *Industrial application blockchain practice cases*. https://mp.weixin.qq.com/s?__biz=MzUxMzc4MjA4NQ==&mid=2247484874&idx=1&sn=8e0af725d36cdd2c5969b39dc91733ed&chksm=f94ebde0ce3934f669ccbbd3d1063897bbbee93e5196ad5d2b3c55d7d60a394936635c9c99b1&mpshare=1&srcid=0814HgTw2ah9yUHfINldH7VL&sharer_sharetime=1628948606761&sharer_shareid=3f439b70854717410bbd97cd511f119b&from=singlemessage&scene=1&subscene=10000&clicktime=1630039298&enterid=1630039298&ascene=1&devicetype=android-29&version=28000a3d&nettype=WIFI&abtest_cookie=AAACAA%3D%3D&lang=zh_CN&exportkey=AxbisCB%2Fo%2FxIBv6SsogS%2FAk%3D&pass_ticket=rr0HBDyFaypryLmw2%2Bgr5c%2Fa%2F4txJeBnfQLqo6oCAIRej4aOGCXxfFxyv8BAPUJI&wx_header=1

Šarac, M., Pavlović, N., Bacanin, N., Al-Turjman, F., & Adamović, S. (2021). Increasing privacy and security by integrating a Blockchain Secure Interface into an IoT Device Security Gateway Architecture. *Energy Reports*, *7*, 8075–8082. Advance online publication. doi:10.1016/j.egyr.2021.07.078

Saxena, S., Bhushan, B., & Ahad, M. A. (2021). Blockchain based solutions to secure IoT: Background, integration trends and a way forward. *Journal of Network and Computer Applications*, *181*, 103050. Advance online publication. doi:10.1016/j.jnca.2021.103050

Scholten, K., & Fynes, B. (2017). Risk and Uncertainty Management for Sustainable Supply Chains. In Sustainable Supply Chains (pp. 413-436). doi:10.1007/978-3-319-29791-0_19

Scott, W. R. (2008). *Institutions and organizations: Ideas and interests* (3rd ed.). SAGE Publications.

Scott, W. R. (2008). Institutions and Organizations: Ideas and Interests. Academic Press.

Shaikh, A. A., Sharma, R., & Karjaluoto, H. (2020). Digital innovation & enterprise in the sharing economy: An action research agenda. *Digital Business*, *1*(1), 100002. Advance online publication. doi:10.1016/j.digbus.2021.100002

Smart City of China. (2021). https://mp.weixin.qq.com/s?__biz=MzA3ODA1MzMwNw==&mid=2650542117&idx=1&sn=94ec06a764d893d8bd6c0e60d10e0545&chksm=87401af1b03793e758d565e3c7a3f0d5b21029e62caff6e8d3d64002301d69427c10d5f80f3e&mpshare=1&srcid=0814Ry69kbJB4NxF8GIsJu4a&sharer_sharetime=1628948491962&sharer_shareid=3f439b70854717410bbd97cd511f119b&from=singlemessage&scene=1&subscene=10000&clicktime=1630219119&enterid=1630219119&ascene=1&devicetype=android-29&version=28000a3d&nettype=WIFI&abtest_cookie=AAACAA%3D%3D&lang=zh_CN&exportkey=A3%2Ftehxk17AJjE2UCFxIVHk%3D&pass_ticket=Ug8WmXDfzeZqV%2BuFb4h9aKcdozrVzzMS8T2Rn5UWSFwbBqI3chjjcsw25hOdTLnA&wx_header=1

Steuer, B., Staudner, M., & Ramusch, R. (2021). Role and potential of the circular economy in managing end-of-life ships in china. *Resources, Conservation and Recycling*, *164*, 105039. doi:10.1016/j.resconrec.2020.105039 PMID:32929303

Terrada, L., Khaïli, M. E., & Ouajji, H. (2020). Multi-Agents System Implementation for Supply Chain Management Making-Decision. *Procedia Computer Science*, *177*, 624–630. doi:10.1016/j.procs.2020.10.089

Turban, E., Outland, J., King, D., Lee, J. K., Liang, T.-P., & Turban, D. C. (2018). Electronic Commerce 2018. *Electronic Commerce*, *2018*. Advance online publication. doi:10.1007/978-3-319-58715-8

Wang, J., Liu, J., Wang, F., & Yue, X. (2021a). Blockchain technology for port logistics capability: Exclusive or sharing. *Transportation Research Part B: Methodological*, *149*, 347–392. doi:10.1016/j.trb.2021.05.010

Wang, L., Luo, X. R., Lee, F., & Benitez, J. (2021b). Value creation in blockchain-driven supply chain finance. *Information & Management*, 103510. Advance online publication. doi:10.1016/j.im.2021.103510

Wang, L., Ma, Y., Zhu, L., Wang, X., Cong, H., & Shi, T. (2021c). Design of integrated energy market cloud service platform based on blockchain smart contract. *International Journal of Electrical Power & Energy Systems*, *135*, 107515. Advance online publication. doi:10.1016/j.ijepes.2021.107515

Wang, P., Valerdi, R., Zhou, S., & Li, L. (2015). Introduction: Advances in IoT research and applications. *Information Systems Frontiers*, *17*(2), 239–241. doi:10.100710796-015-9549-2

Blockchain, W. (2021). *China information chip another step forward.* https://mp.weixin.qq.com/s/uyhguvWakwK8j-vGbXo0uA

Wei, X., Prybutok, V., & Sauser, B. (2021). Review of supply chain management within project management. *Project Leadership and Society*, *2*, 100013. Advance online publication. doi:10.1016/j.plas.2021.100013

Weiguan Tech. (2019). *Tianjin TBC Blockchain Cross-border Trade Through train- the world's first demonstration project*. Author.

Weilian & Puhuayongdao. (2018). *2018 China's Blockchain (non-financial) Application Market Survey Report*. www.pwccn.com

Xie, Z., Wang, J., & Miao, L. (2021). Big data and emerging market firms' innovation in an open economy: The diversification strategy perspective. *Technological Forecasting and Social Change*, *173*, 121091. Advance online publication. doi:10.1016/j.techfore.2021.121091

Xinhua. (2015). *Smart, green, healthy and safe--focus on consumption development during the 13th Five-Year Plan period*. http://www.gov.cn/xinwen/2015-11/10/content_5006890.htm

Xinhua. (2017). *The development of China's digital economy promotes global openness and sharing*. http://www.gov.cn/xinwen/2017-12/04/content_5244456.htm

Xinhua. (2021a). *China's digital economy has reached 35.8 trillion yuan*. http://www.gov.cn/xinwen/2020-11/23/content_5563612.htm

Xinhua. (2021b). *"Zhejiang Fair Online" system online all-weather multi-directional intelligent supervision platform economy*. http://www.gov.cn/xinwen/2021-02/26/content_5589087.htm

Ya, W. (2016). Committee member Guo Guangchang: we will focus on building a "smart economy" to improve total factor productivity. *Xinhua*. http://www.gov.cn/xinwen/2016-03/11/content_5052414.htm

Ying, Z. (2017). The eight cities of Shenyang Economic Zone jointly build smart city clusters. *Liaoning Daily*. http://www.gov.cn/xinwen/2017-09/25/content_5227290.htm

Ying, Z. (2020). Wisdom for a Better Future- Sidelights of the 2020 World Digital Economy Conference. *Xinhua*. http://www.gov.cn/xinwen/2020-09/14/content_5543181.htm

Yuan, G., Ye, Q., & Sun, Y. (2021). Financial innovation, information screening and industries' green innovation— Industry-level evidence from the OECD. *Technological Forecasting and Social Change*, *171*, 120998. Advance online publication. doi:10.1016/j.techfore.2021.120998

Zhang, C., Ni, Z., Xu, Y., Luo, E., Chen, L., & Zhang, Y. (2021a). A trustworthy industrial data management scheme based on redactable blockchain. *Journal of Parallel and Distributed Computing*, *152*, 167–176. doi:10.1016/j.jpdc.2021.02.026

Zhang, R., Song, M., Li, T., Yu, Z., Dai, Y., Liu, X., & Wang, G. (2021b). Democratic learning: Hardware/software co-design for lightweight blockchain-secured on-device machine learning. *Journal of Systems Architecture*, *118*, 102205. Advance online publication. doi:10.1016/j.sysarc.2021.102205

Zhang, T., Li, J. J., & Jiang, X. (2021c). Supply chain finance based on smart contract. *Procedia Computer Science*, *187*, 12–17. doi:10.1016/j.procs.2021.04.027

Zhang, Y., Mao, M., Rau, P.-L. P., Choe, P., Bela, L., & Wang, F. (2013). Exploring factors influencing multitasking interaction with multiple smart devices. *Computers in Human Behavior*, *29*(6), 2579–2588. doi:10.1016/j.chb.2013.06.042

Zhou, D., Kautonen, M., Dai, W., & Zhang, H. (2021). Exploring how digitalization influences incumbents in financial services: The role of entrepreneurial orientation, firm assets, and organizational legitimacy. *Technological Forecasting and Social Change*, *173*, 121120. Advance online publication. doi:10.1016/j.techfore.2021.121120

Zorzini, M., Stevenson, M., & Hendry, L. C. (2012). Customer Enquiry Management in global supply chains: A comparative multi-case study analysis. *European Management Journal*, *30*(2), 121–140. Advance online publication. doi:10.1016/j.emj.2011.10.006

Zutshi, A., Grilo, A., & Nodehi, T. (2021). The value proposition of blockchain technologies and its impact on Digital Platforms. *Computers & Industrial Engineering*, *155*, 107187. Advance online publication. doi:10.1016/j.cie.2021.107187

Zweber, J. (2017). Digital Thread and Twin for Systems Engineering: Requirements to Design. *55th AIAA Aerospace Sciences Meeting*. 10.2514/6.2017-0875

Chapter 11
Transformation of Traditional Gas Industries to Blockchain-Enabled Gas Industries:
A Secured Supply Chain Strategy for Tracking Gas

Vladimir Nikolaevich Kustov
Saint Petersburg State University of Railway Transport of Emperor Alexander I, Russia

ABSTRACT

The author considers the main purpose of this chapter to be the presentation of a modern approach to the digital transformation of traditional business processes in the gas industry. Using the example of a pilot project successfully implemented in the gas industry, the author shows the process of synthesizing a high-tech supply chain infrastructure based on blockchain. The presentation begins with a description of the main business processes of the supply chain. The functions for all participants of the system are described and visualized in detail. The main components of the system are considered: digital dispatcher, supply monitor, interaction interfaces, and production environment. A comparative analysis of the security of modern blockchain platforms is provided. The author carefully analyzes the technologies for creating and ensuring the security of smart contracts and offers a step-by-step method for implementing secure smart contracts. At the end of the chapter, the results of choosing the most secure blockchain platforms are presented.

INTRODUCTION

Recently, only a lazy person has not written or talked about blockchain technology. Blockchain – what is it: the technology of the future or self-deception in the light of its little knowledge and applicability today? It is possible to argue, answering this question, for a long time and persistently. This chapter discusses the

DOI: 10.4018/978-1-7998-8697-6.ch011

Copyright © 2022, IGI Global. Copying or distributing in print or electronic forms without written permission of IGI Global is prohibited.

technological features of ensuring the security of this new technology, which often remain "behind the scenes" or represent some superficial, short, and non-revealing description (Kustov & Stankevich, 2019).

The views on blockchain technology expressed by experts in the field of information security and information technologies in print and oral presentations can be defined as opposed and considered at two criteria levels (Kustov & Stankevich, 2018):

1. prospects for implementation;
2. the consequences of performance.

The second criterion directly follows from the first, and both allow us to divide experts into skeptics and enthusiasts. At the first level – "Prospects" – opinions are divided into those that express a sincere belief in blockchain and its existence within a variety of systems and services and those that deny it, referring to the possibility of an alternative, simpler, and, consequently, more reliable approaches to solving specific tasks. The second criterion – "Consequences" - divides experts into those who express unbridled delight in the light of the upcoming "revolution" (Swan, 2018), comparable to the creation of the Internet, and those who associate blockchain with the death of existing information and payment systems (Chris, 2017). To the point, the creator of the blockchain, Satoshi Nakomoto, did not expect such a sad outcome in any way (Satoshi, 2008).

However, in practice, a huge mass of positive examples of the use of new technology prevails (Eman et al., 2020), (Nin et al., 2021), (Ahmed et al., 2021). The gas industry is no exception, and much attention is paid to the distributed registry technology.

So, the author considers the *main purpose* of this chapter to be the presentation of a modern approach to the digital transformation of traditional business processes in the gas industry. In recent years, several blockchain pilot projects have been implemented in the gas industry. Using the example of a pilot project successfully implemented in the gas industry, the author shows the process of synthesizing a high-tech supply chain infrastructure based on blockchain. Three completed pilot projects are particularly indicative:

1. A pilot project to create a supply efficiency management system using blockchain technology.
2. Develop a technological platform prototype for automating concluding, monitoring, and executing contracts based on blockchain technology.
3. Development of a new digital Smart Fuel platform using blockchain technology.

As part of the first project, gas industry specialists tested blockchain technology and the Internet of Things concept in material and technical resources logistics.

Radiofrequency tags (RFID) and satellite positioning sensors (GPS) were installed by technical specialists on the shut-off valves and pipe products purchased for the gas production company. At the shipment stage of pipe product shipment from the manufacturer, a document with information about the delivery was formed after reading the RFID tags. The GPS sensor made it possible to monitor cargo movement to the storage base, the speed of its movement, the number, and the duration of stops on the way. All data received from the devices was recorded by a smart contract and reflected in the blockchain. In the future, information about warehouse and transport operations — entering products into a warehouse, moving to a berth for loading, delivery to a platform in the Pechora Sea — was transmitted according to a similar scheme. The blockchain provided an inextricable link between the physical delivery, all concurrent processes, and document flow and allowed all participants to access reliable information in encrypted form.

The successful implementation of the pilot project confirmed the possibility of using blockchain technology in supply chain management. The gas industry is considering the prospects for further using the potential of the blockchain and replicating the experience gained.

"Blockchain in deliveries has allowed us to create an ecosystem for the interaction of all participants in the process, such as the manufacturer, inspector, logistics operator, warehouse, and consumer. We see potential in the development and further application of the technology" (Karaev, 2018).

According to the second project, a prototype of a technological platform was developed on the basis of blockchain technology, which provides for the automation of the process of concluding, monitoring, and executing contracts. This system also assumes automatic arbitration and automatic calculation of gas payments. The developed system is open to all participants of the contractual process, and it is completely protected from unauthorized interference and unauthorized changes. The gas industry is currently actively working on implementing automating the support of the contractual process for gas supplies. At the initial stage, this work is carried out only for large industrial gas consumers. "The digital economy is the future that has already come. This project is a vivid example of a combination of industry, technological and financial expertise, in which all participants benefit" (Vanurina, 2019).

As part of the third project, a new Smart Fuel platform was developed based on the blockchain, designed to accelerate mutual settlements between the fuel operator and the airline.

As a result of its use, the settlement time was reduced from four days to fifteen seconds. "The Smart Fuel digital system simplifies the work of our partners as much as possible and increases the financial security of mutual settlements. Our solution allows us to take into account all the needs of airlines, reduce import dependence on foreign services, and has a high potential for scaling for the aviation industry" (Egorov, 2021).

Because of the implementation of the pilot projects mentioned above, the following estimates of their economic efficiency were obtained:

1. Reducing administrative and commercial costs by 5-10% (thanks to the pilot projects) allows large oil and gas companies to save 0.4-0.7 billion dollars.
2. One of the largest oil and gas companies estimated that the use of blockchain in the oil and gas business increases the company's efficiency by 10-15%.
3. This oil and gas company believes that implementing the pilot project will allow the company to save up to 10% of tax costs.

Limiting the scope of this chapter, the author further examines in more detail the stages of work on only one of these projects. To create and implement modern technologies at gas industry enterprises, a pilot project was carried out on the topic "Managing the quality of material and technical resources and supply efficiency using Blockchain technology," consisting of the following main stages:

1. Research and graphical visualization of the main business processes of the supply efficiency management system at gas industry enterprises using Blockchain technology.
2. Comparative analysis of blockchain platforms, testing, and selection of a platform for implementation. Let's take a closer look at the pilot design process by the steps listed above.

RESEARCH AND GRAPHICAL VISUALIZATION OF THE MAIN BUSINESS PROCESSES OF THE SUPPLY EFFICIENCY MANAGEMENT SYSTEM

The urgent need to develop a system for tracking the supply of MTR at gas industry enterprises is due to the very complex and time-consuming interaction of supply participants who have their separate information systems (IS). Data processing in the existing supply system is carried out exclusively centrally using data processing Centers (DPC). There was a need to compare data processing processes centrally with the help of a data center and decentralized with the help of distributed registry technology (blockchain). The results of the comparison are presented in Table 1.

As can be seen from Table 1, the use of Blockchain technology in data processing has significant advantages:

- Increasing the level of trust,
- Control of the business process by all participants of the process,
- Control of user access by consensus decision,
- Ensuring the automatically guaranteed fulfillment of contractual obligations through the use of smart contracts,
- Using the built-in certified cryptographic protection tools (CCPT),
- Guaranteed data immutability,
- The absence of expensive and security-sensitive DPC,
- Using standard communication channels,
- Increased reliability due to profound territorial decentralization,
- Extensive scaling of the proposed solution based on the use of boxed versions of the developed product.

The listed set of very significant advantages is a weighty argument in favor of using Blockchain technology.

As for the current situation in the existing supply system, as can be seen from Figure 1, the existing supply system was completely outdated, redundant, and did not meet modern concepts. The main components of a typical information system (IS) of an ancient supply chain, shown in Figure 1, are:

- IS operator;
- Operator IS;
- IS of the Customer (gas company);
- IS of the Transport company;
- Manufacturer IS;
- The Inspector IS.

All information systems were heterogeneous. Each gas company created its own corporate IS. Communication channels were not standardized. As shown in Figure 1, during the interaction of the Transport Company's IS ↔ the Customer's IS, and the operator IS ↔ the inspector IS, the most archaic methods of communication were observed, up to the "pigeon mail", of course, allegorically.

Three types of communication were actively used: telephone (IS of the inspector ↔ IS of the Operator), regular mail (IS of the Manufacturer ↔ IS of the Customer), paper document management: IS of the Manufacturer ↔ IS of the Operator, IS of the Transport Company ↔ IS of the Inspector. Sometimes non-traditional types of communication were also used (for example, courier delivery) for the Customer's IS ↔ The Transport Company's IP. The customers were the largest gas and gas transportation companies. Large telecommunications companies acted as operators, logistics operators acted as transport companies, metallurgical, and pipe enterprises acted as producers, since the main supply was pipe products. The supervisory gas company specially created for this purpose acts as an Inspector.

In this situation, it was decided to reorganize the supply chain. The main goal of the reorganization was to create a supply process controlled by a program code (a special software platform). The general scheme of the pilot project is shown in Figure 2.

Figure 1. General view of the supply chain

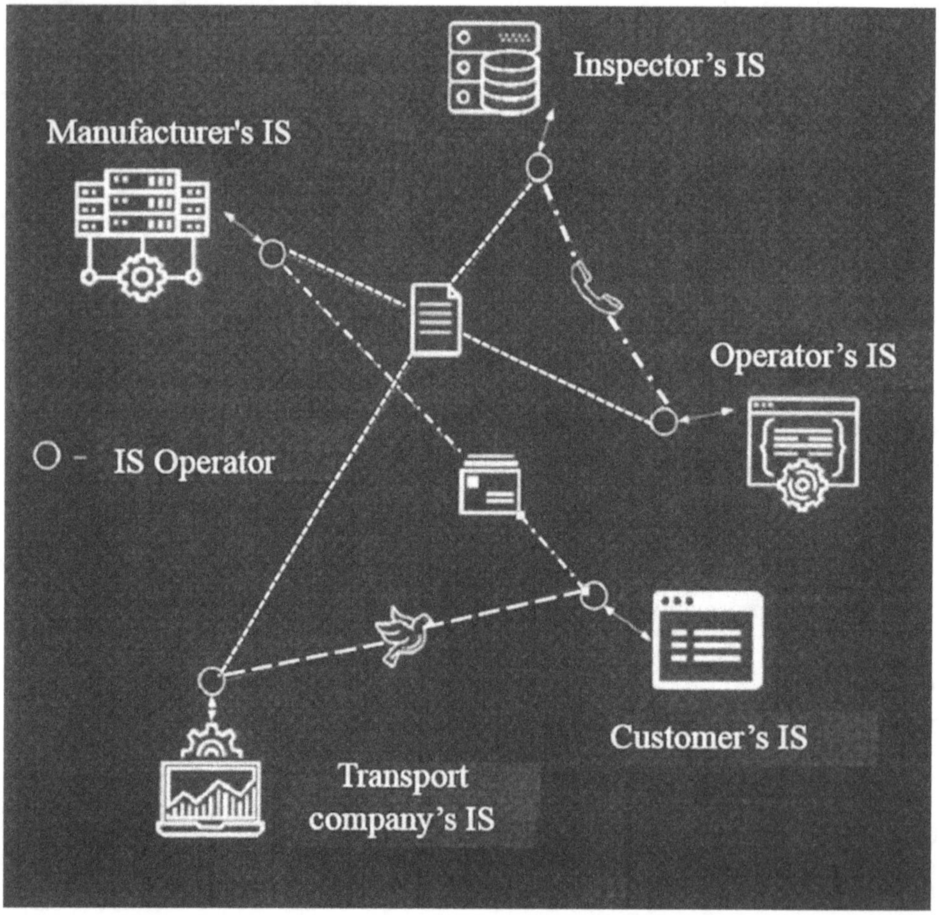

Table 1. Comparison of CDP and blockchain applications in the pilot project

No	Requirements for the implementation of the project	Centralized data processing (CDP)	The technology of distributed registries
1	The ability to integrate the participant's IP directly with the data storage and processing point in the participant's infrastructure.	Centralized data processing. Disadvantage: the need for all participants to trust the operator.	Storage and processing of data for all participants in the process. Advantage: there is no need to trust the operator.
2	It is necessary to be able to audit the implementation of the business process by all participants.	Closed code that provides a business process. Disadvantage: the inability to check the logic of the business process by all participants.	Open source code that provides a business process. Advantage: the ability to check the logic of the business process by all participants).
3	It is necessary to control the rights of users on the participant's side.	Availability of centralized user access control. Disadvantage: the ability to disconnect participants by a centralized solution.	Distributed user access control. Advantage: restriction of participants by consensus decision/
4	Ensuring guaranteed performance of obligations.	Lack of guaranteed fulfillment of obligations within the system. Disadvantage: the need to trust the developer.	Ensuring guaranteed fulfillment of obligations within the system. Advantage: provided by the properties of smart contracts.
5	Ensuring the immutability of historical data over time, the need to differentiate data access managed by data owners.	Hashing and encryption. Disadvantage: the use of third-party cryptographic tools. It is necessary to purchase certified funds.	Hashing and encryption. Disadvantage: the use of third-party cryptographic tools. It is necessary to purchase certified funds.
6	Ensuring the immutability of historical data over time.	The operations "create", "read", "change", "delete" data are supported.	The "create" and "read" data operations are supported. Advantage: immutability of data.
7-9	Reducing the cost of implementing, replicating, and supporting the solution.	The need to connect the process participants to the operator's capacities. Disadvantage: loss of control.	Advantage: there is no need to connect participants to the operator's capacities.
		The need for reliable high-speed communication channels. Disadvantage: high costs.	Advantage: standard communication channels.
		The need to provide a fault-tolerant infrastructure. Disadvantage: high costs.	Reliability is ensured by territorial decentralization. Advantage: the costs are distributed to the participants.
10	The need to scale the solution to a large number of participants in the process.	Disadvantage: dependence on the operator's resources.	Advantage: scaling depends on the resources of the participants.
11	The need for the legal significance of the transmitted and stored information.	Disadvantage non-certified cryptographic means of the EDI operator.	Advantage: the presence of certified crypto funds on the platform for two platforms in the Russian Federation, three more platforms are being certified.
12	The need to ensure transparency of the project life cycle as a whole, including at subsequent stages.	Replication of data at subsequent stages of the project lifecycle. Disadvantage: requires integration with the developed solution.	Advantage: The ability to replicate data for use by solutions based on blockchain platforms from the boxed version.

The main element of the pilot project is the Product environment; the main component is the blockchain platform, which stores a log of all events in the system in transactions. In addition, other main components can be distinguished in this diagram of the pilot project, such as:

- Delivery contract;

- Production;
- Payment;
- Input control.

These processes interact with the Blockchain platform through the interfaces of the SAP ERP system. In addition, the following processes also became integral elements of the pilot project:

- Inspection control;
- Delivery.

As interfaces for interaction with the Blockchain platform, these processes, respectively, use the products developed during the implementation of the pilot project:

- Digital Inspector;
- Supply monitor.

Figure 2. General scheme of the pilot project

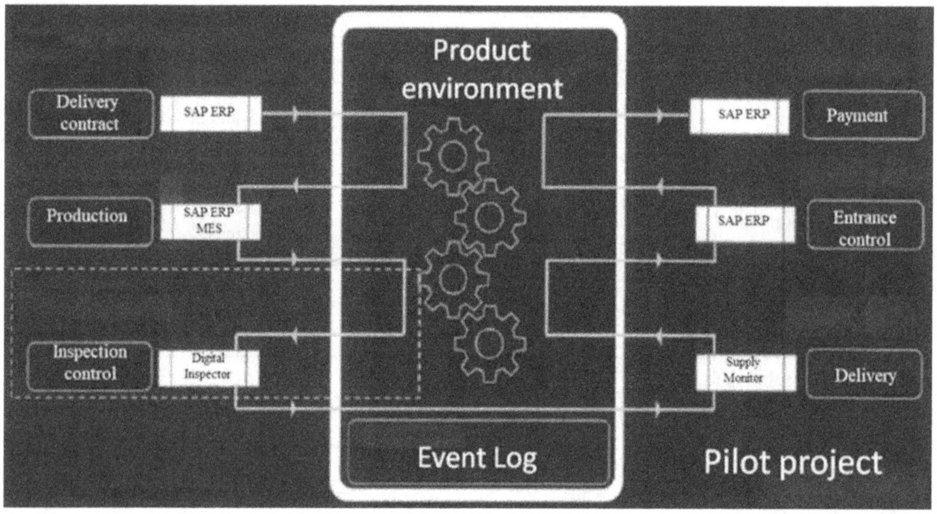

In general, the diagram of providing the implemented platform with an entire supply lifecycle is shown in Figure 3.

The following stages act as the life cycle stages by the widely used "BUY-SHIP-PAY" technology. At the Production stage, a Digital Inspector is used for inspection supervision, and its use ensures a complete rejection of paper document management during inspections. Obtaining the initial data for the digital inspector is provided by objective control sensors that fully cover the entire production process with their observation.

At the delivery stage, the use of a Delivery Monitor is provided. It provides 100% train tracking and accurate cargo arrival forecast. GPS trackers on cars are also used for monitoring, providing objective information about the delivery.

Figure 3. Diagram of providing the implemented platform with an entire supply lifecycle

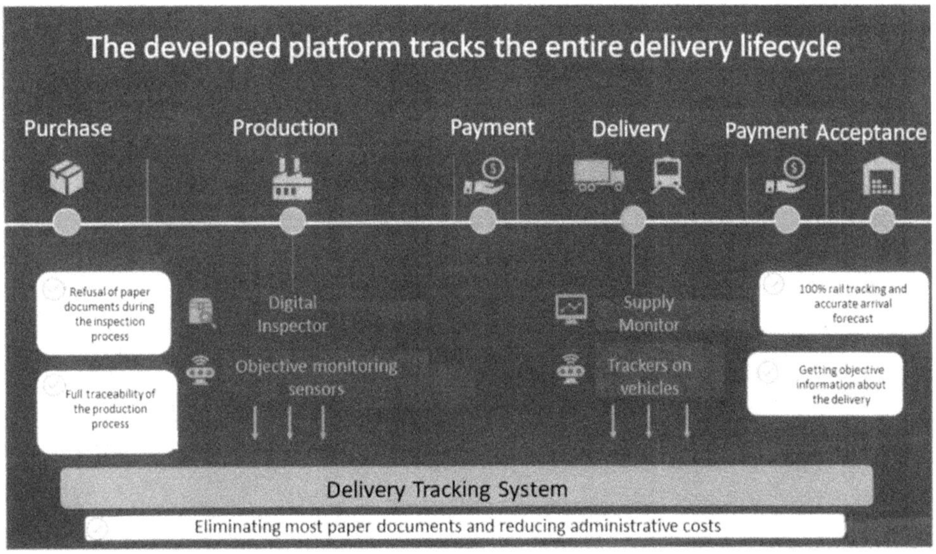

Automatic data processing is provided at all stages marked in green using a Delivery Tracking System operating on the Blockchain platform.

This system eliminates the majority of paper documents and reduces administrative costs.

Figure 4 shows a diagram of the delivery process before the reorganization ("As it was"). The diagram contains the following stages: Placing specifications at the factory, Inspection control, shipment and acceptance of products, and Mutual settlements.

Figure 4. Diagram of the delivery process before the reorganization ("As it was")

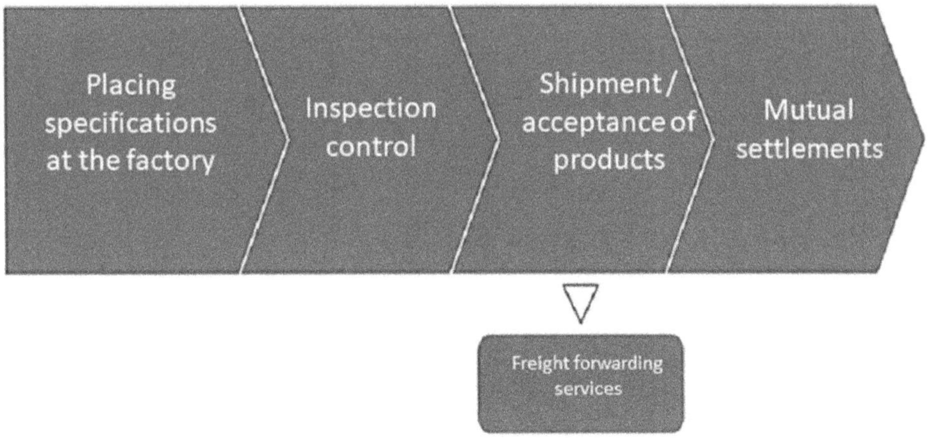

Figure 5 shows a diagram of the delivery process after the reorganization.

Figure 5. Diagram of the delivery process after the reorganization ("As it became")

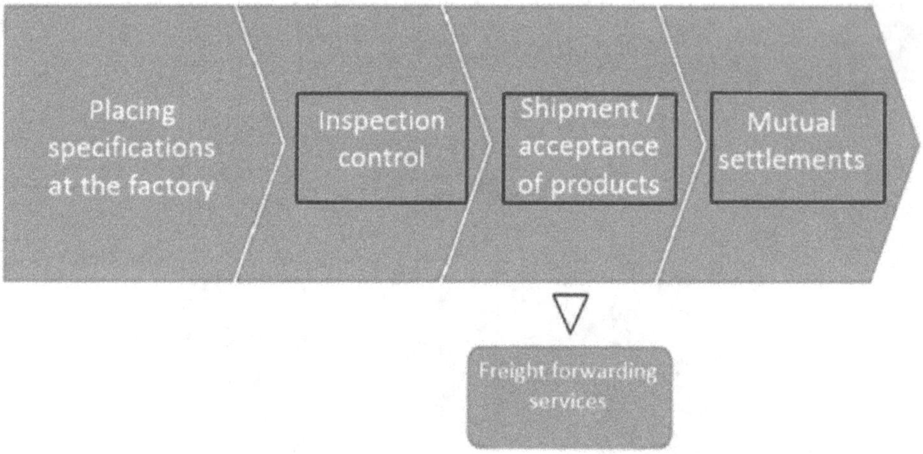

The scheme, in general, is almost identical to the one shown in Figure 4. However, significant changes in the stages framed in red in Figure 5 will be noted below. Both schemes provide freight forwarding services at the stage of shipment and acceptance of products.

For each stage of the delivery process, detailed transaction chains have been developed, implemented by the implemented platform. An example of such a transaction chain for the first stage of the diagram (see Figure 4) is shown in Figure 6

Figure 6. Inspection control "As it was"

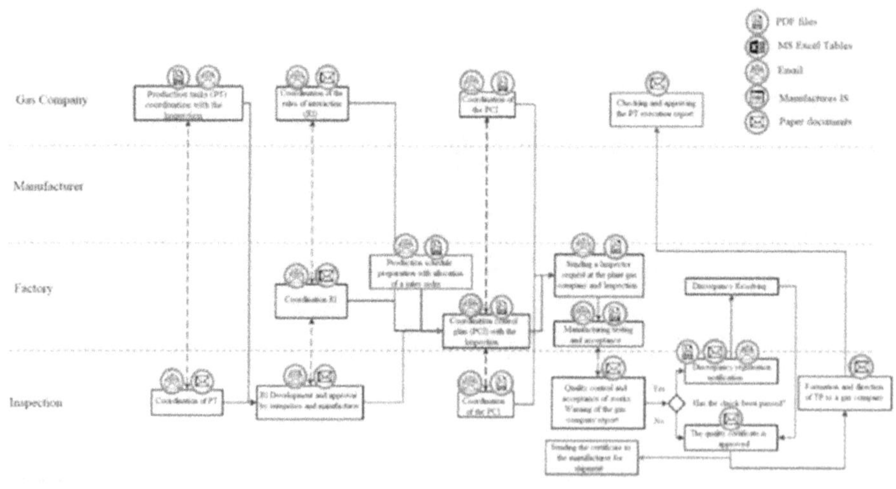

This diagram shows the transaction chains for each performer.

Participation in the following transactions is provided for the Gas Company (Customer):

1. Coordination of production tasks (PT) with the inspection.

2. Coordination of the rules of interaction (RI).
3. Coordination of the control plan (PCI).
4. Checking and approving the PT execution report.

Participation in the following transactions is provided for the factory's company:

1. Coordination RI.
2. Production schedule preparation with the allocation of a sales order.
3. Coordination of the control plan (PCI) with the inspection.
4. Sending an inspector request at the plant, gas company, and inspection.
5. Manufacturing, testing, and acceptance.
6. Discrepancy Resolving.

Participation in the following transactions is provided for the inspection:

1. Coordination of PT.
2. RI Development and approval by enterprises and manufacturers.
3. Coordination of the PCI.
4. Quality control and acceptance of works. Warning of the gas company's report.
5. Sending the certificate to the manufacturer for shipment.
6. Discrepancy registration notification.
7. The quality certificate is approved.
8. Formation and direction of TP to a gas company.

The document type is indicated in unique icons (PDF file, MS Excel table, paper document, postal item). Transactions are interconnected by links that implement the logic of the corresponding business process.

Figure 7. Inspection control "As it became."

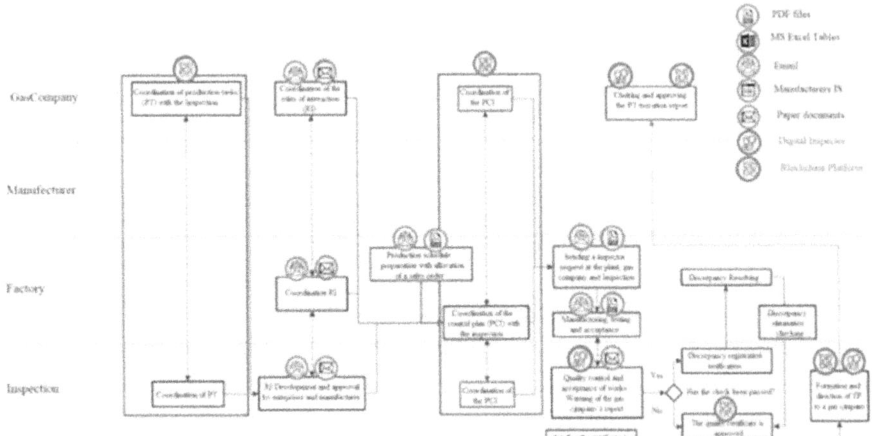

Figure 7 shows the business process inspection control transaction diagram after the reorganization "As it became." The logic of the business process has not changed. However, the processing of transactions marked in red involves the participation of new components of the business process: the Blockchain platform and the Digital Inspector. The documents processed by these components are marked with the corresponding red icons.

Figure 8. Model of digital document flow and data exchange of participants in contractual relations

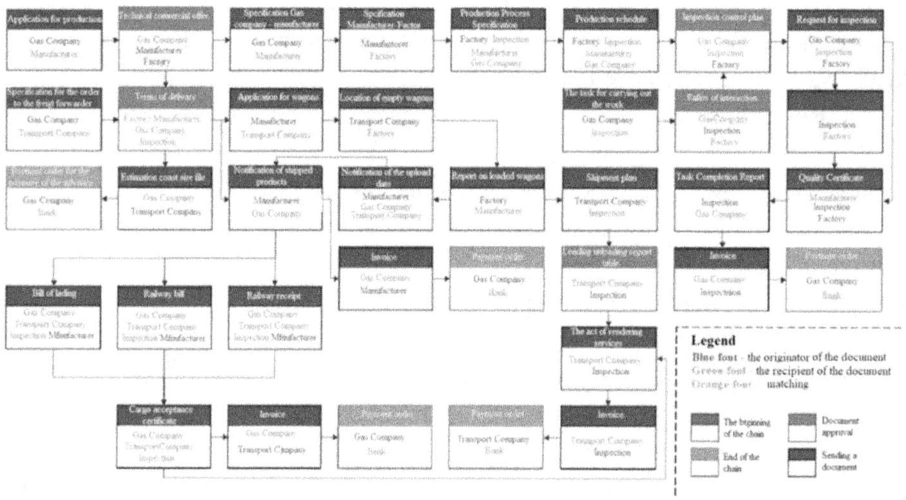

During the implementation of this stage, a Model of digital document management and data exchange of participants in contractual relations was also developed, shown in Figure 8. For each element in the document chain, the document's title is given in the block's header displaying the document. The lower part of the block contains the names of the subjects interacting with this document, performing the roles: the drafter of the document (indicated in blue), the recipient of the document (indicated in green), and the approving person (indicated in orange). The initial document in the chain is indicated in blue, and the final document is green. In addition, the sent documents are indicated in black, and the documents requiring approval are indicated in orange. The digital document management Model developed at this stage significantly simplified code writing at the smart contract development stage and helped avoid errors.

Then the chains of documentation transactions were developed for the two main stages of the pipe product delivery process:

1. Production of products – Inspection control / Payment of inspection control;
2. Logistics / Payment for manufacturing.

Figure 9 shows an example of a chain of documentation transactions for the Production of products – Inspection control / Payment of inspection control stage. For each transaction, the name of the forwarded document and the participants of the interaction are indicated. In addition, the type of operation is specified by the legend: document forwarding (white), control event (red), request (yellow), execution (green).

Figure 9. The chain of documentation transactions at the stage: production of products – inspection control / payment of inspection control

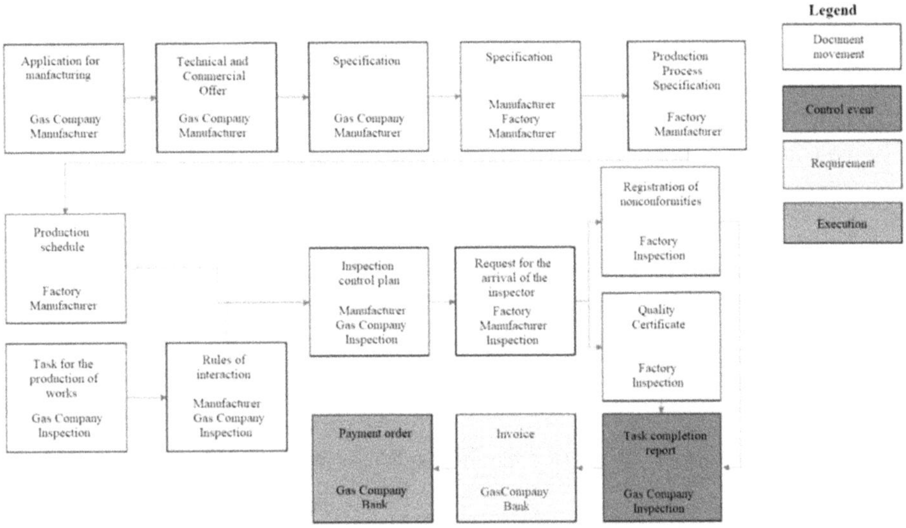

The development of documentation transaction chains completes the first stage of the pilot project. At the second stage of the pilot project, a comparative analysis of blockchain platforms, their testing and the choice of a platform for implementation were performed.

COMPARATIVE ANALYSIS OF BLOCKCHAIN PLATFORMS AND THE CHOICE OF A PLATFORM FOR IMPLEMENTATION

Information Security Requirements (When Developing Smart Contracts)

According to statistics, more than 70% of smart contracts carry vulnerabilities (Report, 2019). There is not yet a proven software package that allows you to fully investigate the code of smart contracts by static and dynamic analysis in a fully automatic mode and find vulnerabilities (Shapiev, 2019) in them that can cause harm in millions of dollars.

Blockchain technology has tremendous popularity and is being implemented everywhere. In static code analysis, the program is analyzed without its actual execution and dynamic analysis in the execution process. In most cases, static analysis means analysis carried out using automated source or executable code tools, performed without running the program.

This term is usually applied to analysis performed by automated tools, and human analysis is called program concept, program understanding, or code mapping. In most cases, the analysis is performed on different versions of the source code. Since the Solidity programming language and the term smart contract itself is pretty new and used directly in the modern sphere of the crypto economy, many potential vulnerabilities can lead to substantial financial losses. Thus, the developer of a smart contract, or an entire project, is obliged to pay attention to checking his code for vulnerabilities.

At the moment, the dynamic analysis of smart contracts is reduced to checking the code in actual conditions, either in the blockchain platform or in its test version. In general, dynamic code analysis is a method of analyzing program code directly during its execution. The process of dynamic analysis can be divided into several stages:

- Preparation of source codes;
- Conducting a trial run of the code and collecting the necessary information;
- Analysis of the extracted data.

During the trial run, we can execute the program on both real and virtual simulators. In this case, we must obtain the executable file from the source code. It is impossible to analyze the code containing problems of compiling or assembling the file in this way. With the help of dynamic analysis, the following data can be obtained:

- Resources used - the execution time of the code as a whole or its modules;
- Number of web requests;
- Cyclomatic complexity;
- Code errors;
- Memory leaks;
- Vulnerabilities in the code.

The dynamic analysis allows you to ensure that the project is working well or identifies errors, showing that it is necessary to fix them. Dynamic analysis is more advantageous from the point of view of improving quality since it does not allow you to lose sight of the program's shortcomings, as, for example, with static analysis. However, even if no defects were detected during the analysis, this does guarantee no "100%"defects since the full coverage of the program with tests does not mean that there are no errors in the code since the dynamic analysis cannot detect logical errors.

Simplified Methodology for Finding Vulnerabilities in Smart Contracts

To write a secure functioning smart contract, you need to go through several stages of security development:

- Design,
- Development,
- Testing.

Design (Writing a Specification)

This process is also called the development of system requirements. Before writing a smart contract, you need to describe its concept, actions, processes, and interaction. It is worth discussing these actions with the customer and approving all the requirements. Next, define the plan and the dependence of the processes in the smart contract. Analyze all current vulnerabilities and think about the security of operations.

Development

This stage consists of the process of implementing smart contracts. To successfully write secure code, you need to analyze the current vulnerabilities in code development and the features of the development language. It is essential to do this before writing it since it will be difficult to fix errors and vulnerabilities in the code in the future. After that, you can start writing secure code.

Testing

This stage is testing and investigating the written code of a smart contract for the presence of vulnerabilities. For this stage, the developer can write tests independently. Still, it will be much easier to use a ready-made set of tests, thanks to which you can find vulnerabilities in smart contracts.

We should be borne in mind that a full security check costs a lot of money. Therefore, it will also take time. Consequently, it is always easier to write and initially secure a contract than to fix vulnerabilities later. It is also possible to use external audits at this stage. A visual representation of the actions for implementing a secure and functioning smart contract in the IDEF0 methodology has the form shown in Figure 10.

Figure 10. Stages of developing a secure smart contract

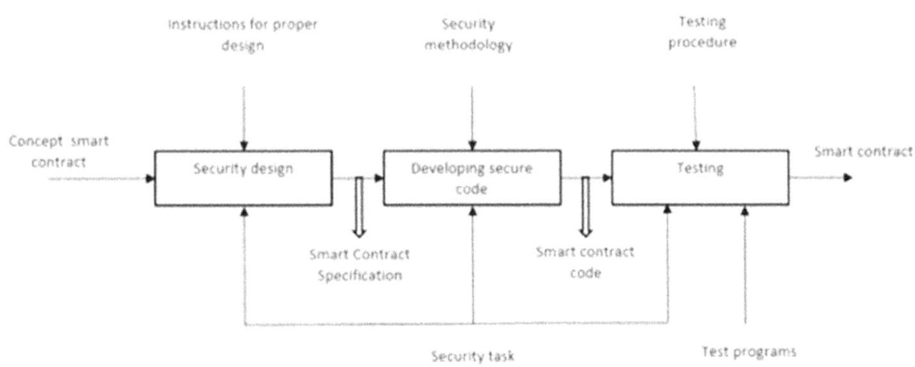

The next stage is the development of secure code. For this, you will need a method for ensuring the security of a smart contract. In addition, a security specialist is engaged in the development, which creates a security task, and at the exit from this stage, a secure code should appear.

The last stage in the IDEFO methodology (functional modeling methodology and graphical notation intended for formalization and description of business processes) is testing, where the testing procedure is the control tool, and the developer and test programs, analyzers are the mechanism. In the end, after passing all the stages, a secure smart contract is obtained.

Structure of the Methodology

As it was written above, this security technique is needed to develop a secure smart contract code. A smart contract (using the example of Ethereum) is developed in a specially created Solidity language (Official, 2018), (Dannen, 2018). It is a statistically typed JavaScript-like programming language.

For convenience, the methodology was divided into three parts. The user of the method will write a properly functioning and secure smart contract code simply.

The methodology includes three stages:

1. Study and understanding of known code writing vulnerabilities that are not related to the solidity programming language and the blockchain environment, but which are also relevant in these areas;
2. Features of the solidity language, without which a smart contract working will not work;
3. Recommendations for the correct and safe functioning of smart contracts in the EVM Ethereum itself.

A visual representation of the methodology plan is shown in Figure 11.

Figure 11. The plan of the methodology for ensuring the security of a smart contract

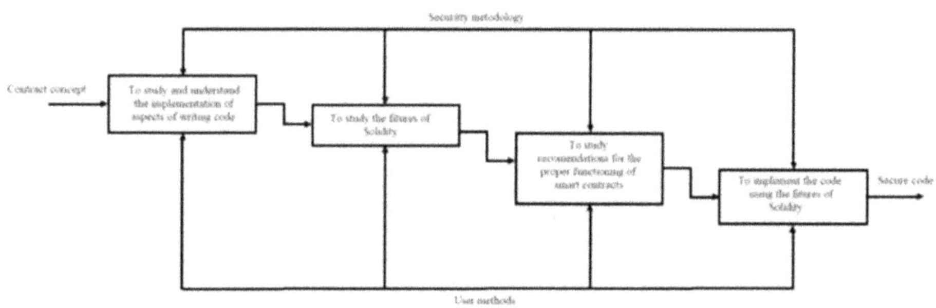

Vulnerabilities and Problems that Arise When Writing Smart Contracts

The security of smart contracts must be reliably ensured. There are many examples of how the vulnerabilities of smart contracts lead to very significant economic losses, and here are just two examples.

Just following intuition instead of best practices may only lead to unwanted loopholes. The well-known DAO (Decentralized Autonomous Organisation) hack can be considered a prime example of overlooked side effects in smart contracts. The Ethereum-based DAO began as the world's largest crowdfunding project yet quickly turned into one of the most memorable failures when exploiting a recursive call pattern resulted in the sudden removal of DAO funds. The following hard fork of the Ethereum blockchain to undo the damage of over $50 million (see https://www.zeit.de/digital/internet/2016-06/the-dao-blockchain-ether-hack) only fueled controversy.

Just as severe, with damage totaling $30 million (see https://www.coindesk.com/30-million-ether-reported-stolen-parity-wallet-breach), was the Parity wallet breach related to Ethereum in July 2017. Careless use of a delegate call command in a critical library enabled the attacker to gain ownership of a multi-signature wallet and to redirect all of its funds

For a smart contract to be secure and an attacker could not break it or send tokens to himself, you need to remember typical and well-known errors when writing code for applications. It is especially true for smart contracts since the developer will not correct mistakes after sending them to the blockchain in the future.

Below is an up-to-date list of errors that we can use to avoid for the correct operation of programs, namely smart contracts, with explanations:

- ***Buffer overflow*** is one of the most well-known computer systems and application hacking methods available in smart contracts. A phenomenon that occurs when an application or program writes data outside of the buffer allocated in memory. Overflow occurs due to incorrect work with the entered data and the memory allocated for them and in the absence of strict protection on the part of the application for the entered values. Since smart contracts can read the user's data, you need to remember the restriction of the data entered. If you restrict the buffer in the array when creating it and do not check what the user entered, then an attacker has a chance to rewrite part of the smart contract, respectively, to get data or access to it.
- ***Vulnerability of using format strings***. These are errors when there is no control over the input-output field and the use of a format string, thanks to which the input-output of arguments occurs. Therefore, it is possible to compromise the processor's memory: getting password values, addresses. The user can access it and write values to the memory cells, thanks to which a buffer overflow is possible. And it is also possible to get data from any memory area that the processor can process.
- ***Checking the arguments.*** The developer should understand that the user can enter anything in the smart contract input field. The user can enter data that can be interpreted into the program and change something meaningful that can disrupt the operation of the smart contract or can execute arbitrary code. You should limit the data entered or provide for the output of errors with explanations. The data may not fall within the acceptable interval, especially true with smart contracts since the process may affect financial transactions.
- ***Vulnerabilities of corrupted input.*** They also occur in cases when the data entered by the user is transmitted to the interpreter without sufficient control. The user can set the input data so that the running interpreter will execute a completely different command that the authors of the vulnerable program intended.

Specific Vulnerabilities and Errors Affecting the Security of Smart Contracts Written in the Solidity Language

Visibility and Delegate Call: In solidity, as in other programming languages, the functions public and private are provided. Anyone can call the first ones, the second ones can be reached only within the contract. There is a handy Delegatecall function. It is the basis for implementing libraries and modular code. It also allows you to load code from another address at runtime dynamically. The storage, current address, and balance are still related to the calling contract, and only the code is taken from the called address. However, it has vulnerabilities since an attacker can gain access to the contract ownership with the owner function during the delegation process. So when using the Delegate function, you need to be careful and check what it interacts with function.

Front-Running Attack*:* In the blockchain, all transactions are processed and recorded in the block by miners. There is a pool of transactions, and usually, the miner arranges them in the order of the commission and then processes them. Therefore, an attacker can view all transactions, find the right one and send the same one. Still, with a higher commission, his transaction will be in priority, and there is a high probability that it will be processed and written to the block faster than the first transaction. This vulnerability is especially relevant in lotteries and sweepstakes.

Sending the Ether to the Contract: Solidity has a self-destruct function: it deletes the smart contract and sends all tokens to a specific address. The nuance is that the address may be a contract whose backup function may not be performed. That means that if a contract function has a conditional operator that depends on the fact that the balance of this contract is below a certain amount, this operator can potentially be bypassed by the user. If you send a return function, the contract cannot receive ether, but the backup function is not called if you select the self-destruct contract as the target. So it would be best if you never used the contract balance as a means of protection.

Calling the Unknown*:* In this case, the attacker's contract can first claim leadership by sending a sufficient amount of ether to an insecure contract. Then the transactions of another player who tries to claim the leadership will be rejected due to the revert function. Despite a simple attack, this leads to permanent denial of service of the contract, which makes it useless.

Small Address Attack: Since the user can work with the exchange, he can enter an incorrect address, which is less in the number of bits. Since a fixed-length string is fed to the EVM, the EVM complements it with insignificant zeros if the string is smaller than it. Accordingly, the number of tokens may change because of this in the encoding. And the entry in the blockchain will not be at all the one that the user wanted. It is important to check for the correct number of characters in the address in the smart contract, and if this check is not passed, then do not carry out transactions.

Here are some examples of the source texts of smart contracts in which the vulnerabilities are present:

Race Condition Type: The vulnerability lies in the possibility of calling the external code again, during the execution of the contract code. This can lead to different function calls interacting in destructive ways. Example of a smart contract code with this vulnerability:

```
mapping (address} => uint) private userBalances;

  function wthdrawBalance() public  {
         uint amountToWithdraw = userBalances[msg.sender];
         require(msg.sender.call.value(amountToWithdraw)(); // 1
  /* In line 1, the external code is called, which can be called again
       until the end of the first call */
         userBalances[msg.sender] = Ø;
}
```

Dependence on the timestamp. When writing a smart contract, you need to keep in mind that the node offering the next block can write a timestamp into it based on its interests. Thus, it can influence the execution of a contract relying on the timestamp value in its code. Example of a smart contract code with this vulnerability:

```
uint someVariable = now + 1;
  if (now % 2 == 0) { // now installed by the miner
        // important code
}
  if ((someVariable - 100) % 2 == 0) { // someVariable depends on now
        // important code
}
```

Data type overflow. Data type overflow is dangerous because the value change may occur according to logic not provided by the developer. This vulnerability can occur both with the upper bound of the data type and with the lower one. Example of a smart contract code with this vulnerability:

```
mapping (addres => uint256) public balanceOf
// Unsafe option
  function transfer(addres _to, uint256 _value) {
          /* Checking the availability of the amount to send */
        require(balanceOf[msg.sender] => _value);
          /* Add and subtract new balances */
        balanceOf[msg.sender] -= _value;
        balanceOf[_to] += _value;
}
 // Safe option
   function transfer(addres _to, uint256 _value) {
   /* Checking the availability of the amount to send and checking for overflow */
         require(
         balanceOf[msg.sender] -=value &&
         balanseOf[_to} + _value >= balanceOf[_to]
         );
   /* Change Balances */
         balanceOf[msg.sender] -= _value;
         balanceOf[_to] += _value;
 }
```

Justification of the Choice of Tested Platforms

Based on all the collected data, it can be concluded that it is advisable to test the following number of platforms:

1) Hyperledger;
2) Corda;
3) Apla;
4) Exonum;
5) Universa;
6) Quorum.

Currently, the developers of all platforms listed above may change the concept or release. The main criterion is the availability of a distribution kit (a significant version according to the platform's numbering of software versions). As it turned out, not all platforms have reached the stage of a major public release. Also, each of the above platforms has a test network that will allow you to conduct load testing with minimal costs to purchase internal cryptocurrency or platform tokens. Due to this circumstance, it is essential to make a basic configuration of each platform and identify potential aspects for testing.

As a result, we can conclude that now we have selected platforms that close the list of tasks from the point of view of technologies - a centralized database, the main functional criteria of which are to prevent downtime, the same results of processing identical transactions, the availability of protection mechanisms against forgery, transaction rollbacks and violations of legitimacy.

Security Requirements (Authentication and Access Control Methods, Logging, Corporate Certificates)

The comparative characteristics of the platforms under consideration are presented in Table 2.

Table 2. The results of the comparison of blockchain platforms.

Requirement	Hyperledger Fabric	Corda	Waves Vostok	Apla	Ethereum
Availability of an authentication mechanism with the possibility of integration with the LDAP directory service	Carried out by the development Integration module	Identically	Identically	Carried out by the development Integration module (it is possible to use built-in tools)	No information available
Availability of access control mechanisms (DAC RB AC)	There is no need to develop an integration module	Identically	Identically	It has an access control mechanism	No information available
Availability of a system for logging events occurring in the system	The blockchain contains a transaction log that various existing systems can analyze	Identically	Identically	Identically	No information available
Availability of a notification system (alarm system) about events occurring in the system	It is carried out through the development of an integration module	Identically	Identically	Identically	No information available

continues on following page

Table 2. Continued

Requirement	Masterchain	Bifury Exonum	SAP Leonardo	Universa	Quorum
The possibility of using SHA-3 as a cryptographic hash function	Open Sours, modification required	SHA-256 is used; changing the algorithm is possible only in the open version (not Enterprise)	SHA-256 is used, a closed platform, it is impossible to change the hash function	SHA-256 is used, the possibility of changing the hash function is not defined	No information available
The ability to import corporate certificates for signing transactions	There is a possibility of implementation	There is no possibility	Identically	Identically	No information available
Requirement	**Masterchain**	**Bifury Exonum**	**SAP Leonardo**	**Universa**	**Quorum**
Availability of an authentication mechanism with the possibility of integration with the LDAP directory service	No information available	Carried out by the development Integration module	No information available	Carried out by the development Integration module. The function is under development.	Carried out by the development Integration module
Availability of access control mechanisms (DAC RB AC)	There is no mechanism	There is no need to develop an integration module	No information available	There is no mechanism, feature in the development	There is no need to develop an integration module
Availability of a system for logging events occurring in the system	The blockchain contains a transaction log that various existing systems can analyze	Identically	No information available	Identically	Identically
Availability of a notification system (alarm system) about events occurring in the system	It is carried out through the development of an integration module	Identically	No information available	Identically	Identically
The possibility of using SHA-3 as a cryptographic hash function	No information available	Modification is required; SHA-3 is not implemented by default in the platform	No information available	The hashing method is not defined in the documentation	There is a possibility of using SHA-3
The ability to import corporate certificates for signing transactions	No information available	There is no possibility	No information available	There is no possibility	Identically

METHODS AND MEANS OF FORMAL VERIFICATION OF THE PROGRAM CODE OF SMART CONTRACTS

Verification of the program code is verifying the results of its work for compliance with specifications (requirements formulated from the outside).

In the formulation of the problem of this work, the concept of verification is not used in a strictly mathematical sense. Verification, in the strict sense, really works with ready-made requirements received from the outside. In addition to verifying compliance, it implies a preliminary analysis of the subject area and identification of requirements that contribute to the most secure functioning of contracts.

In addition to the requirements, each smart contract has a specific business logic, the requirements for which can only be collected separately. Verification of specific requirements for adequacy, unambiguity, completeness, consistency, and other important properties can only be carried out separately for each smart contract and verification of the smart contract code for compliance with these specific requirements.

The process of collecting and analyzing business requirements is a separate task, different from the task of this work. Formal verification of program code is a more strict concept, meaning formal proof of compliance or non-compliance of the code results with formal specifications.

Currently, three approaches to formal verification of programs are most widely used •

- Symbolic execution,
- Checking models,
- Verification using automatic proof of theorems.

Each of these approaches should be discussed in detail.

Symbolic Execution

The main idea of symbolic execution is that if the value of a variable is unknown, then when analyzing the code, it is indicated by some symbol, and further operations with this variable are performed as operations with this symbol.

It turns out that the whole process of reasoning, in this case, can be represented as an algorithm, which means that it can be done automatically, which is successfully used by many modern verifiers. With automatic verification, the conditions for the values of variables are formed somewhat differently. All possible branches of the program execution are sorted out one by one. When analyzing each branch, a set of conditions is compiled for the values of variables under which the program follows this branch. When each new condition appears, the entire set of conditions is checked for satisfiability.

If it turns out that many conditions are impossible at some point, it means that the program cannot follow this branch. The conditions are checked for feasibility by the SMT (Satisfaction Modulo Theories) solver.

Symbolic execution gives very decent results, applicable in practice, for real industrial programs. For example, the Microsoft SAGE system uses the symbolic execution approach, which is used to verify various Microsoft products: both typical applications, such as PowerPoint, and the Windows operating system itself. Of course, in the verifiers used in practice, the analysis process is complex and non-trivial, and real verifiers use various optimizations to simplify this process.

A PVS-static code analyzer in C, C++, C#, and Java is designed mainly to help developers in these languages. One of the ideas used in its work is symbolic execution. Symbolic execution serves as the basis for many verifiers designed for analyzing a variety of programs. There are tools for analyzing smart contracts of the Ethereum network that use symbolic execution: Mythril, Oyente, Manticore (it also allows you to analyze ELF files). We should also mention SMT-solvers, without the use of which no tool for symbolic execution can do.

Software code verification systems refer to such solvers as Z3, Spacer, Cvc3, Yices, Alt-Ergo, Gappa, veriT. SMT solvers are used in symbolic execution and in other approaches, which will be discussed later.

Checking Models

This approach is based on the fact that the system's behavior is represented in a specific model. As a rule, the model describes the system in a simplified form. The behavior of the described model must be checked for compliance with specific regulations that must be set along with the model itself. When it comes to the verification of temporal (ital. - the tempo of models that take into account cause-and-effect relationships in time conditions), the rules for compliance with which the behavior of the model is checked take into account the time aspect. This means that in the formulations of the rules, there are such concepts as "never," "always," "ever," "eventually." Examples of such rules are the following statements: "the balance of a certain account will never be zero", "if a message is sent, it will eventually be processed".

Verifiers that implement model verification are based on a serious scientific theory, described step by step (Velder et al., 2011). Different verifiers based on model verification use different working schemes. It would be superfluous to dwell in detail on the theory of mathematical logic and consider all the algorithms used by different tools for the overview part so that we will give one of the verification schemes used, in particular, by the SPIN verifier.

The user describes the system's behavior in the built-in programming language (in the case of SPIN, the Promela language). The verifier looks at the system being checked as a finite automaton, each state is characterized by a set of values of all global variables. The user also sets rules (statements that take into account the time aspect). For compliance, you need to check the system's behavior. By negating these statements, another finite automaton is constructed specially. Then the intersection of the languages generated by these two automata is constructed. If the intersection is empty, the verification was successful since the negations of the rules we set cannot come true. If the intersection is not empty, it serves as an example of a case when the system's behavior violates the rules we have set. Many verifiers are based on checking temporal models: SPIN (the most famous), Eldarica, Uppaal, NuSMV.

Automatic Proof of Theorems

In the most general terms, verification using automatic proof of theorems looks like this.

Both the system specification and its implementation are written as formulas in a certain logic. Let's denote the specification formula φ, the implementation formula - ψ. We need to check the expression $\psi \rightarrow \varphi$ for truth. The system meets the specifications if and only if this expression is true. For the proof $\psi \rightarrow \varphi$, programs for automatic proof of theorems are used. Such programs are based on a theory developed by mathematical logic. Many algorithms used for automatic verification of theorems belong to the same theory. Here we will present a very brief introductory introduction to mathematical logic. Automated theorem-proving programs usually use first-order predicate logic. There is a complete set of variables in this logic, a set of functional and predicate symbols of a given arity. Arity refers to the number of arguments of a functional or predicate symbol.

A term is a variable or string of the form $f(t_1, t_2,..., t_n)$, where f is the functional symbol of arity n and t_i are terms. Constants can be considered as functions of arity 0. The predicate has the form $P(t_1, t_2,..., t_n)$, where P is the predicate symbol of arity n, and t_i are terms.

Propositions are predicates, logical combinations of propositions or propositions equipped with quantification of existence or universality. There are also many types of typed logic, and each variable has a type. Each function symbol has many argument types and a result type, and each predicate symbol has many argument types but no result type. Quantifications in this logic are also typed.

In predicate logic, there are rules for inference and obtaining consequences, according to which the validity of one or more sentences follows the validity of another sentence. The algorithm for automatic proof of theorems is reduced to the application of these inference rules. Automatic proof requires inference rules and a strategy for how to search for proof. For example, a strategy may suggest using inference rules from the end, starting with the sentence that needs to be proved.

The strategies used by the programs for proving theorems are based on algorithms for traversing in width and depth. The proof problem has twice the exponential complexity concerning the length of the sentence being proved. That is why automatic proof programs are usually interactive since, in this case, the user can help the program build a proof, which significantly reduces the complexity of the task.

Interaction with the automatic proof system requires a highly qualified user.

We note Coq, Simplify, Isabelle/HOL, HOL 4, HOL Light, Mizar among the tools for automatic proof used to verify program code.

Protection of Hyperleger and Exonum Services from Errors

In writing the functions of Hyperleger and Exonum smart contracts, which describe some business logic for working with objects stored in the blockchain, the programmer may make mistakes. Some of these errors can be found by the compiler itself and will be eliminated in time. Others can lead to the following consequences:

1. ***Emergency stop of the blockchain node.*** A program that implements the node's logic and executes the code of the services can terminate and output an error. Implementing the code of services on Rust, Exonum or Golang platforms in Hyperleger may happen because the situations of calling the panic function were not correctly handled, or the functions that explicitly cause panic were not taken into account. For services in Java, Node.js, this situation may occur due to non-intercepted exceptions.
2. ***Emergency termination of an external API*** call that changes the network state or does not change it. Similar to the previous case, there may be a situation when the REST API request handler will not be able to terminate correctly. This will not cause the node to stop, but the program executing the request will not receive an error message or a result.
3. ***The node hangs.*** If the transaction processing function has a high computational complexity or enters an erroneous state with an eternal cycle, the network nodes will not be able to perform the transaction.
4. ***The external API handler freezes.*** In case of a programmer error, the external REST API handler thread may never be complete, or it will run for an unacceptably long time, consuming the resources of network nodes. The Hyperleger and Exonum blockchains are private, and only a limited set of nodes can create transactions in them. Therefore, they do not have a built-in mechanism for protecting against DOS, and all responsibility for the absence of such situations falls on the programmer.
5. ***Littering of the network.*** Since the smart contract can make transactions in calculating the next block, the network can constantly increase the size of the blockchain indefinitely.
6. ***Invalid calls inside transaction calculation functions***. Functions that calculate transactions should not depend directly or indirectly on external data sources since transactions should result on any node.

7. ***Recursive calls between the functions of smart contracts*** can violate the logic of their operation or an eternal loop in the handler thread.
8. ***Inconsistency of transaction calls.*** The service can store data both locally on each node and globally. In the Exonum blockchain, the hash of the current state of the service is returned by the state_hash function; in Hyperleger, the PutState function writes the data stored in blocks. At the same time, you need to carefully ensure that the data loaded into the blocks does not depend on the local data stored on the node. Otherwise, each node of the network will calculate it differently, and the transaction will not be consistent when the block is enabled.

Some of the errors described above are listed in the DASP-10 list compiled for the Ethereum blockchain. Due to the richer execution model of smart contracts (services) compared to Ethereum, other errors in writing functions become possible in the Hyperleger and Exonum blockchains.

It is necessary to perform thorough testing of the services to avoid the occurrence of these errors. However, insufficiently large projects, it becomes more difficult to find an error using tests. The reason is that tests can check only a finite set of program execution paths. When adding new functions and branches to the code, the number of input data variants that need to be included in the test grows non-linearly. A combinatorial explosion of variants occurs.

Recommendations for Developing a Methodology for Formal Verification of Smart Contracts

As a result of the analysis of the languages of development of services of the Hyperleger and Exonum platforms, the following conclusions were made:

1. You need to verify the transaction functions and event handler functions separately. Transaction functions should be calculated the same way on different nodes, and at other times, the values returned to it should not depend on the node's local memory or external data. The verification method should check this and allow you to deal with such errors. Handler functions can use both local variables and freely access external data.
2. Denial of Service check. It is necessary to take into account all situations when the service may be blocked. For each cycle, it is essential to estimate the number of iterations for recursion to evaluate its depth. In the Golang and Rust languages, avoiding all constructs that explicitly or implicitly cause panic is necessary. In the Java language, it is essential to catch all exceptions. The verifier must detect all situations that can lead to hanging any called function of the contract or their combinations.
3. Access control. Although blockchains are private, and a limited set of nodes can make transactions in them, it is necessary to consider the risk of an attack on such nodes. There are no built-in authentication tools for transaction requests in blockchains; there is only a way to confirm such a right through the public key mechanism:
    a. There are three types of REST API requests in Exonum. The first type is public read requests; any client can make them, they do not change the state of the blockchain, but they can change the state of local node variables. The second type is requests for transactions, and they must be signed with private keys. The third is administrative requests for configuring contracts.

The secrecy of storing private keys ensures security. At the same time, access to the node itself is not provided by additional authentication mechanisms.

b. The Hyperledger Fabric blockchain supports authentication in the parallel Hyperleger composer (OAuth) and fabric-rest (JWT) projects.

Following the service's business logic, the verification method should detect potential opportunities for violating access rights to contract functions.

When building smart contracts for the Hyperleger and Exonum platforms, it is necessary to perform automated verification. You need to use either ready-made verification utilities (Java) or develop specialized verification tools for verification. The conditions to be checked must be drawn up following the requirements of business logic and to verify the correctness of the operation of the blockchain itself. The verification algorithm should look like a set of mandatory requirements applied to the functions responsible for supporting the execution of transactions and for processing network events.

CONCLUSION

The presented chapter discusses the materials of a pilot project to create a supply efficiency management system using blockchain technology. The description of the project begins with the study of the main business processes of the supply chain. A detailed description and visualization of functions for all system participants is given: the customer, the manufacturer, the inspection, the transport company. The system's main components are considered: a digital dispatcher, a supply monitor, interaction interfaces, and a production environment. A detailed comparative analysis of the security of most modern blockchain platforms is also presented. A distinctive feature is a thorough review of the technology for creating and ensuring the secure implementation of decentralized applications and smart contracts. The author offers a step-by-step method for implementing secure smart contracts. At the end of the chapter, the selection results of the most secure blockchain platforms are presented. The successful implementation of the pilot project confirmed the possibility of using blockchain technology in supply chain management. It showed prospects for further using the potential of blockchain and replicating the experience gained. Blockchain in the supply chain has allowed creating an ecosystem for the interaction of all participants in the process, such as the manufacturer, inspector, logistics operator, warehouse, and consumer. The approach discussed in the chapter certainly has the potential to develop and further apply blockchain technology.

REFERENCES

Ahmed, A. A., Bassem, A. A., Irfan, M., Khan, M., Salvador, E. V., & Jialiang, P. (2021). Quantum-inspired blockchain-based cybersecurity: Securing smart edge utilities in IoT-based smart cities. *Information Processing & Management*, *58*(4), 102549. doi:10.1016/j.ipm.2021.102549

Chris, J. S. (2017). *Who will be killed by blockchain: 4 small business areas that will soon disappear.* https://incrussia.ru/understand/kogo-ubet-blokchejn-4-sfery-malogo-biznesa-kotorye-skoro-ischeznut/

Dannen, K. (2018). *Introduction to Ethereum and Solidity*. Samizdat.

Egorov, V. (2021). *Gazprom Neft sells its blockchain platform in the form of an NFT token.* (https://beincrypto.ru/gazprom-neft-prodaet-reliz-sobstvennoj-blokchejn-platformy-v-vide-nft-tokena/)

Eman, M. A., Abdullah, M. I., Passent, M. E., Oh-Young, S., & Ali, K. B. (2020). DITrust chain: Towards blockchain-based trust models for sustainable healthcare IoT systems. *IEEE Access: Practical Innovations, Open Solutions*, *8*, 111223–111238. doi:10.1109/ACCESS.2020.2999468

Karaev, A. (2018). *"Gazprom Neft" has tested blockchain and the Internet of Things in logistics.* (https://www.gazprom-neft.ru/press-center/news/v-gazprom-nefti-ispytali-blokcheyn-i-internet-veshchey-v-logistike/)

Kustov, V. N., & Stankevich, T. L. (2018). Once Again about Blockchain Technology. *Intellectual Technologies on Transport*, (3), 38–46.

Kustov, V. N., & Stankevich, T. L. (2018). Blockchain Prospects: a Dialogue between a Skeptic and an Optimist. *Bulletin of Scientific Conferences, 1*(37), 77-84.

Kustov, V. N., & Stankevich, T. L. (2019). Blockchain Technology: a Story of Ingenious Simplicity or Enlightened Thinking. How to protect yourself from blockchain? *Information Protection. INSIDE, 2*(86), 11-18.

Nin, H. L., Mohamed, E., Shanka, K., Gupta, B. B., & Ahmed, A. A. (2021). Secure blockchain enabled Cyber–physical systems in healthcare using deep belief network with ResNet model. *Journal of Parallel and Distributed Computing*, *153*, 150–160. doi:10.1016/j.jpdc.2021.03.011

Official documentation on the Solidity language from the Ethereum Foundation. (2018). https://solidity.readthedocs.io/en

Report of the company Positive Technologies. (2019). *Initial Coin Offering. Threats to information security*. https://www.ptsecurity.com/upload/corporate/ru-ru/analytics/ICO-Threats-rus.pdf

Roadmap for the development of the. (2019). *End-to-end digital technology "of the Distributed Registry System"*. Rostec.

Satoshi, N. (n.d.). *Bitcoin. A Peer-to-Peer Electronic Cash System*. https://bitcoin.org/bitcoin.pdf

Shapiev, M. M. (2019). Vulnerabilities of smart contracts and ways of their exploitation. *Scientific Electronic Journal "Meridian", 10*(28), 1-5.

Swan, M. (2018). Blockchain: The scheme of a new economy. Olymp-Business Publishing House.

Vanurina, V. (2019). *Gazprom is switching to blockchain*. https://news.rambler.ru/other/41980326-gazprom-perehodit-na-blokcheyn/

Velder, S. E., Lukin, M. A., Shalyto, A. A., & Yaminov, B. R. (2011). *Verification of automaton programs [Verifikatsiya avtomatnykh program]*. Nauka.

Chapter 12
Recent Trends in Logistics Management:
Past, Present, and Future

Kannadhasan S.
https://orcid.org/0000-0001-6443-9993
Cheran College of Engineering, India

Nagarajan R.
Gnanamani College of Technology, India

Srividhya G.
Gnanamani College of Technology, India

Xiaolei Wang
Aalto University, Finland

ABSTRACT

The purpose of this chapter is to broaden the discussion about the various logistics solutions used by industrial firms to improve customer satisfaction and to assess their effect. This study seeks to discover and suggest new connections between logistics management solution theory and customer satisfaction using semi-structured interviews. Twelve small and mid-sized Algerian industrial firms from various industries participated in the semi-structured interviews. Their 22 top supply chain and logistics managers were questioned to determine their perceptions of what is essential to their suppliers and how logistics management is crucial for them to be happy customers. In today's highly competitive global economy, businesses are under increasing pressure to discover innovative methods to generate value and deliver it to their consumers.

DOI: 10.4018/978-1-7998-8697-6.ch012

Copyright © 2022, IGI Global. Copying or distributing in print or electronic forms without written permission of IGI Global is prohibited.

INTRODUCTION

Nearly 25 years ago, consumer satisfaction with customer service was the focus of business research. Business consultants, companies, and operational management have worked together to identify the characteristics of companies that consistently delight their customers, develop techniques for measuring customer satisfaction, and implement continuous quality improvement mechanisms that respond to customer feedback. Customer service and satisfaction are essential for every firm looking to evaluate its performance and guarantee its survival, regardless of whether the study was performed by and for the business sector. Product prices gradually increased throughout the 1950s and 1960s, resulting in many crises and restricted buying power. Business consultants were looking for a solution that balanced customer happiness, cost, and quality. Furthermore, the fierce competition at the period pushed businesses to seek a competitive edge. According to the study, logistics management may help a company achieve customer satisfaction, cost, and value advantage.

Transportation fleet management, order fulfilment, logistics design, inventory, supply, and third-party logistics service provider administration are all examples of logistics management. Customer service, sourcing, procurement, production planning, scheduling, packing, and assembly are all examples of logistics management. Logistics management is an important part of strategic, operational, tactical, and operational planning and execution at all levels (Achumba.,et.al,2013). In today's competitive market, businesses must run at peak efficiency and provide great service to be profitable. In the fast moving consumer products sector, three variables have been discovered to influence warehouse efficiency and effectiveness: warehouse management system simplicity/complexity, product slotting methods, and warehouse layout design. The capacity of the company to efficiently manage the warehouse, minimise costs, and fulfil orders is crucial to its success. It is important to note that warehouse management presents significant difficulties for businesses. Because of changes in the way raw materials, intermediate commodities, and final products are handled, the function and significance of warehouses in the American economy has shifted significantly(Albernaz.,et.al, 2014). Warehouse management is becoming more generally recognized as a necessity in today's market, where customer satisfaction and service have become a crucial element in a company's capacity to stand out from the competitors. To ensure optimal performance throughout the business, the warehouse operating system must be built for receiving inventory, fast order fulfilment, automated validation of warehouse operations, and accurate inventory management.

The success of physical product distribution relies heavily on the warehousing network. Leading companies are seen to use and execute various warehousing techniques, including as capacity switching, hub networking, cobbling, and outsourcing. For enhancing warehouse design techniques, both analytic and simulation models are suggested. Analytic models are often design-oriented, which means they look at a lot of different options rapidly to find a solution. Simulation models, on the other hand, are often analysis-oriented. They can offer an opinion on a design, but they are generally restricted in their capacity to explore the design area. To gain more flexibility in evaluating warehouse issues, both methods must be integrated. Aside from new supply chain trends, technological advancements have a significant effect on storage. Many formerly manual activities have now been mechanised or even automated. Robots may be employed to arrange arriving goods on pallets in an automated warehouse (Dobler Burt.,et.al,2006). Each pallet's contents are transmitted to a central computer, which allocates the pallet to a vacant storage space. Incoming pallets are transported to the storage buffer by conveyors or guided vehicles, and pallets are stored in the correct location in the storage area by automated Storage/Retrieval equipment.

The part of the supply chain process that organises, executes, and manages the efficient, effective, forward, reverse flow, goods, services, related information of origin, and point of consumption in order to meet customer requirements, according to the Council of Logistics Management. In layman's terms, having the right product in the right location at the right time in the right condition means having the right thing in the right place at the right time in the right condition. On the other side, the supply chain includes all of the processes involved in fulfilling a customer's request. It starts with the supplier and extends to production, distribution, retail, and, finally, the customer (Kandampully.J.,et.al, 2003). Supply chain management is the management of goods, information, and money as they move through the supply chain from supplier to manufacturer to wholesaler to retailer to customer. Developing new technologies, businesses may gain strategic competitive advantages in a variety of management activities, such as logistics and supply chain management. The application's degree of success, on the other hand, is determined by the technology it employs, as well as the presence of appropriate organisational infrastructure, culture, and management practises. In the logistics sector, information, communication, and automation technologies have dramatically improved the speed with which data is recognised, collected, processed, analysed, and sent while maintaining a high degree of accuracy and dependability. Technology can help businesses improve their competitiveness and performance. It makes a major contribution to supply chain performance by enhancing the logistics system's overall performance and efficiency. Many modern technologies are utilised in logistics in industrialised countries, but acceptance in India is sluggish. As the Indian economy liberalises, competition is intensifying, and the only way to stay ahead of the pack is to invest in technology-enabled processes (C.R. Kothari et al., 2008).

Manufacturing demand and sales are erratic, leading in fierce international rivalry. As a consequence of the rapid rate of change in global markets, many manufacturing companies have been pushed to become more responsive to changing customer expectations and needs for more value-added products and services(Chepkoeh.A,et.al,2019). The most important approach for manufacturing companies to succeed in today's competitive market is to offer value-added, high-quality, and creative products. To remain competitive, many Malaysian industrial firms have implemented a variety of improvement initiatives and established new operational philosophies (Cooper.D.R, et.al,2015). Since the 1980s, SCM has gradually grown in popularity in manufacturing firms and has become an essential component of company strategy.

SUPPLY CHAIN MANAGEMENT

Due to rising consumer demand, digitization in the supply chain and logistics network is becoming more dynamic. This digitization provides simple access to consumer requirements by efficiently sharing product/service delivery tracking information. The tracking information is guaranteed by the integration of businesses involved in the supply chain process, whose job it is to create mapping between different systems. The integration of data or information across different companies usually resulted in high expenses and sluggish dissemination. This study looks at how blockchain technology may be used to integrate supply chains. This technology works by integrating with the cloud, which provides a cost-effective business strategy for digital supply chains. Furthermore, via increased visibility, this technology may aid in the disruption of digital supply chain networks. Continuous monitoring is possible with such visibility, resulting in better supply chain performance. Due to the inherent dangers, adoption of this technology in the logistics and supply chain sector is sluggish, and some businesses are cautious about its deployment. However, it is anticipated that blockchain will gain the required trust and extend its acceptance across all industries.

The primary goal of this study was to determine if the construction sector was ready to use blockchain technology. A construction business in Finland was chosen as the test case to see whether blockchain technology might be used there. According to the findings, there are significant potentials/opportunities to use block-chain in the construction industry, particularly in local and international logistics and sales. This technology also benefits construction projects in terms of openness and visibility throughout the whole value chain. Blockchain technology is made up of three components: private key cryptography, a peer-to-peer network, and software. It keeps track of transactions on an open distributed ledger without exposing the identities of the people involved. This technology can perform transactions and document exchanges rapidly, while also providing security and flexibility to any transaction at a lesser cost than conventional methods.

The blockchain database may be both write-controlled and read-controlled, meaning that any of the blockchain's members can write and read into it. A read-write-controlled database, such as Bitcoin, is one example. Traditional database systems provide less confidentiality and trust than blockchain databases. Blockchain requires a significant amount of encryption in order to preserve information secrecy. The architecture, or how related technologies are integrated with one another, is the primary distinction between a blockchain and a conventional database. A client-server network architecture is used to operate a conventional database system. A client may update records in a database that is kept on a centralized server if they have the appropriate rights. The administrator is in charge of such a centralized database system, and authorization to access the database is needed. The blockchain database, on the other hand, is a decentralised database in which each member maintains, calculates, and updates new entries. It enables members to share information without the need for a central administrator.

A blockchain database enables a network of users to establish a shared system of record by transacting at the same time. Due to its decentralised management, the blockchain database removes the dangers of a centralised system, where anybody with the appropriate access rights may delete or alter the data. In a blockchain, current information may be kept alongside historical data, while in a centralised database system, all data is up-to-date at any given time. The speed of a blockchain database is comparable to that of a centralised database system.

Bitcoin, Ethereum, and ICOs (initial coin offerings) are examples of blockchain applications in the financial sector, and they are increasingly being acknowledged as real commodities with purpose, value, and scarcity. The blockchain technology underpins all of these coins.The combination of vision, culture, method, and strategy to arrange an optimum flow of high-quality, low-cost goods is known as supply chain management, cost-effective components from dependable and innovative suppliers, resulting receiving high-quality, competitively that they designed and manufactured (SCM). SCM is a term that refers to all supply chain activities, which includes delivering the correct products to the appropriate consumers in the right amount and on time. SCM is a contemporary competitiveness problem that is gaining traction in global manufacturing companies' production and strategic planning. Customers' expectations for improved product quality, more product variety, and better customer service, as well as increasing worldwide competition and rising natural resource prices, have presented manufacturing firms with new difficulties.

On a daily basis, today's businesses interact with suppliers and customers from all over the world. Many Malaysian manufacturing firms have implemented SCM to reduce waste and errors, improve corporate performance, and maintain or improve overall firm performance as a result of the changing global business environment. SCM is gaining popularity because it is seen as a strong motivator and strategic tool for companies looking to succeed in the marketplace. As a result, academics are beginning to see SCM as having the potential to aid in performance improvement. The availability of appropriate quality and quantity raw materials will have a major effect on the final product's availability, quality, and quantity. Raw material management is critical to a manufacturing company's overall success is shown in Figure 1. Aside from demand and other factors such as competitor activities and the general price index, the raw material condition in terms of efficient management and good planning has an impact on a business's level of activity, turn-over, and final profit. In every production process, determining the economic, reorder level, and minimum and maximum stock levels is critical.

Material forecasting, planning, inventory control, scrap control, and disposal are all responsibilities of the material function, as is providing management with information on purchases and inventories in compliance with financial laws and regulations. A deeper examination of these positions shows the difficulties of adhering to the principles of balanced raw material management. Material management, which is defined as the coordination of activities in a manufacturing organization in order to enhance Procurement, transportation, stocking, and usage of inputs efficiency is therefore essential to production operations and management. Material management's effectiveness and efficiency have a direct impact on the organization's overall success. In order to accomplish continuous production cycles and improved operational efficiency, raw material management in a manufacturing company requires special attention and scrutiny. Maintaining a sufficient stock level may also free up operational capital that might be put to better use elsewhere.

Figure 1. Supply Chain Management

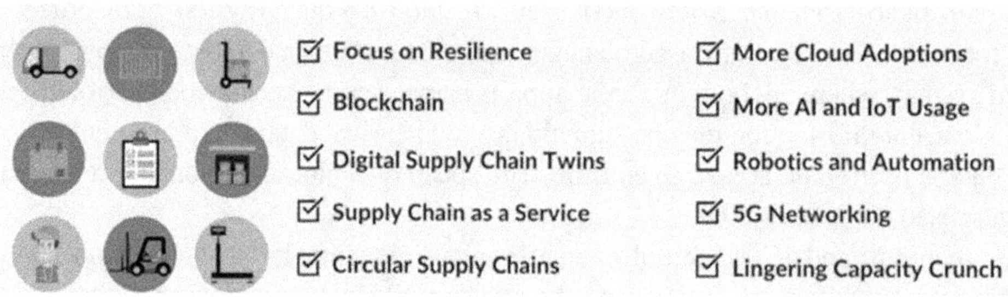

Warehouses are designed with additional space in mind, as well as the handling of boards and other materials. The terms used in the explanation of the key task primary distribution centre are "stockroom and focus dispersion," which are mutual, controlled, and effective. In an interims chain structure, warehousing and setup are two completely distinct portions with equal capability. Warehousing is the storage of products, inventories, information, and other items in a specified area or structure. The products are redesigned and repackaged at a warehouse. On a larger size, this item will mainly seem bundled, but on a smaller scale, it will appear unbundled. In other words, one of the most essential things that this distribution centre can accomplish is to prevent the under bump goliath manufactured goods from spreading too far. The downstream distribution centre operations are usually more focused in these sectors. When the object is treated as a landscape, it becomes even more unique. After all, the less time you spend dealing with the unit, the more handling costs you'll have to pay. Although the distribution centre will serve a broad variety of closures, the most of them will have the same flow texture. To put it another way, they receive a big cargo, put it on fast healing, recover and sort SKUs, distribute them to consumers, and maintain the supply chain. The buyer's administration, the store system, traders, and transportation are all part of the chain, as are the organization's composition, collection, innovation, and expertise in grouping and transporting products.

These exercises identify the flow from raw material to client, as well as change and update data linked to assets. Raw teeth and components are getting more and more complete with the item being supplied to the end customer, according to the exercise network inventory asset revise characteristics. To put it simply, it's a network inventory or commercial relationship between a company, a supplier, and a client. The collection, which includes providers, industry's focus, distribution centres, rationing focus, and retail outlets, stocks, and completed items, also mentions raw materials, work-in-progress stocks, and completed items that flow between administrations, as well as an event production of warehouses. According to the study, Indian businesses have long overlooked the importance of the coordinations sector, which continues to be one of the most underutilized areas in the country. While the distribution centre market is inefficient in its oversight, it may cause major disruptions across the manufacturing network. The ability to associate with areas in India is no longer particularly reassuring, as it has resulted in substantial losses in the item's transportation, dispersion, and capacity. Given India's significant development in organized retail and producing activities, market testimonies are progressively gaining momentum in the intermediate cycle, as each has sparked interest in storage, giving the industry a boost. According to Brobdingnagian, the fundamental market problems are divided into a few categories. To begin, the stockroom reviewed the organization of a big enterprise that was experiencing problems. Second, Company Repositioning operating and auxiliary structure indicated that this task would require a lot of thinking. Third, the current and coordinated framework for stockroom duties, as well as the action of the specialized and operational units was informed of regular sharp repositioning of the zone organization.

This paper's main goal is to demonstrate that it is the best in class at streamlining three groups that attract stockroom supply and circulation focuses in the examination work to listen carefully in order to improve the proficiency of request picking and client pick, as well as staggered rack stockpiling distribution centre conveyance through the application. Identifying the optimum accumulation position for a big number of products in the stockroom is the most significant element in determining distribution centre efficiency. Capacity responsibilities are influenced by factors such as capacity framework size and structure, material handling frameworks, item quality, request patterns, turnover rates, and lodging requirements. Has shown that a series of capacity projects using random, committed, or class-based methods and a transversal higher factor and a transversal higher factor may be the most effective approach to increasing the potential report on how companies should manage the capacity stockroom framework's arranging and control exercises.

Reporting surveys are used to explain the current, traditional arrangement stockroom framework, to suggest another way to make the arranging more productive and reduce reaction time, in order to maintain a distribution rapidly changing client requests. The research ends with recommendations for related organizational activities, including putting more effort into creating new models rather than maintaining existing ones. Capacity units should evaluate the whole retail network, from the supplier to the end customer, while making decisions. This necessitates a comprehensive knowledge of the interactions between the different components and activities. The article describes an information system that enables users to operate logistics terminals in both automated and manual modes, as well as alter the parameters of products receiving and shipping operations based on workload. Based on the time requirements, amount, and product range, the created software offers real-time analysis and shows the receiving, sending, and distributing operations.

In corporate logistics, supply chain management, physical distribution, materials management, and even rhocrematics have all been utilised. Regardless of its name, business logistics is an important part of management in most companies, whether they are manufacturing or service-oriented. The process of planning, executing, controlling, efficient, cost-effective, raw materials, stocks, products, and related information from point of origin to meet customer needs, as defined by the Council of Logistics Management. The global economy is becoming more linked than ever before. Companies are pursuing, or have already implemented, global strategies in which their goods are intended for a worldwide market and manufactured wherever low-cost raw materials, components, and labour are available, or they produce locally and sell globally. Supply and distribution lines are stretched in both instances as compared to a company that wants to produce and sell locally. Not only did the trend emerge naturally as a consequence of businesses seeking to save costs or expand their markets, but it was also helped by trade-friendly government frameworks. As businesses adopt a more global perspective of their operations, logistics performance and costs will play a larger role in globalization/internationalization. Since a result, logistics becomes more important inside the company, as logistics expenses, particularly transportation costs, account for a substantial portion of overall costs. If a business wishes to locate foreign suppliers for its resources or produce its products in other countries, for example, the goal is to earn more money. Although material and labour costs may be cheaper, if transportation and inventory costs increase, logistics costs are likely to rise as well. Shows a compromise that may result in a greater profit by cutting material, labour, and administrative costs but sacrificing logistics and tariffs. Outsourcing improves the supply chain's value, but it requires tighter logistics cost control to product management.

With the advent of Web Services, it is now theoretically possible to create a consistent interface for solution developers, which opens up new commercial possibilities. The ELPIF architecture offers a single generic interface on which any Shipping Service Providers may develop their Web Services and then register them in UDDI Registries so that other businesses can discover and utilize them. The ideas contained in ELPIF may be extended to various domains, even though we are focused on the shipping sector.Shipping services would be able to follow a paradigm of what might be termed a generic shipping service by integrating Web Services with a common interface approach. This is important because it enables a shipping service client to create code that uses the generic shipping model and then use the dynamic data binding method to access a particular shipping service implementation at run time. Developers do not need to alter their development environments to create or utilize Web Services since they can be implemented in any programming language. As a result, the architectural flexibility of our framework may benefit any client application. XML enables the transmission of business data across businesses in most integration systems by offering a cross-platform solution to data encoding and data formatting. SOAP, for example, is based on XML and provides a straightforward method to package data for transmission between systems. UDDI enable programmable components to be put on remote-accessible Web sites. We can not only offer interoperability for our clients, but we can also utilize our multi-platform approach to create superior products and solutions that enable any industry to conduct transactions quickly and effectively by using the aforementioned technologies.

The adoption of RL will also assist businesses in realising their corporate social duty to preserve the environment and encourage them to learn more about better product recovery methods. This research may assist decision-makers in properly implementing RL by providing information on the obstacles that are influencing its operations. With the assistance of various stakeholder views and potential deliberate efforts, uncertainty about the adoption of RL may be reduced. Enterprises will also benefit from the adoption of RL. Stakeholders must have a shared knowledge of important RL elements since they are critical in the development of holistic organizational strategies and the successful implementation of RL. Companies may create a priority list of RL adoption action plans once they are aware of the difficulties. This study results have major commercial consequences to a number of RL stakeholders, industry practitioners, academic and government makers. The study contains a number of flaws that may be solved with further investigation. Initially, it concentrated only on the obstacles to RL implementation in Pakistan's industrial sector. The findings, on the other hand, may be utilized and modified in other nations, taking into account variations in laws and regulations, RL maturity, and corporate structures. Second, this research relied on SEM, which required a high sample size; future studies might utilize MCDM techniques like AHP, ANP, DEMATEL, and others to uncover significant RL obstacles in other nations. Third, it may be useful to establish long-term plans to promote RL in poor nations. It may also be investigated if there is a connection between RL adoption and adoption obstacles.

By improving product quality and service while reducing costs, a well-functioning supply chain management (SCM) system may provide companies a long-term competitive advantage. Despite the literature's focus on the significance of supply chain integration for productivity, empirical evidence to assess the impacts on performance is lacking. As a consequence, the purpose of this research was to see how SCM affected the quality and performance of hotel services. The goal of this research was to see how supply chain management affects the quality of hotel service. As a result, fast food outlets, particularly McDonald's, were chosen as sample units. The number of answers obtained throughout the research was more than anticipated, resulting in more empirical data to examine and analyse. As can be observed from the findings, McDonald's has to enhance its packaging tests, delivery department, and menu variety offerings.Outbound logistics performance, like other kinds of supply chain performance, necessitates assessment and evaluation methods that show possibilities to enhance an organization's performance. This research examines how a third-party logistics firm may successfully and efficiently assist a manufacturing company's export logistics. We examine how a third-party logistics business might assist a manufacturing company in lowering its cost of products sold, as well as if there is evidence that employing a third-party logistics company is cost-effective. Finally, we offer suggestions to assist in the selection and hiring of a third-party logistics provider for the manufacturing sector. A self-administered questionnaire was utilised to gather the information. The supply chain operations reference was used to evaluate this (SCOR). In terms of lowering order management costs, service efficiency was not very responsive, with the majority of respondents stating that GGBL's relationship with DHL is worse than before.

In addition, the responsive service efficiency of GGBL outbound logistics operations with DHL was investigated using order delivery cost as a measure to see whether it could be improved. According to the research, it was much worse than prior surgeries. Similarly, improvements in the cash-to-cash cycle time were found to be similar to prior DHL agreements. This implies that the cash-to-cash cycle time in GGBL's outbound logistics with DHL hasn't altered much, and they may still enhance performance. According to the majority of respondents, the degree to which third-party logistics companies fulfil expectations matches prior engagements in terms of satisfaction. This demonstrates that GGBL has a lot of work to do to enhance the effectiveness of its third-party logistics partnership in order to increase satisfaction among all parties concerned.

The results showed that the model's link between logistics management and manufacturing performance had mixed outcomes, with a significant association between incoming logistics and performance and a non-significant relationship between outbound logistics and performance. As a consequence, it's unclear if logistics management can help a business improve its performance. According to the findings, manufacturing leaders should search for ways to enhance their outbound operations; consider utilizing performance-enhancing drivers like information technology, as well as outsourcing outbound activities.

LOGISTICS MANAGEMENT

The globalisation process allows for the sale of identical products at different prices from different manufacturers. There is intense competition as a result of the increased supply on the market, and some companies are battling to remain viable. Information technology advancements have resulted in a larger flow of knowledge throughout the world, leading in better producer and consumer education. Companies can only stay in business if they continuously lowering product costs and adding new features to their products on a regular basis. As a result, the company's continued intense development is critical to its survival on both local and worldwide markets. Both locally and globally, globalisation had a significant effect on manufacturing. Globalization widened the market and increased competition, causing consumers to put more expectations on producers to improve quality, serviceability, and flexibility while keeping prices low. Improving logistics performance was one method to increase efficiency in manufacturing companies. As a result, if manufacturing companies wanted to improve their efficiency and flexibility, they needed new methods to manage product flow from the manufacturing site to the end customer.

Logistics management is an essential management technique that may be used in today's companies. Logistics management reduces overall operating expenses and improves the effectiveness of a company's commercial activities. Reduced lead times afforded by seamless material flow from the upstream to the downstream end of the supply chain may enhance organizational competitiveness when coupled with a responsive strategy. This strategy will guarantee that end consumers receive good value for their money while also reducing industry uncertainty. Many reasons led to the growth of logistics management in the form we know it today, including deregulation, competitive forces, information technology, globalisation, and profit leverage. The goal of logistics management was to increase the number, size, and placement of factories and warehouses while controlling distribution costs is shown in Figure.2.. As a result, Logistics management has excelled in inventory control and transportation, as well as in the operational side of Logistics.

To enhance their performance, businesses use a variety of business improvement methods. Supply chain management and logistics have long been seen as critical components of a company's ability to compete. Logistics and supply chain management have received a lot of attention since the early 1980s. On the other hand, supply chain management is a difficult topic to grasp, and many writers have emphasized the need of precise definitional structures and conceptual frameworks in this area. We provide a lesson on current research in logistics and supply chain operations management in this article. This page begins with an explanation of the terms logistics and supply chain management, which will aid you in comprehending the breadth of the research articles that follow. The main aim of this website is to demonstrate how these studies contribute from various research perspectives and to address a range of current problems in this area. Finally, we discuss our findings as well as future study possibilities in this area.

Figure 2. Logistics Management

The management of product transit between the point of origin and the site of consumption in order to satisfy specific needs, such as those of consumers or companies, is referred to as logistics. Food, liquids, and abstract notions like time, information, particles, and energy are all part of logistics. Information transfer, material handling, manufacturing, packing, inventory, shipping, storage, and, in certain cases, security are all part of the logistics of physical things. Dedicated simulation tools may be used to simulate, analyse, visualise, and optimise logistics complexity. Import and export logistics are driven by the desire to utilise as little resources as feasible. Despite the fact that the preceding definition of logistics is not universal, it is likely to be accepted in this case. The Council of Logistics Management, now known as the Council of Supply Chain Management Professionals, defines inventory management as the process of planning, implementing, controlling, and ensuring an efficient and effective flow of goods, services, and information from point of origin in order to meet customer requirements.

As this term is expressed in Chinese, the idea of logistics is centered on product flow. It is also emphasized the significance of product storage, transportation, distribution, packaging, and processing. Despite the fact that corporate logistics covers a broad variety of operations, traditional logistics research has mostly concentrated on logistics infrastructure, transportation, and inventory planning. The term supply chain management seems to be even less defined than logistics. According to the authors, SCM has been poorly defined, and "there is a considerable degree of variation in people's views. Nonetheless, we provide a generally accepted definition that is very broad, not limited to any one academic field, and properly reflects the vast range of problems that this term is often used to address. Supply chain management is defined as the systematic, strategic coordination of traditional business operations and strategies inside a firm and across businesses in the supply chain with the goal of improving the individual company's and supply chain's long-term performance.

The words logistics and supply chain are frequently used interchangeably in academics and business because they are intimately related to product circulation over its whole life cycle, and both have been considered as the fundamental unit of competitive analysis in model management science. The phrase "supply chain" refers to a broader notion that encompasses, among other things, network sourcing, supply pipeline management, value chain management, and value stream management. Furthermore, since the supply chain is made up of a range of organisations, the majority of which are businesses, the idea of logistics has nothing to do with the concept of organisation, which is the polar opposite of supply chain.

One of the most significant aspects of supply chain management is that businesses want to enhance the supply chain as a whole rather than cutting costs or increasing profits at the expense of their supply chain partners. As a result, one of the most fundamental supply chain management ideas is that supplier networks, not individual companies, compete. Game theory, like incentive theory, is an essential study technique for supply chain management in situations when information is lacking.

Manufacturing businesses need optimal production planning and scheduling. It guarantees efficient manufacturing, consistent delivery, and cost savings. Large variations in demand, on the one hand, and a strong need for balanced output, on the other, are common challenges for businesses. Flexible responses are often difficult due to rigid manufacturing planning. There aren't many stochastic techniques for optimizing sequencing. Lead times are lengthy, procedures are inefficient, and in-process inventories are large as a consequence of this. Some manufacturers may consider creating a corporate vision that maximizes operational excellence, offers insightful analytics, implements and measures strategic initiatives, and identifies and manages risks to assist their businesses transition to "ruthless competitor" status. To accomplish so, businesses should concentrate on consistent business processes and create well-defined and linked business, technological, and operational strategies that enhance flexibility and speed while also allowing them to profitably react to market changes.

Supply management tactics, such as sourcing and commodity and supplier development, as well as overall cost management and performance assessment, should all be included in these efforts. In order for the company's overarching strategic vision to succeed, corporate leaders, business unit managers, programme managers, and operational employees must all support it. Master Production Scheduling (MPS) is the process of scheduling things across time that have a significant effect on lower-level components or have capacity needs. End items, intermediate components, or a pseudo item that depicts things gathered for the sake of planning are all examples of master planned items. Making a production plan requires a range of inputs, ranging from supply chain to operations to assembly line capacity planning. With this complexity comes a major divergence between the sales order input team and the production line orders, which are frequently accepted without evaluating acceptable lead times or dependencies, leaving manufacturing with a difficult task.

It's not simple to ensure that productivity is maximized while also controlling expenses. Within and across businesses, the SCM synchronizes and amalgamates these flows. The primary responsibility of a The goal of a supply chain executive or manager is to reduce cycle time by managing the supply chain. The supply chain should be planned and implemented in such a manner that it coordinates the supply system. As a result, supply chain management is critical for collecting consumer needs, forecasting, establishing schedules, buying and managing inventories, regulating manufacturing orders, and optimizing customer satisfaction. Traditionally, the design of an MPS and the management of the SCM have been looked at independently, and each issue has been addressed without the outcomes being linked. This results in synchronisation issues, product loss and theft, delivery delays, poor inventory management, excessive transportation expenses, and other issues.

As a result, it's critical to synchronies production plant planning activities with plant capacity, storage capacity, shipping capacity, and disaggregated demand at the retail level. Another essential guideline to follow in the MPS-SCM system is the customer service level. This idea is based on a number of distinct performance metrics. The order fill rate refers to the percentage of client requests that are fulfilled from stock. There is no need to consider supplier and production wait times for this small percentage of client orders. At every level of the system, the order fill rate may be assessed in terms of a central warehouse, a field warehouse, or stock. The stock out rate is the inverse of the fill rate, and it shows the number of orders that are lost due to a stock out. The number of backordered orders is the total number of orders that have not yet been fulfilled. To offer the greatest possible customer service, order fill rate, stock out rate, and backorder levels must all be optimized. Another measure is on-time delivery probability, which is defined as the proportion of customer orders completed on time, that is, before the agreed-upon date. Manufacturing Logistics is concerned with the opportunities and difficulties presented by a certain industry. These options allow for the deployment of a collection of critical resources to assist industrial processes, or they involve a series of critical logistical chores. The process of identifying customer end-item needs and fulfilling them starts with manufacturing logistics. The planning, scheduling, and management of all operations that result in inventory acquisition, processing, shipping, and storage is known as manufacturing logistics. Order acceptance, production planning and scheduling, inventory management, inventory distribution, and the creation of related decision procedures and decision support systems are among these tasks.

Material, information, and service flow across business, industry, and national borders are studied from a wider manufacturing logistics perspective. Multiple facilities and firms, as well as integration of manufacturing and service functions such as sales, marketing, and information technology, as well as integration with traditional logistics functions such as transportation, warehousing, and distribution, may be required to coordinate these complex activities. Many issues in industrial logistics research have been thoroughly investigated, yet many challenges remain unsolved from a wider perspective. Important elements of the business environment must be addressed, or at the very least be consistent with, significant contributions to manufacturing logistics.

Various sources of ambiguity and inaccurate information in the application domains, limits of legacy systems and organisational structures, issues identified, product and technology life-cycle effects, outsourcing opportunities, strategic alliances, and the company's long-term viability The primary business environment for manufacturing logistics is a dynamic element that changes over time. Technological advancements, corporate partnerships, and global competitive positioning may all have a significant impact on the industrial logistics environment. In today's competitive climate, logistics and supply chain management techniques are becoming more popular, since success is evaluated not only by actions and decisions, but also by improvements in return on investment and profitability. In the hotel and service sectors, logistics and supply chain management are considered operations management techniques, although they may be used to assist add value to their facilities.

Hotels, restaurants, event organising, theme parks, transportation, cruise lines, and other tourism-related professions are all part of the hospitality industry. The hotel industry is a multibillion-dollar business that survives on people's leisure time and money. Facility maintenance, direct operations (waiters, housekeepers, porters, culinary workers, and so on) as well as administration, marketing, and human resources are all part of a hospitality unit, such as a restaurant, hotel, or amusement park. The supply chain is crucial in the hotel and catering sectors. In order to improve customer service, workers in this industry must develop excellent relationships with suppliers and work with a reliable ordering system. Spend intelligence tools, in addition to inventory management systems, are used by cutting-edge hospitality chains to gather, rationalise, and analyse historical and real-time purchasing data.

Online supply chain logistics providers are a new type of Logistics Company. These companies help internet companies integrate their operations with other logistics companies so that they may fulfill their customers' needs effectively and efficiently. These service providers work with both online sellers and third-party logistics providers, integrating selling and flow operations across the supply chain to highlight the significance of logistics transport providers who link suppliers, manufacturers, sellers, and consumers.

As a consequence, logistics management has become more important in the market, and the amount of trade in many countries has grown significantly. As a consequence, logistics management is increasingly seen as an important component of a country's competitiveness. Customers' wants and expectations for products can only be met if goods and services are delivered on time and at a fair cost. Six logistics capabilities that may influence a company's performance are logistics information management, tight loop capability, supply chain integration, supply chain coordination, conformance capability, and institutional incentives. In today's economic environment, logistics management strategy is critical to an organization's entire corporate governance, especially in the areas of asset management and cash flow. An effective transportation system should increase efficiency while also improving service quality and lowering operational costs. Both the public and commercial sectors must collaborate to improve the transportation business.

This research will also help academics and researchers. The findings of this study will add to the body of information that already exists, in addition to the many other studies of similar kind that have been performed. A lot of challenges have to be addressed throughout the study. Respondents' views on the study variables were limited by closed-ended questions in the questionnaire; this was remedied, however, by ensuring that the questionnaire's questions were able to enable the gathering of data that completely and objectively addressed all of the research factors. Because respondents suppressed critical information in a variety of ways throughout the study, the researcher had to guarantee the participants of anonymity so that they could freely provide the information is shown in Figure.3.. Furthermore, the University's official statement of support for the concept reduced the risk of being attacked as a consequence of the research.

Responding to respondents' queries about why the research was important to them was another issue. The researcher had to reassure them that she was willing to share her results with the company in order to aid in the adoption of policies that would enhance the organization's performance and, as a result, provide long-term employment. It is focused with choosing the best choice possible, in which all alternatives are deemed rational, and each anticipates the probable actions and responses of its opponents. This idea has been used to a variety of political and competitive strategic exchanges. Game theory is made up of three parts. The first of the three is the player. These are the people who work in the corporate world. Corporate executives, companies, and individual company owners are all frequent sights. The second element is the strategies that players may use at different points during the game. This part also contains the game's rules, which are used to specify the sequences of all possible moves and actions. The outcomes of each possible method, as well as the anticipated payoffs based on those findings, are presented in the final section.

This is a formal investigation of decision-making in which a large number of actors are required to make decisions that have a significant impact on the interests of other players. This term refers to circumstances in which the activities of a large number of participants are interdependent, whether they are people, organizations, companies, or a mix of all three. According to these specialists, there are two approaches to this Non-cooperative theory and cooperative theory is two types of theories. When the players may get a larger benefit by working together rather than alone, the former applies. Because transportation and customer happiness, which are variables in this research, need a high degree of global collaboration among all supply chain actors, this theory applies in this case. Collaboration is becoming increasingly important in order to enhance global logistics performance. They go on to say that a new collaboration model has shown to be effective in lowering worldwide costs and improving logistical service rates. This concept, especially the cooperative approach, is critical since a well-managed transportation system will almost definitely improve customer satisfaction by ensuring timely delivery of medical supplies. Because they handle the quantitative and qualitative mismatch between material availability and demand in production, marketing, and consuming, storage systems are important components of a logistics system. According to them, the main objectives of a logistics storage system are to organize a logical system of storage activities at minimum cost, to make effective use of all components, to identify and mobilize excess unneeded property, and to have timely and comprehensive inventory information. Monitoring material use is critical since it aids in the discovery of cost reductions and overruns.

Figure 3. Digital Logistic Management

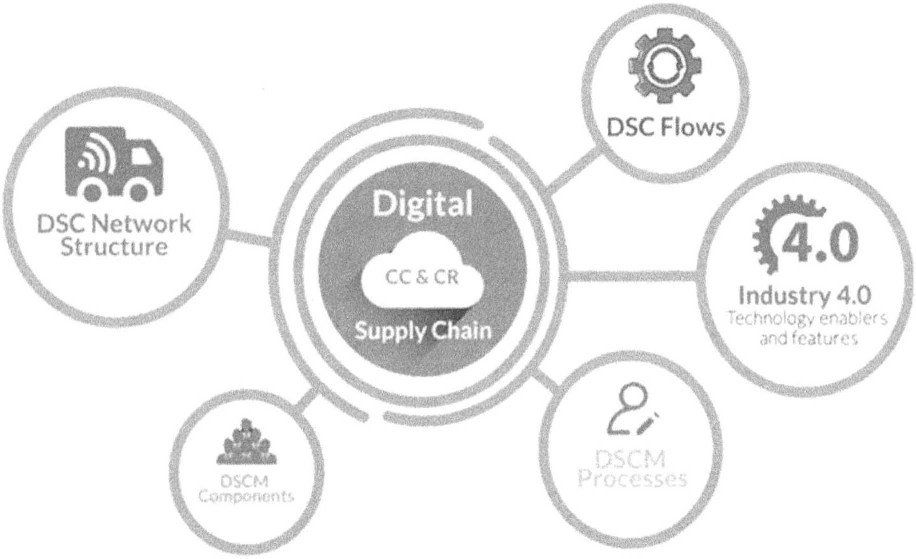

For an organization's efficiency, the warehouse layout is just as essential. Reduced time spent moving from one place to another to choose things may help an organisation become more productive. Hand-held Radio Frequency readers, as well as pick-to-light and voice recognition systems, have been used by world-class warehouse operations, showing the importance of technology in warehouse operations. Warehouses were forced to phase out hard copy pick tickets because they were prone to inefficiencies and human error.

Storage systems may be constructed at the beginning, middle, and end of freight traffic or industrial processes to provide for temporary product storage and timely material resource delivery to industrial and commercial facilities in response to internal market requirements. They go on to say that there should be storage facilities between production and transportation, as well as between the times when products leave manufacturing units and reach consumers, to level out the erratic production, consumption, and operating cycles of different forms of transportation. As a consequence, the whole promotion of material flow from producers to consumers via the logistics chain must take into account the presence of a network of different storage systems. According to them, a warehouse is a complex technical structure that consists of many linked components, has a specified structure, and performs a range of activities in order to convert material flow, as well as the manufacturing and processing of consumer goods. As a consequence, rather than being thought of as a distinct entity, a warehouse should be considered an integral component of the supply chain.

CONCLUSION

The expansion of a supply chain leads to a greater knowledge of the whole chain, making common standards simpler to implement. Supply chain development will be the foundation of competitiveness in many sectors in the future age of hyper-competition, both implicitly and openly. As a consequence of supply chain analysis waste or duplicate activities, suppliers and logistics networks are urged to synchronies and minimize non-core operations. Regardless of the difficulties, developing a dependable and efficient supply chain may become a core skill, if not a differentiator, for any business. Supplier relationships and collaborations are critical in hotel logistics and supply chain management. Long-term cooperation benefits both the business and its suppliers by allowing them to profit from a direct, long-term connection while also encouraging collaborative problem-solving and planning. These strategic alliances allow hotels to work successfully with a select group of essential suppliers that are eager to share product success and cooperate to save time and effort. Client satisfaction rises as a result of relationships, and they are less likely to move on to the next hotel. As customer customization and personalized service have become more important, building relationships has become more important for company sustainability. Hotels may use the relationships to differentiate themselves from their competitors, keep customers loyal, and pass on value.

REFERENCES

Achumba, I. C., Ighomereho, O. S., & Akpor-Robaro, M. O. (2013). Security challenges in Nigeria and the implications for business activities and sustainable development. *Journal of Economics and Sustainable Development*, *4*(2), 79–99.

Adetunji, O. M., & Owolabi, A. A. (2016). Firm performance and its drivers: How important are the industry and firm-level factors. *International Journal of Economics and Finance*, *8*(11), 60–77. doi:10.5539/ijef.v8n11p60

Agu, A. O., Obi-Anike, H. O., & Eke, C. N. (2016). Effect of inventory management on the organizational performance of the selected manufacturing firms. *Singaporean Journal of Business, Economics, and Management Studies*, *5*(4), 56–69.

Ahmad, A. A. (2017). Factors affecting the organizational performance of manufacturing firms. *International Journal of Engineering Business Management*, *9*, 1–9. doi:10.1177/1847979017712628

Albernaz, H., Maruyama, U. G., Maciel, M. S., & Correa, F. R. (2014). Implementation of distribution centers as logistics competitive advantage: Study on oil company distributor in southeast Brazil. *Independent Journal of Management & Production*, *5*(4), 1089–1106. doi:10.14807/ijmp.v5i4.243

Chambers, D., & Lacey, N. (2011). *Modern Corporate Finance: Theory and Practice* (6th ed.). Hayden-McNeil.

Chepkoech, A. (2019, May 28). Retrieved October 24, 2019, from www.nation.co.ke: https://www.nation.co.ke/ health/Why-Kenya-imports-drugs/3476990-5135300-h7o9f9/index.html

Cohen, S., & Rousell, J. (2005). *Strategic Supply Chain Management: The five disciplines for top performance*. Mc Graw- Hill.

Cooper, D., & Schindler, P. (2006). *Business Research Methods*. Mc Graw Hill.

Cooper, D. R., & Gutowski, T. G. (2015). Environmental Impact of Reuse. *Journal of Industrial Ecology*, 1–14.

Dick, A., & Basu, K. (1994). Customer Loyalty: Toward an integrated conceptual framework. *Journal of the Academy of Marketing Science*, *22*(2), 99–113. doi:10.1177/0092070394222001

Dobler & Burt. (2006). Purchasing management (6th ed.). McGraw Hill International Edition.

Goldsby, T., & Martichenko, R. (2005). *Lean Six Sigma Logistics: Strategic Development to Operational Success*. J. Ross Publishing, Inc.

Jessop, D., & Morrison, A. (1994). *Storage and supply of materials* (6th ed.). London: Financial Times.

Kandampully, J. (2003). *B2B Relationships and Networks in the Internet Age*. Journal Management Decisions.

Kothari, C. R. (2008). *An introduction to operational Research*. Vikas Publishing.

Koumanakos, D. P. (2008). The effect of inventory management on firm performance. *International Journal of Productivity and Performance Management*, *57*, 355–369.

Lambert. (2006). *Supply Chain Management: Processes, Partnerships, Performance*. Supply Chain Management Institute.

Compilation of References

Abeyratne, S. A., & Monfared, R. P. (2016). Blockchain ready manufacturing supply chain using distributed ledger. *International Journal of Research in Engineering and Technology*, *5*(09), 1–10. doi:10.15623/ijret.2016.0509001

Abou-Nassar, E. M., Iliyasu, A. M., El-Kafrawy, P. M., Song, O. Y., Bashir, A. K., & Abd El-Latif, A. A. (2020). DITrust chain: Towards blockchain-based trust models for sustainable healthcare IoT systems. *IEEE Access: Practical Innovations, Open Solutions*, *8*, 111223–111238. doi:10.1109/ACCESS.2020.2999468

Achumba, I. C., Ighomereho, O. S., & Akpor-Robaro, M. O. (2013). Security challenges in Nigeria and the implications for business activities and sustainable development. *Journal of Economics and Sustainable Development*, *4*(2), 79–99.

Addo-Tenkorang, R., & Helo, P. T. (2016). Big Data Applications in Operations/Supply-chain Management: A Literature Review. *Computers & Industrial Engineering*, *101*, 528–543. doi:10.1016/j.cie.2016.09.023

Adebayo, A., Rawat, D. B., Njilla, L., & Kamhoua, C. A. (2019). Blockchain-enabled information sharing framework for cybersecurity. *Blockchain for Distributed Systems Security*, 143-158.

Adetunji, O. M., & Owolabi, A. A. (2016). Firm performance and its drivers: How important are the industry and firm-level factors. *International Journal of Economics and Finance*, *8*(11), 60–77. doi:10.5539/ijef.v8n11p60

Aggarwal, V., Sharma, K., Kaushik, N., Bhushan, B., & Himanshu. (2021). Integration of Blockchain and IoT (B-IoT): Architecture, Solutions, & Future Research Direction. *IOP Conf. Series: Materials Science and Engineering, 1022*. 10.1088/1757-899X/1022/1/012103

Agrawal, R., Verma, P., Sonanis, R., Goel, U., De, A., Kondaveeti, S. A., & Shekhar, S. (2018, April). Continuous security in IoT using blockchain. In *2018 IEEE International Conference on Acoustics, Speech and Signal Processing (ICASSP)* (pp. 6423-6427). IEEE. 10.1109/ICASSP.2018.8462513

Agrawal, T. K., & Pal, R. (2019). Traceability in textile and clothing supply chains: Classifying implementation factors and information sets via Delphi study. *Sustainability*, *11*(6), 1698. doi:10.3390u11061698

Agu, A. O., Obi-Anike, H. O., & Eke, C. N. (2016). Effect of inventory management on the organizational performance of the selected manufacturing firms. *Singaporean Journal of Business, Economics, and Management Studies*, *5*(4), 56–69.

Aheleroff, S., Zhong, R. Y., & Xu, X. (2020). A Digital Twin Reference for Mass Personalization in Industry 4.0. *Procedia CIRP*, *93*, 228–233. doi:10.1016/j.procir.2020.04.023

Ahmad, A. A. (2017). Factors affecting the organizational performance of manufacturing firms. *International Journal of Engineering Business Management*, *9*, 1–9. doi:10.1177/1847979017712628

Ahmed, A. A., Bassem, A. A., Irfan, M., Khan, M., Salvador, E. V., & Jialiang, P. (2021). Quantum-inspired blockchain-based cybersecurity: Securing smart edge utilities in IoT-based smart cities. *Information Processing & Management*, *58*(4), 102549. doi:10.1016/j.ipm.2021.102549

Aitzhan, N. Z., & Svetinovic, D. (2016). Security and privacy in decentralized energy trading through multi-signatures, blockchain and anonymous messaging streams. *IEEE Transactions on Dependable and Secure Computing*, *15*(5), 840–852. doi:10.1109/TDSC.2016.2616861

Akmeemana, C. (2017). *Blockchain Takes Off: How Distributed Ledger Technology Will Transform Airlines*. Academic Press.

Akter, S., Michael, K., Uddin, M. R., McCarthy, G., & Rahman, M. (2020). Transforming business using digital innovations: The application of AI, blockchain, cloud and data analytics. *Annals of Operations Research*, •••, 1–33.

Alazab, M., Alhyari, S., Awajan, A., & Abdallah, A. B. (2020). Blockchain technology in supply chain management: An empirical study of the factors affecting user adoption/acceptance. *Cluster Computing*, *24*(1), 83–101. doi:10.100710586-020-03200-4

Albernaz, H., Maruyama, U. G., Maciel, M. S., & Correa, F. R. (2014). Implementation of distribution centers as logistics competitive advantage: Study on oil company distributor in southeast Brazil. *Independent Journal of Management & Production*, *5*(4), 1089–1106. doi:10.14807/ijmp.v5i4.243

Ali, M. H., Chung, L., Kumar, A., Zailani, S., & Tan, K. H. (2021). A sustainable Blockchain framework for the halal food supply chain: Lessons from Malaysia. *Technological Forecasting and Social Change*, *170*, 120870. Advance online publication. doi:10.1016/j.techfore.2021.120870

Aliyu, S., Tom, A. M., Haruna, I., Taiye, M. A., & Barakat, M. M. (2018). The Role of Blockchain Technology Applications in Supply Chain Management. *International Journal of Computer Mathematics*, 1.

Al-Jaroodi, J., & Mohamed, N. (2019). Blockchain in Industries: A Survey. *IEEE Access: Practical Innovations, Open Solutions*, *7*, 36500–36515. doi:10.1109/ACCESS.2019.2903554

Alladi, T., Chamola, V., Sahu, N., & Guizani, M. (2020). Applications of blockchain in unmanned aerial vehicles: A review. *Vehicular Communications*, *23*, 100249. doi:10.1016/j.vehcom.2020.100249

Allied Market Research. (2018). *Global Connected Logistics Market Expected to Reach $27,722 Million by 2023*. https://www.alliedmarketresearch.com

Al-Rakhami, M. S., & Al-Mashari, M. A. (2021). Blockchain-Based Trust Model for the Internet of Things Supply Chain Management. *Sensors (Basel)*, *21*(5), 1759. doi:10.339021051759 PMID:33806319

Al-Talib, M., Melhem, W. Y., Anosike, A. I., Garza Reyes, J. A., Nadeem, S. P., & kumar, A. (2020). Achieving resilience in the supply chain by applying IoT technology. *Procedia CIRP*, *91*, 752–757. doi:10.1016/j.procir.2020.02.231

Andoni, M., Robu, V., Flynn, D., Abram, S., Geach, D., Jenkins, D., McCallum, P., & Peacock, A. (2019). Blockchain technology in the energy sector: A systematic review of challenges and opportunities. In *Renewable and Sustainable Energy Reviews* (Vol. 100, pp. 143–174). Elsevier Ltd. doi:10.1016/j.rser.2018.10.014

Anitha, K., Palaksha Reddy, K., Krishnamoorthy, N., & Jaiswal, S. (2021). IoT's in enabling the supply chain visibility and connectivity and optimization of performance. *Materials Today: Proceedings*. Advance online publication. doi:10.1016/j.matpr.2020.12.343

Anwar. (2019). *Connect2Smallports project: South Baltic small ports – Gateway to the integrated and sustainable European transport system*. Accessed on 10th November 2021. Available: http://bth.diva-portal.org/smash/record.jsf?pid=diva2%3A1361852&dswid=7361.M

Arner, D. W. (2016). FinTech, RegTech and the Reconceptualization of Financial Regulation. Academic Press.

Aslam, J., Saleem, A., Khan, N. T., & Kim, Y. B. (2021). Factors influencing blockchain adoption in supply chain management practices: A study based on the oil industry. *Journal of Innovation & Knowledge*. doi:10.1016/j.jik.2021.01.002

Assesment, S. (2021). *Industrial application blockchain practice cases*. https://mp.weixin.qq.com/s?__biz=MzUxMzc4MjA4NQ==&mid=2247484874&idx=1&sn=8e0af725d36cdd2c5969b39dc91733ed&chksm=f94ebde0ce3934f669ccbbd3d1063897bbbee93e5196ad5d2b3c55d7d60a394936635c9c99b1&mpshare=1&srcid=0814HgTw2ah9yUHfINldH7VL&sharer_sharetime=1628948606761&sharer_shareid=3f439b70854717410bbd97cd511f119b&from=singlemessage&scene=1&subscene=10000&clicktime=1630039298&enterid=1630039298&ascene=1&devicetype=android-29&version=28000a3d&nettype=WIFI&abtest_cookie=AAACAA%3D%3D&lang=zh_CN&exportkey=AxbisCB%2Fo%2FxIBv6SsogS%2FAk%3D&pass_ticket=rr0HBDyFaypryLmw2%2Bgr5c%2Fa%2F4txJeBnfQLqo6oCAIRej4aOGCXxfFxyv8BAPUJI&wx_header=1

Atlam & Wills. (2019). Technical aspects of blockchain and iot. In *Advances in Computers* (Vol. 115, pp. 1–39). Elsevier.

Atlam, H. F., Azad, M. A., Alzahrani, A. G., & Wills, G. (2020). A Review of Blockchain in Internet of Things and AI Big Data. *Cognitive Computation*, *4*, 28.

Atlam, H. F., & Wills, G. B. (2019). Chapter One - Technical aspects of blockchain and IoT. In S. Kim, G. C. Deka, & P. Zhang (Eds.), *Role of Blockchain Technology in IoT Applications* (Vol. 115, pp. 1–39). Elsevier. doi:10.1016/bs.adcom.2018.10.006

Aung, M. M., & Chang, Y. S. (2014). Traceability in a food supply chain: Safety and quality perspective. *Food Control*, *39*, 172–184. doi:10.1016/j.foodcont.2013.11.007

Axon, L., & Goldsmith, M. (2017, July). PB-PKI: A Privacy-aware Blockchain-based PKI. In SECRYPT (pp. 311-318). doi:10.5220/0006419203110318

Aziz, M. F., Khan, A. N., Shuja, J., Khan, I. A., Khan, F. G., & Khan, A. R. (2019). A lightweight and compromise-resilient authentication scheme for IoTs. *Transactions on Emerging Telecommunications Technologies*, 3813. doi:10.1002/ett.3813

Azzi, R., Chamoun, R. K., & Sokhn, M. (2019). The power of a blockchain-based supply chain. *Computers & Industrial Engineering*, *135*, 582–592. doi:10.1016/j.cie.2019.06.042

Babich, V., & Hilary, G. (2020). Distributed ledgers and operations: What operations management researchers should know about blockchain technology. *Manufacturing & Service Operations Management*, *22*(2), 223–240. doi:10.1287/msom.2018.0752

Babun, L., Denney, K., Celik, Z. B., McDaniel, P., & Uluagac, A. S. (2021). A survey on IoT platforms: Communication, security, and privacy perspectives. *Computer Networks*, *192*, 108040. Advance online publication. doi:10.1016/j.comnet.2021.108040

Babu, R., & Jayashree, K. (2016). *Prominence of IoT and Cloud in Health Care. International Journal of Advanced Research in Computer Engineering & Technology*, *5*(2), 420–424.

Bahga, A., & Madisetti, V. K. (2016). Blockchain platform for industrial internet of things. *Journal of Software Engineering and Applications*, *9*(10), 533–546. doi:10.4236/jsea.2016.910036

Bai, C., & Sarkis, J. (2020). A supply chain transparency and sustainability technology appraisal model for blockchain technology. *International Journal of Production Research*, *58*(7), 2–7. doi:10.1080/00207543.2019.1708989

Bajaj. (2018). Blockchain and IoT based Smart Container Management for Global Supply Chain Traceability. *IJARIIE*, *4*(4).

Balci, G. (2021). Digitalization in container shipping: Do perception and satisfaction regarding digital products in a non-technology industry affect overall customer loyalty? *Technological Forecasting and Social Change*, *172*, 121016. Advance online publication. doi:10.1016/j.techfore.2021.121016

Bamakan, S. M. H., Faregh, N., & ZareRavasan, A. (2021). Di-ANFIS: An integrated blockchain–IoT–big data-enabled framework for evaluating service supply chain performance. *Journal of Computational Design and Engineering*, *8*(2), 676–690. doi:10.1093/jcde/qwab007

Bamakan, S. M. H., Motavali, A., & Babaei Bondarti, A. (2020). A survey of blockchain consensus algorithms performance evaluation criteria. In *Expert Systems with Applications* (Vol. 154, p. 113385). Elsevier Ltd. doi:10.1016/j.eswa.2020.113385

Bandara, E., Tosh, D., Foytik, P., Shetty, S., Ranasinghe, N., & De Zoysa, K. (2021). Tikiri—Towards a lightweight blockchain for IoT. *Future Generation Computer Systems*, *119*, 154–165. doi:10.1016/j.future.2021.02.006

Banerjee, A. (2018). Blockchain Technology: Supply Chain Insights from ERP. In Advances in Computers (Vol. 111, pp. 69–98). Academic Press Inc. doi:10.1016/bs.adcom.2018.03.007

Barenji, A. V., Li, Z., & Wang, W. M. (2018). Blockchain cloud manufacturing: Shop floor and machine level. *Smart SysTech 2018: European Conference on Smart Objects, Systems and Technologies*, (pp. 1–6). Academic Press.

Bartoletti, M., & Pompianu, L. (2017, April). An empirical analysis of smart contracts: platforms, applications, and design patterns. In *International conference on financial cryptography and data security* (pp. 494-509). Springer. 10.1007/978-3-319-70278-0_31

Beck, R., Avital, M., Rossi, M., & Thatcher, J. B. (2017). Blockchain Technology in Business and Information Systems Research. *Business & Information Systems Engineering*, *59*(6), 381–384. doi:10.100712599-017-0505-1

Begum, A., Tareq, A. H., Sultana, M., Sohel, M. K., Rahman, T., & Sarwar, A. H. (2020). Blockchain attacks analysis and a model to solve double spending attack. *International Journal of Machine Learning and Computing*, *10*(2), 352–357.

Behnke, K., & Janssen, M. F. W. H. A. (2020). Boundary conditions for traceability in food supply chains using blockchain technology. *International Journal of Information Management*, *52*, 101969. doi:10.1016/j.ijinfomgt.2019.05.025

Ben-Daya, M., Hassini, E., & Bahroun, Z. (2017). Internet of Things and Supply Chain Management: A Literature Review. *International Journal of Production Research*. Advance online publication. doi:10.1080/00207543.2017.1402140

Bhandarkar, V. V., Bhandarkar, A. A., & Shiva, A. (2019). Digital stocks using blockchain technology the possible future of stocks? *International Journal of Management*, *10*(3). Advance online publication. doi:10.34218/IJM.10.3.2019/005

Birkel, H., & Müller, J. M. (2021). Potentials of industry 4.0 for supply chain management within the triple bottom line of sustainability – A systematic literature review. *Journal of Cleaner Production*, *289*, 125612. Advance online publication. doi:10.1016/j.jclepro.2020.125612

Blockchain, W. (2021). *China information chip another step forward*. https://mp.weixin.qq.com/s/uyhguvWakwK8j-vGbXo0uA

Blockchains. (2020, February). Benefits of Blockchain In Logistics Industry. *Benefits of Blockchain In Logistics Industry*. Retrieved July 17, 2021, from https://101blockchains.com/blockchain-in-logistics/

Bodkhe, U., Tanwar, S., Parekhi, K., Khanpara, P., Tyagi, S., Kumar, N., & Alazab, M. (2020). Blockchain for Industry 4.0: A Comprehensive Review Special Section on Deep Learning Algorithms for Internet of Medical Things. *IEEE Access: Practical Innovations, Open Solutions*, *8*, 79764–79800. doi:10.1109/ACCESS.2020.2988579

Bogart, S., & Rice, K. (2015). The blockchain report: Welcome to the internet of value. *Needham Insights*, *5*, 1–10.

Boison, D. K., & Antwi-Boampong, A. (2019). Blockchain ready port supply chain using a distributed ledger. In NB! ICT Innovation, Regulation, Multi Business Model Innovation, and Technology (pp. 1–32). Multi-agent.

Bonilla, S., Silva, H., Terra da Silva, M., Franco Gonçalves, R., & Sacomano, J. (2018). Industry 4.0 and Sustainability Implications: A Scenario-Based Analysis of the Impacts and Challenges. *Sustainability*, *10*(10), 3740. Advance online publication. doi:10.3390u10103740

Bonkenburg, T. (2016). *Robotics in logistics*. DHL Customer Solutions & Innovation, Troisdorf.

Bose, A., Aujla, G. S., Singh, M., Kumar, N., & Cao, H. (2019, August). Blockchain as a service for software defined networks: A denial of service attack perspective. In 2019 IEEE Intl Conf on Dependable, Autonomic and Secure Computing, Intl Conf on Pervasive Intelligence and Computing, Intl Conf on Cloud and Big Data Computing, Intl Conf on Cyber Science and Technology Congress (DASC/PiCom/CBDCom/CyberSciTech) (pp. 901-906). IEEE. doi:10.1109/DASC/PiCom/CBDCom/CyberSciTech.2019.00166

Bosu, A., Iqbal, A., Shahriyar, R., & Chakraborty, P. (2019). Understanding the motivations, challenges and needs of Blockchain software developers: A survey. *Empirical Software Engineering*, *24*(4), 2636–2673. doi:10.100710664-019-09708-7

Brandl, N. (2016). *Siegeszug der Cloud.* https://logistik-heute.de

Buterin, V. (2014). A next-generation smart contract and decentralized application platform. *White Paper, 3*(37).

Buterin, V., & Associates. (2014). A next-generation smart contract and decentralized application platform. *White Paper, 3*.

Cachin, C. (2016, July). Architecture of the hyperledger blockchain fabric. In *Workshop on distributed cryptocurrencies and consensus ledgers* (*Vol. 310*, No. 4). Academic Press.

Carter, C. R., & Rogers, D. S. (2008). A framework of sustainable supply chain management: Moving toward new theory. *International Journal of Physical Distribution & Logistics Management*, *38*(5), 360–387. doi:10.1108/09600030810882816

Casino, F., Dasaklis, T. K., & Patsakis, C. (2019). A systematic literature review of blockchain-based applications: Current status, classification and open issues. *Telematics and Informatics*, *36*, 55–81. doi:10.1016/j.tele.2018.11.006

Castro, M., & Liskov, B. (1999, February). Practical byzantine fault tolerance. In OSDI (Vol. 99, No. 1999, pp. 173-186). Academic Press.

Centobelli, P., Cerchione, R., Vecchio, P. D., Oropallo, E., & Secundo, G. (2021). Blockchain technology for bridging trust, traceability and transparency in circular supply chain. *Information & Management*, 103508. Advance online publication. doi:10.1016/j.im.2021.103508

Černý, M., Gogola, M., Kubaľák, S., & Ondruš, J. (2021). Blockchain technology as a new driver in supply chain. *Transportation Research Procedia*, *55*, 299–306. doi:10.1016/j.trpro.2021.06.034

Cha, S. C., Chen, J. F., Su, C., & Yeh, K. H. (2018). A blockchain connected gateway for BLE-based devices in the internet of things. *IEEE Access, 6*, 24639-24649.

Chakraborty, R. B., Pandey, M., & Rautaray, S. S. (2018). Managing computation load on a blockchain–based multi–layered internet–of–things network. *Procedia Computer Science*, *132*, 469–476. doi:10.1016/j.procs.2018.05.146

Chambers, D., & Lacey, N. (2011). *Modern Corporate Finance: Theory and Practice* (6th ed.). Hayden-McNeil.

Chang, J. (2017). *Blockchain: The immutable ledger of transparency in healthcare technology*. Accessed on November 4th, 2021, Available: https://medium.com/@sidebench/blockchainthe-immutable-ledger-of-transparency-in-healthcare-technology-a4a64b1d5594

Chang, J., Katehakis, M. N., Melamed, B., & Shi, J. (Junmin). (2018). Blockchain Design for Supply Chain Management. SSRN *Electronic Journal*. doi:10.2139/ssrn.3295440

Chang, S. E., & Chen, Y. (2020). When blockchain meets supply chain: A systematic literature review on current development and potential applications. In *IEEE Access* (Vol. 8, pp. 62478–62494). Institute of Electrical and Electronics Engineers Inc. doi:10.1109/ACCESS.2020.2983601

Chang, Y., Iakovou, E., & Shi, W. (2020). Blockchain in global supply chains and cross border trade: A critical synthesis of the state-of-the-art, challenges and opportunities. *International Journal of Production Research*, *58*(7), 2082–2099. doi:10.1080/00207543.2019.1651946

Chanson, M., Bogner, A., Bilgeri, D., Fleisch, E., & Wortmann, F. (2019). Blockchain for the IoT: Privacy-preserving protection of sensor data. *Journal of the Association for Information Systems*, *20*(9), 1274–1309. doi:10.17705/1jais.00567

Chartered Institute of Procurement and Supply (CIPS). (n.d.). *What Is Procurement and Supply?* CIPS.

Chen, J., Cai, T., He, W., Chen, L., Zhao, G., Zou, W., & Guo, L. (2020). A Blockchain-Driven Supply Chain Finance Application for Auto Retail Industry. *Entropy 2020, 22*(1), 95. doi:10.3390/e22010095

Chen, S., Shi, R., Ren, Z., Yan, J., Shi, Y., & Zhang, J. (2017). A blockchain-based supply chain quality management framework. In *2017 IEEE 14th International Conference on e-Business Engineering (ICEBE)* (pp. 172–176). 10.1109/ICEBE.2017.34

Chen, X. (2019). *Cross-border trade blockchain white paper*. Academic Press.

Cheng, S., Zeng, B., & Huang, Y. Z. (2017). Research on application model of blockchain techonology in distributed electricity market. *IOP Conference Series: Earth and Enviornmental Sciene*, 93.

Chen, I.-R., Guo, J., & Bao, F. (2014). Trust management for service composition in SOA-based IoT systems. *Proceedings of the IEEE Wireless Communications and Networking Conference (WCNC)*, 3444-3449. 10.1109/WCNC.2014.6953138

Chen, Y., Chen, H., Han, M., Liu, B., Chen, Q., & Ren, T. (2020). A Novel Computing Power Allocation Algorithm for Blockchain System in Multiple Mining Pools Under Withholding Attack. *IEEE Access: Practical Innovations, Open Solutions*, *8*, 155630–155644. doi:10.1109/ACCESS.2020.3017716

Chepkoech, A. (2019, May 28). Retrieved October 24, 2019, from www.nation.co.ke: https://www.nation.co.ke/ health/Why-Kenya-imports-drugs/3476990-5135300-h7o9f9/index.html

Chicarino, V., Albuquerque, C., Jesus, E., & Rocha, A. (2020). On the detection of selfish mining and stalker attacks in blockchain networks. *Annales des Télécommunications*, *75*(3-4), 1–10. doi:10.100712243-019-00746-2

China Financial Information Industry Association (CFIIA). (2021). *2021 Global Blockchain Innovative Application Demonstration Case Set*. Author.

Chris, J. S. (2017). *Who will be killed by blockchain: 4 small business areas that will soon disappear*. https://incrussia.ru/understand/kogo-ubet-blokchejn-4-sfery-malogo-biznesa-kotorye-skoro-ischeznut/

Chuen, D. L. (2015). *Handbook of Digital Currency*. Bitcoin.

Chung, G., Gesing, B., Chaturvedi, K., & Bodenbenner, P. (2018). *Logistics trend radar*. DHL Customer Solutions & Innovation.

Churyumov, A. (2016). *Byteball: A decentralized system for storage and transfer of value*. https://byteball. org/Byteball. pdf

Cleland-Huang, J., Hayes, J. H., Zisman, A., Egyed, A., Grünbacher, P., & M¨ader, P. (2012). Traceability fundamentals. In *Software and Systems Traceability* (pp. 3–22). Springer. doi:10.1007/978-1-4471-2239-5

Clohessy, T., Acton, T., & Rogers, N. (2019). Blockchain Adoption: Technological, Organisational and Environmental Considerations. *Business Transformation through Blockchain*, 47–76. doi:10.1007/978-3-319-98911-2_2

CloudB. (2021). http://www.heiyunworld.com/

Cohen, S., & Rousell, J. (2005). *Strategic Supply Chain Management: The five disciplines for top performance*. Mc Graw- Hill.

Coita, D. C., Abrudan, M. M., & Matei, M. C. (2019). *Effects of the Blockchain Technology on Human Resources and Marketing: An Exploratory Study*. doi:10.1007/978-3-030-12453-3_79

Cole, R., Stevenson, M., & Aitken, J. (2019). Blockchain technology: Implications for operations and supply chain management. *Supply Chain Management, 24*(4), 469–483. doi:10.1108/SCM-09-2018-0309

Cong, L. W. (2021). Internet of Things: Business Economics and Applications. In M. Pompella (Ed.), *Review of Review of BusinessBusiness* (Vol. 41, pp. 15–30). University of Siena.

Connor, T. (2001). *Still waiting for Nike to do it*. Global Exchange.

Cooper, D. R., & Gutowski, T. G. (2015). Environmental Impact of Reuse. *Journal of Industrial Ecology*, 1–14.

Cooper, D., & Schindler, P. (2006). *Business Research Methods*. Mc Graw Hill.

Cooper, M. C., Lambert, D. M., & Pagh, J. D. (1997). Supply Chain Management: More Than a New Name for Logistics. *International Journal of Logistics Management, 8*(1), 1–14. doi:10.1108/09574099710805556

Council of Supply Chain Management Professionals (CSCMP). (2013). *SCM Definitions and Glossary of Terms*. https://cscmp.org/CSCMP/Academia/SCM_Definitions_and_Glossary_of_Terms/CSCMP/Educate/SCM_Definitions_and_Glossary_of_Terms.aspx?hkey=60879588-f65f-4ab5-8c4b-6878815ef921

Council of Supply Chain Management Professionals (CSCMP). (2018). *CSCMP's definition of supply chain management*. Author.

Crosby, M., & Nachiappan, P. (2016). Blockchain technology: Beyond bitcoin. *Applied Innovation Review, 2*(6-10), 71.

Cui, G., Shi, K., Qin, Y., Liu, L., Qi, B., & Li, B. (2017). Application of block chain in multi-level demand response reliable mechanism. *2017 3rd International Conference on Information Management (ICIM)*, 337–341.

Da Xu, L., Lu, Y., & Li, L. (2021). Embedding blockchain technology into IoT for security: A survey. *IEEE Internet of Things Journal*.

Dabbagh, M., Choo, K.-K. R., Beheshti, A., Tahir, M., & Safa, N. S. (2021). A survey of empirical performance evaluation of permissioned blockchain platforms: Challenges and opportunities. *Computers & Security, 100*, 102078. Advance online publication. doi:10.1016/j.cose.2020.102078

Dai, J., Xie, L., & Chu, Z. (2021). Developing sustainable supply chain management: The interplay of institutional pressures and sustainability capabilities. *Sustainable Production and Consumption, 28*, 254–268. doi:10.1016/j.spc.2021.04.017

Daim, T., Lai, K. K., Yalcin, H., Alsoubie, F., & Kumar, V. (2020). Forecasting technological positioning through technology knowledge redundancy: Patent citation analysis of IoT, cybersecurity, and Blockchain. *Technological Forecasting and Social Change*, *161*, 120329. Advance online publication. doi:10.1016/j.techfore.2020.120329

Dannen, K. (2018). *Introduction to Ethereum and Solidity*. Samizdat.

Davies, S., & Likens, S. (2018). *PwC's global Blockchain survey*. Accessed on October 8, 2021. Available: https://www.pwc.com/jg/en/publications/blockchain-is-here-next-move.pdf

Di Vaio, A., & Varriale, L. (2020). Blockchain technology in supply chain management for sustainable performance: Evidence from the airport industry. *International Journal of Information Management*, *52*, 102014. doi:10.1016/j.ijinfomgt.2019.09.010

Dick, A., & Basu, K. (1994). Customer Loyalty: Toward an integrated conceptual framework. *Journal of the Academy of Marketing Science*, *22*(2), 99–113. doi:10.1177/0092070394222001

Dietrich, F., Ge, Y., Turgut, A., Louw, L., & Palm, D. (2021). Review and analysis of blockchain projects in supply chain management. *Procedia Computer Science*, *180*, 724–733. doi:10.1016/j.procs.2021.01.295

Ding, K., Jiang, P., Leng, J., & Cao, W. (2016). Modeling and analyzing of an enterprise relationship network in the context of social manufacturing. *Proceedings of the Institution of Mechanical Engineers. Part B, Journal of Engineering Manufacture*, *230*(4), 752–769. doi:10.1177/0954405414558730

Dinh, T. T. A., Liu, R., Zhang, M., Chen, G., Ooi, B. C., & Wang, J. (2018). Untangling Blockchain: A Data Processing View of Blockchain Systems. *IEEE Transactions on Knowledge and Data Engineering*, *30*(7), 1366–1385. doi:10.1109/TKDE.2017.2781227

Dobler & Burt. (2006). Purchasing management (6th ed.). McGraw Hill International Edition.

Dobrovnik, M., Herold, D. M., Fürst, E., & Kummer, S. (2018). Blockchain for and in Logistics: What to Adopt and Where to Start. *Logistics*, *2*(3), 18. doi:10.3390/logistics2030018

Dogo, E. M., Salami, A. F., Aigbavboa, C. O., & Nkonyana, T. (2019). Taking Cloud Computing to the Extreme Edge: A Review of Mist Computing for Smart Cities and Industry 4.0 in Africa. Edge Computing, 107–132.

Dolgui, A., Ivanov, D., Potryasaev, S., Sokolov, B., Ivanova, M., & Werner, F. (2020). Blockchain-oriented dynamic modelling of smart contract design and execution in the supply chain. *International Journal of Production Research*, *58*(7), 2184–2199. doi:10.1080/00207543.2019.1627439

Dong, Z., Luo, F., & Liang, G. (2018). Blockchain: A secure, decentralized, trusted cyberinfrastructure solution for future energy systems. *Journal of Modern Power Systems and Clean Energy*, *6*(5), 958–967. doi:10.100740565-018-0418-0

Dorri, A., Kanhere, S. S., & Jurdak, R. (2016). *Blockchain in internet of things: challenges and solutions.* arXiv preprint arXiv:1608.05187.

Dorri, A., Kanhere, S. S., Jurdak, R., & Gauravaram, P. (2017, March). Blockchain for IoT security and privacy: The case study of a smart home. In *2017 IEEE international conference on pervasive computing and communications workshops (PerCom workshops)* (pp. 618-623). IEEE.

Duan, J., Zhang, C., Gong, Y., Brown, S., & Li, Z. (2020). A content-analysis based literature review in blockchain adoption within food supply chain. *International Journal of Environmental Research and Public Health*, *17*(5), 1784. doi:10.3390/ijerph17051784 PMID:32182951

Dubey, R., Gunasekaran, A., Bryde, D. J., Dwivedi, Y. K., & Papadopoulos, T. (2020). Blockchain technology for enhancing swift-trust, collaboration and resilience within a humanitarian supply chain setting. *International Journal of Production Research, 58*(11), 3381–3398. doi:10.1080/00207543.2020.1722860

Dubovec, M. (2005). The problems and possibilities for using electronic bills of lading as collateral. *Ariz. J. Int'l & Comp. L., 23*, 437.

Durach, C. F., Blesik, T., Düring, M., & Bick, M. (2020). Blockchain Applications in Supply Chain Transactions. *Journal of Business Logistics*. doi:10.1111/jbl.12238

Dutta, P., Choi, T. M., Somani, S., & Butala, R. (2020). Blockchain technology in supply chain operations: Applications, challenges and research opportunities. *Transportation Research Part E, Logistics and Transportation Review, 142*, 102067. doi:10.1016/j.tre.2020.102067 PMID:33013183

Dwivedi, Roy, Karda, Agrawal, & Amin. (2021). Blockchain-Based Internet of Things and Industrial IoT: A Comprehensive Survey. Hindawi Security and Communication Networks.

Dwivedi, S. K., Amin, R., & Vollala, S. (2020). Blockchain based secured information sharing protocol in supply chain management system with key distribution mechanism. *Journal of Information Security and Applications, 54*, 102554. doi:10.1016/j.jisa.2020.102554

Dwivedi, Y. K., Hughes, L., Ismagilova, E., Aarts, G., Coombs, C., Crick, T., & Williams, M. D. (2019). Artificial Intelligence (AI): Multidisciplinary perspectives on emerging challenges, opportunities, and agenda for research, practice and policy. *International Journal of Information Management*, 101994.

Economist. (2015). *Blockchain: The great chain of being sure about things*. Accessed 05.11.2021, Available: https://www.economist.com

Egels-Zandén, N., Hulthén, K., & Wulff, G. (2015). Trade-offs in supply chain transparency: The case of Nudie Jeans Co. *Journal of Cleaner Production, 107*, 95–104. doi:10.1016/j.jclepro.2014.04.074

Egorov, V. (2021). *Gazprom Neft sells its blockchain platform in the form of an NFT token.* (https://beincrypto.ru/gazprom-neft-prodaet-reliz-sobstvennoj-blokchejn-platformy-v-vide-nft-tokena/)

Eisenhardt, K. M., & Graebner, M. E. (2007). Theory Building From Cases: Opportunities And Challenges. *Academy of Management Journal, 50*(1), 25–32. doi:10.5465/amj.2007.24160888

Elder, S. D., Zerriffi, H., & Le Billon, P. (2013). Is Fairtrade certification greening agricultural practices? An analysis of Fairtrade environmental standards in Rwanda. *Journal of Rural Studies, 32*, 264–274. doi:10.1016/j.jrurstud.2013.07.009

Ellul, Galea, Ganado, Mccarthy, & Pace. (2020). Regulating blockchain, dlt and smart contracts: a technology regulator's perspective. *ERA Forum, 21*, 209–220.

Ernest, A., Hourt, N., & Larimer, D. (2017). *U.S. Patent Application No. 15/298,177*. US Patent Office.

Etemadi, N., Van Gelder, P., & Strozzi, F. (2021). An ism modeling of barriers for blockchain/distributed ledger technology adoption in supply chains towards cybersecurity. *Sustainability (Switzerland), 13*(9), 4672. doi:10.3390u13094672

Fang, W., Chen, W., Zhang, W., Pei, J., Gao, W., & Wang, G. (2020). Digital signature scheme for information non-repudiation in the Blockchain: A state of the art review. *EURASIP Journal on Wireless Communications and Networking*.

Feng, T. (2016). An agri-food supply chain traceability system for China based on RFID. *13th International Conference on Service Systems and Service Management (ICSSSM)*, 1-6.

Figorilli, S., Antonucci, F., Costa, C., Pallottino, F., Raso, L., Castiglione, M., & Menesatti, P. (2018). A blockchain implementation prototype for the electronic open source traceability of wood along the whole supply chain. *Sensors (Basel), 18*(9), 3133. doi:10.339018093133 PMID:30227651

Filimonau, V., & Naumova, E. (2020). The blockchain technology and the scope of its application in hospitality operations. *International Journal of Hospitality Management, 87*, 102383. doi:10.1016/j.ijhm.2019.102383

Fiorentino, S., & Bartolucci, S. (2021). Blockchain-based smart contracts as new governance tools for the sharing economy. *Cities (London, England), 117*, 103325. Advance online publication. doi:10.1016/j.cities.2021.103325

Firdaus, A., Ab Razak, M. F., Feizollah, A., Hashem, I. A. T., Hazim, M., & Anuar, N. B. (2019). The rise of "blockchain": Bibliometric analysis of blockchain study. *Scientometrics, 120*(3), 1289–1331. doi:10.100711192-019-03170-4

Fosso Wamba, S., Kamdjoug, K., Robert, J., Bawack, R. G., & Keogh, J. (2018). Bitcoin, Blockchain, and FinTech: A Systematic Review and Case Studies in the Supply Chain. *Prod. Plan. Control.*

Fosso Wamba, S., Kala Kamdjoug, J. R., Epie Bawack, R., & Keogh, J. G. (2020). Bitcoin, Blockchain and Fintech: A systematic review and case studies in the supply chain. *Production Planning and Control, 31*(2–3), 115–142. doi:10.1080/09537287.2019.1631460

Fotiou, N., Siris, V. A., & Polyzos, G. C. (2018). Interacting with the Internet of Things Using Smart Contracts and Blockchain Technologies. In *Lecture Notes in Computer Science* (Vol. 11342, pp. 443–452). Springer.

Framework Agreement on Facilitation of Cross-Border Paperless Trade in Asia and the Pacific (FA-CPT). (2016). Economic and Social Commission for Asia and the Pacific, E/ESCAP/RES/72/4.

Francisco, K., & Swanson, D. (2018). The Supply Chain Has No Clothes: Technology Adoption of Blockchain for Supply Chain Transparency. *Logistics, 2*(1), 2. doi:10.3390/logistics2010002

Frentrup, M., & Theuvsen, L. (2006). *Transparency in supply chains: Is trust a limiting factor?* Tech. rep.

Freuden, D. (2018) Hybrid Blockchain: the best of both public and private. *BRAVE NEW Coin.* https://bravenewcoin.com/insights/hybrid-blockchains-the-best-of-both-public-and-private

Frick, N. R. J., Wilms, K. L., Brachten, F., Hetjens, T., Stieglitz, S., & Ross, B. (2021). The perceived surveillance of conversations through smart devices. *Electronic Commerce Research and Applications, 47*, 101046. Advance online publication. doi:10.1016/j.elerap.2021.101046

Fu, Y., & Zhu, J. (2019). Big production enterprise supply chain endogenous risk management based on blockchain. *IEEE Access: Practical Innovations, Open Solutions, 7*, 15310–15319. doi:10.1109/ACCESS.2019.2895327

Galvin, D. (2017). *IBM and Walmart: Blockchain for food safety.* PowerPoint Presentation.

George, R. V., Harsh, H. O., Ray, P., & Babu, A. K. (2019). Food quality traceability prototype for restaurants using blockchain and food quality data index. *Journal of Cleaner Production, 240*, 118021. doi:10.1016/j.jclepro.2019.118021

Gohil & Thakker. (2021). Blockchain-integrated technologies for solving supply chain challenges. *Modern Supply Chain Research and Applications, 3*(2), 78-97. doi:10.1108/MSCRA-10-2020-002

Gokalp, E., Coban, S., & Gokalp, M. O. (2019, November 1). Acceptance of Blockchain Based Supply Chain Management System: Research Model Proposal. *1st International Informatics and Software Engineering Conference: Innovative Technologies for Digital Transformation, IISEC 2019 - Proceedings.* 10.1109/UBMYK48245.2019.8965502

Gökalp, E., Gökalp, M. O., & Çoban, S. (2020). Blockchain-Based Supply Chain Management: Understanding the Determinants of Adoption in the Context of Organizations. *Information Systems Management*, 1–22. doi:10.1080/10580530.2020.1812014

Gold, S., & Heikkurinen, P. (2018). Transparency fallacy: Unintended consequences of stakeholder claims on responsibility in supply chains. *Accounting, Auditing & Accountability Journal.*

Goldsby, T., & Martichenko, R. (2005). *Lean Six Sigma Logistics: Strategic Development to Operational Success.* J. Ross Publishing, Inc.

Goudos, S. K., Dallas, P. I., Chatziefthymiou, S., & Kyriazakos, S. (2017). A Survey of IoT Key Enabling and Future Technologies: 5G, Mobile IoT, Semantic Web, and Applications. *Wireless Personal Communications*, *97*(2), 1645–1675. doi:10.100711277-017-4647-8

Grover, P., Kar, A. K., Janssen, M., & Ilavarasan, P. V. (2019). Perceived usefulness, ease of use and user acceptance of blockchain technology for digital transactions–insights from user-generated content on Twitter. *Enterprise Information Systems*, *13*(6), 771–800. doi:10.1080/17517575.2019.1599446

Guerreiro, S., van Kervel, S. J., & Babkin, E. (2013, July). Towards Devising an Architectural Framework for Enterprise Operating Systems. In ICSOFT (pp. 578-585). Academic Press.

Gu, J., Goetschalckx, M., & McGinnis, L. F. (2007). Research on warehouse operation: A comprehensive review. *European Journal of Operational Research*, *177*(1), 1–21. doi:10.1016/j.ejor.2006.02.025

Gulati, K., Kumar Boddu, R. S., Kapila, D., Bangare, S. L., Chandnani, N., & Saravanan, G. (2021). A review paper on wireless sensor network techniques in Internet of Things (IoT). *Materials Today: Proceedings*. Advance online publication. doi:10.1016/j.matpr.2021.05.067

Guo, J., Zhou, S., Chen, J., & Chen, Q. (2021). How information technology capability and knowledge integration capability interact to affect business model design: A polynomial regression with response surface analysis. *Technological Forecasting and Social Change*, *170*, 120935. Advance online publication. doi:10.1016/j.techfore.2021.120935

Hackius, N., & Petersen, M. (2017). Blockchain in logistics and supply chain: trick or treat? In *Digitalization in Supply Chain Management and Logistics: Smart and Digital Solutions for an Industry 4.0 Environment. Proceedings of the Hamburg International Conference of Logistics (HICL)* (vol. 23, pp. 3-18). Berlin: epubli GmbH.

Hackius, N., & Petersen, M. (2017). Blockchain in logistics and supply chain: trick or treat? *Digitalization in Supply Chain Management and Logistics: Smart and Digital Solutions for an Industry 4.0 Environment. Proceedings of the Hamburg International Conference of Logistics (HICL)*, 23, 3–18.

Hackius, N., Reimers, S., & Kersten, W. (2019). *The Privacy Barrier for Blockchain in Logistics: First Lessons from the Port of Hamburg. Logistics Management.* Springer.

Han, H. (2018). Upgrading informaion consumption and expanding the digital economy Electronic information consumption adds luster to smart life. *Economic Daily*. http://www.gov.cn/xinwen/2018-04/17/content_5283099.htm

Hangzhou Bureau of Statistics. (2020). Hangzhou Statistical Yearbook.

Härtinga, R., Sprengela, A., Wottlea, K., & Rettenmaiera, J. (2020). Potentials of Blockchain Technologies in Supply Chain Management – A Conceptual Model 24th International Conference on Knowledge-Based and Intelligent Information & Engineering Systems. *Procedia Computer Science*, *176*, 1950–1959. doi:10.1016/j.procs.2020.09.334

Hasan, H., AlHadhrami, E., AlDhaheri, A., Salah, K., & Jayaraman, R. (2019). Smart contract-based approach for efficient shipment management. *Computers & Industrial Engineering*, *136*, 149–159. doi:10.1016/j.cie.2019.07.022

Hashemi, S. H., Faghri, F., Rausch, P., & Campbell, R. H. (2016, April). World of empowered IoT users. In *2016 IEEE First International Conference on Internet-of-Things Design and Implementation (IoTDI)* (pp. 13-24). IEEE.

Hayouni, H., & Hamdi, M. (2016, April). Secure data aggregation with homomorphic primitives in wireless sensor networks: A critical survey and open research issues. In *2016 IEEE 13th International Conference on Networking, Sensing, and Control (ICNSC)* (pp. 1-6). IEEE. 10.1109/ICNSC.2016.7479039

Héder, M. (2017). From NASA to EU: The evolution of the TRL scale in Public Sector Innovation. *The Innovation Journal*, *22*(2), 1–23.

Hegde, B., Ravishankar, B., & Appaiah, M. (2020). Agricultural Supply Chain Management Using Blockchain Technology. *International Conference on Mainstreaming Block Chain Implementation*, 1-4. 10.23919/ICOMBI48604.2020.9203259

Hellani, H., Sliman, L., Samhat, A. E., & Exposito, E. (2021). On Blockchain Integration with Supply Chain: Overview on Data Transparency. *Logistics*, *5*(3), 46. doi:10.3390/logistics5030046

Helo, P., & Hao, Y. (2019). Blockchains in operations and supply chains: A model and reference implementation. *Computers & Industrial Engineering*, *136*, 242–251. doi:10.1016/j.cie.2019.07.023

Helo, P., & Shamsuzzoha, A. H. M. (2020, June). Real-time supply chain—A blockchain architecture for project deliveries. *Robotics and Computer-integrated Manufacturing*, *63*, 101909. Advance online publication. doi:10.1016/j.rcim.2019.101909

Hijazi, A. A., Perera, S., Alashwal, A. M., Alashwal, A. M., & Calheiros, R. N. (2019). Blockchain Adoption in Construction Supply Chain: A Review of Studies Across Multiple Sectors. *CIB World Building Congress,* 17–21. https://www.researchgate.net/publication/333879452

Hofmann, E., & Rüsch, M. (2017). Industry 4.0 and the current status as well as prospects on logistics. *Computers in Industry*, *89*, 23–34. doi:10.1016/j.compind.2017.04.002

Holland, M. (2017). *Rückkehr von Petya – Kryptotrojaner legt weltweit Firmen und Behörden lahm.* Academic Press.

Holland, M., Nigischer, C., & Stjepandić, J. (2017). Copyright protection in additive manufacturing with blockchain approach. In *Transdisciplinary Engineering: A Paradigm Shift* (pp. 914–921). IOS Press.

Hu, Q. (2019). *Two Session Observation Smart in action.* http://www.eeo.com.cn/2019/0306/349511.shtml

Huang, J., Mei, Z., & Li, Z. (2020). Business and financial information integration and voluntary management earnings forecasts. *China Journal of Accounting Research*, *13*(3), 291–307. doi:10.1016/j.cjar.2020.07.002

Hughes, L., Dwivedi, Y. K., Misra, S. K., Rana, N. P., Raghavan, V., & Akella, V. (2019). Blockchain research, practice and policy: Applications, benefits, limitations, emerging research themes and research agenda. *International Journal of Information Management*, *49*, 114–129. doi:10.1016/j.ijinfomgt.2019.02.005

Iansiti, M., & Lakhani, K. (2017). The truth about blockchain. *Harvard Business Review*. Available on https://hbr.org/2017/01/the-truthaboutblockchain?utm_source=datafloq&utm_medium=ref&utm_campaign=datafloq

IBM. (2020). *Vaccine distribution on Blockchain.* Accessed on October 27, 2021. Available: https://www.ibm.com/blockchain/solutions/vaccine-distribution

Ikeda, K., & Hamid, M. N. (2018). Applications of Blockchain in the Financial Sector and a Peer-to-Peer Global Barter Web. In *Advances in Computers* (Vol. 111, pp. 99–120). Academic Press Inc. doi:10.1016/bs.adcom.2018.03.008

Ilin, V., & Simić, D. (2013). From traditional ICT solutions towards cloud computing in logistics. *Proceedings of the 1st Logistics International Conference*, 78-83.

Infrastructure, N., & Opportunities, N. (2020). *The White Paper on The Development of China's Smart Economy*. https://www.cdrf.org.cn/jjhdt/5455.htm

Internet, X. (2001). *509 Public Key Infrastructure. Data Validation and Certification Server Protocols*. Network Working Group Request for Comments: 3029. https://www.ipa.go.jp/security/rfc/RFC3029EN.html

Iredale, G. (2020, November). History of Blockchain Technology: A Detailed Guide. *History of Blockchain Technology: A Detailed Guide*. Retrieved July 17, 2021, from https://101blockchains.com/history-of-blockchain-timeline/

Issaoui, Y., Khiat, A., Bahnasse, A., & Ouajji, H. (2019). Smart logistics: Study of the application of blockchain technology. *Procedia Computer Science*, *160*, 266–271. doi:10.1016/j.procs.2019.09.467

iThink Logistics Blog. (2019). *11 Major Innovations in the Logistics Industry*. Accessed on 11th November 2012.Available: https://ithinklogistics.com/blog/11-major-innovations-done-to-transform-the-logistics-industry/

ITU-T. (2002). *Recommendation X.842 information technology security techniques guidelines for the use and management of trusted third party services*. https://www.itu.int/rec/T-REC-X.842

Ivanov, D., Dolgui, A., & Sokolov, B. (2019). The impact of digital technology and Industry 4.0 on the ripple effect and supply chain risk analytics. *International Journal of Production Research*, *57*(3), 829–846. doi:10.1080/00207543.2018.1488086

Jabbar, S., Lloyd, H., Hammoudeh, M., Adebisi, B., & Raza, U. (2021). Blockchain-enabled supply chain: Analysis, challenges, and future directions. *Multimedia Systems*, *27*(4), 787–806. doi:10.100700530-020-00687-0

Jain. (2019). Security Issues in Blockchain based Applications. *International Journal of Engineering and Advanced Technology, 8*(6S).

Jain, G., Singh, H., Chaturvedi, K. R., & Rakesh, S. (2020). Blockchain in logistics industry: In fizz customer trust or not. *Journal of Enterprise Information Management*, *33*(3), 541–558. doi:10.1108/JEIM-06-2018-0142

Jamil, S. (2021). From digital divide to digital inclusion: Challenges for wide-ranging digitalization in Pakistan. *Telecommunications Policy*, *45*(8), 102206. Advance online publication. doi:10.1016/j.telpol.2021.102206

Janssen, M., Weerakkody, V., Ismagilova, E., Sivarajah, U., & Irani, Z. (2020). A framework for analyzing Blockchain technology adoption: Integrating institutional, market, and technical factors. *International Journal of Information Management*, *50*, 302–309. doi:10.1016/j.ijinfomgt.2019.08.012

Javaid, M. (2021). Blockchain technology applications for Industry 4.0: A literature-based review. *Blockchain: Research and Applications*. doi:10.1016/j.bcra.2021.100027

Jayashree, K., & Babu, R. (2018). Privacy in the Internet of Things. *The Internet of Things in the Modern Business Environment*. doi:10.4018/978-1-5225-2104-4.ch005

Jessop, D., & Morrison, A. (1994). *Storage and supply of materials* (6th ed.). London: Financial Times.

Jia, C., Cai, Y., Yu, Y. T., & Tse, T. H. (2016). 5W+ 1H pattern: A perspective of systematic mapping studies and a case study on cloud software testing. *Journal of Systems and Software*, *116*, 206–219. doi:10.1016/j.jss.2015.01.058

Jiang, S. (2021). Blockchain competition: The tradeoff between platform stability and efficiency. *European Journal of Operational Research*. Advance online publication. doi:10.1016/j.ejor.2021.05.031

Jua. (2021). *Zhongqi Anlian- the best supply chain finance solution providers*. https://mp.weixin.qq.com/s?__biz=MzI0NTExMjc1Nw==&mid=2247484946&idx=1&sn=4094f4e4b0c4610be3517005a5c2bb13&chksm=e952ccc8de2545de4d0cc309eb0ad5db70784a645f6f006ec7c1a453b0ea664923127d6dba8e&token=510349077&lang=zh_CN#rd

Kamath, R. (2018). Food traceability on blockchain: Walmart's pork and mango pilots with IBM. *The Journal of the British Blockchain Association*, *1*(1), 3712. doi:10.31585/jbba-1-1-(10)2018

Kamble, S., Gunasekaran, A., & Arha, H. (2018). Understanding the blockchain technology adoption in supply chains-Indian context. *International Journal of Production Research, 25.*

Kamble, S., Gunasekaran, A., & Arha, H. (2019). Understanding the Blockchain technology adoption in supply chains-Indian context. *International Journal of Production Research*, *57*(7), 2009–2033. doi:10.1080/00207543.2018.1518610

Kamran, M., Khan, H. U., Nisar, W., Farooq, M., & Rehman, S.-U. (2020). Blockchain and internet of things: A bibliometric study. *Computers & Electrical Engineering*, *81*, 106525. doi:10.1016/j.compeleceng.2019.106525

Kandampully, J. (2003). *B2B Relationships and Networks in the Internet Age*. Journal Management Decisions.

Karaev, A. (2018). *"Gazprom Neft" has tested blockchain and the Internet of Things in logistics.* (https://www.gazprom-neft.ru/press-center/news/v-gazprom-nefti-ispytali-blokcheyn-i-internet-veshchey-v-logistike/)

Karafiloski & Mishev. (2017). Blockchain solutions for big data challenges: A literature review. In *IEEE EUROCON 2017-17th International Conference on Smart Technologies* (pp. 763–768). IEEE.

Karale, A. (2021). The Challenges of IoT Addressing Security, Ethics, Privacy, and Laws. *Internet of Things*, *15*, 100420. Advance online publication. doi:10.1016/j.iot.2021.100420

Kayikci, Y., Kazancoglu, Y., Lafci, C., & Gozacan, N. (2021). Exploring barriers to smart and sustainable circular economy: The case of an automotive eco-cluster. *Journal of Cleaner Production*, *314*, 127920. Advance online publication. doi:10.1016/j.jclepro.2021.127920

Kennedy, Z. C., Stephenson, D. E., Christ, J. F., Pope, T. R., Arey, B. W., Barrett, C. A., & Warner, M. G. (2017). Enhanced anti-counterfeiting measures for additive manufacturing: Coupling lanthanide nanomaterial chemical signatures with blockchain technology. *Journal of Materials Chemistry. C, Materials for Optical and Electronic Devices*, *5*(37), 9570–9578. doi:10.1039/C7TC03348F

Kersten, W., & Schroder, M. (2015). Supply Chain Risk management for Industries 4.0. Industry 4.0 Management, 31(3), 36–40.

Khan, M. A., & Salah, K. (2018). IoT security: Review, blockchain solutions, and open challenges. *Future Generation Computer Systems*, *82*, 395–411. doi:10.1016/j.future.2017.11.022

Koh, L., Dolgui, A., & Sarkis, J. (2020). Blockchain in transport and logistics – paradigms and transitions. *International Journal of Production Research*, *58*(7), 2054–2062. doi:10.1080/00207543.2020.1736428

Korpela, K., Hallikas, J., & Dahlberg, T. (2017). Digital Supply Chain Transformation toward Blockchain Integration. *Proceedings of the 50th Hawaii International Conference on System Sciences*. 10.24251/HICSS.2017.506

Ko, T., Lee, J., & Ryu, D. (2018). Blockchain Technology and Manufacturing Industry: Real-Time Transparency and Cost Savings. *Sustainability*, *10*(11), 4274. doi:10.3390u10114274

Kothari, C. R. (2008). *An introduction to operational Research.* Vikas Publishing.

Koumanakos, D. P. (2008). The effect of inventory management on firm performance. *International Journal of Productivity and Performance Management*, *57*, 355–369.

Kravitz, D. W., & Cooper, J. (2017, June). *Securing user identity and transactions symbiotically: IoT meets blockchain. In 2017 Global Internet of Things Summit (GIoTS)*. IEEE.

Krings, K., & Schwab, J. (2021). *Blockchain technology in supply chains: What are the opportunities for sustainable development? (No. 2/2021)*. Briefing Paper.

Kruijff, J., & Weygand, H. (2017, June). Using Enterprise Ontology to Gain a Better Understanding of the Blockchain Advances in Information Technology Engineering. *Lecture Notes in Computer Science*, 29–43. doi:10.1007/978-3-319-59536-8_3

Kshetri, N. (2017). Blockchain's roles in strengthening cybersecurity and protecting privacy. *Telecommunications Policy*, *41*(10), 1027-1038.

Kshetri, N. (2017). Blockchain's roles in strengthening cybersecurity and protecting privacy. *Telecommunications Policy*, *41*(10), 1027–1038. doi:10.1016/j.telpol.2017.09.003

Kshetri, N. (2018). 1 Blockchain's roles in meeting key supply chain management objectives. *International Journal of Information Management*, *39*, 80–89. doi:10.1016/j.ijinfomgt.2017.12.005

Kshetri, N. (2021). Blockchain and sustainable supply chain management in developing countries. *International Journal of Information Management*, *60*, 102376. Advance online publication. doi:10.1016/j.ijinfomgt.2021.102376

Kulkarni, M., & Patil, K. (2020). Block Chain Technology Adoption for Banking Services- Model based on Technology-Organization-Environment theory. SSRN *Electronic Journal*. doi:10.2139/ssrn.3563101

Kumar, R., & Sharma, R. (2021). Leveraging Blockchain for Ensuring Trust in IoT: A Survey. *Journal of King Saud University - Computer and Information Sciences*. doi:10.1016/j.jksuci.2021.09.004

Kumar, N. M., & Mallick, P. K. (2018). Blockchain technology for security issues and challenges in IoT. *Procedia Computer Science*, *132*, 1815–1823. doi:10.1016/j.procs.2018.05.140

Kumar, N., & Ganguly, K. K. (2020). External diffusion of B2B e-procurement and firm financial performance: Role of information transparency and supply chain coordination. *Journal of Enterprise Information Management*.

Kumar, S., & Bhatia, M. S. (2021). Environmental dynamism, industry 4.0 and performance: Mediating role of organizational and technological factors. *Industrial Marketing Management*, *95*, 54–64. doi:10.1016/j.indmarman.2021.03.010

Kupriyanovsky, V., Namiot, D., & Sinyagov, S. (2016). Cyber-physical systems as a base for the digital economy. International Journal of Open Information Technologies, 4(2), 18-25.

Kustov, V. N., & Domrachev, A. A. (2011). Transboundary Trust Space as a Component of an International E-Commerce Soft-Infrastructure. *APEC PROJECT Supply Chain Connectivity: e-Commerce as the Main Driver and Integration Too*, 85-96.

Kustov, V. N., & Stankevich, T. L. (2018). Blockchain Prospects: a Dialogue between a Skeptic and an Optimist. *Bulletin of Scientific Conferences*, *1*(37), 77-84.

Kustov, V. N., & Stankevich, T. L. (2019). Blockchain Technology: a Story of Ingenious Simplicity or Enlightened Thinking. How to protect yourself from blockchain? *Information Protection. INSIDE*, *2*(86), 11-18.

Kustov, V. N., & Stankevich, T. L. (2019). Blockchain Technology: a Story of Ingenious Simplicity or Enlightened Thinking. How to protect yourself from blockchain? *J. Information Protection*, *2*(86), 11-18.

Kustov, V. N., & Silanteva, E. S. (2020). Mutual recognition mechanism of legally significant e-documents and data in the cross-border document flow. *Journal of Physics: Conference Series*, *1703*(1), 012011. doi:10.1088/1742-6596/1703/1/012011

Kustov, V. N., & Stankevich, T. L. (2018). Once Again about Blockchain Technology. *Intellectual Technologies on Transport*, (3), 38–46.

Kustov, V. N., & Stankevich, T. L. (2018). Once Again, about Blockchain Technology. *J. Intellectual Technologies on Transport*, (3), 38–46.

Laksch, J. S., & Borsato, M. (2019). Method for digital evaluation of existing production systems adequacy to changes in product engineering in the context of the automotive industry. *Advanced Engineering Informatics*, *42*, 100942. Advance online publication. doi:10.1016/j.aei.2019.100942

Lamba, K., & Singh, S. P. (2017). Big Data in Operations and Supply Chain Management: Current Trends and Future Perspectives. *Production Planning and Control*, *28*(11–12), 877–890. doi:10.1080/09537287.2017.1336787

Lambert. (2006). *Supply Chain Management: Processes, Partnerships, Performance*. Supply Chain Management Institute.

Lamport, L. (2019). A new solution of Dijkstra's concurrent programming problem. In Concurrency: the Works of Leslie Lamport (pp. 171-178). doi:10.1145/3335772.3335782

Larson, P. D., & Halldorsson, A. (2004). Logistics versus Supply Chain Management: An International Survey. *International Journal of Logistics: Research and Applications, 7*(1).

Latif, R. M. A., Farhan, M., Rizwan, O., Hussain, M., Jabbar, S., & Khalid, S. (2021). Retail level Blockchain transformation for product supply chain using truffle development platform. *Cluster Computing*, *24*(1), 1–16. doi:10.100710586-020-03165-4

Lee Kuo Chuen, D. (2015). *Handbook of digital currency* (1st ed.). Elsevier. Available http://EconPapers.repec.org/RePEc:eee:monogr:9780128021170

Lee, C. K. M., & Yaqiong Lv, K. K. H. (2018, April 18). Design and Application of Internet of Things-based Warehouse Management System for Smart Logistics. *International Journal of Production Research*, *56*(8), 2753–2768. Advance online publication. doi:10.1080/00207543.2017.1394592

Leng, K., Bi, Y., Jing, L., Fu, H. C., & Van Nieuwenhuyse, I. (2018). Research on agricultural supply chain system with double chain architecture based on blockchain technology. *Future Generation Computer Systems*, *86*, 641–649. doi:10.1016/j.future.2018.04.061

Lewenberg, Y., Sompolinsky, Y., & Zohar, A. (2015). Inclusive block chain protocols. *International Conference on Financial Cryptography and Data Security*, 528–547. 10.1007/978-3-662-47854-7_33

Liang, X., Shetty, S., Tosh, D., Kamhoua, C., Kwiat, K., & Njilla, L. (2017, May). Provchain: A blockchain-based data provenance architecture in a cloud environment with enhanced privacy and availability. In *2017 17th IEEE/ACM International Symposium on Cluster, Cloud and Grid Computing (CCGRID)* (pp. 468-477). IEEE. 10.1109/CCGRID.2017.8

Li, B.-H., Zhang, L., Wang, S.-L., Tao, F., Cao, J. W., Jiang, X. D., ... Chai, X. D. (2010). Cloud manufacturing: A new service-oriented networked manufacturing model. *Jisuanji Jicheng Zhizao Xitong*, *16*, 1–7.

Lim, M. K., Li, Y., Wang, C., & Tseng, M.-L. (2021). A literature review of blockchain technology applications in supply chains: A comprehensive analysis of themes, methodologies and industries. *Computers & Industrial Engineering*, *154*, 107133. doi:10.1016/j.cie.2021.107133

Lin, W., Huang, X., Fang, H., Wang, V., Hua, Y., Wang, J., Yin, H., Yi, D., & Yau, L. (2020). Blockchain technology in current agricultural systems: From techniques to applications. *IEEE Access: Practical Innovations, Open Solutions*, *8*, 143920–143937. doi:10.1109/ACCESS.2020.3014522

Litke, A., Anagnostopoulos, D., & Varvarigou, T. (2019). Blockchains for supply chain management: Architectural elements and challenges towards a global scale deployment. *Logistics*, *3*(1), 5. doi:10.3390/logistics3010005

Liu, J., Jiang, P., & Leng, J. (2017). A framework of credit assurance mechanism for manufacturing services under social manufacturing context. *2017 13th IEEE Conference on Automation Science and Engineering (CASE)*, 36–40.

Liu, B., Yu, X. L., Chen, S., Xu, X., & Zhu, L. (2017, June). Blockchain based data integrity service framework for IoT data. In *2017 IEEE International Conference on Web Services (ICWS)* (pp. 468-475). IEEE. 10.1109/ICWS.2017.54

Liu, H. (2020). Blockchain and bills of lading: Legal issues in perspective. In *Maritime Law in Motion* (pp. 413–435). Springer. doi:10.1007/978-3-030-31749-2_19

Liu, Z., Liu, Z., Zhang, L., & Lin, X. (2018). MARP: A distributed MAC layer attack resistant pseudonym scheme for VANET. *IEEE Transactions on Dependable and Secure Computing*, *17*(4), 869–882. doi:10.1109/TDSC.2018.2838136

Li, W., Zhong, Y., Wang, X., & Cao, Y. (2013). Resource Virtualization and Service Selection in Cloud Logistics. *Journal of Network and Computer Applications*, *36*(6), 1696–1704. doi:10.1016/j.jnca.2013.02.019

Li, Y., Dai, J., & Cui, L. (2020). The impact of digital technologies on economic and environmental performance in the context of industry 4.0: A moderated mediation model. *International Journal of Production Economics*, *229*, 107777. Advance online publication. doi:10.1016/j.ijpe.2020.107777

Li, Z., Ge, R. Y., Guo, X. S., & Cai, L. (2021). Can individual investors learn from experience in online P2P lending? Evidence from China. *The North American Journal of Economics and Finance*, *58*, 101524. Advance online publication. doi:10.1016/j.najef.2021.101524

Li, Z., Liu, L., Barenji, A. V., & Wang, W. (2018). Cloud-based manufacturing blockchain: Secure knowledge sharing for injection mould redesign. *Procedia CIRP*, *72*, 961–966. doi:10.1016/j.procir.2018.03.004

Lockl, J., Schlatt, V., Schweizer, A., Urbach, N., & Harth, N. (2020). Toward trust in Internet of Things ecosystems: Design principles for blockchain-based IoT applications. *IEEE Transactions on Engineering Management*, *67*(4), 1256–1270. doi:10.1109/TEM.2020.2978014

Longo, F., Nicoletti, L., & Padovano, A. (2019). *Blockchain-enabled supply chain: An experimental study*. Elsevier. https://www.sciencedirect.com/science/article/pii/S0360835219304139

Lyons, G. (2017). Getting smart about urban mobility – Aligning the paradigms of smart and sustainable. *Transportation Research Part A, Policy and Practice*, *115*, 4–14. doi:10.1016/j.tra.2016.12.001

Macrinici, D., Cartofeanu, C., & Gao, S. (2018). Smart contract applications within blockchain technology: A systematic mapping study. In Telematics and Informatics (Vol. 35, Issue 8, pp. 2337–2354). Elsevier Ltd. doi:10.1016/j.tele.2018.10.004

Maier, D., Maier, A., Aşchilean, I., Anastasiu, L., & Gavriş, O. (2020). The relationship between innovation and sustainability: A bibliometric review of the literature. *Sustainability*, *12*(10), 4083. doi:10.3390u12104083

Mainelli, M., & Milne, A. (2016). *The impact and potential of blockchain on the securities transaction lifecycle*. Academic Press.

Makhdoom, I., Abolhasan, M., Abbas, H., & Ni, W. (2019). Blockchain's adoption in IoT: The challenges, and a way forward. In *Journal of Network and Computer Applications* (Vol. 125, pp. 251–279). Academic Press. doi:10.1016/j.jnca.2018.10.019

Manyika, J., Chui, M., Groves, P., Farrell, D., Van Kuiken, S., & Doshi, E. A. (2013). Open data: Unlocking innovation and performance with liquid information. *McKinsey Global Institute*, *21*, 116.

Mao, D., Wang, F., Hao, Z., & Li, H. (2018). Credit evaluation system based on blockchain for multiple stakeholders in the food supply chain. *International Journal of Environmental Research and Public Health, 15*(8), 1627. doi:10.3390/ijerph15081627 PMID:30071695

Marsal-Llacuna, M. L. (2018). Future living framework: Is blockchain the next enabling network? *Technological Forecasting and Social Change, 128*, 226–234. doi:10.1016/j.techfore.2017.12.005

Mathivathanan, D., Mathiyazhagan, K., Rana, N. P., Khorana, S., & Dwivedi, Y. K. (2021). Barriers to the adoption of blockchain technology in business supply chains: A total interpretive structural modelling (TISM) approach. *International Journal of Production Research, 59*(11), 3338–3359. doi:10.1080/00207543.2020.1868597

Mazzei, D., Baldi, G., Fantoni, G., Montelisciani, G., Pitasi, A., Ricci, L., & Rizzello, L. (2020). A Blockchain Tokenizer for Industrial IOT trustless applications. *Future Generation Computer Systems, 105*, 432–445. doi:10.1016/j.future.2019.12.020

Mehta, D., & Senn-Kalb, L. (2021). *In-depth: Industry 4.0 2021*. Academic Press.

Meng & Qian. (2018). The Blockchain Application in Supply Chain Management: Opportunities, Challenges and Outlook. *The 3rd Symposium on Distributed Ledger Technology.*

Methodology of formation of transboundary trust environment and the requirements for its creation, functioning and development. (2017). *XXIII International Conference on Soft Computing and Measurement (SCM'2020) Journal of Physics: Conference Series*. https://www.unescap.org/resources/methodology-formation-transboundary-trustenvironment-and-requirements-its-creation-0/

Mettler, M. (2016, September). Blockchain technology in healthcare: The revolution starts here. In *2016 IEEE 18th international conference on e-health networking, applications and services (Healthcom)* (pp. 1-3). IEEE.

Moavenzadeh, J. (2013). *How can supply chains drive growth?* Accessed on 02.11.2021. Available https://www.weforum.org

Modi, D., & Zhao, L. (2020). Social media analysis of consumer opinion on apparel supply chain transparency. *Journal of Fashion Marketing and Management*.

Mohanta, B. K., Jena, D., Panda, S. S., & Sobhanayak, S. (2019). Blockchain technology: A survey on applications and security privacy challenges. *Internet of Things, 8*.

Monaco, E. (2019). What FinTech Can Learn from High-Frequency Trading: Economic Consequences, Open Issues and Future of Corporate Disclosure. In T. Lynn, J. G. Mooney, P. Rosati, & M. Cummins (Eds.), *Disrupting Finance* (pp. 51–70). Springer Nature Switzerland AG. doi:10.1007/978-3-030-02330-0_4

Montecchi, M., Plangger, K., & Etter, M. (2019). It's real, trust me! Establishing supply chain provenance using blockchain. *Business Horizons, 62*(3), 283–293. doi:10.1016/j.bushor.2019.01.008

Moore, M. (2012). 'Mass suicide' protest at Apple manufacturer Foxconn factory. *The Telegraph, 11*.

Morgan, T. R., Richey, R. G. Jr, & Ellinger, A. E. (2018). Supplier transparency: Scale development and validation. *International Journal of Logistics Management, 29*(3), 959–984. doi:10.1108/IJLM-01-2017-0018

Morris, D. Z. (2017). *Bitcoin hits a new record high, but stops short of $20,000*. Fortune.com.

Mukherjee, S., Chittipaka, V., & Baral, M. M. (2021). Developing a Model to Highlight the Relation of Digital Trust With Privacy and Security for the Blockchain Technology. IGI Global. doi:10.4018/978-1-7998-8081-3.ch007

Müller, J. M., Veile, J. W., & Voigt, K.-I. (2020). Prerequisites and incentives for digital information sharing in Industry 4.0 – An international comparison across data types. *Computers & Industrial Engineering*, *148*, 106733. Advance online publication. doi:10.1016/j.cie.2020.106733

Nakamoto, S. (2008). Bitcoin: A peer-to-peer electronic cash system. *Decentralized Business Review, 21260.*

Nakamoto. (2008). *Blockchain, "A peer-to-peer distributed ledger System" (electronic cash system).* Academic Press.

Nakamoto, S. (2008). *Bitcoin: A peer-to-peer electronic cash system.* Decentralized Business Review.

Nakasumi, M. (2017). Information Sharing for Supply Chain Management based on Block Chain Technology. *IEEE 19th Conference on Business Informatics.*

Nartey, C., Tchao, E. T., Gadze, J. D., Keelson, E., Klogo, G. S., Kommey, B., & Diawuo, K. (2021). On Blockchain and IoT Integration Platforms: Current Implementation Challenges and Future Perspectives Hindawi. *Wireless Communications and Mobile Computing*, *2021*, 6672482. doi:10.1155/2021/6672482

National Bureau of Statistics. (2020). *E-procurement amount (10 billion yuan).* Author.

Nespoli, P., Díaz-López, D., & Gómez Mármol, F. (2021). Cyberprotection in IoT environments: A dynamic rule-based solution to defend smart devices. *Journal of Information Security and Applications*, *60*, 102878. Advance online publication. doi:10.1016/j.jisa.2021.102878

Network Working Group. (2013). *Request for Comments 6960 Internet X.509 Public Key Infrastructure Online Certificate Status Protocol – OCSP*. https://tools.ietf.org/html/rfc6960/

Nicoletti, B. (2018). Fintech and Procurement Finance 4.0. In Procurement Finance (pp. 155-248). doi:10.1007/978-3-030-02140-5_6

Nin, H. L., Mohamed, E., Shanka, K., Gupta, B. B., & Ahmed, A. A. (2021). Secure blockchain enabled Cyber–physical systems in healthcare using deep belief network with ResNet model. *Journal of Parallel and Distributed Computing*, *153*, 150–160. doi:10.1016/j.jpdc.2021.03.011

Ni, W., & Sun, H. (2019). The effect of sustainable supply chain management on business performance: Implications for integrating the entire supply chain in the Chinese manufacturing sector. *Journal of Cleaner Production*, *232*, 1176–1186. doi:10.1016/j.jclepro.2019.05.384

Nofer, M., Gomber, P., Hinz, O., & Schiereck, D. (2017). Blockchain. *Business & Information Systems Engineering*, *59*(3), 183–187. . doi:10.1007/s12599-017-0467-3

North, D. (1990). *Institutions, Institutional Change and Economic Performance*. Cambridge University. doi:10.1017/CBO9780511808678

Notheisen, B., Cholewa, J. B., & Shanmugam, A. P. (2017). Trading real-world assets on blockchain. *Business & Information Systems Engineering*, *59*(6), 425–440. doi:10.100712599-017-0499-8

Nwosu, A. U., & Goyal, S. B. (2020). Blockchain Transforming Cyber-attacks in Healthcare Industry. *World Congress on Information and Communication Technologies.*

O'Sullivan, M., & Sheahan, C. (2019). Using Serious Games to Inform Mass Customization Production Methods from the Fuzzy Front-End of New Product Development. *Procedia Manufacturing*, *38*, 478–487. doi:10.1016/j.promfg.2020.01.061

OASIS Digital Signature Services eXtended (DSS-X) TC. (2007). https://www.oasis-open.org/committees/tc_home.php?wg_abbrev=dss-x

Official documentation on the Solidity language from the Ethereum Foundation. (2018). https://solidity.readthedocs.io/en

Onik, M. M. H., Aich, S., Yang, J., Kim, C.-S., & Kim, H.-C. (2019). Blockchain in Healthcare: Challenges and Solutions. In *Big Data Analytics for Intelligent Healthcare Management*. Elsevier Inc. doi:10.1016/B978-0-12-818146-1.00008-8

Pal & Yasar. (2020). Internet of Things and Blockchain Technology in Apparel Manufacturing Supply Chain Data Management. *Procedia Computer Science, 170*, 450–457.

Paliwal, V., Chandra, S., & Sharma, S. (2020). Blockchain technology for sustainable supply chain management: A systematic literature review and a classification framework. *Sustainability*, *12*(18), 7638. doi:10.3390u12187638

Panarello, A., Tapas, N., Merlino, G., Longo, F., & Puliafito, A. (2018). Blockchain and iot integration: A systematic survey. *Sensors (Basel)*, *18*(8), 2575. doi:10.339018082575 PMID:30082633

Pavithran, D., Shaalan, K., Al-Karaki, J. N., & Gawanmeh, A. (2020). Towards building a blockchain framework for IoT. *Cluster Computing*, *23*(3), 2089–2103. doi:10.100710586-020-03059-5

Pawade, R., Biradar, S., Rakshita, S., Ramegowda, S., & Rumma, S. S. (2021). A Comprehensive Review on Blockchain Technology for Interactive Healthcare Systems. *International Journal of Engineering Research & Technology*.

People's Daily. (2021). *China's digital economy has become more dynamic*. http://www.gov.cn/xinwen/2021-03/22/content_5594357.htm

Perboli, G., Musso, S., & Rosano, M. (2018). Blockchain in logistics and supply chain: A lean approach for designing real-world use cases. *IEEE Access: Practical Innovations, Open Solutions*, *6*, 62018–62028. doi:10.1109/ACCESS.2018.2875782

Pilkington, M. (2016). Blockchain Technology: Principles and Applications. In *Research Handbook on Digital Transformations*. Edward Elgar Publishing.

Pinna, A., Ibba, S., Baralla, G., Tonelli, R., & Marchesi, M. (2019). A massive analysis of ethereum smart contracts empirical study and code metrics. *IEEE Access: Practical Innovations, Open Solutions*, *7*, 78194–78213. doi:10.1109/ACCESS.2019.2921936

Pinto, R. (2019). *What role will Blockchain play in cybersecurity?* Forbes Technology Council. Accessed on 9th November 2021 Available: https://www.forbes.com/sites/forbestechcouncil/2019/04/03/what-role-will-blockchains-play-in-cybersecurity/#4c84e231295c

Pongnumkul, S., Siripanpornchana, C., & Thajchayapong, S. (2017). Performance Analysis of Private Blockchain Platforms in Varying Workloads. *Proceedings of the 2017 26th International Conference on Computer Communication and Networks (ICCCN)*, 1–6. 10.1109/ICCCN.2017.8038517

Popper & Lohr. (2017). *Blockchain: A Better Way to Track Pork Chops, Bonds, Bad PeanutButter?* Academic Press.

Prümmer, M., Bergs, T., Arntz, K., & Lürken, C. (2019). Periphery evaluation for interlinked manufacturing systems in industrial tooling. *Procedia CIRP*, *81*, 470–475. doi:10.1016/j.procir.2019.03.120

PTI Blog. (2019). *5 Big Challenges for Digital Logistics*. PIT's Container Terminal Automation Conference (CTAC). Accessed on 9th November 2021, Available: https://www.porttechnology.org/news/pti_blog_5_big_challenges_for_digital_logistics/

Punter, A. D. (2013). *Supply chain failures. A study of the nature, causes and complexity of supply chain*. Academic Press.

Pureswaran, V. (2015). *Empowering the edge-practical insights on a decentralized Internet of Things*. IBM Institute for Business Value.

Purohit, S. K., & Sharma, A. K. (2015). Database Design for Data Mining driven Forecasting Software Tool for Quality Function Deployment. *International Journal of Information and Electronic Business*, *7*(4), 39–50.

Qian, X. A., & Papadonikolaki, E. (2020). Shifting trust in construction supply chains through blockchain technology. *Engineering, Construction, and Architectural Management*, *28*(2), 584–602. doi:10.1108/ECAM-12-2019-0676

Queiroz, M. M., Telles, R., & Bonilla, S. H. (2019). Blockchain and supply chain management integration: a systematic review of the literature. In Supply Chain Management (Vol. 25, Issue 2, pp. 241–254). Emerald Group Publishing Ltd. doi:10.1108/SCM-03-2018-0143

Queiroz, M. M., Fosso Wamba, S., De Bourmont, M., & Telles, R. (2020). Blockchain adoption in operations and supply chain management: Empirical evidence from an emerging economy. *International Journal of Production Research*. Advance online publication. doi:10.1080/00207543.2020.1803511

Qu, F., Haddad, H., & Shahriar, H. (2019). Smart Contract-Based Secured Business-to-Consumer Supply Chain Systems. *IEEE International Conference on Blockchain*, 580-585. 10.1109/Blockchain.2019.00084

Raheem, D., Shishaev, M., & Dikovitsky, V. (2019). Food system digitalization as a means to promote food and nutrition security in the barents region. *Agriculture*, *9*(8), 168. doi:10.3390/agriculture9080168

Rahul Raman, Sushmitha, & Nalini. (2021). A Survey Paper on Blockchain Technologies in Supply Chain Management. *International Journal of Research in Engineering and Science, 9*(6), 79-86.

Ramezani, J., & Camarinha-Matos, L. M. (2020). Approaches for resilience and antifragility in collaborative business ecosystems. *Technological Forecasting and Social Change*, *151*, 119846. doi:10.1016/j.techfore.2019.119846

Rao, J. J., & Kumara, V. (2017). Review of supply chain management in manufacturing systems. In *International Conference on Innovative Mechanisms for Industry Applications (ICIMIA) Bangalore* (pp. 759–762). 10.1109/ICIMIA.2017.7975567

Raschendorfer, A., Mörzinger, B., Steinberger, E., Pelzmann, P., Oswald, R., Stadler, M., & Bleicher, F. (2019). On IOTA as a potential enabler for an M2M economy in manufacturing. *Procedia CIRP*, *79*, 379–384. doi:10.1016/j.procir.2019.02.096

Rathee, P. (2020). Introduction to blockchain and IoT. In *Advanced Applications of Blockchain Technology* (pp. 1–14). Springer. doi:10.1007/978-981-13-8775-3_1

Rawat, D. B., Parwez, M. S., & Alshammari, A. (2017, October). Edge computing enabled resilient wireless network virtualization for the Internet of Things. In *2017 IEEE 3rd International Conference on Collaboration and Internet Computing (CIC)* (pp. 155-162). IEEE. 10.1109/CIC.2017.00030

Rawat, D., Chaudhary, V., & Doku, R. (2021). Blockchain technology: Emerging applications and use cases for secure and trustworthy smart systems. *Journal of Cybersecurity and Privacy*, *1*(1), 4–18. doi:10.3390/jcp1010002

Rawat, D. B., & Bajracharya, C. (2017). *Vehicular cyber-physical systems*. Springer. doi:10.1007/978-3-319-44494-9

Rawat, D. B., & Ghafoor, K. Z. (Eds.). (2018). *Smart cities cybersecurity and privacy*. Elsevier.

Rawat, D. B., Rodrigues, J. J., & Stojmenovic, I. (Eds.). (2015). *Cyber-physical systems: from theory to practice*. CRC Press. doi:10.1201/b19290

Rejeb, A., Keogh, J. G., & Treiblmaier, H. (2019). *Leveraging the Internet of Things and Blockchain Technology in Supply Chain Management Future Internet*. Academic Press.

Rejeb, A., Simske, S., Rejeb, K., Treiblmaier, H., & Zailani, S. (2020). Internet of Things research in supply chain management and logistics: A bibliometric analysis. *Internet of Things*, *12*, 100318. Advance online publication. doi:10.1016/j.iot.2020.100318

Report of the company Positive Technologies. (2019). *Initial Coin Offering. Threats to information security.* https://www.ptsecurity.com/upload/corporate/ru-ru/analytics/ICO-Threats-rus.pdf

Reyna, A., Martín, C., Chen, J., Soler, E., & Díaz, M. (2018). On blockchain and its integration with IoT. Challenges and opportunities. *Future Generation Computer Systems, 88*, 173–190. doi:10.1016/j.future.2018.05.046

Roadmap for the development of the. (2019). *End-to-end digital technology "of the Distributed Registry System"*. Rostec.

Rose, S., Spinks, N., & Canhoto, A. (2014). Management Research : Applying the Principles. In *Management Research*. Routledge. doi:10.4324/9781315819198

RothJ.SchärF.SchöpferA. (2019). The Tokenization of assets: using blockchains for equity crowdfunding. Available at SSRN 3443382. doi:10.2139/ssrn.3443382

Rowley, J. (2002). Using case studies in research. *Management Research News, 25*(1), 16–27. doi:10.1108/01409170210782990

Saberi, S., Kouhizadeh, M., Sarkis, J., & Shen, L. (2019a). Blockchain technology and its relationships to sustainable supply chain management. *International Journal of Production Research, 57*(7), 2117–2135. doi:10.1080/00207543.2018.1533261

Salah, K., Rehman, M. H. U., Nizamuddin, N., & Al-Fuqaha, A. (2019). Blockchain for AI: Review and open research challenges. *IEEE Access: Practical Innovations, Open Solutions, 7*, 10127–10149. doi:10.1109/ACCESS.2018.2890507

Šarac, M., Pavlović, N., Bacanin, N., Al-Turjman, F., & Adamović, S. (2021). Increasing privacy and security by integrating a Blockchain Secure Interface into an IoT Device Security Gateway Architecture. *Energy Reports, 7*, 8075–8082. Advance online publication. doi:10.1016/j.egyr.2021.07.078

Satoshi, N. (2008). *Bitcoin. A Peer-to-Peer Electronic Cash System.* https://bitcoin.org/bitcoin.pdf

Satoshi, N. (n.d.). *Bitcoin. A Peer-to-Peer Electronic Cash System.* https://bitcoin.org/bitcoin.pdf

Saurabh, S., & Dey, K. (2021). Blockchain technology adoption, architecture, and sustainable agri-food supply chains. *Journal of Cleaner Production, 284*, 124731. doi:10.1016/j.jclepro.2020.124731

Saxena, S., Bhushan, B., & Ahad, M. A. (2021). Blockchain based solutions to secure IoT: Background, integration trends and a way forward. *Journal of Network and Computer Applications, 181*, 103050. Advance online publication. doi:10.1016/j.jnca.2021.103050

Sayeed, S., & Marco-Gisbert, H. (2019). Assessing blockchain consensus and security mechanisms against the 51% attack. *Applied Sciences (Basel, Switzerland), 9*(9), 1788. doi:10.3390/app9091788

Scand. (2020, September). *6 Ways Blockchain Can Improve Logistics*. Retrieved July 17, 2021, from https://scand.com/company/blog/blockchain-for-logistics/

Schär, F. (2021). Decentralized finance: On blockchain-and smart contract-based financial markets. *FRB of St. Louis Review*.

Schlecht, L., Schneider, S., & Buchwald, A. (2021). The prospective value creation potential of Blockchain in business models: A delphi study. *Technological Forecasting and Social Change, 166*, 120601. doi:10.1016/j.techfore.2021.120601

Scholten, K., & Fynes, B. (2017). Risk and Uncertainty Management for Sustainable Supply Chains. In Sustainable Supply Chains (pp. 413-436). doi:10.1007/978-3-319-29791-0_19

Scott, W. R. (2008). Institutions and Organizations: Ideas and Interests. Academic Press.

Scott, W. R. (2008). *Institutions and organizations: Ideas and interests* (3rd ed.). SAGE Publications.

Semunab, S. N., & Noor, N. M. (2016). Implementation of Wireless Mobile RFID Reader in Real-World Industry Environment. *Journal Technology*, *78*(5–10), 74–82.

Sengupta, J., Ruj, S., & Bit, S. D. (2020). A comprehensive survey on attacks, security issues and blockchain solutions for IoT and IIoT. *Journal of Network and Computer Applications*, *149*, 102481. doi:10.1016/j.jnca.2019.102481

Seo, Y.-J., Dinwoodie, J., & Roe, M. (2014). Measures of supply chain collaboration in container logistics. *Maritime Economics & Logistics*. Advance online publication. doi:10.1057/mel.2014.26

Shafagh, H., Burkhalter, L., Hithnawi, A., & Duquennoy, S. (2017, November). Towards blockchain-based auditable storage and sharing of iot data. In *Proceedings of the 2017 on cloud computing security workshop* (pp. 45-50). 10.1145/3140649.3140656

Shaikh, A. A., Sharma, R., & Karjaluoto, H. (2020). Digital innovation & enterprise in the sharing economy: An action research agenda. *Digital Business*, *1*(1), 100002. Advance online publication. doi:10.1016/j.digbus.2021.100002

Shapiev, M. M. (2019). Vulnerabilities of smart contracts and ways of their exploitation. *Scientific Electronic Journal "Meridian"*, *10*(28), 1-5.

Sharma, P. K., Moon, S. Y., & Park, J. H. (2017). Block-VN: A distributed blockchain-based vehicular network architecture in smart city. *Journal of Information Processing Systems, 13*(1), 184-195.

Sharma, T. K. (2017). *List of best open source Blockchain platforms*. Blockchain Council. Available: https://www.blockchain-council.org/blockchain/list-of-best-open-source-blockchain-platforms/

Sharma, A. K., & Khandait, S. P. (2016). A Novel Software Tool to Generate Customer Needs tor Effective Design of Online Shopping Websites. *International Journal of Information Technology and Computer Science*, *83*(3), 85–92. doi:10.5815/ijitcs.2016.03.10

Sharma, A. K., & Khandait, S. P. (2017). A Novel Fuzzy Integrated Customer Needs Prioritization Software Tool for Effective Design of Online Shopping Websites. *International Journal of Operations Research and Information Systems (IJORIS)*, *8*(4), 23–38.

Sharma, A. K., Mehta, I. C., & Sharma, J. R. (2009). Development of Fuzzy Integrated Quality Function Deployment Software - A Conceptual Analysis. *I-Manager's Journal on Software Engineering*, *3*(3), 16–24. doi:10.26634/jse.3.3.190

Sharma, A., Tiwari, S., Arora, N., & Sharma, S. C. (2021). Introduction to Blockchain. In *Blockchain Applications in IoT Ecosystem* (pp. 1–14). Springer. doi:10.1007/978-3-030-65691-1_1

Sharma, P. K., Kumar, N., & Park, J. H. (2020). Blockchain technology toward green iot: Opportunities and challenges. *IEEE Network*, *34*(4), 263–269. doi:10.1109/MNET.001.1900526

Sharples, M., & Domingue, J. (2016, September). The blockchain and kudos: A distributed system for educational record, reputation and reward. In *European conference on technology enhanced learning* (pp. 490-496). Springer. 10.1007/978-3-319-45153-4_48

Sheel, A., & Nath, V. (2019). Effect of blockchain technology adoption on supply chain adaptability, agility, alignment and performance. *Management Research Review*, *42*(12), 1353–1374. doi:10.1108/MRR-12-2018-0490

Shin, D. D. H. (2019). Blockchain: The emerging technology of digital trust. *Telematics and Informatics*, *45*(September), 101278. Advance online publication. doi:10.1016/j.tele.2019.101278

Shoaib, M., Lim, M. K., & Wang, C. (2020). An integrated framework to prioritize blockchain-based supply chain success factors. *Industrial Management & Data Systems*, *120*(11), 2103–2131. doi:10.1108/IMDS-04-2020-0194

Silanteva, E. S., & Kustov, V. N. (2020). Technological aspects of the trust in the cross-border paperless exchange. *Journal of Physics: Conference Series*, *1703*(1), 012049. doi:10.1088/1742-6596/1703/1/012049

Simi, Ć., & Ilin, V. (2017). Utilizing big data for safety and sustainable mobility. *Proceedings of the 6th International Conference "Towards a Humane City"*, 317-323.

Smart City of China. (2021). https://mp.weixin.qq.com/s?__biz=MzA3ODA1MzMwNw==&mid=2650542117&idx=1&sn=94ec06a764d893d8bd6c0e60d10e0545&chksm=87401af1b03793e758d565e3c7a3f0d5b21029e62caff6e8d3d64002301d69427c10d5f80f3e&mpshare=1&srcid=0814Ry69kbJB4NxF8GIsJu4a&sharer_sharetime=1628948491962&sharer_shareid=3f439b70854717410bbd97cd511f119b&from=singlemessage&scene=1&subscene=10000&clicktime=1630219119&enterid=1630219119&ascene=1&devicetype=android-29&version=28000a3d&nettype=WIFI&abtest_cookie=AAACAA%3D%3D&lang=zh_CN&exportkey=A3%2Ftehxk17AJjE2UCFxIVHk%3D&pass_ticket=Ug8WmXDfzeZqV%2BuFb4h9aKcdozrVzzMS8T2Rn5UWSFwbBqI3chjjcsw25hOdTLnA&wx_header=1

Software Electronic Signatures and Infrastructures (ESI) Policy requirements for certification authorities issuing public-key certificates. (2013). https://www.etsi.org/deliver/etsi_ts/102000_102099/102042/02.04.01_60/ts_102042v020401 p.pdf

Sompolinsky, Y., Lewenberg, Y., & & Zohar, A. (2016). SPECTRE: a fast and scalable cryptocurrency protocol. *IACR Cryptol. ePrint Arch.*

Song, J. M., Sung, J., & Park, T. (2019). Applications of blockchain to improve supply chain traceability. *Procedia Computer Science*, *162*, 119–122. doi:10.1016/j.procs.2019.11.266

Sripathi, L. (2019). *Adoption of Blockchain technology in food supply chain management*. Academic Press.

Steiner, J., Baker, J., Wood, G., & Meiklejohn, S. (2015). *Blockchain: the solution for transparency in product supply chains*. Available at: provenance. org/whitepaper.

Steuer, B., Staudner, M., & Ramusch, R. (2021). Role and potential of the circular economy in managing end-of-life ships in china. *Resources, Conservation and Recycling*, *164*, 105039. doi:10.1016/j.resconrec.2020.105039 PMID:32929303

Sullivan, C., & Burger, E. (2017). E-residency and blockchain. *Computer Law & Security Review, 33*(4), 470-481.

Sun, H., Hua, S., Zhou, E., Pi, B., Sun, J., & Yamashita, K. (2018). Using Ethereum Blockchain in Internet of Things:A Solution for Electric Vehicle Battery Refueling. In *Lecture Notes in Computer Science* (Vol. 10974, pp. 3–17). Springer.

Sunny, J., Undralla, N., & Pillai, V. M. (2020). Supply chain transparency through blockchain-based traceability: An overview with demonstration. *Computers & Industrial Engineering*, *150*, 106895. doi:10.1016/j.cie.2020.106895

Surendra Yadav, V., & Singh, A. R. (n.d.). *A Systematic Literature Review of Blockchain Technology in Agriculture*. Academic Press.

Swan, M. (2018). Blockchain: The scheme of a new economy. Olymp-Business Publishing House.

Szabo, N. (1997). Formalizing and securing relationships on public networks. *First Monday*, *2*(9). Advance online publication. doi:10.5210/fm.v2i9.548

Tadejko, P. (2015). Application of Internet of Things in Logistics – Current Challenges. *Economics and Management*, *7*(4), 54–64.

Tandon, A. (2019). An empirical analysis of using blockchain technology with internet of things and its application. *International Journal of Innovative Technology and Exploring Engineering*, *8*, 1470–1475.

Tan, K. H., Zhan, Y. Z., Ji, G., Ye, F., & Chang, C. (2015). Harvesting Big Data to enhance supply chain innovation capabilities: An analytic infrastructure based on deduction graph. *International Journal of Production Economics*, *165*, 223–233. doi:10.1016/j.ijpe.2014.12.034

Tapscott, D., & Kaplan, A. (2019). *Blockchain Revolution in Education and LifeLong Learning: Preparing for Disruption, Leading the Transformation*. www.blockchainresearchinstitute.org/contact-us

Taylor, E., & Cremer, A. (2016). *Volkswagen takes 18 billion hit over emissions scandal*. Tech. rep., Reuters.

TBG17 CCL (Core Component Library). (2020). *Submission Guidelines and Procedures*. UN/CEFACT/TBG17/N004 Draft Version 3.0.

Terrada, L., Khaïli, M. E., & Ouajji, H. (2020). Multi-Agents System Implementation for Supply Chain Management Making-Decision. *Procedia Computer Science*, *177*, 624–630. doi:10.1016/j.procs.2020.10.089

The software package "Trusted Third Party Services "Litoria DVCS." (2017). Program Description, 72410666.00044-01 13 01, 36 p.

Thistlethwaite, G. (2018, July). *How blockchain is changing the logistics industry*. Retrieved July 17, 2021, from https://www.gbnews.ch/blockchain-logistics-industry/

Thompson, C. (2016). *How does the Blockchain work? The Blockchain review by intrepid*. Accessed on 9th November 2021, Available: https://medium.com/blockchain-review/the-difference-between-a-privatepublic-consortium-blockchain-799ae7f022bc

Tian, F. (2016). An agri-food supply chain traceability system for China based on RFID & blockchain technology. *13th International Conference on Service Systems and Service Management (ICSSSM)*, 1-6. 10.1109/ICSSSM.2016.7538424

Tian, Z., Zhong, R. Y., Vatankhah Barenji, A., Wang, Y. T., Li, Z., & Rong, Y. (2021). A blockchain-based evaluation approach for customer delivery satisfaction in sustainable urban logistics. *International Journal of Production Research*, *59*(7), 2229–2249. doi:10.1080/00207543.2020.1809733

Tijan, E., Aksentijević, S., Ivanić, K., & Jardas, M. (2019). Blockchain technology implementation in logistics. *Sustainability*, *11*(4), 1185. doi:10.3390u11041185

Tipmontian, Alcover, & Rajmohan. (2020). Impact of Blockchain Adoption for Safe Food Supply Chain Management through System Dynamics Approach from Management Perspectives in Thailand. *Proceedings*, *39*(1), 14. doi:10.3390/proceedings2019039014

Tönnissen, S., & Teuteberg, F. (2018). Using blockchain technology for business processes in purchasing – Concept and case study-based evidence. *Lecture Notes in Business Information Processing*, *320*, 253–264. doi:10.1007/978-3-319-93931-5_18

Tosh, D. K., Shetty, S., Foytik, P., Njilla, L., & Kamhoua, C. A. (2018, October). Blockchain-empowered secure internet-of-battlefield things (iobt) architecture. In MILCOM 2018-2018 IEEE Military Communications Conference (MILCOM) (pp. 593-598). IEEE.

Trade data element Directory (TDED) UNTDED. (2005). ISO 7372:2005, Vol. 1 Data Elements.

Treiblmaier, H. (2018). The impact of the blockchain on the supply chain: A theory-based research framework and a call for action. *Supply Chain Management*, *23*(6), 545–559. doi:10.1108/SCM-01-2018-0029

Tschorsch, F., & Scheuermann, B. (2016). Bitcoin and beyond: A technical survey on decentralized digital currencies. *IEEE Communications Surveys and Tutorials*, *18*(3), 2084–2123. doi:10.1109/COMST.2016.2535718

Tsiulin, S., Reinau, K. H., Hilmola, O. P., Goryaev, N., & Karam, A. (2020). Blockchain-based applications in shipping and port management: a literature review towards defining key conceptual frameworks. *Review of International Business and Strategy.*

Turban, E., Outland, J., King, D., Lee, J. K., Liang, T.-P., & Turban, D. C. (2018). Electronic Commerce 2018. *Electronic Commerce, 2018.* Advance online publication. doi:10.1007/978-3-319-58715-8

Tuteja & Shankar. (2021). A Novel Technique for Securing Supply Chain Management using Blockchain. *Turkish Journal of Physiotherapy and Rehabilitation, 32*(2), 3467–3487.

Uddin, M. A., Stranieri, A., Gondal, L., & Balasubramanian, V. (2021). *A Survey on the Adoption of Blockchain in IoT: Challenges and Solutions. Blockchain, Research and Applications.* doi:10.1016/j.bcra.2021.100006

UN ESCAP. (2016). *Framework Agreement on Facilitation of Cross-border Paperless Trade in Asia and the Pacific.* https://treaties.un.org/doc/source/docs/ESCAP_RES_72_4-E.pdf

UNCITRAL. (2001). *Model Law on Electronic Signatures.* https://uncitral.un.org/en/texts/ecommerce/modellaw/electronic_signatures/

Vafadarnikjoo, A., Badri Ahmadi, H., Liou, J. J. H., Botelho, T., & Chalvatzis, K. (2021). Analyzing blockchain adoption barriers in manufacturing supply chains by the neutrosophic analytic hierarchy process. *Annals of Operations Research*, 1–28. doi:10.100710479-021-04048-6

van Hoek, R. (2019). Unblocking the chain – findings from an executive workshop on blockchain in the supply chain. *Supply Chain Management, 25*(2), 255–261. doi:10.1108/SCM-11-2018-0383

Vanurina, V. (2019). *Gazprom is switching to blockchain.* https://news.rambler.ru/other/41980326-gazprom-perehodit-na-blokcheyn/

Velder, S. E., Lukin, M. A., Shalyto, A. A., & Yaminov, B. R. (2011). *Verification of automaton programs [Verifikatsiya avtomatnykh program].* Nauka.

Verhoeven, P., Sinn, F., & Herden, T. (2018). Examples from Blockchain Implementations in Logistics and Supply Chain Management: Exploring the Mindful Use of a New Technology. *Logistics, 2*(3), 20. doi:10.3390/logistics2030020

Villegas-Ch, W., Palacios-Pacheco, X., & Román-Cañizares, M. (2020). Integration of IoT and Blockchain to in the Processes of a University Campus. *Sustainability, 12*(12), 4970. doi:10.3390u12124970

Violino, S., Pallottino, F., Sperandio, G., Figorilli, S., Antonucci, F., Ioannoni, V., Fappiano, D., & Costa, C. (2019). Are the innovative electronic labels for extra virgin olive oil sustainable, traceable, and accepted by consumers? *Foods, 8*(11), 529. doi:10.3390/foods8110529 PMID:31731433

Violino, S., Pallottino, F., Sperandio, G., Figorilli, S., Ortenzi, L., Tocci, F., & Costa, C. (2020). A full technological traceability system for extra virgin olive oil. *Foods, 9*(5), 624. doi:10.3390/foods9050624 PMID:32414115

Viriyasitavat, W., Da Xu, L., Bi, Z., & Sapsomboon, A. (2020). Blockchain-based business process management (BPM) framework for service composition in industry 4.0. *Journal of Intelligent Manufacturing, 31*(7), 1737–1748. doi:10.100710845-018-1422-y

Virto, L. R. (2018). A preliminary assessment of the indicators for Sustainable Development Goal (SDG) 14 "Conserve and sustainably use the oceans, seas and marine resources for sustainable development". *Marine Policy, 98*, 47–57. doi:10.1016/j.marpol.2018.08.036

Vis, I. F. A. (2006). Survey of research in the design and control of automated guided vehicle systems. *European Journal of Operational Research, 170*(3), 677–709. doi:10.1016/j.ejor.2004.09.020

Vogelsteller, F., & Buterin, V. (2015). *ERC-20 token standard. Ethereum Foundation.* Stiftung Ethereum.

Wamba, S. F., & Queiroz, M. M. (2020). Blockchain in the operations and supply chain management: Benefits, challenges and future research opportunities. In *International Journal of Information Management* (Vol. 52, p. 102064). Elsevier Ltd., doi:10.1016/j.ijinfomgt.2019.102064

Wang, M., Wu, Y., Chen, B., & Evans, M. (2021). Blockchain and Supply Chain Management: A New Paradigm for Supply Chain Integration and Collaboration. *Operations and Supply Chain Management, 14*(1), 111 – 122.

Wang, G., Gunasekaran, A., Ngai, E. W. T., & Papadopoulos, T. (2016). Big Data Analytics in Logistics and Supply Chain Management: Certain Investigations for Research and Applications. *International Journal of Production Economics, 176*, 98–110. doi:10.1016/j.ijpe.2016.03.014

Wang, J., Liu, J., Wang, F., & Yue, X. (2021a). Blockchain technology for port logistics capability: Exclusive or sharing. *Transportation Research Part B: Methodological, 149*, 347–392. doi:10.1016/j.trb.2021.05.010

Wang, L., Luo, X. R., Lee, F., & Benitez, J. (2021b). Value creation in blockchain-driven supply chain finance. *Information & Management*, 103510. Advance online publication. doi:10.1016/j.im.2021.103510

Wang, L., Ma, Y., Zhu, L., Wang, X., Cong, H., & Shi, T. (2021c). Design of integrated energy market cloud service platform based on blockchain smart contract. *International Journal of Electrical Power & Energy Systems, 135*, 107515. Advance online publication. doi:10.1016/j.ijepes.2021.107515

Wang, P., Valerdi, R., Zhou, S., & Li, L. (2015). Introduction: Advances in IoT research and applications. *Information Systems Frontiers, 17*(2), 239–241. doi:10.100710796-015-9549-2

Wang, Q., Zhu, X., Ni, Y., Gu, L., & Zhu, H. (2020). Blockchain for the IoT and industrial IoT: A review. *Internet of Things, 10*, 100081. doi:10.1016/j.iot.2019.100081

Wang, Y., Han, J. H., & Beynon-Davies, P. (2019). Understanding blockchain technology for future supply chains: A systematic literature review and research agenda. *Supply Chain Management, 24*(1), 62–84. doi:10.1108/SCM-03-2018-0148

Wannenwetsch, H. (Ed.). (2014). *Integrierte Materialwirtschaft, Logistik und Beschaffung* (5th ed.). Springer. doi:10.1007/978-3-642-45023-5

Weber, I., Xu, X., Riveret, R., Governatori, G., Ponomarev, A., & Mendling, J. (2016, September). Untrusted business process monitoring and execution using blockchain. In *International Conference on Business Process Management* (pp. 329-347). Springer. 10.1007/978-3-319-45348-4_19

Weiguan Tech. (2019). *Tianjin TBC Blockchain Cross-border Trade Through train- the world's first demonstration project.* Author.

Weilian & Puhuayongdao. (2018). *2018 China's Blockchain (non-financial) Application Market Survey Report.* www.pwccn.com

Wei, X., Prybutok, V., & Sauser, B. (2021). Review of supply chain management within project management. *Project Leadership and Society, 2*, 100013. Advance online publication. doi:10.1016/j.plas.2021.100013

White Paper on a Reference Data Model. (2017). Centre for Trade Facilitation and Electronic Business, Twenty-third session.

Williams, Z., Lueg, J. E., & LeMay, S. A. (2008). Supply chain security: An overview and research agenda. *International Journal of Logistics Management, 19*(2), 254–281. doi:10.1108/09574090810895988

Wollschlaeger, M., Sauter, T., & Jasperneite, J. (2017). The Future of Industrial Communication: Automation Networks in the Era of the Internet of Things and Industry 4.0. *IEEE Industrial Electronics Magazine, 11*(1), 17–27. doi:10.1109/MIE.2017.2649104

Wong, L. W., Leong, L. Y., Hew, J. J., Tan, G. W. H., & Ooi, K. B. (2020). Time to seize the digital evolution: Adoption of blockchain in operations and supply chain management among Malaysian SMEs. *International Journal of Information Management, 52*, 101997. doi:10.1016/j.ijinfomgt.2019.08.005

Wong, L.-W., Tan, G. W.-H., Lee, V.-H., Ooi, K.-B., & Sohal, A. (2020). Unearthing the determinants of Blockchain adoption in supply chain management. *International Journal of Production Research, 58*(7), 2100–2123. doi:10.1080/00207543.2020.1730463

Wu, H., Cao, J., Yang, Y., Tung, C. L., Jiang, S., Tang, B., Liu, Y., Wang, X., & Deng, Y. (2019). Data management in supply chain using blockchain: challenges and a case study. *Proceedings - International Conference on Computer Communications and Networks, ICCCN.* 10.1109/ICCCN.2019.8846964

Wu, H., Li, Z., King, B., Miled, Z. B., Wassick, J., & Tazelaar, J. (2017). A distributed ledger for supply chain physical distribution visibility. *Information (Basel), 8*(4), 137. doi:10.3390/info8040137

Xcube, L. A. (2020, April). *How Companies Worldwide are Using Blockchain Technology in Their Manufacturing Processes.* Retrieved July 17, 2021, from https://www.xcubelabs.com/blog/how-companies-worldwide-are-using-blockchain-technology-in-their-manufacturing-processes/

Xiao, Z., Li, Z., Yang, Y., Chen, P., Liu, R. W., Jing, W., Pyrloh, Y., Sotthiwat, E., & Goh, R. S. M. (2020). Blockchain and IoT for Insurance: A Case Study and Cyberinfrastructure Solution on Fine-Grained Transportation Insurance. *IEEE Transactions on Computational Social Systems, 7*(6), 1409–1422. doi:10.1109/TCSS.2020.3034106

Xie, J., Tang, H., Huang, T., Yu, F. R., Xie, R., Liu, J., & Liu, Y. (2019). A Survey of Blockchain Technology Applied to Smart Cities: Research Issues and Challenges. *IEEE Communications Surveys and Tutorials, 21*(3), 2794–2830. doi:10.1109/COMST.2019.2899617

Xie, Z., Wang, J., & Miao, L. (2021). Big data and emerging market firms' innovation in an open economy: The diversification strategy perspective. *Technological Forecasting and Social Change, 173*, 121091. Advance online publication. doi:10.1016/j.techfore.2021.121091

Xinhua. (2015). *Smart, green, healthy and safe--focus on consumption development during the 13th Five-Year Plan period.* http://www.gov.cn/xinwen/2015-11/10/content_5006890.htm

Xinhua. (2017). *The development of China's digital economy promotes global openness and sharing.* http://www.gov.cn/xinwen/2017-12/04/content_5244456.htm

Xinhua. (2021a). *China's digital economy has reached 35.8 trillion yuan.* http://www.gov.cn/xinwen/2020-11/23/content_5563612.htm

Xinhua. (2021b). *"Zhejiang Fair Online" system online all-weather multi-directional intelligent supervision platform economy.* http://www.gov.cn/xinwen/2021-02/26/content_5589087.htm

XML Key Management Specification (XKMS 2.0). (2005). *Version 2.0 W3C Recommendation.* https://www.w3.org/TR/xkms2/

Xu, R., Zhang, L., Zhao, H., & Peng, Y. (2017). Design of network media's digital rights management scheme based on blockchain technology. *2017 IEEE 13th international symposium on autonomous decentralized system (ISADS)*, 128–133.

Xu, Z., Liu, Y., Zhang, J., Song, Z., Li, J., & Zhou, J. (2019). Manufacturing Industry Supply Chain Management Based on the Ethereum Blockchain. *2019 IEEE International Conferences on Ubiquitous Computing Communications (IUCC) and Data Science and Computational Intelligence (DSCI) and Smart Computing, Networking and Services (SmartCNS)*, 592-596. 10.1109/IUCC/DSCI/SmartCNS.2019.00124

Ya, W. (2016). Committee member Guo Guangchang: we will focus on building a "smart economy" to improve total factor productivity. *Xinhua*. http://www.gov.cn/xinwen/2016-03/11/content_5052414.htm

Yadav, S., & Singh, S. P. (2020). Blockchain critical success factors for sustainable supply chain. *Resources, Conservation and Recycling*, *152*, 104505. doi:10.1016/j.resconrec.2019.104505

Yadav, V. S., Singh, A. R., Raut, R. D., & Govindarajan, U. H. (2020). Blockchain technology adoption barriers in the Indian agricultural supply chain: An integrated approach. *Resources, Conservation and Recycling*, *161*, 104877. doi:10.1016/j.resconrec.2020.104877

Yang, C. S. (2019a). Maritime shipping digitalization: Blockchain-based technology applications, future improvements, and intention to use. *Transportation Research Part E, Logistics and Transportation Review*, *131*, 108–117. doi:10.1016/j.tre.2019.09.020

Yang, H., & Tate, M. (2012). A descriptive literature review and classification of cloud computing research. *Communications of the Association for Information Systems*, *31*(1), 2. doi:10.17705/1CAIS.03102

Ying, Z. (2017). The eight cities of Shenyang Economic Zone jointly build smart city clusters. *Liaoning Daily*. http://www.gov.cn/xinwen/2017-09/25/content_5227290.htm

Ying, Z. (2020). Wisdom for a Better Future- Sidelights of the 2020 World Digital Economy Conference. *Xinhua*. http://www.gov.cn/xinwen/2020-09/14/content_5543181.htm

Yin, W., Wen, Q., Lin, W., Zhang, H., & Jin, Z. (2015). An Anti-quantum Transaction Authentication Approach in Blockchain. *IEEE Access: Practical Innovations, Open Solutions*, *14*.

Yu, Wang, & Zhu. (2019). Blockchain technology for the 5g-enabled internet of things systems: Principle, applications and challenges. *5G-Enabled Internet of Things*.

Yuan, Y., & Wang, F.-Y. (2016). Towards blockchain-based intelligent transportation systems. *2016 IEEE 19th international conference on intelligent transportation systems (ITSC)*, 2663–2668.

Yuan, G., Ye, Q., & Sun, Y. (2021). Financial innovation, information screening and industries' green innovation—Industry-level evidence from the OECD. *Technological Forecasting and Social Change*, *171*, 120998. Advance online publication. doi:10.1016/j.techfore.2021.120998

Yu, F. R., & He, Y. (2019). A service-oriented blockchain system with virtualization. *Trans. Blockchain Technol. Appl.*, *1*, 1–10.

Yu, F. R., Liu, J., He, Y., Si, P., & Zhang, Y. (2018). Virtualization for distributed ledger technology (vDLT). *IEEE Access: Practical Innovations, Open Solutions*, *6*, 25019–25028. doi:10.1109/ACCESS.2018.2829141

Yusof, H., Farhana Mior Badrul Munir, M., Zolkaply, Z., Jing, L. C., Yu Hao, C., Swee Ying, D., Seang Zheng, L., Yuh Seng, L., & Kok Leong, T. (2018). Behavioral Intention to Adopt Blockchain Technology: Viewpoint of the Banking Institutions in Malaysia. *International Journal of Advanced Scientific Research and Management*, *3*. www.ijasrm.com

Zachariadis, M., Hileman, G., & Scott, S. V. (2019). Governance and control in distributed ledgers: Understanding the challenges facing blockchain technology in financial services. *Information and Organization*, *29*(2), 105–117. doi:10.1016/j.infoandorg.2019.03.001

Zakhary, V., Amiri, M. J., Maiyya, S., Agrawal, D., & Abbadi, A. E. (2019). *Towards global asset management in blockchain systems.* arXiv preprint arXiv:1905.09359.

Zeilinger, M. (2018). Digital art as 'monetized graphics': Enforcing intellectual property on the blockchain. *Philosophy & Technology*, *31*(1), 15–41. doi:10.100713347-016-0243-1

Zelbst, P. J., Green, K. W., Sower, V. E., & Bond, P. L. (2019). The impact of RFID, IIoT, and Blockchain technologies on supply chain transparency. *Journal of Manufacturing Technology Management*, *31*(3), 441–457. doi:10.1108/JMTM-03-2019-0118

Zhang. (2016). A Secure System for Pervasive Social Network-Based Healthcare. *Special Section on Trust Management in Pervasive Social Networking (TruPSN).*

Zhang, C., Ni, Z., Xu, Y., Luo, E., Chen, L., & Zhang, Y. (2021a). A trustworthy industrial data management scheme based on redactable blockchain. *Journal of Parallel and Distributed Computing*, *152*, 167–176. doi:10.1016/j.jpdc.2021.02.026

Zhang, P., Schmidt, D. C., White, J., & Lenz, G. (2018). Blockchain Technology Use Cases in Healthcare. In *Advances in Computers* (Vol. 111, pp. 1–41). Academic Press Inc. doi:10.1016/bs.adcom.2018.03.006

Zhang, R., Song, M., Li, T., Yu, Z., Dai, Y., Liu, X., & Wang, G. (2021b). Democratic learning: Hardware/software co-design for lightweight blockchain-secured on-device machine learning. *Journal of Systems Architecture*, *118*, 102205. Advance online publication. doi:10.1016/j.sysarc.2021.102205

Zhang, T., Li, J. J., & Jiang, X. (2021c). Supply chain finance based on smart contract. *Procedia Computer Science*, *187*, 12–17. doi:10.1016/j.procs.2021.04.027

Zhang, Y., Mao, M., Rau, P.-L. P., Choe, P., Bela, L., & Wang, F. (2013). Exploring factors influencing multitasking interaction with multiple smart devices. *Computers in Human Behavior*, *29*(6), 2579–2588. doi:10.1016/j.chb.2013.06.042

Zhang, Y., & Wen, J. (2017). The IoT electric business model: Using blockchain technology for the internet of things. *Peer-to-Peer Networking and Applications*, *10*(4), 983–994. doi:10.100712083-016-0456-1

Zhao, G., Liu, S., Lopez, C., Lu, H., Elgueta, S., Chen, H., & Boshkoska, B. M. (2019). Blockchain technology in agri-food value chain management: A synthesis of applications, challenges and future research directions. *Computers in Industry*, *109*, 83–99. doi:10.1016/j.compind.2019.04.002

Zheng, Z., Xie, S., Dai, H., Chen, X., & Wang, H. (2017). An overview of blockchain technology: Architecture, consensus, and future trends. 2017 IEEE international congress on big data (BigData congress), 557–564.

Zheng, Z., Xie, S., Dai, H., Chen, X., & Wang, H. (2017). An overview of Blockchain technology: architecture, consensus, and future trends. *IEEE 6th international congress on big data*. Accessed on 5th November 2021. Avalaible:https://www.researchgate.net/publication/318131748_An_Overview_of_Blockchain_Technology_Architecture_Consensus_and_Future_Trends

Zheng, Z., Xie, S., Dai, H.-N., Chen, X., & Wang, H. (2018). Blockchain challenges and opportunities: A survey. *International Journal of Web and Grid Services*, *14*(4), 352–375. doi:10.1504/IJWGS.2018.095647

Zhong, R. Y., Newman, S. T., Huang, G. Q., & Lan, S. (2016b). Big Data for Supply Chain Management in the Service and Manufacturing Sectors: Challenges, Opportunities, and Future Perspectives. *Computers & Industrial Engineering*, *101*, 572–591. doi:10.1016/j.cie.2016.07.013

Zhou, D., Kautonen, M., Dai, W., & Zhang, H. (2021). Exploring how digitalization influences incumbents in financial services: The role of entrepreneurial orientation, firm assets, and organizational legitimacy. *Technological Forecasting and Social Change*, *173*, 121120. Advance online publication. doi:10.1016/j.techfore.2021.121120

Zhu, H., & Zhou, Z. Z. (2016). Analysis and outlook of applications of blockchain technology to equity crowdfunding in China. *Financial Innovation, 2*(1), 1-11.

Zhu, S., Song, J., Hazen, B. T., Lee, K., & Cegielski, C. (2018). How supply chain analytics enables operational supply chain transparency: An organizational information processing theory perspective. *International Journal of Physical Distribution & Logistics Management*, *48*(1), 47–68. doi:10.1108/IJPDLM-11-2017-0341

Zorzini, M., Stevenson, M., & Hendry, L. C. (2012). Customer Enquiry Management in global supply chains: A comparative multi-case study analysis. *European Management Journal*, *30*(2), 121–140. Advance online publication. doi:10.1016/j.emj.2011.10.006

Zutshi, A., Grilo, A., & Nodehi, T. (2021). The value proposition of blockchain technologies and its impact on Digital Platforms. *Computers & Industrial Engineering*, *155*, 107187. Advance online publication. doi:10.1016/j.cie.2021.107187

Zweber, J. (2017). Digital Thread and Twin for Systems Engineering: Requirements to Design. *55th AIAA Aerospace Sciences Meeting*. 10.2514/6.2017-0875

About the Contributors

S. B. Goyal completed PhD in the Computer Science & Engineering in 2012 from India and served many institutions in many different academic and administrative positions. He is holding 19+ years experience at national and international level. He has peerless inquisitiveness and enthusiasm to get abreast with the latest development in the IT field. He has good command over Industry Revolution (IR) 4.0 technologies like Big-Data, Data Science, Artificial Intelligence & Blockchain, computer networking, deep learning etc. He is the first one to introduce IR 4.0 including Blockchain technology in the academic curriculum in Malaysian Universities. He had participated in many panel discussions on IR 4.0 technologies at academia as well as industry platforms. He is holding 19+ years' experience in academia at National & International level. He is serving as a reviewer or guest editors in many Journals published by Inderscience, IGI Global, Springer. He is contributing as a Co-Editor in many Scopus books. He had contributed in many Scopus/ SCI Journal/ conferences. Currently, Dr Goyal is associated as a Director, Faculty of Information Technology, City University, Malaysia.

Nijalingappa Pradeep is working as Professor in Computer Science and Engineering, Bapuji Institute of Engineering and Technology, Davangere, Karnataka, India affiliated to Visvesvaraya Technological University, Belagavi, Karnataka, India. He is having 18 years of academic experience, which includes teaching and research experience. He has worked at various verticals starting from Lecturer to Associate Professor. His research areas of interest include Machine Learning, Pattern Recognition, Medical Image Analysis, Knowledge Discovery Techniques, and Data Analytics. He is presently guiding TWO research scholars on Knowledge Discovery and Medical Image Analysis. He has successfully edited book published by IGI Publishers and Elsevier, USA. Two edited books to be published by Elsevier and Scrivener Publishing, Wiley are in progress. He has published more than 20 research articles published in refereed journals and also one Indian Patent application is published and one Australian Patent is granted. He is a reviewer of various International Conferences and few journals. He is a Professional member in IEEE, ACM, ISTE and IEI. Also, he is a Technical Committee Member for Davangere Smart City, Davangere.

Mangesh M. Ghonge is currently working at Sandip Institute of Technology and Research Center, Nashik, Maharashtra, India. He received his Ph.D. in Computer Science & Engineering from Sant Gadge Baba Amravati University, Amravati, India and an M.Tech degree in Computer Science & Engineering from Rashtrasant Tukadoji Maharaj Nagpur University, Nagpur, India. He authored/co-authored more than 60 published articles in prestigious journals, book chapters, and conference papers. Besides, Dr. Mangesh Ghonge authored/edited 10 international books published by recognized publishers such as Springer, IGI Global, CRC Press Taylor & Francis, Wiley-Scrivener, Nova. He has been invited as a resource person for many workshops/FDP. He has organized and chaired many national/international conferences and conducted various workshops. He received a grant from the Ministry of Electronics and Information Technology (MeitY) and DST. He is editor-in-chief of International Journal of Research in Advent Technology (IJRAT), E-ISSN 2321-9637. He is also guest editor for SCIE indexed journal special issue. He worked as a reviewer for Scopus/SCIE Indexed journals.

Renjith V. Ravi is presently employed as Associate Professor in the department of electronics and communication engineering of M.E.A Engineering college, Malappuram, Kerala, India. He has published 10 articles in various international journals and conferences and having an experience of around 10 years of in Teaching and Research. He has completed his Ph.D in Electronics and Communication Engineering in 2019, M.E. in Embedded System Technology in 2011 and B.Tech in Electronics and Communication Engineering in 2007. He is the reviewer of various reputed international journals from Elsevier, Springer, Inderscience, IGI Global, etc.

* * *

Monica Agrawal is an accomplished academician, administrator, trainer and counsellor she specializes in the areas of Human resources, blockchain & organisational behaviour. Areas of interest include stress management, leadership, student distraction & women empowerment. Has approx. 21 years of teaching, administrative and research experience. Have several research publications in the journals of national and international repute. Attended and participated in various national and international conferences on contemporary issues.

Manimaran Aridoss pursued Bachelor of Science from Bharathidasan University, Trichy in 2006, Master of Computer Applications from Anna University in year 2009 and Ph.D from Bharathidasan University in 2018. He is currently working as Assistant Professor in Department of Computer Applications, Madanapalle Institute of Technology & Science, Andhra Pradesh. He has published 9 research papers in reputed International Journals and participated more than 15 workshops on latest technologies like Big Data, Cloud Computing, Data Science, Network Simulators and Research Proposals. His main research work focuses on Network Security, Cloud Computing and Internet of Things. He has 4 years of Teaching Experience and 4 years of Research Experience.

Swati Bansal is working in Shrada University and her area of interest is Employability, Distraction, HRM, and blockchain.

Rohit Bansal is working as an Assistant Professor in the Department of Management Studies in Vaish College of Engineering, Rohtak. With a rich experience of 13 years, he has achieved growth through robust and proactive academic initiatives. He has authored & edited 8 books as well as published 95 research papers and chapters in journals of repute including edited books. His area of interest includes marketing management, human resource management, organizational behavior, and services marketing. He is on Editorial Advisory Board as a member of 110 national and international peer-reviewed journals. He is Managing Editor of International Journal of 360° Management Review & International Journal of Techno-Management Research. He served as a member of the advisory committee in many international conferences. He has acted as Session Chair in 4th International Online Conference on "Recent Advancements in Interdisciplinary Research" organized by the Foundation of Innovative Research held on May 8-9, 2020. He Received the "Excellence in Teaching Award" in Edge India Times Award organized by Edge India Publications Private Limited held on 15th November 2020 through virtual mode.

Manish Mohan Baralis working as an Assistant Professor in the Department of Operations, GITAM Institute of Management, GITAM (Deemed to be University), Visakhapatnam. He is an engineering graduate from KIIT University, Bhubaneswar, Odisha, MBA in International Business from GITAM University, Visakhapatnam, and pursued his Ph.D. in Management from Birla Institute of Technology Mesra, Ranchi. He has publications in reputed journals and high indexed book chapters. He has published in reputed journals like the International Journal of Logistics Management, FIIB Business Review, etc. He has presented more 12 papers in various conferences and has also received three best papers and best paper presented awards. His research areas include Information Technology, Cloud Computing, Supply Chain Management, Artificial Intelligence, Operations Research, and Quality Management. He has expertise in statistical techniques like SEM and MCDM techniques like TOPSIS, Fuzzy TOPSIS, etc.

Sachin Chauhan has rich Academic and Administrative experience of about 14 years in different management institutions. During this tenure he has published more than 20 research papers in national and international journals of repute and attended various conferences and seminars also he has participated in more than 15 fdp's.

Gaurav Choudhary received a Ph.D. in Information Security Engineering from Soonchunhyang University, South Korea. He has done a Master of Technology in Cyber Security from the Sardar Patel University of Police and received a Chancellor Gold Medal for Academic Excellence. He is presently working as a Postdoctoral Researcher at DTU Compute, Department of Applied Mathematics and Computer Science, Technical University of Denmark (DTU). Prior to joining DTU, he has also worked as an Assistant Professor in the School of Computer Science, University of Petroleum and Energy Studies (UPES), and School of Computer Science and Engineering (SCSE) at VIT Bhopal University. In his Ph.D. tenure, he worked at Mobile Internet Security Laboratory (MobiSec Lab), South Korea as a Cyber Security Researcher on various projects funded by reputed organizations such as the Institute for Information and Communications Technology Promotion (IITP), National Research Foundation of Korea (NRF), and the Air Force Office of Scientific Research (AFOSR), USA. His current research interests include Threat Intelligence, IoT and CPS Security, Cyber Security, Vulnerability Assessment, 5G Security, Drone Security, and Cryptography. He has authored or co-authored many reputed SCI journal/conference papers and book chapters.

Chandramohan Dhasarathan is currently Assistant Professor, Computer Science & Engineering Department, Thapar Institute of Engineering & Technology, Patiala, Punjab, India. His area of interest includes Pervasive & Ubiquitous Computing, Privacy and Security, Distributed Web Service, Web Service (Evaluation) Testbed, Software Metrics, GVANET and Cloud Computing, Opportunistic Computing, Evolutionary Computing, Service Computing, Software Engineering, Multi-Agent, Fog & Edge Computing, Underwater Communication. Currently he is working on E-Waste Management, Disaster Management, Bio-Inspired Algorithms and Privacy Preserving Generic Framework for Cloud Data Storage, Optimization approach for minimizing Agro-crops.

Emanuela Hanes is an independent researcher. Her cooperation includes the Vienna University FH BFI Campus Wien. Her research interests include China-EU business strategies, RegTech, FinTech, Cryptocurrencies, Geopolitics, Chinese Strategic Planning and Development Policies.

Jabir Mumtaz is an assistant professor in Department of Mechanical Engineering (CUST). His research focuses is in Production Planning and Scheduling, Operations Management, Industrial System Optimization, Manufacturing Processes and Artificial Intelligent Optimization Algorithms. Currently working on as research project related to industry 4.0 and digital twins to introduce smart manufacturing techniques in conventional industries.

Jayashree K. is presently working as a Professor in the Department of Computer Science and Engineering at Rajalakshmi Engineering College, Chennai. She has completed her Masters in Embedded System Technologies from Anna University and Bachelors in Computer Science and Engineering from Madras University. Her areas of interest includes Data Analytics, Cloud Computing and distributed computing. She is a member of ACM.

Rafael Kunst is a professor and Researcher at the Applied Computing Graduate Program of the University of Vale do Rio dos Sinos (Unisinos), Brazil, where he is also a member of the Software Innovation Laboratory – SOFTWARELAB. He is also an ad-hoc consultant for the Brazilian Ministry of Education. He holds a Ph. D. and an M.Sc. degree in Computer Science; both received from the Federal University of Rio Grande do Sul (UFRGS). His current research interests involve next-generation mobile communications, such as 5G and 6G, military communications, Industry 4.0, smart cities, Internet of Things, and the application of Big Data Analytics and Machine Learning to optimize telecommunications. He has extensive experience as a consultant, coordinating and participating in projects with companies from Brazil and abroad. In 2020 he was a visiting professor at the IBM Watson IoT Center - Munich, Germany.

Vladimir Kustov is a doctor of technical sciences in 1994. Specialty: 20.02.12 – System analysis, modeling of military operations and systems, computer technologies in military Affairs (technical Sciences). Professor since 1995. Professor of the Department of Informatics and information security, St. Petersburg state University of Railways of Emperor Alexander I (PGUPS), St. Petersburg, Russia. Education: Perm higher command and engineering militery school in 1972 with a degree in “aircraft control systems and ground-based test and launch electrical equipment for them”. More than 40 years of teaching and research experience. 16 candidates of technical Sciences and 4 doctors of technical Sciences were trained. Research interests: information security, electronic signature validation protocols, trusted third-party technology, cryptography and steganography, noise-proof coding, distributed registry technology (blockchain). More than 230 publications with a total volume of more than 80 printed pages, 14 copyright certificates for inventions, 5 copyright certificates for programs. Member of the dissertation Council, member of the IEEE.

Zhiruo Liu is an independent researcher. Her research interests include supply chain finance, Chinese economy, and business analytics.

Subhodeep Mukherjee is a PhD student at the GITAM Institute of Management, GITAM (Deemed to be University), Visakhapatnam, India. He obtained his Master's degree from the Birla Institute of Technology, Mesra, Ranchi India. His main research interests include food supply chain management, cloud computing, blockchain technologies. He has publications in reputed journals and high indexed book chapters. He has presented more nine papers in various conferences and has also received two best papers and best paper presented awards. His main research interests include food supply chain management, cloud computing, blockchain technologies. He has expertise in statistical techniques like SEM, etc.

Arulkumar N. is currently working as an Assistant Professor at Christ (Deemed to be University), Bangalore, India. He received a Ph.D. degree in Computer Science from Bharathidasan University, India in 2019. His research areas are Computer Networks, Cyber Security, and the Internet of Things (IoT). He published more than 30 research papers in both journals and conferences. He published 4 patents in the fields of physics, communication and computer science. He has chaired many technical sessions and delivered more than 15 invited talks at the national and international levels. He has completed more than 33 certifications from IBM, Google, Amazon, etc. He passed the CCNA: Routing and Switching Exam in 2017. Additionally, he also passed the Networking Fundamentals in the year 2017 exam from Microsoft.

Naveen Kumar N. is working as Associate Professor, in Madanapalle Institute of Technology and science, Madanapalle, Andhra Pradesh. He has done his Doctorate from Sri Venkateswara University, Tirupati, in the area of " An Efficient Approach To Remove High Density Salt And Pepper Noise Using Stationary Waverley Transform" in the year 2014". He completed his Master of Computer Applications from Sri Venkateswara university, Tirupati, in the year 2005. He has 10 years of experience in research and teaching. His areas of interest include Nural Networks, Image Processing and Data Analysis. He guided 50 PG Projects. He is the author of more than 13 research papers published in various national & international journals with high Impact Factor and citations. He acted as the committed member in various national and international conferences which is funded by AICTE & UGC. In addition to regular duties. He organized more than 60 social awareness programs which will educate the society under National Cadet Corps from 2016-2021.

R. Nagarajan received his B.E. in Electrical and Electronics Engineering from Madurai Kamarajar University, Madurai, India, in 1997. He received his M.E. in Power Electronics and Drives from Anna University, Chennai, India, in 2008. He received his Ph.D in Electrical Engineering from Anna University, Chennai, India, in 2014. He has worked in the industry as an Electrical Engineer. He is currently working as Professor of Electrical and Electronics Engineering at Gnanamani College of Technology, Namakkal, Tamilnadu, India. His current research interest includes Power Electronics, Power System, Soft Computing Techniques and Renewable Energy Sources.

Babu R. is a Research Scholar in Anna University. He has completed his Masters in Software Engineering with a merit of 2nd rank in the University and Bachelors in Computer Science and Engineering from Rajalakshmi Engineering College affiliated to Anna University. His areas of interest include Web Services, Service Oriented Architecture, Cloud Computing, Big Data Analytics and Internet of Things. He is a life member of CSI and served as a Management Committee Member for three years. He has received Active Participation Award – Youth from CSI. He also received Faculty Excellence Award from Infosys in Faculty Enablement Program for three successive years.

Krati Reja is currently pursuing the B.Tech Degree in Computer Science Engineering with specialization in Cyber Security and Digital Forensics from Vellore Institute of Technology, Bhopal. Her current research interests includes Blockchain , Artificial intelligence , Cryptography.

Srinivasan S. P. is presently working as a Controller of Examinations & Professor in the Department of Mechanical Engineering at the Rajalakshmi Engineering College, Chennai, India. He obtained his B.E. degree in Production Engineering from St. Peter's Engineering College from Madras University, Chennai, India in 1997.He got his Master degree M.E in Industrial Engineering from the College of Engineering, Guindy , Anna University, Chennai in January 2000. He received his PhD degree from Anna university in 2011 in the field of Supply chain management. He has been engaged in teaching, research and consultancy. He has published a number of research papers in International journals and presented many papers in various International conferences. He has also published a text book titled 'Dynamics of Machines' in 2003. He is also a visiting faculty in the Department of Industrial Engineering, Anna University Chennai. He has extensively traveled and presented seminars in leading technical institutions in India and abroad. He has taught subjects like Engineering mechanics, Engineering Graphics, Engineering Materials & Metallurgy, Production planning & control, Total Quality Management, Industrial Robotics, Facility Planning & Layout design, Quality & Reliability Engineering etc.,. His current research interest towards the agriculture supply chain management with application in the field of alternate fuels, production management, Transportation and logistics, decision support system, optimization techniques. He is also a Chief Superintendent at Rajalakshmi Engineering College for Anna University exams 2011-17. He has successfully implemented 5S & Kaizen concepts in the Department of Mechanical Engineering and also extended it to the entire campus at Rajalakshmi Engineering College. He won the Platinum award from ABK-AOTS DOSOKAI kaizen competition award. In this connection he won the Platinum award from ABK AOTS DOSOKAI Kaizen competition. He is also an executive council member of Chinmaya mission, Chennai. He is a life member of various professional bodies includes Institute of Engineers (IEI), ISTE, IIIE, ,NIQR,ASME, IAENG and IACSIT. He was chairman for the Indian Institution of Industrial Engineering – Chennai chapter. He has successfully completed his sabbatical Training at Lucas TVS Company in 2011 for a month period. He has attended an Internship on Energy studies at Trier University – Germany during 2014. Currently working on 'IoT in the field of supply chain management' & 'Additive manufacturing in medical applications.

Shishir Kumar Shandilya is the Deputy Director of SECURE – Centre of Excellence in Cyber Security and Division Head of Cyber Security and Digital Forensics at VIT Bhopal University. He is working as a Principal Consultant to the Govt. of India for Technology Development and Assessment in Cyber Security. He also holds the position of Executive Director of National Cyber Defense Research Centre, New Delhi. He is a Visiting Researcher at Liverpool Hope University-United Kingdom, a Cambridge University Certified Professional Teacher and Trainer, ACM Distinguished Speaker and a Senior Member of IEEE. He is a NASSCOM Certified Master Trainer for Security Analyst SOC (SSC/Q0909: NVEQF Level 7) and an Academic Advisor to National Cyber Safety and Security Standards, New Delhi. He has received the IDA Teaching Excellence Award for distinctive use of technology in Teaching by Indian Didactics Association, Bangalore (2016) and Young Scientist Award for two consecutive years, 2005 and 2006, by Indian Science Congress and MP Council of Science and Technology. He has seven books published by Springer Nature-Singapore, IGI-USA, River-Denmark and Prentice Hall of India. His recently published book is on Advances in Cyber Security Analytics and Decision Systems by Springer.

Ashish K. Sharma is presently working as an Associate Professor, Dept. of CSE, Raisoni College of Engineering (GHRCE), Autonomous Institution in Nagpur. Prior to this, he was associated with IT industry in the areas of Training, Software and Web Development. He has total experience of 25 years, which includes Academic, Industrial and Software and Web Development. He has published many research papers, Nationally and Internationally in Conferences and Journals of repute that includes Taylor & Francis, Actapress, IGI Global, Inderscience and MECS-Press. He has also published National and International patents. He is also on the Editorial and Review Board of some journals. He is Microsoft Certified Professional (MCP) and also hold Brainbench certification. He is an Approved Supervisor of G H Raisoni Amravati University (GHRU) for PhD in CSE. Presently supervising 5 PhD students. Also an Approved Supervisor of Nagpur University (RTMNU) for M.E. by Research in CSE. One student awarded M.E. by Research under him. His thrust areas are Data Mining, Databases, Soft Computing, DSS, Data Science and Machine Learning.

Durgesh M. Sharma is currently working as an Assistant Professor, Department of AI, G H Raisoni College of Engineering, Autonomous Institute in Nagpur. Earlier, he worked as an Assistant Professor, Department of Information Technology, Manoharbhai Patel Institute of Engineering and Technology, India. He has a total of 11 years of Academic Experience. He has published several National and International research papers in Conferences and Journals. He has been granted one Patent by the Government of India. He is also a Reviewer of peer-reviewed journals. Presently, he is pursuing a Ph.D. from the Vellore Institute of Technology, Bhopal. His research interest domains are Machine Learning, Artificial Intelligence, Cyber-Physical Systems (CPS), and Data Mining.

Ekaterina Silanteva is General Director, New Space of Trade LLC, Moscow, Russia. Education: Lomonosov Moscow State University, School of Public Administration, 2013, Manager in Public and Municipal Administration, Lomonosov Moscow State University, School of Public Administration, 2017, PhD Candidate. 08.00.05: Economy and Management of the National Economy. More than 10 years of teaching and research experience. A number of studies have been conducted at the intersection of Economics and IT for international organizations such as ECE, UNESCAP and Crown Agents. She is an UNNExT expert and is engaged in research work in the field of cross-border paperless trade. Research interests: information security, electronic signature validation protocols, trusted third-party technology, mutual recognition mechanisms, cryptography and steganography, distributed registry technology (blockchain), IT performance assessment, development of competitive strategies for IT companies. She has more than 10 scientific publications with a total volume of more than 10 printed pages.

Ram Singh is Sr. Assistant Professor & Coordinator Department of Commerce, Quantum School of Business, Quantum University Roorkee India. Dr. Singh has completed his Ph.D. degree in Commerce from HNB Garhwal Central University Srinagar Uttarakhand India. Currently, Dr. Singh is a member and secretary of Research Council of Quantum University, member of BOF/BOS (Commerce), a member of Editorial Board of numeral Journals, and Reviewer in various peer reviewed National and International Journals of Accounting, Finance & General Management. He has published 2 books and several research papers & articles in different SCOPUS/UGC listed/Peer-Reviewed journals. Besides this, he has also attended various FDPs, workshops, national & international webinars conducted by renowned institutions & organizations. He also presented papers in various national & International Seminars & Conferences and published more than a dozen articles/Chapters in proceedings of seminars & Conferences.

Poshan (Sam) Yu is a Lecturer in Accounting and Finance in the International Cooperative Education Program of Soochow University (China). He is also an External Professor of FinTech and Finance at SKEMA Business School (China), a Visiting Professor at Krirk University (Thailand) and a Visiting Researcher at the Australian Studies Centre of Shanghai University (China). Sam leads FasterCapital (Dubai, UAE) as a Regional Partner (China) and serves as a Startup Mentor for AIC RAISE (Coimbatore, India). His research interests include financial technology, regulatory technology, public-private partnerships, mergers and acquisitions, private equity, venture capital, start-ups, intellectual property, art finance, and China's "One Belt One Road" policy.

Index

Recommended Reference Books

IGI Global's reference books are available in three unique pricing formats: Print Only, E-Book Only, or Print + E-Book.

Shipping fees may apply.

www.igi-global.com

ISBN: 978-1-7998-1048-3
EISBN: 978-1-7998-1049-0
© 2020; 605 pp.
List Price: US$ **285**

ISBN: 978-1-5225-8933-4
EISBN: 978-1-5225-8934-1
© 2020; 667 pp.
List Price: US$ **295**

ISBN: 978-1-7998-0357-7
EISBN: 978-1-7998-0359-1
© 2020; 451 pp.
List Price: US$ **235**

ISBN: 978-1-7998-0070-5
EISBN: 978-1-7998-0071-2
© 2020; 144 pp.
List Price: US$ **175**

ISBN: 978-1-5225-6980-0
EISBN: 978-1-5225-6981-7
© 2019; 339 pp.
List Price: US$ **235**

ISBN: 978-1-5225-5390-8
EISBN: 978-1-5225-5391-5
© 2018; 125 pp.
List Price: US$ **165**

Do you want to stay current on the latest research trends, product announcements, news, and special offers?

Join IGI Global's mailing list to receive customized recommendations, exclusive discounts, and more.
Sign up at: **www.igi-global.com/newsletters.**

Publisher of Peer-Reviewed, Timely, and Innovative Academic Research

IGI Global
PUBLISHER of TIMELY KNOWLEDGE

www.igi-global.com Sign up at www.igi-global.com/newsletters facebook.com/igiglobal twitter.com/igiglobal linkedin.com/igiglobal

Ensure Quality Research is Introduced to the Academic Community

Become an Evaluator for IGI Global Authored Book Projects

The overall success of an authored book project is dependent on quality and timely manuscript evaluations.

Applications and Inquiries may be sent to:
development@igi-global.com

Applicants must have a doctorate (or equivalent degree) as well as publishing, research, and reviewing experience. Authored Book Evaluators are appointed for one-year terms and are expected to complete at least three evaluations per term. Upon successful completion of this term, evaluators can be considered for an additional term.

If you have a colleague that may be interested in this opportunity, we encourage you to share this information with them.

IGI Global Author Services

Providing a high-quality, affordable, and expeditious service, IGI Global's Author Services enable authors to streamline their publishing process, increase chance of acceptance, and adhere to IGI Global's publication standards.

Benefits of Author Services:

- **Professional Service:** All our editors, designers, and translators are experts in their field with years of experience and professional certifications.
- **Quality Guarantee & Certificate:** Each order is returned with a quality guarantee and certificate of professional completion.
- **Timeliness:** All editorial orders have a guaranteed return timeframe of 3-5 business days and translation orders are guaranteed in 7-10 business days.
- **Affordable Pricing:** IGI Global Author Services are competitively priced compared to other industry service providers.
- **APC Reimbursement:** IGI Global authors publishing Open Access (OA) will be able to deduct the cost of editing and other IGI Global author services from their OA APC publishing fee.

Author Services Offered:

English Language Copy Editing
Professional, native English language copy editors improve your manuscript's grammar, spelling, punctuation, terminology, semantics, consistency, flow, formatting, and more.

Scientific & Scholarly Editing
A Ph.D. level review for qualities such as originality and significance, interest to researchers, level of methodology and analysis, coverage of literature, organization, quality of writing, and strengths and weaknesses.

Figure, Table, Chart & Equation Conversions
Work with IGI Global's graphic designers before submission to enhance and design all figures and charts to IGI Global's specific standards for clarity.

Translation
Providing 70 language options, including Simplified and Traditional Chinese, Spanish, Arabic, German, French, and more.

Hear What the Experts Are Saying About IGI Global's Author Services

*"Publishing with IGI Global has been **an amazing experience** for me for sharing my research. The **strong academic production** support ensures quality and timely completion."* – **Prof. Margaret Niess, Oregon State University, USA**

*"The service was **very fast, very thorough, and very helpful** in ensuring our chapter meets the criteria and requirements of the book's editors. I was **quite impressed and happy** with your service."* – **Prof. Tom Brinthaupt, Middle Tennessee State University, USA**

Learn More or Get Started Here:

For Questions, Contact IGI Global's Customer Service Team at cust@igi-global.com or 717-533-8845

IGI Global
PUBLISHER of TIMELY KNOWLEDGE
www.igi-global.com

IGI Global
PUBLISHER of TIMELY KNOWLEDGE
www.igi-global.com

Celebrating Over 30 Years of Scholarly Knowledge Creation & Dissemination

InfoSci®-Books

A Database of Nearly 6,000 Reference Books Containing Over 105,000+ Chapters Focusing on Emerging Research

InfoSci®-Books Database

The **InfoSci®-Books** is a database of nearly 6,000 IGI Global single and multi-volume reference books, handbooks of research, and encyclopedias, encompassing groundbreaking research from prominent experts worldwide that spans over 350+ topics in 11 core subject areas including business, computer science, education, science and engineering, social sciences, and more.

Open Access Fee Waiver (Read & Publish) Initiative

For any library that invests in IGI Global's InfoSci-Books and/or InfoSci-Journals (175+ scholarly journals) databases, IGI Global will match the library's investment with a fund of equal value to go toward **subsidizing the OA article processing charges (APCs) for their students, faculty, and staff** at that institution when their work is submitted and accepted under OA into an IGI Global journal.*

INFOSCI® PLATFORM FEATURES

- Unlimited Simultaneous Access
- No DRM
- No Set-Up or Maintenance Fees
- A Guarantee of No More Than a 5% Annual Increase for Subscriptions
- Full-Text HTML and PDF Viewing Options
- Downloadable MARC Records
- COUNTER 5 Compliant Reports
- Formatted Citations With Ability to Export to RefWorks and EasyBib
- No Embargo of Content (Research is Available Months in Advance of the Print Release)

**The fund will be offered on an annual basis and expire at the end of the subscription period. The fund would renew as the subscription is renewed for each year thereafter. The open access fees will be waived after the student, faculty, or staff's paper has been vetted and accepted into an IGI Global journal and the fund can only be used toward publishing OA in an IGI Global journal. Libraries in developing countries will have the match on their investment doubled.*

To Recommend or Request a Free Trial:
www.igi-global.com/infosci-books
eresources@igi-global.com • Toll Free: 1-866-342-6657 ext. 100 • Phone: 717-533-8845 x100

IGI Global
PUBLISHER of TIMELY KNOWLEDGE
www.igi-global.com

IGI Global
PUBLISHER of TIMELY KNOWLEDGE
www.igi-global.com

Publisher of Peer-Reviewed, Timely, and Innovative Academic Research Since 1988

IGI Global's Transformative Open Access (OA) Model: How to Turn Your University Library's Database Acquisitions Into a Source of OA Funding

Well in advance of Plan S, IGI Global unveiled their OA Fee Waiver (Read & Publish) Initiative. Under this initiative, librarians who invest in IGI Global's InfoSci-Books and/or InfoSci-Journals databases will be able to subsidize their patrons' OA article processing charges (APCs) when their work is submitted and accepted (after the peer review process) into an IGI Global journal.

How Does it Work?

Step 1: **Library Invests in the InfoSci-Databases:** A library perpetually purchases or subscribes to the InfoSci-Books, InfoSci-Journals, or discipline/subject databases.

Step 2: **IGI Global Matches the Library Investment with OA Subsidies Fund:** IGI Global provides a fund to go towards subsidizing the OA APCs for the library's patrons.

Step 3: **Patron of the Library is Accepted into IGI Global Journal (After Peer Review):** When a patron's paper is accepted into an IGI Global journal, they option to have their paper published under a traditional publishing model or as OA.

Step 4: **IGI Global Will Deduct APC Cost from OA Subsidies Fund:** If the author decides to publish under OA, the OA APC fee will be deducted from the OA subsidies fund.

Step 5: **Author's Work Becomes Freely Available:** The patron's work will be freely available under CC BY copyright license, enabling them to share it freely with the academic community.

Note: *This fund will be offered on an annual basis and will renew as the subscription is renewed for each year thereafter. IGI Global will manage the fund and award the APC waivers unless the librarian has a preference as to how the funds should be managed.*

Hear From the Experts on This Initiative:

"I'm very happy to have been able to make one of my recent research contributions **freely available** along with having access to the **valuable resources** found within IGI Global's InfoSci-Journals database."

– **Prof. Stuart Palmer,** Deakin University, Australia

"Receiving the support from IGI Global's OA Fee Waiver Initiative **encourages me to continue my research work without any hesitation**."

– **Prof. Wenlong Liu**, College of Economics and Management at Nanjing University of Aeronautics & Astronautics, China

For More Information, Scan the QR Code or Contact:
IGI Global's Digital Resources Team at eresources@igi-global.com.

IGI Global
PUBLISHER of TIMELY KNOWLEDGE

Are You Ready to Publish Your Research?

IGI Global
PUBLISHER of TIMELY KNOWLEDGE

IGI Global offers book authorship and editorship opportunities across 11 subject areas, including business, computer science, education, science and engineering, social sciences, and more!

Benefits of Publishing with IGI Global:

- Free one-on-one editorial and promotional support.
- Expedited publishing timelines that can take your book from start to finish in less than one (1) year.
- Choose from a variety of formats, including: Edited and Authored References, Handbooks of Research, Encyclopedias, and Research Insights.
- Utilize IGI Global's eEditorial Discovery® submission system in support of conducting the submission and double-blind peer review process.
- IGI Global maintains a strict adherence to ethical practices due in part to our full membership with the Committee on Publication Ethics (COPE).
- Indexing potential in prestigious indices such as Scopus®, Web of Science™, PsycINFO®, and ERIC – Education Resources Information Center.
- Ability to connect your ORCID iD to your IGI Global publications.
- Earn honorariums and royalties on your full book publications as well as complimentary copies and exclusive discounts.

Join Your Colleagues from Prestigious Institutions, Including:

Australian National University

Massachusetts Institute of Technology

Johns Hopkins University

Harvard University

Columbia University in the City of New York

Learn More at: www.igi-global.com/publish

or Contact IGI Global's Aquisitions Team at: acquisition@igi-global.com

Purchase Individual IGI Global InfoSci-OnDemand Book Chapters and Journal Articles

InfoSci®-OnDemand

Pay-Per-View Articles and Chapters from IGI Global

For More Information, Visit: www.igi-global.com/e-resources/infosci-ondemand

Browse through nearly 150,000+ articles/chapters to find specific research related to their current studies and projects that have been contributed by international researchers from prestigious institutions, including MIT, Harvard University, Columbia University, and many more.

Easily Identify, Acquire, and Utilize Published Peer-Reviewed Findings in Support of Your Current Research:

Accurate and Advanced Search: Utilize the advanced InfoSci-OnDemand search engine to identify research in your area of interest.

Affordably Acquire Research: Provide an affordable alternative to purchasing an entire reference book or scholarly journal.

Fast and Easy One-Click Shopping: Simply utilize the OnDemand "Buy Now" button on the webpage.

Instantly Download/Access Your Content: Receive an immediate link to download your InfoSci-OnDemand content to your personal computer and device.

Access Anywhere, Anytime, and on Any Device: Additionally, receive access to your OnDemand articles and chapters through a personal electronic library.

Benefit from the InfoSci Platform Features: Providing formatted citations, full-text PDF and HTML format, no embargo of content, no DRM, and more.

"It really provides **an excellent entry into the research literature of the field**. *It presents a manageable number of* **highly relevant sources** *on topics of interest to a wide range of researchers. The sources are* **scholarly, but also accessible** *to 'practitioners'."*

- Ms. Lisa Stimatz, MLS, University of North Carolina at Chapel Hill, USA

Interested in Additional Savings and Acquiring Multiple Articles and Chapters Through InfoSci-OnDemand?

Subscribe to InfoSci-OnDemand Plus

Learn More

www.ingramcontent.com/pod-product-compliance
Lightning Source LLC
LaVergne TN
LVHW081328021026
849161LV00010BA/2647